Blessed

Blessed

A History of the American
Prosperity Gospel

KATE BOWLER

OXFORD
UNIVERSITY PRESS

OXFORD
UNIVERSITY PRESS

Oxford University Press is a department of the University of Oxford.
It furthers the University's objective of excellence in research,
scholarship, and education by publishing worldwide.

Oxford   New York
Auckland   Cape Town   Dar es Salaam   Hong Kong   Karachi
Kuala Lumpur   Madrid   Melbourne   Mexico City   Nairobi
New Delhi   Shanghai   Taipei   Toronto

With offices in
Argentina   Austria   Brazil   Chile   Czech Republic   France   Greece
Guatemala   Hungary   Italy   Japan   Poland   Portugal   Singapore
South Korea   Switzerland   Thailand   Turkey   Ukraine   Vietnam

Oxford is a registered trade mark of Oxford University Press
in the UK and certain other countries.

Published in the United States of America by
Oxford University Press
198 Madison Avenue, New York, NY 10016

© Oxford University Press 2013

Library of Congress Cataloging-in-Publication Data
Bowler, Kate.
Blessed : a history of the American prosperity gospel / Kate Bowler.
p.   cm.
Includes bibliographical references and index.
ISBN 978-0-19-982769-5
1. Faith movement (Hagin)—United States.
2. United States—Church history—20th century. I. Title.
BR1643.5.B68   2013
277.3'083—dc23   2012038602

9

Printed in the United States of America
on acid-free paper

To my parents,
for their loving home.
And to Toban,
for bringing it with us
on all life's journeys.

Contents

Acknowledgments

IN A STUDY of divine money, I certainly enjoyed an embarrassment of riches. I experienced an abundance of care, support, and guidance when undertaking this project. I can never express the full measure of gratitude I owe my family. My husband, Toban, offered his support with characteristic sweetness. I imagine perfection looks a lot like a husband who (without caring what I chose for my profession) happily chats about "our book" while making dinner. And sanctification is surely sharing a home office with me. My mother and father approached every obstacle in my life as an opportunity to be helpful. When health problems prevented me from finishing the manuscript, they drove across the continent just to offer editorial and culinary support. In a calculus I will never understand, they actually seemed grateful. I could not have made it over the finish line without my siblings, Amy, Maria, and brother-in-law John, who cheerfully helped at different stages of my dissertation. And to my extended family, Chelsea, her friendship demands a book of its own.

This book began as a dissertation and benefited immeasurably from the support of my committee. My advisor, Grant Wacker, makes mentorship a ministry. His insistence on clarity, compassion, and active verbs made it impossible to form thoughts without first wondering WWGD. Tom Tweed always went above and beyond to give me the tools to think critically. He approached every argument with a young scholar's needs at heart: wit, care, and a razor blade. Mark Chaves forced me to come to grips with actual social science, while Glenn Hinson brought storytelling back to history for me. Julie Byrne made everything look easy.

A wonderful community of scholars helped me along. Scott Billingsley, Phil Sinitiere, Shayne Lee, Gerardo Marti, Larry Eskridge, Kathryn Lofton, Ed Harrell, Katie Hladky, Wallace Best, Arlene Sánchez Walsh, Jonathan Walton, Tamelyn Tucker-Worgs, and Matt Sutton enriched my work by their example and wise counsel. David Roebuck of the Dixon Pentecostal

Research Center, Darrin Rodgers of the Flower Pentecostal Heritage Center, and Mark Roberts of the Holy Spirit Research Center not only made every resource available, but pointed me in the right direction countless times. I have benefited from the deft research support of Jacki Price-Linnartz, Rob Stansel, and the diligent Mike Suh, who pretended to find this fascinating for an entire summer. Heather Moffitt's keen editorial work on my dissertation saved me from more errors than I can count. Cyrus Schleifer's social network analysis work was beautifully done. Portions of Chapter 4 were included in Candy Gunther Brown's *Global Pentecostal and Charismatic Healing* (Oxford 2011). Her editorial pen and rich insights continue to improve my thinking.

This research was aided with the generous support of the Centre for Research on Canadian Evangelicalism, whose intellectual powerhouse, John Stackhouse, oversaw my research on Canadian iterations of the prosperity gospel. My travel to Israel with Benny Hinn in 2008 was made possible by an international travel grant from Duke University.

At Duke Divinity I found a theological home and a community of endless support. Many thanks to my doctoral cohort—especially Mandy McMichael, Heather Vacek, Angela Tarango, Wen Reagan, Sarah Ruble, Elesha Coffman, Brendan Pietsch, Joshua Vis, and Seth Dowland—for nurturing these ideas over so many years. If my new colleagues tired of lecture after lecture on Joel Osteen, they never let me know it. In hallowed halls where Masterpiece Theatre always seems to be playing faintly in the background, they encouraged me to be myself. In particular, Richard Hays, Laceye Warner, and Edgardo Colón-Emeric made special efforts to support my research. Dave Odom and Bill Lamar from Leadership Education at Duke Divinity made Herculean efforts on my behalf. A special thank you goes to my students, who not only bought me Joel Osteen's board game but took up the questions posed by the prosperity gospel with compassion and rigor. I am so grateful for the opportunity to be a part of their lives and our common pursuit of service to the church.

Many thanks to Cynthia Read, Sasha Grossman, Joellyn Ausanka, and the editorial staff at Oxford University Press for their many efforts in bringing this book into the cold light of day. Judith Heyhoe of Duke Divinity School cast her expert editorial eye on my work for two long years, bringing it so much closer to what it ought to be. And thank you to David Steinmetz, who always seemed to think I was worth reading without having read a word.

Finally, I owe a debt of appreciation to the many people in the pulpits and the pews who shared their lives with me, especially the members of Durham's Victorious Faith Center. "Gratitude bestows reverence," observed John Milton, "allowing us to encounter everyday epiphanies, those transcendent moments of awe that change forever how we experience life and the world." This work has been deepened by their everyday epiphanies.

Blessed

Introduction

THE VICTORIOUS FAITH CENTER sign blinked red. The church was squat and wide, an inauspicious storefront sandwiched between a nail salon and a payday loan office in a Durham, North Carolina, mini-mall. For years I had been studying churches with triumphant names like World Overcomers and Victory International to trace an emerging movement, famous for promises like the one before me in bright neon: Victorious Faith. The movement goes by different names, ranging from the slightly pejorative (Health and Wealth or Name It and Claim It) to the vaguely descriptive (Faith or Word of Faith) to the blunt shorthand, the prosperity gospel. Though it is hard to describe, it is easy to find. The prosperity gospel is a wildly popular Christian message of spiritual, physical, and financial mastery that dominates not only much of the American religious scene but some of the largest churches around the globe.

The pastor and first lady of the Victorious Faith Center agreed to meet to discuss my study of the prosperity movement, and I was eager to discover their connections to the larger ministerial networks that dominate this movement.[1] As I launched into a description of my study, I felt the emotional temperature drop. No, the pastor stated firmly, his teachings had no historical precedent; they were born from revelation. This was an independent, nondenominational church built on faith alone. "What about the church's name?" I asked. It had come to him in a dream. The conversation lapsed into uncomfortable silence as I realized that this line of questioning violated his sense of integrity as a revelator. Flushed, I mentally tabulated the odds of quickly finding another church. Perhaps I should have visited Destiny Church down the street or found a recommended local ministry from a famous prosperity preacher's website. In the yawning pause, a magazine on the coffee table caught my eye. It was *The Word of Faith*, the official publication of the flagship Word of Faith institution, Rhema Bible Training Center in Broken Arrow, Oklahoma. The sight of the magazine prompted a different line of questioning. Where did he go to school? Where did he turn for spiritual inspiration? What ministries did the church support? The hidden structures of the prosperity movement began to emerge. Pastor Walton had spent several years learning from the televangelist host of *Success-N-Life*, Robert Tilton, at his Bible school in Texas. He has sustained the momentum of his ministry by reading prosperity publications and by taking intermittent trips to witness divine healer Benny Hinn's crusades. The local church "sows" money like seeds into the international ministries of celebrities like Creflo Dollar, Kenneth Hagin, and Joel Osteen. While Pastor Walton sees his insights and preaching bubbling up from the wellsprings of scripture and personal revelation, in song, sermon, and giving, his Sunday mornings at the Victorious Faith Center also closely resemble thousands of similar churches dotting the American religious landscape.

The seeming independence of churches like the Victorious Faith Center has puzzled pastors, scholars, and media pundits alike. Few know how to measure the breadth of the prosperity movement or even how to lay the tape. The prosperity gospel is not bounded strictly by region, as its celebrities hail from Seattle to New York, Houston to Chicago, and even around the globe. Denominational markers do not offer many clues, since most of its largest churches claim nondenominational status. Few leaders advertise themselves a "prosperity preacher," even if they sermonize weekly about divine finances. Congregational size also proves inconclusive: while famous prosperity-preaching congregations like Lakewood Church or World Changers Church International crowd the list of American megachurches, countless small congregations proclaim an equally fervent prosperity gospel. Likewise, these congregational estimates cannot account for the millions of Americans who spice up their spiritual lives by watching their favorite televangelists, reading their publications, or attending their conferences.

Common sense also sends researchers in the wrong direction. The prosperity gospel cannot be conflated with fundamentalism, pentecostalism, evangelicalism, the religious right, the so-called black church, or any of the usual suspects (though it certainly overlaps with each).[2] The prosperity message favors theological conservatism, and yet, organizationally it is unlike other conservative movements that tend to produce mandates and institutions with ironclad purpose. The prosperity gospel lacks the semblance of this well-oiled institutional machinery, leading many observers to conclude that its celebrities operate as theological and institutional independents, rising, persisting, and falling haphazardly. They appear to be solo evangelists—fireflies that flicker on and off, here and there, each burning brightly and then fading without consistency or connection.

This confusion is largely because the prosperity gospel thrives in diverse forms on the American religious terrain. In Houston, Joel Osteen, known as the "smiling preacher," inspired his 38,000-member congregation through humorous and lightly theological sermons salted with insights from his latest self-help bestseller, *I Declare! 31 Promises to Speak Over Your Life*.[3] Nielsen Media christened him America's most-watched inspirational figure, with a weekly audience of seven million.[4] T. D. Jakes, dubbed by *Time* magazine as one of America's most influential new religious leaders, built a financial empire with his 30,000-member congregation, media conglomerate, and more than two dozen books on emotional healing.[5] Creflo Dollar, pastor of Atlanta's 30,000-member World Changers Church International, traded Osteen's smiles for fatherly admonitions, urging his mostly black church members to increase their wealth by increasing their faith. The Ohio pastor Rod Parsley earned a national reputation as a prosperity preacher and self-proclaimed pit bull for the religious right. Frederick Price, the Los Angeles pastor of Crenshaw Christian Center, lambasted traditional Christianity as a "slave religion" and implored his 22,000-member congregation to use prosperity theology to overcome barriers to black upward mobility.[6] Joyce Meyer eschewed a conventional church ministry altogether and toured America's largest cities with a message of abundance and hope heard largely by audiences of white, middle-aged women. These independent ministers and others like them, taken together, operate as a major force in American religion, generating vast audiences and financial donations.

Millions of Americans fell in love with the prosperity gospel and its new kind of preacher. Charming though not effusive, polished but not slick, these favored few could as easily have appeared on *Piers Morgan Tonight* as behind their megachurch Sunday pulpits. Podcasts, Internet streaming, and daily television programming carried their sermons to millions. They cultivated their fame with personal appearances in sold-out arenas. The megachurch ministerial elite dominated not only religious media networks, like Pat Robertson's Christian Broadcasting Network or the Trinity Broadcasting Network, but secular outlets as well, becoming mainstays on stations like Black Entertainment Television. Some climbed the charts of the *New York Times* bestsellers list, and all found their titles lining the religion/inspiration aisles from Walmart to Barnes & Noble. The Senate buzzed about these celebrities' high profit margins, while bloggers and media pundits debated each ministerial expenditure.[7] Loved or hated, they were never forgotten. At almost any moment, day or night, the American public could tune in to see these familiar faces and a consistent message: God desires to bless you.

By the turn of the twenty-first century, a dozen or so prosperity preachers had become household names and powerful players in the American religious scene. To their congregations, they acted as pastors, prophets, and visionaries. They attracted spiritual tourists and members alike to their church complexes, thickets of offices, television production studies, classrooms, and sanctuaries. They put on hard hats and cut ribbons for their latest building projects and then quickly set a new goal in their church's sights. Their biographies—from their childhood, conversion, and family life to their rise to fame and their empire building—became the narrative glue of virtually every sermon, book, and piece of merchandise to emerge from their churches. To their fellow pastors, they were sovereigns of ministerial kingdoms, whose coveted endorsements, preaching platforms, and financial support fueled the aspirations of the thousands below them.

To the secular media, these prosperity leaders represented the Christianity of the American marketplace. With microphones pinned to their lapels, they preached upbeat messages of God's goodness and human potential. They knew the questions would naturally turn to their own wealth and defended their personal jets and real estate assets with examples of their altruistic motives. And to popular religious audiences, they served as America's counselors, self-help advisors as trusted as professional therapists. Audiences cheered as T. D. Jakes appeared easily alongside Dr. Phil on the psychologist's hit television show, two relationship experts with cures for the country's ills. In those roles, faith celebrities became leaders of a popular religious force. These ministers, and others like them, constituted the national leadership of the prosperity movement, commanding some of the country's largest spiritual audiences through pulpits and television cameras. Surveys continued to find popular support for its cause. A recent *Time* poll found that 17 percent of Christians surveyed identified themselves as part of such a movement, while 31 percent believed that God increases the riches of those who give. A full two-thirds agreed that God wants people to prosper.[8] A Pew survey reported that 43 percent of all Christian respondents agreed that the faithful receive health and wealth. A 2008 Pew study found that three-in-four Latino believers, across all Christian denominations, agreed with the statement: "God will grant financial success and good health to all believers who have enough faith."[9] American audiences had made this gospel their own.

This book seeks to show how millions of American Christians came to see money, health, and good fortune as divine. My attempt to answer how this took place follows three lines of argumentation. First, these chapters introduce readers to the major figures and features of the twentieth-century American prosperity gospel, from touring mesmerists and meta-physical sages to pentecostal healers, Reformed optimists, Episcopal ecstatics, and Republican stumpers. Progressing chronologically, I trace the movement's roots in the late nineteenth century to its flowering in the pentecostal revivals of the World War II years and maturity in the ripe individualism of post-1960s America.

Second, this book is an attempt to describe not only the rise of a discrete movement but also a transformation of popular religious imagination that has not yet ended. Americans began to question an ethic of self-denial as a stony orthodoxy barren of the Gospel's abundant promises. Believers of all stripes started to claim supernatural promises for joy, healing, sanctification, provision, self-worth, business sense, family unity, heavenly tongues, and Holy Spirit fire come down. But the movement did not simply foster hope. The prosperity gospel guaranteed a special form of Christian power to reach into God's treasure trove and pull out a miracle. It represented the triumph of American optimism over the realities of a fickle economy, entrenched racism, pervasive poverty, and theological pessimism that foretold the future as dangling by a thread. Countless listeners reimagined their ability as good Christians—and good Americans—to leapfrog over any obstacles.

Third, the following chapters seek to familiarize readers with the unifying themes of the prosperity gospel and the diverse people who speak its language. The prosperity gospel, I argue, centers on four themes: *faith, wealth, health,* and *victory*.[10] (1) It conceives of *faith* as an activator, a power that unleashes spiritual forces and turns the spoken word into reality. (2) The movement depicts faith as palpably demonstrated in *wealth* and (3) *health*. It can be measured in both the wallet (one's personal wealth) and in the body (one's personal health), making material reality the measure of the success of immaterial faith. (4) The movement expects faith to be marked by *victory*. Believers trust that culture holds no political, social, or economic impediment to faith, and no circumstance can stop believers from living in total victory here on earth. All four hallmarks emphasize demonstrable results, a faith that may be calculated by the outcome of a successful life, no matter whether they express this belief through what I call "hard prosperity" or "soft prosperity." Hard prosperity

judges people's faith by their immediate circumstances, while soft prosperity appraises believers with a gentler, more roundabout, assessment.
(For an extended discussion of the term "prosperity gospel," see appendix
B.) Though believers argue that Christian prosperity differs from worldly
acquisitiveness, these Christians recognize that their message inscribes
materiality with spiritual meaning. Inverting the well-worn American
mantra that things must be seen to be believed, their gospel rewards those
who believe *in order to* see. In their confidence that they are promised
faith, wealth, health, and *victory,* they count themselves blessed.

A *Caution*

Given the controversies that swirl around the prosperity gospel, a few cau-
tionary words should be kept in mind. First, I believe that, at a fundamental level, American desires for the "good life" are basic and ordinary. That
is not to say that everyone has the same standards of adjudicating quality
of life, but that when many people say "prosperity," they mean survival.
People long for the necessities that sustain life and rejoice when those
goods overflow. As an academic, writing in a scholarly world dominated by
the upper-middle class, it is not unusual to see prosperity read pejoratively
as indulgence or fetish instead of a humdrum part of everyday living.
Writing beneath the neo-Gothic spires of Duke University, built as part of
James B. Duke's tobacco empire, I am undoubtedly a beneficiary of a gospel of wealth. More than once, believers have reminded me that in studying
the prosperity gospel, I have also been blessed and shown favor. As they
prayed lavish blessings over my work, I could hardly forget how we all
hope to see our small efforts multiplied.

Second, religion and money have never stood more than an arm's
length apart. Economic status divides us all into strata, groupings of taste,
habit, and lifestyle. It largely dictates where we live, with whom we associate, and what horizons we imagine for ourselves. Prosperity (and the
fluctuating criteria by which we measure how much is enough) is both the
substance of ethical debate and a deeply rooted means by which we adjudicate our place in the world. Religious beliefs, practices, habits, and institutions naturally assign value to these economic accidents or consequences,
making prosperity a crucial arena of spiritual meaning making.

Third, this book examines only one of America's prosperity gospels;
that is, there have been many forms of Christian thinking about money.
This book might easily have begun with Max Weber's beloved Puritans,

ended with apocalyptic speculation about the effects of the recession, and still been incomplete. I have chosen a much narrower genealogy of one pentecostal offshoot dubbed "*the* prosperity gospel," despite the fact that in American religious history, countless clergy and laypeople have speculated about the relationship between God's favor and hunger or plenty. Recipes for success have contained a changing list of ingredients, and American religion could hardly exhaust its possibilities. It cannot serve as an organizing theme for the whole of American religious history because it rarely evoked a common response. American believers, at times, expressed ambivalence about the importance of wealth or declared it incompatible with virtue. Many Christians, peering through the eye of a needle, declared prosperity an undesirable end.

Fourth, the prosperity gospel, though much reviled by the media and academics alike, deserves sustained attention. After a public lecture, I am frequently told that there is nothing to study in the prosperity gospel except naked greed. There is good religion, and then there is *Bad Religion*.[11] While the faith movement strikes many observers as lying outside the bounds of respectable academic attention, I argue that the prosperity gospel is a decisive theological, economic, and social force shaping American religion. This is not a story about how a few brave souls smuggled money into pentecostalism, but about how American believers learned to use their everyday experiences as spiritual weights and measures.

A Personal Note

I was frantically trying to finish my final papers for my PhD coursework when my fingers slowed and stopped. Some kind of overuse injury had eaten up the strength in my arms and left me unable to perform everyday activities—typing, cooking, driving—I had taken for granted. After a mistaken diagnosis led to an ill-advised surgery and a bout of temporary paralysis, some unfortunate students received expressive emoticons that semester in lieu of final comments. My mother about lost it when the next batch of doctors chatted amiably about removing a rib or two. After the conventional doctors it was a revolving door of acupuncturists, physical therapists, occupational therapists, chiropractors, herbalists, and eventually magnet suppliers and detoxifying footbath specialists.

All the while, I was living my other life, my research life. I spent week after week in prosperity churches, healing services, and financial seminars, observing and interviewing believers in God's abundant provisions.

It is a strange occupation to be a historian of divine well-being as your own is getting away from you. Any ethnographer worth her salt knows that the observer is inescapably a part of the lives she is trying to tell. Looking back on these eight years of research, I suspect it was, in part, owing to the faithfulness of pain that I listened so intently to the promises and the prophets of the American prosperity gospel. It bound me to the stories I heard and the questions I pursued. What is it like to be healed? Can life's circumstances mirror personal faith? Does God often do all things? What is the Christian language of hope? Christians gingerly parse that word, hope. We implicitly know that false hope is the poison in our veins, the log in our eyes. But what qualifies hope as Christian hope? Duke Divinity's Chuck Campbell once observed that hope is divine when it confounds us, even as it claims us, spoken in love, service, and words that no one will believe: words like, "All will be well." These words "posit eternity to those that only want an end, caught in the daily ritual of counting food and time." I am an outsider to the pentecostal tradition but an insider to Christianity and the stubborn assurance that for us, the Gospel is good news. Just how good is for readers and the faithful to decide.

I

Gospels

Confident living rights every wrong;
dynamic power helps me be strong.
"Confident Living," Unity School of Christianity
(New Thought) Hymn

THE ROOTS OF the modern prosperity gospel are long and tangled. To understand the size, success, and diversity of today's movement, we first need to understand certain ways of thinking about spiritual power that emerged and competed for attention early in the twentieth century. This thinking took many forms and went by different names, including mind-cure, success literature, positive thinking, self-help, and prosperity theology. Mystics, businessmen, Manhattan pastors, and storefront prophets alike sermonized its virtues. This was the core: *adherents, acting in accordance with divine principles, relied on their minds to transform thought and speech into heaven-sent blessings.* It focused on the individual rather than groups and emphasized the power of the individual's mind. This chapter traces the development of this thinking about spiritual power in the metaphysical New Thought movement and its growth into more recognizably evangelical gospels of health and wealth. We might envision the prosperity gospel as composed of three distinct though intersecting streams: pentecostalism; New Thought (an amalgam of metaphysics and Protestantism discussed later in this chapter); and an American gospel of pragmatism, individualism, and upward mobility. In this chapter, we see how these divergent traditions flowed across the American religious landscape and into new conduits of health and wealth.

Though little known outside of pentecostal circles, the evangelist E. W. Kenyon serves as our journey's leading guide. His evangelical appropriation of this concept of spiritual power channeled New Thought and pentecostal streams, shaping the prosperity movement into, to borrow a title from Norman Vincent Peale, "A Guide to Confident Living."

New Thought's Mind-Power

Prayer beat the fluttering heart of humanity's connection to the divine. Christians have always sought to access supernatural power for their daily lives, and the chief way they tried to do so was through prayer: requests from helpless humans to an omnipotent God who heard these pleas and might—or might not—answer them as desired by the petitioners. This formula required the pray-ers to acknowledge their own weak position and rely on the One with unlimited bounties. Finding this method irksome, ineffective, or too passive, Christians often sought to *compel* the supernatural to produce their desired results. Many hoped to command (critics would say manipulate) the physical and spiritual planes through the interior world of thought, imagination, meditation, and prayer. The historian of metaphysics Catherine Albanese christened it *mental magic* (as opposed to *material magic*) for its use of vision, imagination, affirmative prayer, and an interiority that focused on self-mastery.[1] What Albanese called mental magic we will call *mind-power* because its discourse of control and efficacy centered on the role of thought and speech. Victorian America was a hotbed of mind-power, bursting with transcendentalism, spiritualism, Free Masonry, Christian Science, and, of particular interest here, an offshoot of Christian Science called New Thought. Out of this miasma came the thinkers who nurtured a particular species of mind-power, planting the seeds of the present-day prosperity gospel.

This type of mind-power surged in the late nineteenth century, accompanying confidence about the progress and potential perfectibility of the human race. The era after the Civil War, often known as the Gilded Age, witnessed a flood of religious ideals that bathed the period with hearty individualism and a bold pragmatism. Self-mastery became an art and occupation, as people sought to consolidate the era's advances with improvements to their own lives. An ethos of self-help prevailed. Personal sewing machines and *Popular Mechanics* magazine harnessed technology for house repair. Gymnasiums appeared in universities and city centers across the country, as people devoted themselves to the pleasure and pursuit of self-taught athletic conditioning. All signs seemed to point to the world's (and humanity's) hidden potential. New scientific inventions like the telegraph, electric light, and discoveries like Koch's Postulates—which demonstrated the role of germs in disease causation—introduced the American masses to invisible *causal* forces.

Ideas about the power of the mind ripened in this climate, the fruit of at least a half century of metaphysical speculation. Ralph Waldo Emerson's philosophical idealism, Swedish mystic Emmanuel Swedenborg's Neoplatonic theory of correspondence, and Helena Blavatsky's theosophical quest for uniform spiritual laws seeded the ground, but it took Phineas Parkhurst Quimby, inventor and healer, to bring ideas about mind-power to maturity.[2] Personal experience led Quimby part of the way. He attempted to cure his tuberculosis with some fresh air, but his carriage ride went awry when his horse balked, forcing him to run beside the horse. Surprisingly, the run offered relief of his symptoms, which signaled to Quimby that the mind could overcome disease. Quimby's suspicions about the power of the mind solidified as he shared his generation's obsession with mesmerism, a hybrid of healing practices and metaphysical thought, based on Franz Anton Mesmer's discovery of hypnosis. Quimby followed in Mesmer's footsteps as a touring mesmerist; later, as a successful physician, he stumbled into discoveries about the human subconscious, including the effectiveness of placebos and the "talking cure," a forerunner of modern psychotherapy. The New England physician eventually concluded that healing occurred because of mental and spiritual alignment, inspiring a generation of positive thinkers to follow the connection between thought and healing.

Mary Baker Eddy, founder of Christian Science, filtered Quimby's conclusions through a Christological framework. As Eddy taught, Jesus came to save the world, not through his divinity, but by demonstrating right thinking. He saw the earth as it truly was: an illusory material realm where the mind tricked people into dangerous misperceptions. The heart of Christianity was knowledge, and believers must be reeducated in the new mental science. Her 1875 manifesto *Science and Health* pressed beyond Quimby's mental science by breaking with any lingering materialism. She disavowed the reality of illness and even death, arguing that suffering resulted from mental errors. Believers must rid themselves of misperceptions that blocked mental and physical restoration. Eddy offered a compelling vision of divine health that promised a true *Christian Science*, spiritual truth with repeatable results. Yet not all who insisted on the power of the mind were willing to call the material illusory. American popular religion came to favor the productive tension of mind and body it found in Eddy's rival and successor: New Thought.

New Thought represents a cluster of thinkers and metaphysical ideas that emerged in the 1880s as the era's most powerful vehicle of mind-power. Three aspects of New Thought became foundational to the twentieth century's views of mind-power. First, it assumed essential unity between God and humanity, declaring that separation from the divine was only a matter of degree. The American religious terrain, plowed deep by the soulful individualism of Ralph Waldo Emerson, was fertile soil for a high anthropology (which is to say, an optimistic theology of human capacity.) As many New Thought authors worked inside a Christian framework, they explored "salvation" not as an act imposed from above by God, but rather an act of drawing out humanity's potential. Second, New Thought taught that the world should be reimagined as thought rather than substance. The spiritual world formed absolute reality, while the material world was the mind's projection. Unlike Christian Science, New Thought never denied the reality of the material world, but saw it as contingent upon the mind. Right standing with the divine required sacred alignment, a mystical connection that won the historian Sydney Ahlstrom's famous label of "harmonial religion."[3] Third, New Thought argued that people shared in God's power to create by means of thought. People shaped their own worlds by their thinking, just as God had created the world using thought. Positive thoughts yielded positive circumstances, and negative thoughts yielded negative situations.[4] These three features—a high anthropology, the priority of spiritual reality, and the generative power of positive thought—formed the main presuppositions of the developing mind-power.

In its infancy, New Thought was largely preoccupied with healing, the same issue that consumed Christian Science and the wider American culture. Like hydropathy, Grahamism, Adventism, homeopathy, and the burgeoning faith cure movement, New Thought offered a religious alternative to the often harsh regimen of standard medical treatments.[5] Bloodletting, mercury-laced purgatives, and arsenic tonics formed common "cures," making orthodox medicine a potentially risky treatment. Warren Felt Evans, New Thought's first author, promulgated the physical benefits of this therapeutic brand of metaphysics with the publication of *The Mental Cure* in 1869. Evans, as a practicing healer and systematizer of New Thought, sought to explain illness as an imbalance resulting from wrong thinking. William James labeled these buoyant ideas, "the religion of healthy-mindedness."[6]

These gospels of health stood on one side of a blurry line between Christian metaphysics and metaphysical Christianity. One prioritized the method of mind-power, while the other concentrated on its relationship to Jesus' death and resurrection. And though pentecostals viewed metaphysics with suspicion and contempt, its ministers who tarried on the subject of faith began to hover close to the line. A little known healer on the margins of pentecostalism, with his blend of evangelical and New Thought theology, first showed them how. His work introduced pentecostalism to a new Christian stream of mind-power.

E. W. Kenyon

Essek William Kenyon flatly rejected the "religion of healthy-mindedness" as counterfeit.[7] In his 55 years as a revivalist, educator, and evangelist in areas of New Thought's greatest influence, he railed against it as a substitution of gospel truth with abstract "principles."[8] Only Christians' rightful use of divine principles could unlock God's treasury of blessings, and Kenyon endeavored to teach them how. He called it "dominating faith."[9] His foundational works on spiritual power articulated a set of universal laws that electrified late nineteenth-century evangelicalism and its offspring, pentecostalism, with confidence in human capabilities.

FIGURE I.I **E. W. Kenyon** Pastor and radio evangelist E. W. Kenyon, pictured with an open bible, encouraged Christians to use their faith to dominate their circumstances. Date unknown.

Source: Flower Pentecostal Heritage Center.

Kenyon took a circuitous path to ministry. He showed early promise when, as a teenager, he served as a preacher and deacon in the Methodist church of Amsterdam, New York. When his spiritual ambitions fizzled, he embarked on a career as an organ salesman, and then as an actor, before he enrolled in dramatic studies at Boston's Emerson College of Oratory. The college's theological impact on Kenyon is a subject of ongoing debate. Yet his tenure at Emerson, home to the New England sage Ralph Waldo Trine and other metaphysical teachers, certainly brought him into contact with the New Thought movement.[10] In 1893, Kenyon married Evva Spurling, an agnostic and divorcée nine years his senior. Shortly after marriage, Kenyon and his new wife embraced the teachings of Keswick Higher Life (a branch of the Holiness movement) and took up the ministerial mantle. For almost a decade, the Kenyons lived as faith healers and ministerial nomads. Kenyon held various Baptist pastorates in Massachusetts, and the couple traveled as evangelists. He became increasingly committed to living by faith, surrendering his livelihood and his possessions for common use. In 1900, Kenyon founded Bethel Bible Institute in Spencer, Massachusetts, using as a model the Faith Training College of faith cure leader Charles Cullis. In 1914, Evva died after a prolonged illness; the same year, Kenyon married a young Nova Scotian named Alice Maud Whitney. In the early 1920s, the Kenyon family, now expanded with a son and daughter, left their fledgling school for California, where he again bounded between pulpits and evangelistic meetings with restless intensity.[11] In 1931, he departed for Washington state where he founded the New Covenant Baptist Church and a radio program *Kenyon's Church of the Air*. In Washington, Kenyon's legacy found its home. His newsletter *Herald of Life* and Seattle Bible Institute began there. Apart from *The Father and His Family* and *The Wonderful Name of Jesus*, Kenyon published most of his major works during this period.

The scaffolding of E. W. Kenyon's theology stood on the bedrock of late nineteenth-century evangelicalism. Kenyon's evangelical piety would have passed muster in the Great Awakening, giving priority to the authority of the Bible, the experience of "new birth," the subsequent need for sanctification, and the necessity of evangelism. Radical evangelicals—and Kenyon with them—argued that sanctification conferred greater power than Christians had yet realized.[12] In Christ's death and resurrection, believers could expect not only the new birth that marked the start of the Christian life but also the transformation wrought by entire sanctification. The doctrine of entire sanctification sprang from the work of the eighteenth-century Englishman John Wesley, who taught that God's grace might set believers on the road to perfect love for Christ by freeing them from the inclination to sin. The doctrine gained new significance in (Wesleyan) Holiness and Reformed circles in the mid-nineteenth century, when believers began to depict entire sanctification not as a process, but as a calculable moment. This baptism of the Holy Spirit, as it was, offered Kenyon a powerful vision of Christian victory over sin.

Quarrels over the timing of the sanctification experience later became one of the early pentecostal movement's thorniest debates. Did it accompany or follow salvation? For E. W. Kenyon, the real question was one of power: What victories could the redeemed Christian expect over sin? Kenyon confidently claimed that Christ had secured not only sanctification but also a plethora of other blessings in the atonement. He preached this view to William H. Durham, who (whether it was because of Kenyon or not) embraced it. Durham's 1910 sermon, later published as "Finished Work of Christ," ignited a firestorm of controversy that, by 1920, had won most pentecostals to the view that sinners found salvation—justification and sanctification—in a single soteriological work of grace.[13] Christ's atoning work may be finished, but for Kenyon this was not the end of the story.[14] His theology held that this profound ontological shift from sinner to saint signaled only the first phase of redemption. To explain, Kenyon appropriated New Thought's focus on mind, spirit, and universal laws to show that Christians could look to the cross not as a promise of things to come, but as a guarantee of benefits *already* granted.

Christ's substitutionary atonement, according to Kenyon, underwrote a series of spiritual and legal transactions. In language reminiscent of New Thought, God was a spirit who created a spiritual universe. The physical world was a shallow material reflection of this preeminent and preexisting spiritual universe. Though clothed in the "temporary dwelling place" of flesh and bones, humans too were *primarily* spirit.[15] Though the priority of spirit seemed a peripheral theological detail, Kenyon drew it into every beginner's course on the gospel. Without it, the cross became difficult to understand. In the Fall, Satan gained legal authority over Adam and became humanity's spiritual father, the consequences of which were sickness, poverty, and death.[16] Without Christ, humanity resembled the inhabitants of Plato's cave, devoid of the light of revelation and "dependent upon [their] senses for [their] protection and life."[17] Their dulled senses could not perceive or access the storehouse of blessing God intended for them. Christ's resurrection united humanity's spiritual nature with God's own, restoring their spiritual vision and legal rights to dominion over the earth. This bifurcation between spiritual and physical worlds lent added meaning to Jesus' death. According to Kenyon, Satan "took Jesus' spirit with him down to the pit of hell where Jesus during three terrible days and nights suffered the tortures of hell's cohorts."[18] The power of sin was broken. Clear-eyed believers henceforth possessed God's ability and authority to rule over the material world.

Christians, now unburdened by sin, hovered only a little lower than angels. Kenyon's anthropology outstripped the boldness of even Higher Life teachers, who, as Kenyon biographer Dale Simmons observed, held up divine union with God as a distant *goal*. Kenyon understood it to be the *starting point*.[19] Jesus' death and resurrection had shifted believers' onto-logical status, making them legal shareholders of certain rights and priv-ileges. At times, Kenyon's Holy Spirit-filled Christians hardly could be identified as human at all, as their total identification with God approached deification. "The World has not known that there is a su-perman in their midst today," Kenyon marveled. "They don't know that every new creation is a superman in the embryo."[20] Believers could not rise to the heights of spiritual supermen without the second phase of their redemption.[21] The next step would be epistemological, as believers learned the inner workings of faith.

Kenyon's theology of faith took inspiration from his involvement with the late nineteenth-century divine healing movement.[22] Alternatively called faith cure, the movement thrived among evangelical Protestants, ordained and lay, from a variety of traditions. Charles Cullis, author of *Faith Cures, or Answers to Prayer in the Healing of the Sick* (1879), inspired a generation of leaders (particularly those in Higher Life and Holiness cir-cles) to take up healing as another provision of the atonement.[23] Kenyon's personal experience with healing paved the way. His conversion and sub-sequent healing within the Keswick Higher Life tradition made him into a preacher, eager to see life as an unfolding victory over sin, but not a healer.[24] Shortly after his conversion in A. J. Gordon's church, he relates that his "poor, sick, wrecked body was instantly made whole."[25] Still, Ken-yon was a reluctant minister for the gospel of health, worried about being called a fanatic.[26] Eventually Evva Kenyon's sheepish attempt at faith heal-ing changed them both, when a tuberculosis-ridden man begged for and received healing after Evva's reluctant hands touched him.

In faith cure, Kenyon discovered the collaboration of belief, mind, and health. Through healing services, published treatises, and the founding of "faith" homes for the sick, advocates sought to overcome illness through the cultivation of faith.[27] Illness, they taught, perished when a patient believed and then acted as one whom God has already healed. Practitioners were encouraged to pray the "prayer of faith," holding God to his guarantee of restored health for all who believe. As the historian Heather Curtis noted, devotional practices of health put faith in motion, "training the senses to ignore lingering pain or symptoms of sickness and disciplining the body to 'act faith' by getting out of bed and serving God through energetic engagement with others."[28] This mental and physical exertion energized the work of faith, translating spiritual fervor into physical wholeness. Kenyon wholeheartedly agreed that Christians must live out their faith in contradiction to their senses. As Kenyon argued, humans, bombarded by "sense knowledge," must be trained to see the spiritual truths ("revelation knowledge") buried beneath.[29] Faith laid claim to these hidden spiritual realities. Kenyon went even further and prescribed more than a faith cure to illness. Believers must not only nourish belief through action; they must unleash the spiritual forces that commanded the universe. Faith, as he defined it, was the "confident assurance based on absolute knowledge that everything is already provided through the operation of certain immutable laws."[30] To explain how this came to be, Kenyon turned back to the beginning, creation. The story of creation accounted for both how God used faith and how humans were created for faith.

"In the beginning was the Word." This familiar opening of John recapitulated the Genesis creation account, and, for Kenyon, summed up creation's most enduring feature—the spoken word. God *spoke* the world into existence, creating light with the words, "Let there be light." In this, Kenyon shared a common New Thought premise that God established the "original Creative Word" in Genesis, making the spoken word the template for activating power.[31] Kenyon, however, stipulated that the divine power poured into the container of words could be called only one thing: faith. "Faith-filled words" not only brought the universe into being but also governed the world as an invisible force.[32] The power of the spoken word simply carried faith to its desired ends.

The "Word" became a signifier with many referents. Kenyon accepted the customary meaning of Jesus Christ as the Word, both God himself and God's message to the world. Scripture housed God's written Word. Yet Kenyon gave priority to the *spoken* Word above all as the source of God's power. Believers speaking God's own Word gained access to the creative power that laid the foundations of the earth. He urged believers to use spoken words, called positive confessions, to tap into this spiritual power. "Faith never rises above its confession," he often repeated.[33] Though Kenyon lambasted New Thought adherents for their proclamations of "I am well, I am well, I am happy, I am happy," he chided their content, not their method. Kenyon advised them to repeat instead: "I am a child of the Living God."[34] New Thought employed the right process with the wrong theology. God sought speakers, not simply believers. Even the unsaved, Kenyon mused, might enjoy the benefits of positive words.[35]

Just as the atonement transferred legal authority from Satan to the faithful, the name of Jesus held forensic significance. Kenyon taught that Jesus transferred the "Power of Attorney" to all those who use his name. Prayer took on binding legal qualities as believers followed Jesus' formula: "If ye shall ask anything in my name, I will do it" (John 14:14). Kenyon replaced the word "ask" with "demand," since petitioners were entitled to the legal benefits of Jesus' name.[36] The Holy Spirit became merely an assistant as Kenyon gave the credit for casting out demons, speaking in tongues, and curing disease to the rightful use of the name of Jesus.

Kenyon's articulation of "overcoming faith"—evangelicalism sparked with mind-power—acted as a flint stone for generations of followers. Kenyon's theology preceded and then overlapped with pentecostalism, and as it did, it brought underlying themes into sharp relief. Faith-filled believers became powerful conduits through which God's power could flow. His amplified anthropology, together with a priority on spiritual reality and the power of thought expressed in word and deed, provided the theological groundwork for some of the most radical pentecostal claims to atonement power. Kenyon's Finished Work theology, as articulated by William Durham, left a lasting imprint on pentecostal ontology. Oneness pentecostals (who understood Jesus alone as God) widely embraced his book *The Wonderful Name of Jesus* (1927) as an articulation of Jesus' singular expression of God's power.[37]

Kenyon's theology represented only a minority strain within pentecostalism. In his lifetime, Kenyon's Bethel Bible Institute, correspondence school, and evangelistic revivals earned him modest fame. Yet the wide reach of his books, periodicals, and national radio ministry gave him lasting theological influence. By the time of his death in 1948, Kenyon's *Herald of Life* boasted a circulation of more than 20,000 people in nearly sixty countries.[38] More indirectly, though no less consequentially, his imprint on pentecostal healing practices bore his legacy to full maturity.

Pentecostalism's Mind-Power

Early pentecostals stood with their feet firmly planted in the material world. Though better known for their heavenly minded experiences of ecstatic worship, speaking in tongues, and focus on the Lord's imminent return, pentecostals also distinguished themselves with radical claims about God's terrestrial blessings. Like their radical evangelical predecessors, they preached a "fourfold" gospel of divine healing, personal salvation, baptism of the Holy Spirit, and Christ's soon return. They claimed the human material body as a primary focus of divine action. As the Zion City evangelist John G. Lake observed, salvation was "an all-inclusive word, including all that God does for the spirit, soul, and body of man."[39] It is not surprising then that many pentecostals found Kenyon useful. Kenyon's relationships with some of the greatest pentecostal leaders of the day—William Durham, Aimee Semple McPherson, John G. Lake, and F. F. Bosworth—led many to mistake him for a pentecostal. He had attended the Azusa Street revival and even applied for ordination by the Assemblies of God in the mid-1920s. For unknown reasons, he never followed through.[40] Though Kenyon kept pentecostalism at arm's length, a strong minority of pentecostals adopted Kenyon's instrumental vision of faith.[41]

Fred F. Bosworth, healing evangelist and radio pioneer, borrowed elements of Kenyon's ideas to form one of the most influential theologies of health.[42] In the 1920s, Bosworth spread his message through popular revivals across the United States and Canada, as well as through his Chicago-based radio program, *National Radio Revival Missionary Crusaders*. This famous deliverance evangelist attracted 12,000 attendees to a single crusade in Ottawa, Ontario. His bestselling manifesto, *Christ the Healer*, popularized the utterly confident view of divine health that all right-thinking Christians may lay claim to perfect health. In the first edition, Bosworth taught readers to "appropriate" healing through faith by belief, action, and praise (rather than "confession.") Like Kenyon, Bosworth urged readers to pray the "prayer of faith" and to act on their healing "while every sense contradicts Him."[43] The body served as a site of healing, blessing, and empowerment. By the edition in 1948, Bosworth offered a simple prescription to "act faith, speak faith, and to think faith."[44] Kenyon's vision of overcoming faith impacted him significantly, and he received permission to include Kenyon's work directly in a new chapter entitled "Our Confessions." What Kenyon called "dominating faith," Bosworth called "appropriating faith" and "victorious faith," "*taking* and *using* what God offers to us."[45]

Bosworth shared Kenyon's conclusion that healing was a legal right, secured by Christ, and accelerated through spiritual effects of positive words. Confession, he wrote, "puts God to work fulfilling His promise" and brings believers' words into reality. He likened the process to a game of checkers: "Our move is to expect what he promises . . . before we *see* the healing. . . . He always moves when it is His turn."[46] A believer's move forced God to move accordingly. They never cried out: "Lord, heal me if it be thy will!"—the qualification marred God's self-imposed promise with doubt. Bosworth parroted Kenyon's words: "A spiritual law that few recognize is that our confession rules us."[47] Pentecostals would have to put their lips, as well as their hearts, to use.

Bosworth's gospel of health would later become an important pillar of the healing revivals of the 1940s. Bosworth worked tirelessly alongside the revival's biggest names as a mentor and specialist in the outworking of faith. He regularly appeared before famed healer William Branham for morning and afternoon "Faith Meetings" to raise their expectations for healing.[48] Gordon Lindsay's *Voice of Healing* frequently reprinted Bosworth's theology of faith, and the young guns of the revival would crowd

FIGURE I.2 Fred F. Bosworth A dapper crowd poses for a shot of F. F. Bosworth's 1931 revival in Chicago, Illinois. The evangelist (pictured in the gray suit and tie on the platform) was famous for his healing manual, *Christ the Healer*, and his packed crusades.

Source: Flower Pentecostal Heritage Center.

around him for tips and teaching. Though Bosworth never preached about prosperity, he placed the righteous individual, speaking faith-filled words, at the heart of divine healing. Though he would have despised the association, his own methods "sanctified" aspects of New Thought mind-power for pentecostal audiences. His theology—and the developing doctrine of verbal power—might be called *metaphysically inflected*, filtered through a first generation of New Thought-inspired pentecostals. As his healing practices and revival techniques proved to be a textbook for later healing revivalists, Bosworth cemented Kenyon's imprint on divine health long after anyone remembered Kenyon's name.

Yet Kenyon's theology also leavened pentecostal ontology, as pentecostals placed great emphasis on God's desire to perfect, not simply redeem, his followers. Their confidence in human perfectibility seemed limitless, as pentecostals wondered how God-like they might become. Earlier we noted Kenyon's insistence that Christians who lived up to their spiritual benefits would become "supermen," and "world-ruler[s] in the spiritual realm."[49] To be sure, most lightly tempered their holy optimism with modesty, reminding one another that Christ alone deserved the glory. The historian Grant Wacker called this early pentecostal confidence "psychological dynamite" for its claims of powerful access to divine authority.[50]

John G. Lake, the Zion City evangelist and missionary to South Africa, laid out one of the strongest pentecostal cases for suprahuman abilities. Credited with pioneering "God-men" theology, Lake's bold claims teetered on self-apotheosis. "God intends us to be gods (John 10:34)," he argued. "There is a God-power and a soul-force in the nature of man that God is endeavoring to bring forth. . . . The man within is the real man. The inner man is the real governor, the true man that Jesus said was a god."[51] Lake, like Bosworth, credited Kenyon and John Alexander Dowie as theological inspirations, and it is tempting to conclude that his soaring anthropology sprang mainly from faith cure and Kenyon's appropriation of mind-power. A lesser known chapter of Lake's ministry, however, established a more direct link to New Thought. Prior to establishing his famous healing ministry in Spokane, Washington, Lake co-served a congregation with New Thought author Albert C. Grier, a partnership that began a lifelong collaboration.[52] The two shared a devotion to divine health and labored together in the church's "healing rooms," areas where trained church members ministered to the sick through counsel and prayer. In 1915, Lake founded his own congregation, comprised largely of former members of the New Thought congregation. He advertised himself as "Dr. John Lake, Miracle

Healing Power," offering his services free of charge to all seeking divine
health. His ministry garnered national attention as reportedly 100,000
people claimed healing.[53] He clearly owed much to Grier's ministry and
the healing rooms erected by Dowie in the late 1800s in Zion City. While
Lake's biographer asserts that the evangelist preached an unequivocally
pentecostal message, Lake's comparatively stronger claims to spiritual
power suggest that New Thought lit the fuse of pentecostalism's psychological dynamite.

Words spoken in prayer, exorcism, worship, or plain conversation took
on added weight, as pentecostals cultivated a popular theology and practice
of verbal power. Their high opinion of the spoken word had begun on
Azusa Street, as pentecostals turned to *glossolalia* (speaking in tongues) as
their spiritual seal. Eager believers demonstrated their divine connection
not by doctrine or ritual, but by speaking in a holy language. (Other physical manifestations might have been chosen to signal the Holy Spirit's presence. For example, the Metropolitan Church Association, headquartered in
Waukesha, Wisconsin, contributed some of the early pentecostal leaders
and the distinction of being called "The Holy Jumpers" because some of its

FIGURE 1.3 John G. Lake Evangelist John G. Lake advertising his healing services
in Spokane, Washington, with a Ford Model A. The wooden sign reads: "Dr. John
G. Lake, Miracle Healing Power, Fourth & McClellan." Circa 1931.
Source: Flower Pentecostal Heritage Center.

members identified jumping as an evidence of spirit-baptism.)[54] Pentecostals stood out in the history of Christianity for they alone required an involuntary ecstatic utterance as a credential for ordination and full participation in the community. Pentecostals cemented the material character of *glossolalia* in doctrinal formulas as "the initial *physical* evidence of speaking in tongues" (emphasis added).[55] The word *physical* was deemed so important that when it was accidentally left out of the Assemblies of God "Statement of Fundamental Truths" in 1916, a special corrective was made a year later.[56] Early debates whether the deaf could speak in tongues using sign language pointed to their enthusiasm for the power of the spoken word and desire for all to participate.[57] The absolutism that charged their doctrine with certainty and their actions with cosmic meaning also fixed words with iron-clad import. These pentecostals relied on prevailing prayer to transmit their pleas not as requests but as contracts, guaranteeing miraculous results.[58] Believers ferreted out the meaning of God's many names for personal use. To the sick, for instance, God revealed himself as *Jehovah-Rapha* ("I am the Lord that healeth thee"). To the fearful, God's redemptive name was *Jehovah-Nissi* ("The Lord Our Banner of Protection"). In each name adherents found a key to personal power. The wide acceptance of Kenyon's *The Wonderful Name of Jesus* and Bosworth's "The Seven Redemptive Names of Jehovah" in *Christ the Healer* popularized the talismanic use of Jesus' name. In pulpits and prayer closets alike, believers intoned his name with a sweet reverence, expecting it to bring their petition, praise, or deliverance to completion.[59]

Early American pentecostalism, intersected with channels of New Thought, had absorbed a high anthropology and view of divine speech that would help shape its theology throughout the rest of the century. In the postwar years, this reedy stream of pentecostal mind-power would become a flood.

Health, Wealth, and Black Metaphysicals

In the early 1900s, Americans found metaphysical religion—and New Thought in particular—lurking everywhere, in Broadway plays, bestselling books, street-corner success manuals, and in the advice husbands heard from their wives when they looked up from *Good Housekeeping*. It had become the prevailing current of American popular religion, as difficult to identify as "religion" proper from the air people breathed. In 1901, William James observed the dawn of this era: "Mind-cure principles are beginning to so pervade the air that one catches their spirit at second hand."[60] Though the institutional forms of New Thought remained dominated by whites, New Thought's widespread popularity guaranteed that all Americans, black and white, breathed it in.[61]

Many African American believers caught the spirit firsthand.[62] The late nineteenth century bore witness to the engagement of African Americans at all social levels with spiritualism, hypnosis, mesmerism, New Thought, and other variations of metaphysical religion.[63] By the close of World War I, new forms of metaphysical religion sprang to life. In the 1920s and 1930s, as the Great Migration pressed African Americans into Northern urban landscapes, a groundswell of alternative religious communities promised religious—and often metaphysical—answers to social and economic problems. Poor, white city-dwellers had dime novels and success manuals to help them live within Leviathan. The flood of new immigrants struggled to move economically upstream. But these new black migrants lived under the double burden of poverty and Jim Crow laws. Though crippling economic and political realities might have led African Americans to despair of the possibility of the pursuit of happiness, an ebullient gospel infused them with new hope. Cross-pollinations of New Thought, pentecostalism, and African-derived traditions (hoodoo, voodoo) began to flourish in the urban north, as leaders like Prophet James Jones, Father Divine, Father George Hurley, and the Reverend Ike promised to smooth the rough edges of capitalism and industrialism with theologies that countered poverty, disease, and despair.[64] They sounded the ram's horn declaring the world to be—despite all evidence to the contrary—fundamentally good and ripe with opportunity.

The rise of black spiritualism, in particular, demonstrated the vitality and fluidity of metaphysical Christianity in urban African American communities. While white spiritualism had found religious solace in séances and otherworldly communications in parlors and auditoriums across the country, black spiritualism was not such a staid and middle-class phenomenon.[65] Nurtured in New Orleans and spread widely in the urban North and South in the 1920s and 1930s, black spiritualism was a transplanted religion for transplanted people. Its leaders were Southern to the bone and brought a voodoo tactility to Sunday mornings. Catholic pageantry reserved for popes and cardinals was imparted to church founders; it reveled in sensuality and color, abundantly using candles, robes, crowns, and scepters. Black spiritualism's fractious and experimental nature produced as many approaches as there were churches. In Detroit's Universal

Hagar's Spiritual Church, Father George Hurley mixed spiritualism with elements of pentecostalism, Catholicism, voodoo, and black nationalism. In Chicago, the First Church of Deliverance might have been mistaken for a pentecostal service but for its focus on séances, religious iconography, and channeling of the spirit world.[66] The congregation swelled from a storefront to a 2,000-member body, known for its jubilant blend of pentecostal worship, Catholic pageantry, and the invocation of spells.[67] Believers around cluttered altars gloried in names like Princess and Queen. By the 1930s, black spiritualists remained a small but rapidly growing religious alternative among urban African Americans.[68]

Black spiritualists adopted and adapted metaphysical religion, but more important, they applied it to the pressing daily questions of scarcity, racism, segregation, and despair. Some black metaphysical gospels promoted individual solutions. Father George Hurley, for example, eschewed programmatic solutions for the urban black poor, urging his followers to counter racism with prayer and positive thinking.[69] Others bent metaphysical ideals toward a communal gospel of self-help. Father Divine's Harlembased Peace Mission protected poverty-stricken believers by providing

FIGURE 1.4 **Sweet Daddy Grace** Founder Bishop Charles Emmanuel "Sweet Daddy" Grace seated beside his second wife, Angelina Montano, at a celebratory occasion in a United House of Prayer church. The men in suits and bow ties, and the women, young and old, in white dresses, necklaces, and crown-like hair pieces made this banquet a regal affair. Between 1932 and 1937.

Source: Scurlock Studio Records, Archives Center, National Museum of American History, Smithsonian Institution.

clothing, food, housing, and job training.[70] In Depression-era America, Father Divine famously fed thousands daily at his Peace Mission banquets, lavish meals that defied segregation by seating black and white members beside one another. Elder "Lightfoot" Solomon Michaux, dubbed the "Happy Am I Preacher," preached a Holiness gospel studded with New Thought to his radio audiences of more than two million, a message he bolstered with comprehensive social welfare programs.[71] Black metaphysical Christianity entwined racial uplift with the power of the mind.

These self-help prophets offered a symbolic materialism. Prophet James F. Jones, famed radio evangelist and black Spiritual leader, gilded much of his worship facility, bestowed lordly titles on his congregation, and stuffed his mansion with expensive furnishings. He would be remembered by the *Saturday Evening Post* as the "Messiah in Mink."[72] (*Jet* magazine constantly portrayed him in a cape and sombrero.[73]) Reverend Clarence Cobbs of Chicago's First Church of Deliverance displayed a penchant for fashionable cars, lavish attire, and cigars.[74] Elder Lightfoot Solomon Michaux simply flashed his gold-toothed smile. Sweet Daddy Grace, founder of the United House of Prayer for All People, famously celebrated his wealth. Though he was closer to an old-fashioned Holiness preacher than a mind-power prophet, his ministry was a spectacle of consumption. He enjoyed a lavish lifestyle, replete with expensive cars, regal attire, and his trademark long hair and fingernails (testifying to his freedom from any form of manual labor). Believers could see his mustached face featured on everything from his own line of toothpaste to the stained-glass windows in his churches.

Yet beyond personal demonstrations of wealth, these leaders showed believers a path to personal fulfillment. These metaphysical gospels promised a winning advantage within the framework of capitalism and industrialism. Father Divine diagnosed the cause (negative thinking) and the cure (positive thinking) for the Great Depression. Reverend Cobbs invested candles, flowers, or other objects with sacred power, asking participants for a monetary donation in exchange for the object (and the blessings it would bring).[75] These messages of divine opportunity formed a bulwark against the everyday losses of living under authorities patrolling the black and white divide. And further, they encouraged desire. Leaders offered prayers, rituals, and sacred objects to help believers resurrect hope. Their followers embraced a gospel that affirmed the material world of the urban North.[76] These uprooted city-dwellers knew what they wanted. They sought a faith that closed the gap between desire and fulfillment.

FIGURE 1.5 Father Divine Father Divine in his trademark suit and tie, standing behind his polished desk. Circa 1932.
Source: Scurlock Studio Records, Archives Center, National Museum of American History, Smithsonian Institution.

In sum, the urban gospels of the interwar period both introduced metaphysical religion to far-flung African American audiences and asserted the importance of prosperity and religious access to the Good Life. To be sure, popular African American magazines derided these preachers, but they captured readers' attention as figures of celebrity and interest. The focus on material blessings, be it a mink or the next meal, established a precedent that later ministers were soon to follow. Their theologies reflected not only the black appropriation of predominantly white metaphysical religion but also the religious innovations of self-help prophets. After World War II, when white pentecostals heralded the righteous acquisition of health and finances, they little knew that a handful of African American believers had been there before them.

These uplift movements throw Kenyon's gospel into stark relief. Fusions of black pentecostalism and metaphysical religion resonated with audiences, forging connections that proved to be electric. Pentecostalism provided a familiar narrative of sin, repentance, and salvation, sealed with

Jesus' death and resurrection. New Thought, in contrast, persisted as a religion of utility. In other words, people found in it a religion they could *use*. The resulting messages combined a Christological framework with the mechanism of mind-power, guaranteeing believers the ability to change their circumstances by tapping into new spiritual powers. Believers could expect their thoughts, emotions, actions, and happenstance to express God-given power and blessings. The fusion of New Thought and pentecostal traditions produced a distinct strand of prosperity theology within African American religion, a live wire that pulsed with nothing short of power.

Gospels of Wealth

Pentecostals, for the most part, had learned to do without. Contrary to the thesis popularized by Anderson's *Visions of the Disinherited*, pentecostals actually lived much the same lives as most Americans. They were, like their neighbors, country-living, working-class folks with the level of education typical of the time.[77] Though they hailed from an economic cross-section of society, most earned a modest living working as laborers, craftsmen, service providers, and, sometimes, professionals, winning ordinary comforts and few excesses. From the patchwork tents of pentecostal camp meetings to the pulpits of prominent leaders such as Charles Fox Parham, Smith Wigglesworth, and Aimee Semple McPherson, few believers projected economic ambitions through a theological lens. Though E. W. Kenyon promised heaven-sent finances, he spoke little of personal prosperity, resting on a shoestring budget to support his lifestyle and ministry.[78] Holy Ghost people cried out for lost souls, healed bodies, miraculous tongues, and the Lord's kingdom to come, but rarely for material blessings that would change their social station. "The natural tendency of prosperity," warned *The Latter Rain Evangel*, "is to inspire us with self-confidence and to turn us away from God."[79] Even if Jesus himself had not recommended it, they might still have preferred to be salt of the earth.

Yet not all Americans smiled when fortune frowned. For the first half of the century, many American Protestants, like the broader American culture, sought religious solutions to their economic troubles. Some wanted Christian sanction for what they already owned, while others searched for tools to attain more. Many simply found a religious language of desire; longing coupled with the comfort that God ordered both the supernatural and mundane in their lives. While pentecostals, Christian Scientists, and New Thought teachers, among others, called for faith, prayer, positive words, and surrender to divine health, a host of voices called for similar principles applied to economic use. These principles later dubbed "positive thinking" by mainline Protestants and "positive confession" by pentecostals, endowed American Christianity with the same power that they granted divine health—the spiritual *means* to achieve results.[80] Again, as with gospels of health, metaphysical religion supplied Christianity with the instrument required to close the gap between earnest faith and divine blessings.

The term "positive thinking" requires some explanation. Often mistaken simply for optimism, positive thinking stressed the power of the mind over matter. It leaned on monism and philosophical idealism to define how life rewarded those with right thinking. Positive thinking was synthetic, mixing the categories of religion, psychology, medicine, and self-help; its prophets were not typically systematizers or intellectuals, but popularizers and doers. By the 1950s, mind-power, recast as positive thinking, earned a lasting place in the popular religious imagination and the American prosperity movement. Inside mainline Protestantism, it was both a reflection of its high view of human nature and potential, as well as an explanation for its middle-to-upper class respectability. Unlike believers of the Holiness and radical evangelical traditions, mainline Protestants did not turn to the power of the mind for health. What they sought, nicely summarized by the title of industrialist Andrew Carnegie's famous essay, was a "Gospel of Wealth."

In the late nineteenth century, the Gilded Age's yawning gap between rich and poor prompted a flurry of Christian responses. Walter Rauschenbusch's Social Gospel and William and Catherine Booth's Salvation Army, to name only two examples, offered Christian solutions to the swelling ranks of the urban poor. Yet not all Christians sought to solve the problems inherited from industrialism and immigration. Some Protestants so identified Christianity with America's good fortune that they flocked to those who would explain the gospel as immanent to the fits and starts of capitalism. Russell H. Conwell (1843–1925), Baptist minister and lawyer, became a prophet of the gospel of wealth with his famous sermon, "Acres of Diamonds." The sermon, preached some 6,000 times, promised listeners that wealth lay within any American's grasp, if they would only accept their Christian duty to work hard and see God's hand through the workings of capitalism. Conwell reinterpreted his Calvinist inheritance for this new corporate age, equating poverty with sin and riches with dutiful virtue. "I say you ought to be rich; you have no right to be poor," he concluded sharply.[81] Much like Horatio Alger's "rags to riches" dime novels, composed of anecdotes of virtue rewarded by financial windfalls, Conwell paired theological and fiscal optimism, resting on a high view of human perfectibility. The message required neither inner divinity nor potent words. Great men—and they were men—were once regular people, separated from the masses by steely character. Conwell preached the American virtues of innovation, pragmatism, and self-reliance dipped in bronze. Modern business simply tested every Christian's nature. Conwell's Wall Street gospel agreed with the unfettered accumulation by the nation's first millionaires and billionaires, sharing the mythical secret that brought an Andrew Carnegie or John D. Rockefeller to the top: sheer will.[82]

This was an American gospel, based on hard work, pragmatism, innovation, self-reliance and openness to risk.[83] The steadfast virtues of thrift, prudence, and persistence—so celebrated as the foundation of the American character—were appended to the imagined traits of frontiersmen, wildcatters, and fortune seekers. It was a muscular Christianity, emphasizing manly exploit and a willingness to seek what is hidden. It valued action over abstraction; it moralized money and finances as markers of thoroughgoing virtue. In Bruce Barton's *The Man Nobody Knows*, biblical injunctions and hard-nosed capitalism demanded that believers work twice as vigorously to achieve success.[84] Soft-palmed men were scorned. The American dream was realized not simply in those who had heaped up treasures but who had all the virtues to earn it or discover it all over again.

Metaphysical Money

For many Americans, however, work and drive were not enough. A little divine assistance might be needed. New Thought began as a prescription for mental and physical well-being. Yet New Thought's early focus on health did not last long; by 1890, New Thought had expanded its vision of what mystical alignment with the divine could bring. It was not simply that the movement's growth and newfound institutional strength fortified the boldness of its convictions. New Thought leaders, as the historian Beryl Satter documented, adopted a new (and contested) focus on desire, prosperity, and materiality.[85] The turn proved permanent. Unity

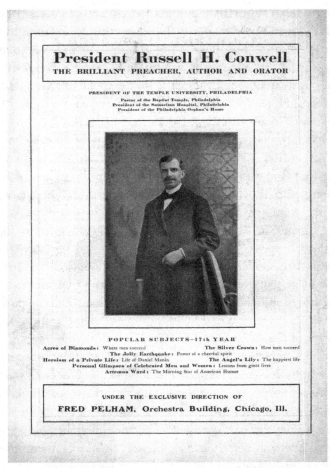

FIGURE 1.6 Russell H. Conwell Russell Conwell's 1908 talent brochure, advertising not only his famous "Acres of Diamonds" speech but also follow-up lectures like "The Silver Crown" (on how to succeed) and "The Angel's Lily" (on living the happiest life.)

Source: Redpath Chautauqua Bureau Records, University of Iowa Libraries, Iowa City, Iowa.

with God, many speculated, could merit both health and material abundance. This strand of metaphysical religion tilted toward knowledge, thought, and "the powers of mind, in individualistic terms, to heal disease, achieve prosperity, and enjoy personal success."[86] Teachers like Frances Lord made prosperity a centerpiece of New Thought, following in the footsteps of Emma Curtis Hopkins, her teacher, who quietly included material abundance as one of the many manifestations of right thinking.[87] Helen Wilmans penned *The Conquest of Poverty* (1899), one of the first examples of prosperity themes within New Thought. Charles and Myrtle Fillmore, founders of the influential Unity School of Christianity, asserted that prosperity was integral to New Thought. Charles Fillmore's aptly titled book *Prosperity* (1936) spoke of a God that Russell Conwell would have recognized—a God of abundant supply. "The Lord is my banker," read Fillmore's rendering of Psalm 23, "my credit is good . . . Yea, though I walk in the very shadow of debt, I shall fear no evil."[88] Yet, unlike Conwell, Fillmore's road to success lay within. Teaching that God was the divine supply, he implored listeners to align themselves with this divine source. This spiritual mutuality would yield financial and spiritual blessings.

Older themes in New Thought faded as metaphysicians like Ralph Waldo Trine trumpeted the movement's new values. Early New Thought, as Albanese argued, centered on themes of correspondence and the tranquil mind, language that evoked images of balance and mental stasis. As New Thought moved into the twentieth century, confidence in the power of the mind—and its corresponding ability to access divine sources—ruptured any concept of the mind as static. Metaphors shifted to "energy," "flows," and "streams" as believers asserted the *instrumentality* of thought.[89] Trine, whose metaphysical inheritance from Ralph Waldo Emerson was stamped even on his name, popularized these emergent themes with his bestseller (two million copies sold) *In Tune with the Infinite* (1897). By the time of his death in 1958, he had become a leader among metaphysical teachers. He implored readers to see themselves as channels of divine energy and learn to be ready vessels for divine flow. Stagnant emotions and thoughts blocked healthy transmission, leading to misery and disease. Right thinking would open the floodgates to the abundant life: "See yourself in a prosperous condition. Affirm that you will before long be in a prosperous condition. . . . You thus make yourself a magnet to attract the things that you desire."[90]

Trine's emphasis never strayed from the theme of self-actualization. In other words, though he addressed other topics, he always majored in inspiration. Like countless authors after him, he insisted that any person could spiritually align him/herself with happiness, health, and fortune. In trumpeting human potential, he evoked readers' desire that spiritual forces could reach into the material world and right any wrongs. Second, his method prized accessibility and popular appeal. Unlike many of New Thought's earliest prophets, Trine eschewed theological precision in favor of usefulness. Rather than descriptive, Trine's work remained prescriptive. He meant it to be followed, not simply read. Third, Trine left a lasting impression. As the author of the first New Thought bestseller, Trine made the so-called everyman his target audience. Trine charted a path to prosperity that appeared compatible with his largely Christian readership, careful to choose Christian language and concepts that would not wrinkle the noses of the Protestant mainstream. New Thought literature followed him, becoming increasingly targeted toward religious nonspecialists and even nonbelievers. Sweeping generalities buried the specifics, allowing New Thought to move beyond its sectarian heritage and into a blurry—but powerful—collection of religious beliefs inextricable from American culture itself.

The "Disappearance" of New Thought

In the first decades of the twentieth century, New Thought ruled a kingdom of ink as its prophets penned innumerable books designed for mass appeal. Theologically thin but thick with guarantees of success, these self-assurance manuals sought availability over respectability. Critics found the publications crude and insincere, as their cheap and often poorly produced manuals papered the city. Yet their broad appeal won them continued relevance.

New Thought's gospel of success evolved into a steady stream of success literature, which crisscrossed among the genres of self-help, business, and metaphysical religion. Success literature found wide readership.[91] By 1905, Orison Swett Marden's *Success Magazine*, boasting a circulation of 300,000, promised just that, success in all aspects of life.[92] William Walker Atkinson (known also as Swami Ramacharaka) became one of the most popular authors of New Thought success literature. His many works, including *The Secret of Success* (1908), *Mind-Power* (1908), and *The Secret of Mental Magic* (1912), popularized New Thought's interest in the power of the mind and its instrumental value. He taught that the conscious mind controlled the unconscious, unlocking the "secret" to attaining what one desired. This high emphasis on mind-power put prosperity under the thinker's control. The Unity School of Christianity, the largest of New Thought's denominations, published *The Christian Business Man* (1922) in an effort to show readers how to apply New Thought principles to the marketplace.[93] Kenyon's own *Sign Posts on the Road to Success* (1938) joined the trend.

New Thought's mental science drew on developments in clinical medicine. Beginning in the 1870s, European neuroscientists began to seek the causes of mental illness. Their investigations coalesced into the field of psychology, devoted to applying scientific inquiry to the workings of the mind. By the 1880s, psychology had begun to take shape as an American academic discipline. Within a generation, New Thought's authors appropriated psychological language with increasing boldness. New Thought pioneer William Atkinson, for instance, showed only glimmers of psychological familiarity at the dawn of the twentieth century. By 1910, Atkinson's *Your Mind and How to Use It: A Manual of Practical Psychology* equated New Thought with the burgeoning field of mental health. Frank Haddock, author of the bestselling *The Power of the Will* (1907), similarly offered New Thought ideas in a psychological form. Haddock repackaged New Thought as an instruction manual for success replete with drills. Without religious references, he taught readers to activate the will and teach it to succeed. The distinction between psychology and religion was equally confused in popular discourse. Fashionable magazines used New Thought and psychological authorities interchangeably, "present[ing] physicians, Protestant ministers, early psychotherapists, and New Thought healers as equally valid schools of modern psychotherapy."[94] This hybrid identity—part metaphysical, part psychological, and part success literature—formed the foundation of "self-help."

New Thought's influence did not weigh heavily on American culture in its institutional form but endured because of its confluence with like-minded ideas.[95] With Horatio Dresser writing for *Good Housekeeping*, Trine for *Woman's Home Companion*, and similar themes enacted through popular novels and plays, New Thought's sectarian differences softened into palatable generalities. As Albanese observed, this may not have been entirely accidental. "It disappeared," wrote Albanese. "It became a part of general culture, so that by effacing its own logo it successfully shaped American mentality in marked and continuing ways."[96] After World War II, it would resurface in the mainline American religious imagination as "positive thinking," equal parts psychology, business, self-help, and metaphysics. In erasing its particularities, New Thought marketed a message that articulated and spiritualized American self-perceptions. New Thought uncovered the hidden truth that Americans longed to hear—that divinity was lodged somewhere in their beings and that their secret powers demanded expression. It represented a powerful combination of two spiritual conclusions, "inner divinity" and "outer power."[97]

Corporate Metaphysics

The gospel of wealth continued to ride the wave of prosperity through the 1920s. As Americans transitioned from the World War I wartime economy to a peacetime order, a flood of new wealth rewarded big business and avid consumerism. The economic leader was lionized; as Brooks Holifield argued, "The First World War—and the economic boom that followed—elevated the manager of massive organizations and the successful businessman to even greater cultural authority."[98] Theologically, too, economic themes took precedent. American Christians' valorization of manly virtue, epitomized by the muscular Christianity of evangelist Billy Sunday, took on a decidedly corporate cast. Jesus himself possessed business acumen, as Bruce Barton's *The Man Nobody Knows* (1924) revealed him to be "an extraordinarily successful executive who forged an organization that 'conquered the world' by the use of modern business methods."[99] As the church modeled big business, lay people turned to a gospel that explained how wealth, capitalism, and devotion coincided.

Soon the economic collapse of the Great Depression tested the gospel of wealth's mettle. Yet while the financial hardships of the American public seemingly severed its love affair with capitalism, new voices arose to defend the virtuous acquisition of wealth. Its champions included salesman Dale Carnegie. Carnegie sold a solution that an impoverished population could afford—positive thinking. He popularized the relationship between thought and wealth acquisition with his bestselling *How to Win Friends and Influence People* (1936). Through radio, print media, and his "Dale Carnegie Course," Carnegie guaranteed a secularized demonstration of the power of positive thinking. His folksy principles, such as "Smile" or "Be a good listener," produced one of the first self-help bestsellers and carved out a place for the power of the mind within a supposedly secular, though overwhelmingly Protestant, sphere. A year after Dale Carnegie taught the American public how to win friends, Napoleon Hill published *Think and Grow Rich!* a New Thought rendering of similar goals. Hill promised to reveal the secret of Andrew Carnegie's success, allowing any person to achieve the good life. Several techniques proved effective, Hill argued. Visualization would unleash the mind's power for the imagined object: "Hold your thoughts . . . on money by concentration, or fixation of attention, with your eyes closed, until you can actually see the physical appearance of the money. Do this at least once each day."[100] Repetition was also key. Hill urged practitioners to repeat instructions to the

unconscious mind, which was "the only known method of voluntary development of the emotion of faith."[101] The mind was energy, and required
visualization and affirmations to be released. Divine Science author
Emmet Fox also assured the masses that resources were only a thought
away, as his bestsellers *The Sermon on the Mount* and *Power Through Con-
structive Thinking* reasserted the reality of divine supply.[102] After all,
quipped Elder Lightfoot Solomon Michaux, "the sun is shining. The birds
are singing. They're not complaining 'bout the depression. Why should
we?"[103]

Though the American economy failed to provide prosperity, it continued to shape Depression-era Protestant thinking. In an exhaustive study
by the Yale psychologist Mark A. May and the Union Seminary theologian William Adams Brown, published as *The Education of American
Ministers*, the authors fretted, "'The modern psychology of business success' guided lay expectations of ministers. The churches wanted 'a
winner, not only of souls, but of dollars and prestige.'"[104] Parishioners

FIGURE 1.7 Napoleon Hill Napoleon Hill reading his New Thought classic *Think
and Grow Rich!*

Source: Library of Congress, Prints & Photographs Division, NYWT&S Collection,
LC-USZ62–136395.

desired spiritual leadership to succeed where the economy had not, producing financial success despite the hard times. Self-help literature obsessed with "business virtue" cluttered the shelves, as the stolid world of business demanded constant introspection. Why did one investor succeed while another failed? Surely market timing, personal connections, or a sixth sense for business answered that question, but the newly minted self-help genre turned to "character" to explain capitalism's unruly favor. The virtuous businessman would succeed where others had failed. As Donald Meyer argued, character became the enduring focus, qualities which mixed and matched religious ideals and practical values. It was the Protestant work ethic restored, which "supplement[ed] the standard 'religious' virtues of faith, hope, charity, etc., with the 'secular' virtues of industry, thrift, honesty, practicality, rationality, and the like."[105] As the economic rollercoaster of the 1920s and 1930s brought Americans high and then low, commerce and Christianity could not be separated as believers read their own religious fortunes by the changing times.

Twice Blessed: The Gospel of Health and Wealth

In 1941 America went to war and in a very short time the economically depressed United States turned into a fiscal powerhouse. Factories churned out millions of weapons, planes, ships, and vehicles; unemployed men donned uniforms and shipped overseas to fight the Germans and Japanese. There was considerable concern in 1945 that the end of hostilities and the return of these men would be the occasion of a renewed depression, but the opposite occurred as North America would see an astonishing period of prosperity and abundance that would last for decades.

Post–World War II America considered itself doubly blessed. The economy boomed, sustaining the nation's largest middle-class in history. Good health required fewer miracles, as medical advances staved off previously deadly illnesses with mass vaccines for polio and tuberculosis. Positive thinking matched the nation's triumphant mood, trumpeting the spiritual activism, high anthropology, and confidence in the mind that resonated through American culture. Even pentecostals found the message irresistible. In the 1940s and 1950s, independent pentecostal healing evangelists began to speak of financial blessings, spiritual laws, and the significance of high-spirited faith. Their new focus on mind-power to win both health *and* wealth would be the start of the modern prosperity movement.

When pentecostal evangelists of the 1940s and 1950s began to unveil laws of financial return, spirit-filled listeners were not the only ones with ears to hear. This developing movement devoted to securing God's blessings had been constructed from multiple religious elements with wide appeal across racial and denominational lines. The sectarian cast of mind-power had long-since faded and softened sharp lines drawn between pentecostalism, New Thought, and the deified qualities attributed to the American character. In its myriad forms, as success literature, popular psychology, faith cure, mind cure, positive thinking, or African American uplift gospels, this genus of mind-power provided Christians with a supplemental set of tools to solve problems. How can I overcome pain with prayer? How can I provide for my family? What must I do to endure? Christianity, infused with mind-power, allowed sufferers greater access to God. Divine principles granted every person admission to God's tender mercies. The emphasis on practice was irrepressible. Truths were "techniques," waiting to be "applied." Self-esteem, health, finances, or divine power itself became transferable goods requiring safe passage from God to the believer or one believer to another. Whether through prayer, hypnotism, the use of placebos, or the power of suggestion, believers cultivated religious practices and techniques to subdue, focus, or activate its hidden powers. This new type of thinking amplified Christian notions of spiritual power, remaking the gospel into a forceful tool for achieving health and wealth.

As the prosperity movement dawned, Essek William Kenyon was living in his twilight years. The grandfather of the modern faith message, he died in 1948, the first year of the post–World War II healing revivals that gave national attention to the incipient prosperity gospel. The postwar generation that rediscovered Kenyon's "overcoming faith" heard it echoed in diversely constituted gospels of health and wealth that resounded in American culture. The African American uplift movements that populated the urban landscape found new Christian audiences through the controversial icon, Reverend Ike. Secular and mainline "positive thinking" reappeared in magazines and television as the self-help messages of Norman Vincent Peale. As the faith movement coalesced in the postwar years, independent pentecostal revivalists immersed their old-time gospel in the same certainty, nurturing an understanding of faith characterized by unyielding confidence. Kenyon's gospel became the primary Christian vehicle of mind-power, a refinement of the mechanism by which the believer's authority and God's power met. His message soon rang out in the testimonies, revelations, and prophecies of a like-minded generation of true believers.

2

Faith

The first step in seeking to produce results by any power is
to contact that power . . .
The second step is to turn it on . . .
The third step is to believe that this power is coming into use and
to accept it by faith.

AGNES SANFORD, 1947

POSTWAR PENTECOSTALS INHERITED a rich legacy of faith. A half century of theologizing and experimentation about the interaction between
belief and action left them more confident than ever that God had greater
things in store. Expectant as they were, many doubted that the old wine-
skins of pentecostal denominations could contain the good news. After
1945, hundreds of ministers broke from their pentecostal denominations
to form independent evangelistic associations, ministries whose lifeblood
was the bold examples and promises of their charismatic founders.[1] Restless and self-reliant, these evangelists nonetheless used each other's magazines, platforms, radio (and later, television) broadcasts, and personal
endorsements to spread their gospel of healing, prophecy, deliverance,
wealth, and faith. It was a wholesale revival that stirred the country with
talk of faith—faith to heal, faith to deliver, faith to prosper, and faith to
unleash God's will by simply speaking true words aloud.

This chapter seeks to show how the modern prosperity gospel was born
out of these postwar pentecostal revivals and spread far beyond them a
decade later by a second revival among mainstream churchgoers. Three
significant shifts occurred in this period. First, the nascent theology of
mind-power that we encountered in chapter 1 went from being a minor
theme to one of major significance. Second, as more and more preachers
adopted this electrified view of faith, a number of these itinerants began to
enlarge the scope of what belief might be expected to produce, adding

health, happiness, and creature comforts to the growing list of miracles. The 1950s saw the first financial miracles creep into testimonies and sermons as a patchwork message of competing and complementary explanations about how faith made belief work. The growing consensus among this network of preachers about how faith had the power to draw both health *and* wealth into believers' lives marked the early formation of this pentecostal offshoot called the prosperity gospel. Third, the prosperity gospel gained momentum and exposure throughout the 1950s and 1960s as one revival crested into another, this time among a significantly larger audience of American Protestants and Catholics.[2] In a single generation, the message became a full-fledged movement identifiable inside and outside of pentecostalism by its expanding network of magazines, conferences, crusades, how-to manuals, bible schools, and fellowships. The prosperity gospel hatched inside pentecostalism soon found that its universal reassurances could carry it far beyond any denominational or sectarian home.

Healing Faith: The 1950s

After World War II, a new generation of pentecostal preachers left their homes and denominations, impatiently calling for a return to the movement's expectant supernatural atmosphere. Most of these ministers were faith healers at heart, as the periodical titles of Oral Roberts's *Healing Waters* (1947), Gordon Lindsay's *Voice of Healing* (1948), and Jack Coe's *Herald of Healing* (1950) attest. Across America, rank-and-file pentecostals gathered under the canvas to hear the principal themes of this revival: healing, prophecy, and evangelism.[3] The centerpiece of each service, observed David Edwin Harrell, "was the miracle—the hypnotic moment when the Spirit moved to heal the sick and raise the dead."[4] Successful ministers guaranteed the miraculous, commanding spiritual forces with ease. The flamboyant revivalist O. L. Jaggers, author of *Everlasting Spiritual and Physical Health*, touted the spirit-filled minister as a divine powerhouse, who "will do VERY LITTLE PRAYING FOR THE SICK . . . HE WILL GIVE COMMANDS THAT THE SICKNESS LEAVE."[5] A hunger for new miracles—beyond the mundane paralytic walking, blind seeing, and deaf hearing—cultivated an atmosphere of supra-supernaturalism, startling claims that shocked crowds and strained credulity.[6] In 1956, the *Miracle Magazine* founder A. A. Allen claimed that "miracle oil" streamed from revival participants' heads and hands, then, when that miracle subsided, a "Cross of Blood" appeared on believers' foreheads. On a separate occasion, a photograph of his revival showed demonic and divine forces doing battle.[7] Cover stories such as "I Took My Cancer to Church in a Jar" chronicled a pastor healed by A. A. Allen who returned to the revival the following night with bottled proof. It wasn't the first time for such a hermetic demonstration. A Minneapolis woman, Mrs. John Iaquinto, had put a cancerous growth in a jar and sent a picture to a healing magazine.[8] (The less astonishing "Too Nervous to Sew Now Sewing for Neighbors" never made the same splash but revealed just how ordinary, ordinary people's desires really were.[9]) The gifted but controversial Franklin Hall penned recipes for miraculous power including *Atomic Power with God thru Prayer and Fasting* (1946) and *Formula for Raising the Dead* (1960). He promoted "Bodyfelt Salvation" as a potent healing substance that warded off emotional distress as well as body odor, a teaching he demonstrated by refusing to wash his own jacket, worn to all crusades, as it was already without "spots or odors."[10] These coat-and-tie pentecostals wanted to take the lid off of organized religion and transform common people into holy (but not fragrant) vessels of divine power.

As their faith and reputations centered on the methods that would spur God to act, itinerant evangelists were looking for "the Spiritual Formula that contains real power."[11] Their efforts were experimental and fundamentally utilitarian, favoring practice over philosophy, and so evangelists typically counseled every possible method available, from silent prayer, anointing oil, anointed kerchiefs, laying on of hands, and the classic prayer of faith. Belief in spoken faith, however, took on added weight. Most midcentury revivalists began to preach with F. F. Bosworth's *Christ the Healer* tucked under their arm, agreeing that faith wielded the authority to confess and possess.[12] Headlines from the influential *The Voice of Healing* magazine, the mouthpiece of the early revival, read "We Are What We Say!" and "The Faith That Takes."[13] W. V. Grant even adopted "He shall have whatsoever he saith" as the slogan of his ministry. So heavy was the emphasis on positive confession that one California radio evangelist dared to hope it might even distract Holy Ghost folk from their overly "negative" fixation on who would face hell's eternal flames.[14]

In the early 1950s, most revivalists applied faith to pentecostalism's healing mandate (with the occasional detour to vim, youth, and long life). They called on a God who, through faith, altered reality in the present, not the future. Christian talk about hope had to be amended, for, as Kenyon claimed, "Hope says, 'I will get it sometime.' Faith says, 'I have it now.'"[15] Christians who confessed that the Lord was *going* to heal and deliver thereby implied

that the Lord had not already done it. Faith demanded the perpetual cultivation of a prophetic imagination. The dapper T. L. Osborn, touring beside
F. F. Bosworth, William Branham, and Gordon Lindsay, became a popular
authority on the uses of faith. Repeating Kenyon's teachings verbatim, he
reminded listeners "you will never rise above your confession." Instead,
"TALK FAITH-TALK" for "anything less signs a package delivered by Satan,
who holds the receipt."[16] Christians must proclaim a reality that they cannot
see but must be believed because the Lord deemed it so. Countless healing
testimonies reified this ideal. The radio and healing evangelist Thomas
Wyatt testified that he recovered from his deathbed when he responded to
God's audible voice saying, "I am the Lord that healeth thee."[17] He denied
his grave condition in whispering back, "The Lord has come and healed
me." He demanded to be lifted up, seated at the dinner table, and assisted in
taking his first steps, acting out his healing despite his pain. The account of
his recovery echoes those of faith cure and early pentecostal practices before
him: "The return of strength was speedy after that, for faith had motivated
action, and action had evidenced faith. The substance of faith had been
grasped. For thirty days faith pushed Tom into act after act, until at the end
of a month not a trace of the old sickness remained."[18] Certainty, rather than
hope, dictated their actions.[19] Healing evangelists had little use for hope,
lamenting the traditional and hope-filled Christians who prevented God
from working on their behalf. Those who prayed that God was *going to* heal
them sealed their own sad fate. Christians must command healing, argued
the author of *Omnipotence Is Yours*, for God has given all the power and authority to speak healing into being.[20] When A. A. Allen preached and sweated
under packed tents, summoning blind eyes to see and withered limbs to
walk, he demanded this faith-in-motion: "ACT YOUR FAITH . . . Leave your
wheel chair. Throw away your crutches. Walk and run! Leap for joy! . . . Quit
'trying to believe.' Simply believe, and ACT."[21]

The master fundraiser Velmer Gardner spoke for his generation when
he explained that faith was "the switch in our hand to turn on all the omnipotent power of our Lord."[22] But what was this switch, precisely? Pentecostal
revivalists toyed with many explanations for precisely *how* God turned faith
into power. A young minister named Kenneth E. Hagin spoke of his 1934
recovery from heart trouble as the moment when he discovered the inner
workings of faith, although almost two decades passed before he heard
God's instructions to "Go teach My people faith!" through radio and publication.[23] To be sure, he was a local attraction rather than a major cam-
paigner, who spent the turbulent decade beating the evangelistic circuit as

an Assemblies of God preacher. A flurry of letters between local pastors and the Assemblies of God headquarters, however, suggests that Hagin was giving the denomination, as one pastor put it, "no small trouble" in his corner of Texas.[24] But the man later credited as the "father" of the prosperity gospel systematized and popularized an explanation for faith's potency. He called it the law of faith, drawing the term from Romans 3:27 (KJV): "Where is boasting then? It is excluded. By what law? Of works? Nay: but by the Law of Faith."

Hagin's law of faith contained two overlapping instruments of power, legal and scientific. He began with E. W. Kenyon's teaching that "Christianity is a legal document" in which believers find rights to salvation, protection, and victory over all circumstances.[25] Jesus' death secured these rights for humanity from Satan and transferred God's "power of attorney" to believers, who became entitled to use God's power as their own.[26] The law of faith itself acted as the contract to secure these Christian liberties, in Kenyon's words, providing "the warranty deed that the thing for which you have fondly hoped is at last yours."[27] These legal benefits afforded followers (to use one of the prosperity gospel's well-worn phrases) "rights and privileges": the safety, health, happiness, and financial security promised to each Christian. In crusades, televised sermons, write-in testimonials, and casual conversation, participants spoke of rights and privileges as shorthand for the abundant blessings believers could command "in Jesus' name." Conversely, those who did not demonstrate God's power—plagued by doubt, poverty, or disease—fell to live "beneath their privileges."[28]

The law of faith, according to Hagin, also acted as a universal causal agent, a power that actualized events and objects in the real world. Faith corresponded to natural forces that, like gravity and electricity, were invisible operators of cause and effect.[29] This faith-force subjected the natural world to its power regardless of human opinion or assent, existing as a force apart from (but available to) humanity. Late nineteenth-century radical evangelicals like A. B. Simpson had likened faith to natural laws harnessed for believers' use, yet for all their talk of victory and the "Higher Life," they never envisioned an independent force or law that turned around to bind God himself.[30] Hagin's generation was willing to make larger theological leaps of faith than their predecessors as they sought gains they could measure.

In the years to come, scholars and adherents alike would remember Hagin as the theological powerhouse behind the prosperity gospel. But he was certainly not alone in calling faith a spiritual law. Preachers great and small were equally convinced that there was a legal spiritual system at work. For example, Reverend Thea Jones preached the "Law of Return" to multiracial crowds under the vaulted ceilings of Philadelphia's old Metropolitan opera house. God first granted him a message of salvation, he wrote, then a message of healing, until God finally revealed to him "the secret to success."[31] Likewise, Hagin did not pioneer the idea that this law could reap financial rewards. But his simpler, almost automated, law of faith invoked a Newtonian paradigm that eventually became his hallmark and, in the late 1960s, the foundation of what many have called the "Word of Faith" movement. Of the many prosperity gospels that emerged from the healing revivals, Word of Faith theology adopted a rarefied form of Kenyon's spiritual laws that introduced listeners to a universe structured by God to respond to a particular kind of Christian invocation. Faith was seen as an absolute law, and as such it operated as a universal and uniform reality; there need not be a leap of faith, as faith would prove itself.

Viewed from afar, we can see aspects of the greater healing revival that formed the rough contours of the earliest prosperity gospels (that is to say, the use of faith for health *and* wealth). An economic message was growing louder and clearer as the decade wore on. It began quite meagerly. W. V. Grant, for example, suggested that businessmen and breadwinners use a "word of wisdom" to guide their business knowhow.[32] By 1953, more and more evangelists had begun to speak of financial miracles. Ministers began to first speak of God's blessings, then God's abundance, as more evangelists began to tease out the implications of John 10:10. The healing revival's most influential network, centered around *The Voice of Healing*, showed slow but steady progress toward a message of abundance. Its

---------------→

FIGURE 2.1 **The Voice of Healing Conferences, 1950–1956** Network diagram of featured speakers at the Voice of Healing conferences, 1950–1956. This represents the major figures of the healing revival using advertisements in its main periodical, *The Voice of Healing*. The connections between preachers shown are performative, as each preacher intersects with another by speaking at the same conference. The more intersections between two individuals equates to a stronger graphical relationship (represented by the darker lines). The greater total number of intersections an individual has the more central they are to the network. This is represented by the location of individuals to one another. The layout is based on a graphing algorithm such that the distance between individuals is proportional to the shortest path linking them and the overall length of ties is minimized. Notice how central "faith building" ministries like T. L. Osborn, W. V. Grant, and Gordon Lindsay were to the revival. A. A. Allen and Oral Roberts, too big to need help, hovered on the outskirts.

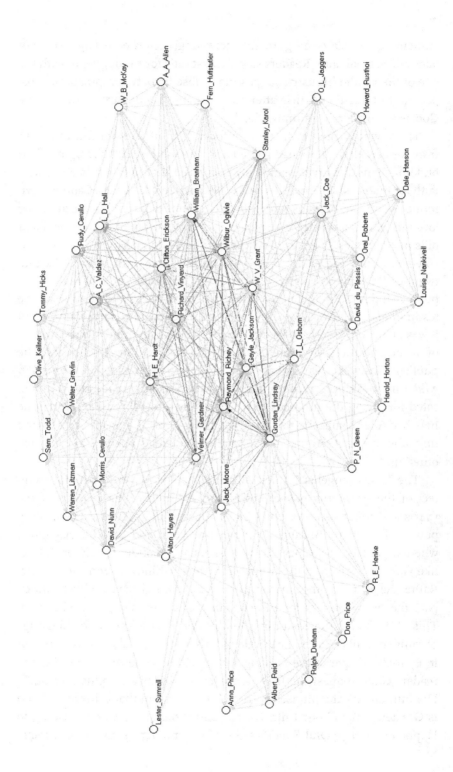

annual conference (see figure 2.1) increasingly featured evangelists with tales of financial faith. Readers saw the first calls for money begin with the rise of their radio ministry, suggesting a close tie between prosperity gospel and fundraising. Article after article inspired audiences to re-imagine God as a provider, not simply a healer.

Those who turned to financially focused ministries tended to be cut from similar cloth. They had gained a reputation for specializing in "faith building," and they had seamlessly combined that faith for healing with faith for finances. The magnetic A. A. Allen made it look easy. Calling down money from the heavens with words such as "believe!" and "claim!" he loved to tell his audience the story of the transformation of his one dollar bills into twenties. "I believe I can command God to perform a miracle for you financially," he said. "When you do, God can turn dollar bills into twenties."[33] Tying prosperity to the soaring supernaturalism of revivals, he published the first popular book on financial miracles and showcased the testimonies of his newly wealthy followers in tents around the country. But it wasn't just his followers' financial success he had in mind, it was also that of his organization. Urging God's people to obey the "law of the tithe," he published risky stories such as "God Told Me to Mortgage My Home," in which he introduced readers to a man who was supernaturally compensated for giving the proceeds of his home loan to Allen. Though no one matched Allen's audacity, this tightly linked network of preachers, receiving up-to-the-moment reports on one another's crusades, seemed to spur each other on.[34]

The Tulsa evangelist Granville Oral Roberts proved to be a major architect of the prosperity gospel, towering over the healing revivals of the 1940s and 1950s as a man of faith. He lacked the preternatural healing power of William Branham, whose prophecy and angelic visitations whetted pentecostals' thirst for new signs and wonders. Neither did he, like Gordon Lindsay, rally diverse ministers behind the common cause. Rather, he eclipsed other ministers because of his shrewd ability to anticipate the new frontiers for ministry in radio, television, and education. This Midas touch provided innumerable demonstrations of the blessings of faith, and, like Hagin, he developed his own vocabulary to account for it. By 1956, his periodical *Healing Waters* had become *Abundant Life*, and readers could request the free pamphlet "God Has a Surplus for You."[35] His influential catchphrases summed up his triumphant theology: "God is Greater," "Turn Your Faith Loose," and "Something Good is Going to Happen to You."[36] Oral Roberts's cheerful reminder to "Expect a Miracle" reconciled two opposing poles—predictability and otherworldliness—that Hagin codified in his law of faith. Faith would cause the supernatural to bend miracles to the will of everyday believers.

Roberts's miraculous youthful recoveries from tuberculosis and stuttering had sent him headlong into his ministerial vocation. Then, in 1947, Roberts uncovered a biblical imperative to prosper tucked into 3 John 2: "Beloved, I wish above all things that thou mayest prosper and be in health even as thy soul prospereth." His 1952 autobiography (the first of many) described it as "the greatest discovery I ever made" and the foundation on which his sprawling ministry stood.[37] His radio program, *Healing Waters* magazine, and first book, *If You Need Healing—Do These Things!* soon followed. Oral Roberts's mushrooming ministry and prosperity theology developed hand-in-hand. His expectations for divine recompense grew with his fundraising needs as his magazine, radio, and (later) television audiences swelled. His 1954 introduction of the "Blessing Pact" promised that God would repay contributors for their donation to Oral Roberts's ministries "in its entirety from a totally unexpected source." The same year he offered his first calculus of spiritual returns, predicting a sevenfold return for donors. His publication *God's Formula for Success and Prosperity* (1956) offered believers a systematic approach to divine blessings, though it stopped short of Hagin's immutable laws.[38]

Experimentalism prevailed over uniformity. Though proponents for divine prosperity were many—just as in early explanations of the law of faith—few preachers offered identical guarantees. The heavily mustached Oscar Buford Dowell turned his expertise managing tent roadshows into his own gospel tent ministry, touring (as his slogan read) "from Dixieland to Canaan's land" with lessons on his law of prosperity.[39] Oral Roberts offered his own formula for prosperity in an assortment of mottos and personal testimonies perfectly suited for advertisement jingles and, later, bumper stickers, because he possessed the kind of good looks and charisma that made churchgoing women really believe that, as he declared, "God is a Good God!" Some ministers confidently promised a hundred-fold return on donations to their organizations,[40] but the majority seemed more comfortable with the explanation that financial miracles operated under some kind of law of divine reciprocity (Luke 6:38 "Give and it shall be given unto you"). These formulas for wealth tended to be heavy on promises, vague on method, and laden with uninterpreted scripture. For example, when the Harry Hampel Deliverance Revivals from Denver, Colorado, took a little time away from railing against Catholic heresies to broadcast the law of faith to claim finances, the result may have puzzled readers. Hampel began with bold assertions about faith as a supernatural law, devoted a chapter to financial prosperity as God's will, but left out how one could achieve it. He simply concluded with a list of familiar scriptures that included references to giving and getting (Luke 6:38), hundredfold return (Mark 10:29–31), tithing (Malachi 3:10–11), and God's abundant provision (Phil 4:19).[41] Prosperity preachers of the decade encouraged an everything-but-the-kitchen-sink approach. Taken together, their wide-ranging prescription for prosperity rested on an ironclad certainty that God, somehow, would provide.

Another revival burning across the Canadian prairies added to this growing consensus on financial faith. Centered largely on power in healing, prophecy, laying on of hands, and the restoration of ancient "fivefold" ecclesial offices (apostles, prophets, missionaries, pastors, and teachers), it was called the "Latter Rain" movement, taken from Joel 2:23, for its belief that it was the last outpouring of the Holy Spirit that preceded the Lord's return. When its leaders began preaching that pentecostals should claim a stronger measure of God's creative power as heaven's true sons and daughters, denominational critics called it an "overrealized eschatology." The fruits of the spirit, as far as they were concerned, were not just ripe. They had spoiled. Not to be deterred by its rejection by pentecostal denominations, its evangelists fanned out across Canada and the United States garnering support in a network of new and existing churches, periodicals, conferences, and Bible schools. Among them, Sylva and Lawrence Iverson and their son Dick Iverson, Franklin Hall, and J. Mattzon Boze (editor of *The Herald of Faith*) became significant leaders in the wider healing revival and some of the earliest proponents of divine wealth.[42]

The radio minister Thomas Wyatt had been washed in the Latter Rain. He founded the popular Wings of Healing ministries with a divine imperative to preach faith for human prosperity. He had whittled his ministerial wisdom down to a simple law of faith: "If we will use faith as an operating force, we can control the physical realm, for faith operates on the basis of spiritual laws which are effective in the physical realm."[43] He taught, like Hagin, that Christians enjoyed direct access to God's creative power and the resulting ability to control the material realm. Despite his triumphant message, Wyatt did not apply this rigorous faith to all aspects of his life and ministry. A rough-and-tumble preacher known for building his institutions himself (often log by log), Wyatt endured hunger, sickness, and even poverty throughout his ministry even after discovering the "faith principle" that ensured steady success. "I had to live on the razor's edge all the time," Wyatt admitted.[44] Neither did he instruct his students otherwise. As a teacher at Des Moines Bible School, he sent his students out to hitchhike the highways and discover God's place for their lives. Wyatt preached theological guarantees but, like many others, experienced everyday life with an ad hoc prosperity gospel.

All revivalists, Latter Rain or otherwise, were preaching upward mobility to people already on the way up. These were the boom years in which many families considered the possibility of home ownership for the first time or were able to enjoy hitherto unobtainable luxuries such as indoor plumbing, a private telephone, and electrical appliances such as stoves and refrigerators. Farm fields were bulldozed to build new subdivisions, and contractors erected instant ranch-style, split-level, and Dutch-colonial homes. A new social space, unknown to the prewar world appeared, variously called the rec room, rumpus room, or family room. There the ever-growing family could watch Oral Roberts, A. A. Allen, or Rex Humbard on increasingly large television sets.[45] A new car was now within the reach of most Americans; Detroit, the unchallenged world automobile capital, turned out chrome-laden land yachts with names denoting a taste for luxury: Bel Air, Imperial, Riviera, and Belvedere.

Pentecostals enjoyed the postwar economic boom as contented middle-class citizens and proved as keen as any American to believe God might have something to do with it.[46] This new generation of pentecostals searched for explanations of how God and the believer's piety worked in tandem. Pentecostals' faith in finances swelled with the postwar economic tides. "We have a different message now, a positive message—we know where we are and what we have, and have been lifted above a life that is always 'walking on egg shells'" summarized one evangelist.[47] Modern capitalism engendered new admiration as a seemingly perfect system of decent wages, high employment rates, and cheaply manufactured goods. The mass marketing and assembly lines churning out cars, ovens, washing machines, lawn mowers, and sectional sofas brought the logic of modernity to believers' homes and driveways. "None can deny that, materially speaking, we have 'never had it so good,'" opined *The Pentecostal Evangel*.[48] Their cosmopolitanism only grew as they earned a modicum of respectability in the public mind.[49] While there is little evidence to suggest that pentecostals were much poorer than other Americans, social location is more than a tally of dollars and cents. It is important to remember that pentecostals felt poor and, worse, discounted.

Pentecostals had experienced the derision of the press and their fellow Christians, further reinforcing the distance they kept between themselves and "the world." The prosperity gospel served to bridge that gap by convincing the sanctified that modernity would not diminish their faith. While some denominations fought for the humble living and standards of modesty that reminded them that they were strangers in a strange land, many white pentecostals were happy to become model suburbanites— their trademark otherworldliness tempered by a bowling league, a pearl necklace, or a dash of makeup here and there.

The newly established Full Gospel Business Men's Fellowship International (FGBMFI) promoted the prosperity gospel as a marvel of modern pentecostal faith. Founded in 1952, the organization spread rapidly as an association of spirit-filled businessmen who gathered in local chapters and annual conferences across the country. The fellowship was not only a sanctified alternative to the weekly meetings and pancake breakfasts of other popular organizations, like the Lion's Club or the Rotary Club, but also a place that reconciled old-time religion with mounting expectations for economic success. Their annual events were rather grand affairs held in high-ceilinged ballrooms; row upon row of long banquet tables where men of commerce could exchange business cards and hear an inspiring message. Whether listening to a baseball player or a Holy Ghost preacher, this participation encouraged spirit-filled men across the country to benefit not only from common wisdom ("Reach for the stars!") but also introduced them to the budding prosperity theology of the healing revivalists. The fellowship served as a faithful companion to independent pentecostal revivalists, not only in its distance from pentecostal denominations but also as a popular platform for ministers like Oral Roberts, John Osteen, Jack Coe, Gordon Lindsay, R. W. Culpepper, William Branham, and Kenneth Hagin. The relationship spurred revivalists and the new organization to lively justifications of godly finances. At the signing of the Articles of Incorporation, G. H. Montgomery, editor of Oral Roberts's *Healing Waters* magazine, preached a rousing sermon denouncing poverty as "of the devil," and its first issue showed how being a Full Gospel Business Man "makes God his Partner and assures him success."[50] Its founder Demos Shakarian rallied them to search for the power of God "available to them for use in their business, to direct and guide them. If our lives are holy and consecrated to God, then we have the boldness to come to Him and ask and receive the things He has intended that we should have."[51] Pentecostal businessmen would learn to invest spiritual meaning in the marketplace and cultivate religious pride in entrepreneurship. The logo showed a firm handshake under a white cross.[52]

Good Americans were good consumers and (so it seemed) good Christians. This nascent culture of acquisitiveness fixed in people's minds the connection between America's fortunes and their own spending power. Personal consumption propelled the economy forward and showed believers the distance their faith could take them. The emerging prosperity gospel further eased the tension between pentecostals' characteristic otherworldliness and a consumer culture more comfortable with drive-in movies, doo-wop, and Easy-Bake Ovens. It encouraged believers to have a faith as rich as they were or, at least, hoped to be.

But more so, the prosperity gospel encouraged them to experience this reversal of fortune as a sign and a wonder. For as much as believers were theological sticklers, this was a theology-in-motion that read spiritual insight backward from circumstance. Whether in the testimonies of miracle seekers at an all-night crusade or Full Gospel businessmen passing the microphone and the meatloaf, the prosperity gospel was deduced from triumphs and failures of yesterday and the day before.

Pentecostal audiences, divided by race and denomination, must have heard these promises of physical, spiritual, and economic transformation with varying conviction. The healing revivals earned some notice from the tens of thousands of Latino pentecostals across the country, particularly as its evangelists often dipped low into the borderlands and Mexico to preach finances alongside healing. In 1955, for example, Evangelist Harry Hampel and Pastor H. M. Menchaca, who acted also as translator, of the Latin-American Assembly of God, stirred Spanish-speaking audiences in Dallas with messages of faith, healing, and salvation.[53] The historical record here runs thin, but revival reports by white, English-speaking preachers offer some clues that others walked in the footsteps of Latino faith healers like Francisco Olazábal (1886–1937).[54] The healing revivals were scattered throughout the Northwest, Midwest, and East Coast states but concentrated in the deeply divided South. African American audiences became a large and coveted audience. For the groundswell of African American pentecostals, locked out of the boom years by segregated housing and a discriminatory labor market, divine prosperity promised an end-run around the political, economic, and social forces of oppression.[55] Photos accompanying testimonies and crusade reports of Oral Roberts, A. A. Allen, and Thomas Wyatt suggest that they earned large followings among African American saints. Soon, black musicians joined them on stage as the supporting cast of revivalism. For those on the margins, the prosperity gospel would be both a siren song and a battle cry.

Most pentecostal denominations, worried about empty promises and empty coffers, withdrew their approval. William Gaston, retired general chairman of the Assemblies of God, bitterly lamented that their churches were "cleaned out" by "lovers of filthy lucre" while missionaries had to beat the bushes for every thin dime.[56] Pentecostal denominations had entered a period of bricks-and-mortar growth, and their expanding administration and governance could best be seen in the rise of their stately new facilities.[57] Abandoning storefronts for steeples, denominations rolled out expanded programs for missions, education, publishing, evangelism, and social services to meet its postwar growth. Despite Gordon Lindsay's call for unity, institutionalization often bred contempt among revivalists.[58] A. A. Allen thumbed his nose at authorities by publishing the Assemblies of God's call for him to withdraw from ministry and his cheeky retort.[59] Upstart independent revivalists and their boisterous services were a challenge that demanded an answer. In 1956, the Assemblies of God took aim at the raucous supernaturalism of healing evangelism, repudiating, among other things, the alleged scriptural foundation for public diagnosis of illness and (likely with Allen's claims in mind) any miraculous "exuding of oil or appearance of blood."[60]

The relationship between faith healers and pentecostal denominations was fraught with difficulty. In the Pentecostal Holiness Church, for example, the prosperity teachings and healing claims of one of their own, Oral Roberts, became the focus of their 1953 General Conference in Memphis, Tennessee. But after Roberts preached a rousing sermon to delegates poised to vote for or against his inclusion in their ranks, the tides turned in his favor. Roberts pledged $50,000 to the Southwestern Pentecostal Holiness College, and the delegates even elected Roberts's ally as bishop.[61]

By the early 1960s, the healing revival had sputtered and slowed. Financial support for its roaming prophets dried up as pentecostals wearily surveyed a spiritual market glutted with miracles, evangelists, and wonders. At the outset of the revival, the famed English pentecostal Donald Gee already fretted that too many believers gauged their faith by their bodies and pocketbooks.[62] Gordon Lindsay, the revival's able publicist, blamed evangelists' ambition and the increasing focus on money.[63] Others were convinced that it faded with the "last rattle of the collection plate."[64] Though Lindsay's God's Master Key to Success and Prosperity (1959) was one of the most popular books on divine wealth, he worried that the revival had gone too far. The garish showmanship that marked excesses of the revival had tainted public perception of the whole. Further, new gains in medicine and nutrition proved so successful that fewer healing miracles seemed necessary. Antibiotics and vaccines conquered the nightmares of previous generations of parents: polio, tuberculosis, whooping cough, and scarlet fever no longer threatened the nursery. The postwar revival had lost credibility and focus. But these faith-building evangelists would not forget the grinding poverty of their former faith and their early life. Having discovered that God's promises for a new generation lay beyond their wildest expectations, they could hardly go back.

Positive Faith: The 1950s

The midcentury healing revivals that lifted the spirits (and expectations) of pentecostals echoed the confidence resonating through postwar American society. Powerful voices trumpeted new Christian formulas for spiritual, physical, and financial abundance. Positive thinking abounded in the years following World War II, as Americans' optimism rose together with the burgeoning consumer culture. Rabbi Joshua Liebman's *Peace of Mind* (1946) introduced self-help to the inspirational mass market, followed shortly by bestsellers such as Claude Bristol's *Magic of Believing* (1948), Father James Keller's *You Can Change the World!* (1948), and Harry Overstreet's *Mature Mind* (1949).[65] Positive thinking was simply a repackaging of earlier metaphysical mind-power, remembered for its psychological cast and emphasis on a cheerful and well-ordered mind. Norman Vincent Peale (1898–1993), Methodist minister and self-help writer, became the principal prophet of this generation. His early successes as a pastor in Brooklyn and Syracuse sealed his reputation as a cheery and anecdotal preacher with a knack for advertising and church growth. In the early 1950s, New Thought ideas began to figure prominently in his writing. As his preaching drew larger crowds, Peale accepted a position at Marble Collegiate Church in New York City, a venerable Reformed Church of America (RCA) pulpit, from which he brought his message to a national audience.

Peale's success stemmed from the fact that he made abstract theology into workable wisdom. The affable preacher made countless appearances around the country and, from the early 1950s, preached weekly to a congregation of 4,000 at Marble Collegiate Church. He reached out to television audiences with his syndicated program, *What's Your Trouble*, which he co-hosted with his wife, Ruth. Listeners tuned into his radio show, *The Art of Living*, which stayed on the air for 40 years. In 1945, he founded his

FIGURE 2.2 **Norman Vincent Peale** A cheery Norman Vincent Peale makes notes at his desk cluttered with letters. He was regularly deluged with fan mail. Circa 1966.
Source: Roger Higgins, *World Telegram & Sun.*

own magazine, *Guideposts*, which gained four million readers over the next half-century.[66] At Peale's peak, his published sermons garnered 150,000 readers, and his syndicated newspaper column claimed an audience of ten million.

Peale's message was timely in two important ways. First, his use of psychological categories caught the rising tide of therapeutic culture in the United States. By the close of the 1930s, the new science of the mind had found mainline Protestant acceptance. Theological reckoning with mental health became commonplace as "pastoral psychology" integrated religious with scientific methods. Richard Cabot's *The Art of Ministering* (1936) and Rollo May's *The Art of Counseling* (1939) signaled that clinical models of pastoral advice-giving were here to stay. Protestant seminaries drew psychology into standard coursework.[67] In 1934, Peale sought the assistance of Smiley Blanton, professor of psychiatry at Cornell University Medical School, to help Peale counsel his parishioners. By 1937, the two had paired up to form the Marble Collegiate Church Clinic, a therapeutic center that integrated psychology and religion. Their co-authored book, *Faith is the Answer: A Psychiatrist and a Pastor Discuss Your Problems* (1940), joined the first waves of mainstream psychological services.[68] Archbishop Fulton J. Sheen's 1954 book *Way to Happiness* and television show *Life Is Worth Living* soon offered a Catholic counterpart with millions of viewers.[69] By the end of World War II, Peale's idioms and impulses had blended into a culture already saturated with psychology.

Second, Peale's theological synthesis of upward mobility with religious buoyancy matched the postwar mood, turning a man into a movement. His blend of Methodist evangelism, Dutch Reformed Calvinism, and New Thought focus on mind-power appeared in earlier works, *The Art of Living* (1937) and *You Can Win* (1938), yet as Peale's writing progressed, New Thought took precedence. In 1952, Peale published *The Power of Positive Thinking*, which became a *New York Times* bestseller for a record-breaking three years and sold a million copies. In it, he folded Christian and psychological categories into a New Thought theme: God's power could be harnessed by "a spirit and method by which we can control and even determine" life's circumstances. Peale taught that any person could access God's power through positive thinking, which directed spiritual energy toward the attainment of health, self-esteem, or business acumen. Much like his New Thought predecessors, Peale promised formulas, patterns of right thought, and the release of power through effective words.[70] He invoked Jesus as Teacher, not Savior, whose instructions on divine flow, source, and energy kept followers "in tune with the Infinite."[71] Yet true to Peale's unique style, the book was not a systematic treatise of thought-power. Rather, it traded precision for anecdotal evidence and warm reassurances. He offered the peppy advice of homemakers, baseball players, American presidents, and traveling salesmen, combined with the wisdom of William James, Ralph Waldo Emerson, and Ralph Waldo Trine.[72] Positive thinking followed a simple formula: "picturize, prayerize, and actualize."[73] This articulation of middle-class aspirations, set on a pedestal by one of America's most popular mainstream preachers, blurred popular and elite religion. Peale's teachings met with heated opposition; his critics excoriated him for having made self-interest into theological fodder.

Peale's sunny sermonizing did not forestall many Americans' grim conclusion that new wealth also brought new dangers. Amidst material prosperity this was also a time of psychological unease. The outbreak of the Korean War and looming threat of the Cold War demanded mental vigilance. Uncertainty fanned the flames of suspicion and incited the hunt for domestic subversion. Hollywood, the armed forces, and the civil service were scoured for instances of divided loyalty and covert communism. The fear of extinction by nuclear weapons found its way into the schoolroom where children practiced "Duck and Cover" drills and into popular culture where fear of the Soviet Union was sublimated into movies about threats from aliens or monsters. Citizens pitted their newly claimed "Judeo-Protestant" identity against godless communism by adding "under God" to the Pledge of Allegiance and "In God We Trust" as the national motto. Evangelical, fundamentalist, and pentecostal periodicals warned their readers in regular prophetic reports that plotted foreordained decline against the rising Red threat.[74]

Even prosperity itself now seemed a menace: what was it doing to the children? School boards and universities produced a flood of social control films meant to tame this new generation who knew nothing of the work ethic and sacrifices of their parents and grandparents. "Are You Popular?" "Table Manners," and "Dating: Dos and Don'ts," sought to mold potentially rebellious youth into pliable students, workers, and consumers. Children were urged to compete for the title of "Posture King," and teens were cautioned of the dangers of early sex and marriage.

The pleasant conformity of the age could not mask many Americans' vague and general unease. Was this all there is? Surely there was more to life than acquisition and display. Existentialism became the philosophical fad of the moment; Sartre and Camus became campus reading. The media discovered "the Beats:" poets, musicians, and hangers-on who were said to reject the crass uniformity of middle-class culture and seek genuine experience in aping the "cool" lifestyle of the urban underclass with its marijuana cigarettes, jazz music, and casual sex. Newsmagazines also uncovered the angst of the suburban housewife whose husband commuted to work in the city and whose children were at school. Bored with the emptiness of her life, she was said to be increasingly turning to the consolations of "mother's little helper"—new lines of tranquilizing drugs, such as Librium and Miltown, meant to soothe the female anxieties that Betty Friedan decried in her bestselling *The Feminine Mystique*. Letters written to Norman Vincent Peale, observed his biographer Carol George, chronicled reader after reader's concerns that their lives were feeble and half-lived.[75] Happy people, it would seem, rarely bought a guide to happiness. Observers dubbed the 1950s' moody mix of sun and clouds "The Age of Anxiety."[76]

It is little wonder that, in the late 1940s and 1950s, Americans brought their worries with them to church on Sundays. To be sure, they had much to be thankful for. Millions of Christians were swept up by the rising economy and enjoyed a rosy status called middle-class. But good fortune was not the only reason to extol God and a sacred economy. The expanding Bolshevik empire continued to threaten the global economic order, replacing controlled capitalism with Soviet-style communism. Be it in positive thinking or pentecostal revivalism, Christianity itself could testify to God's power and the fundamental good of the country's economic underpinning.[77] More Americans wanted to become, as Norman Vincent Peale described his wife Ruth, "a tough-minded optimist."

The exact degree to which pentecostal healing revivalists consciously borrowed from positive thinkers like Norman Vincent Peale (or vice versa) remains uncertain, but the record contains numerous clues that the two traditions frequently overlapped in these early postwar years. In 1949, Oral Roberts began a close partnership with S. Lee Braxton, a prominent pentecostal businessman with a wholehearted devotion to positive thinking. Braxton shared his vast positive-thinking library with Roberts, including *How I Raised Myself from Failure to Success in Selling*, a book Roberts later cited as the most influential he ever read.[78] When the Full Gospel Business Men's Fellowship International was founded with Braxton as vice president, the organization proved to be an institutional expression of Holy Spirit-filled positive thinking. It paraded athletes, corporate giants, itinerant revivalists, and even then Vice President Richard Nixon before a crowd of hungry new capitalists. In 1959, the young Pat Robertson and two fellow pentecostals visited Ruth Peale to demonstrate the importance of speaking in tongues.[79] One suspects that the trio sought to give positive thinking its one missing ingredient: *charismata*. At the very least, pentecostals recognized that they had invested similar ideas and practices with theological significance.

The prosperity gospels emerging from pentecostals and mainline positive thinking shared a belief in the power of Christian speech to achieve results. Both rendered affirmative repetition, visualization, imagination, mood redirection, and voiced scripture as prayerful habits. However, each privileged different sources of authority—positive thinking lauding the science of psychology, and the prosperity gospel upholding *sola scriptura* (by scripture alone); the former spoke of "principles," the latter of "power." In fact, some evangelists criticized positive thinking as effective in a limited way but not quite powerful enough. W. V. Grant, for example, believed that positive thinking could heal bodies but was unable to overcome demonic illnesses.[80]

Unlike positive thinkers, pentecostals had a love for concrete mediators of God's power. Miracle oil, water, handkerchiefs, and squares of tent cloth inspired testimonies as believers explained precisely *how* they received a blessing. Oral Roberts coined the phrase "points of contact" to describe the objects used as springboards to "release your faith toward God."[81] These practices chafed against their simultaneous teaching about God's invisible laws, which already supplied a mechanism for how God transformed faith into blessing. Faith, like gravity, operated as an immutable and repeatable law of cause and effect. What else was necessary? Yet pentecostalism's material devotional culture, older than the rise of the prosperity gospel itself, pervaded prosperity theology as another reflection of its thoroughgoing materialism. If faith could produce material results, health and finances in particular, then why couldn't material objects help faith along?

The 1950s bore witness to a popular search for a religious modus operandi, one that would be both otherworldly and utterly mundane. The Norman Vincent Peales and Oral Roberts of the decade simply reminded people of the goodness of God and the endless possibilities embedded in the everyman's life. In prayer cloths and happy thoughts alike, people discovered the merits of applied Christianity. It was faith they could put to work.

Prosperous Faith: The 1960s

Those who had championed prosperity during the healing revivals now found that their time had come. Its leading lights traded tents for churches, itinerancy for institutions, and most notably, healing for prosperity. These were lean years for tent revivalists, but those evangelists who learned to adapt to the new youthful atmosphere found riches indeed. One after another, the old guard of the healing revivals publicized their discovery of God's gifts of health and wealth.[82] Subtlety was at a premium as evangelists covered their books with images of stuffed wallets, money sacks towering over churches, and gleaming golden keys to personal treasure chests. It was the adolescence of the prosperity gospel.[83]

Old-fashioned evangelistic methods carried the message farther and farther from home. David Nunn, W. V. Grant, and R. W. Culpepper, often side-by-side, pounded the deliverance revival circuit (as their tagline read) "from coast to coast around the world and on the mission fields."[84] Magazine after magazine urged domestic and international readers to claim their financial due.[85] These prosperity evangelists followed the well-trod paths of international pentecostal missionaries and, like them, were on the edge of an encounter with the exploding influence of Christianity in the southern hemisphere. They were beginning to reenvision their strategy of "sending" missionaries when faced with the logistical advantages of training local pastors.[86] T. L. and Daisy Osborn had been leaders in the strategy of co-evangelism whereby they raised funds to allow native evangelists to build their own churches patterned on the Osborn ministry. Christ for the Nations, run by Gordon and Freda Lindsay, which would eventually multiply thousands of churches worldwide, produced their first offshoots in the 1970s.

The preeminence of prosperity theology prompted some teachers to attempt to reconcile divine wealth with the realities of the missionary field. Evangelist David Nunn's *The Healing Messenger* featured emaciated children with distended bellies looking out from the cover under headings such as "Fill My Cup Please." Inside, Nunn taught the principles of financial sowing and reaping, assuring readers that "the proper use of faith brings God's richest blessings to all of us." His magazine encouraged his 140,000 readers to make "Faith Promises" and "Seed Faith Gifts," donations that would bring individual and communal reward: "If you will act in faith today, I believe that this will be the turning point in your life in victory and blessings."[87] The globetrotting minister Lester Sumrall's *World Harvest* chronicled Sumrall's foreign missions with accounts of extraordinary supernaturalism, witchdoctors conquered, and illness vanquished by God's healing power. Even there, articles concerning "God's divine law of compensation" peppered the magazine.[88] Evelyn Wyatt's Keys of Prosperity Pact guaranteed hidden riches as recompense for donations to world evangelism.[89] The Osborns stuffed *Faith Digest* with newsy updates and hundreds of photographs of overseas crusades, interspersed with reminders that prosperity theology yielded abundant returns for American readers. Though compassionate evangelism was in keeping with pentecostal missions, critics pointed out that it failed to answer the question: why not just teach *them* the law of faith?

Many crusade-weary evangelists found divine prosperity to be a message better suited to their new, settled ministries. The *Voice of Healing* favorite Velmer Gardner abandoned his large healing campaigns after claiming exhaustion, and, on the advice of FGBMFI's founder Demos

Three
Easy
Steps
to

PROSPERITY

By LeRoy Jenkins

"YOU CAN HAVE THE DESIRES OF YOUR HEART"

FIGURE 2.3 Leroy Jenkins The 1965 cover of *Three Easy Steps to Prosperity* by evangelist Leroy Jenkins. Believers must take steps to unlock heaven's treasures.

Source: Leroy Jenkins Ministries.

Shakarian, he learned to apply faith to his finances as he had once done for healing. He built a new reputation and a Ramada Inn in Springfield, Missouri.[90] The number of faith-building ministries devoted to prosperity grew in number and presence as new ministerial headquarters and bible schools popped up across Canada and the United States, especially in the Southern states. Gordon Lindsay and his Christ for the Nations ministry established his 40,000 square foot headquarters and a Bible school in Dallas, Texas, adding to the growing number of like-minded faith teachers. Kenneth Hagin finally joined the upper echelon of teachers in founding his own evangelistic association in 1962 with a new headquarters in 1966 in Tulsa, Oklahoma, Oral Roberts's backyard. Even the nomadic LeRoy Jenkins and his idol, A. A. Allen, settled down. Allen built a Bible school in Miracle Valley, Arizona, and Jenkins put away his 10,000-seat tent to found the Church of What's Happening Now.[91]

The southern prairies of Tulsa, Oklahoma, became the prosperity gospel's educational heartland. Oral Roberts University, founded in 1963 was the largest and most ecumenical vision of spirit-filled education fitted with an

FIGURE 2.4 **Oral Roberts University Logo** Oral Roberts University, founded in 1963, summed up its charismatic vision in their logo "Educating the Whole Man" flanked by the words SPIRIT, MIND, BODY.
Source: Kari Sullivan.

unending vision for expansion. In 1974, Hagin founded Rhema Bible Training Center in Tulsa as an official organ of his style of prosperity theology, called "Word of Faith" after his popular magazine of the same name. Hundreds of attempts to duplicate their successes would rise and fall, but these educational centers remained the two most important mouthpieces for the prosperity gospel.

Fundraising strategies grew with the scope of their ministries. In the 1950s, ministers had focused on divine reciprocity ("Give and it shall be given unto you") when asking for offerings and support for their ministries. Few ventured out of discussions of tithing. In the 1960s, their methods focused on covenant-making, pacts between evangelists, believers, and God. There were endless "Blessing Covenants," "Prosperity Covenants," and "Miracle Partnerships" as evangelists explained how a donation to their ministries would open the windows of heaven. Tommy and Daisy Osborn, famous for their overseas evangelism, turned to wholesale prosperity with their "Pact of Plenty," the promise of financial blessings to those who donated (particularly to the Osborn ministry).[92] Soon a flurry of "Prove God" campaigns encouraged believers to test their financial faith and earn their own proof. Gene Ewing, known as a financial troubleshooter for fellow evangelists, published Prove God testimonies like that of M. M. Baker, photographed beside his late model Lincoln:

> Dear Bro. Ewing:
>   During your Memphis, Tenn. crusade I proved God and got one of the miracle billfolds. At the time I was driving a Ford Falcon, but decided it was too small and too light a car, since I travel about 40,000 miles a year. I had been wanting to trade for a Lincoln Continental for some time and less than one week after I proved God, the Lord worked it out and gave me just what I wanted—a Lincoln Continental. I proved God in one of your earlier meetings and God gave us a 1964 12 x 56 Mobile Home and helped me pay off $1,000.00 in bills. The Lord will certainly do what He said He would.[93]

Prove God offerings turned into prove *everything* campaigns, as crusaders like Morris Cerullo urged all Christians to be Proof Producers.

Agricultural imagery flourished as "abundance" and "harvest" entered the Christian vocabulary. The seed faith imagery that Oral Roberts had introduced into the pentecostal vocabulary had produced its own harvest. Cornucopias were portrayed everywhere, overflowing

with fruit, grain, or gleaming coins. The doctrine of "first fruits" (a reference to a harvest oblation found in the Pentateuch) became a standard
classification of donation, second only to tithes. "Plant your FIRST fruits
in the needs of God's work," read the headline of T. L. Osborn's *Faith
Digest*, "EXPECT His ABUNDANT RETURNS for your own needs."[94]
Donors must cull a portion from the *first* of every new piece of income.
Magazines showed preachers in the midst of wheat fields, sheaves of
grain resting on the bibles open in their hands.[95] Though frequently pictured as a spiritual farmer, Oral Roberts urged a measured approach in
his published prayer guides, *Daily BLESSING*. All "Blessing Prayers"
kept the following regimen:[96]

8 a.m. Pray for Spiritual Progress
10 a.m. For Those Without Christ
12:00 p.m. For Healing
6 p.m. For Prosperity
9 p.m. For the World

These prosperity preachers settled into a more consistent theology of
holy words uttered aloud. This consensus surrounding Kenneth Hagin's
theology, and those associated him, became the foundation of the Word of
Faith variety of the prosperity gospel. Kenneth Hagin's exegesis of "Faith
cometh by hearing, and hearing by the word of God" (Romans 10:17) concluded that the cycle of hearing and speaking activated faith. His revelation, recounted in *Hear and Be Healed*, constructed a doctrine that found
widespread acceptance.[97] To accumulate faith, believers engaged in a perpetual process of allowing God's Word to filter into their hearts by hearing
and speaking it out of their mouths. Passively reading scripture was not
enough: it was the act of *hearing* that tied believers to God's power through
faith.

Maintaining faith became a process of imbibing a steady stream of
God's Word. This practice served as a reminder for believers to maintain
their church commitments, because without church attendance saints
could not hear enough to sustain their faith. With the rise of audiocas-
settes, celebrity preachers would quote this verse frequently to promote
their sales, reminding the audience that only a steady diet of the spoken
word could fertilize their hearts. Kenneth Hagin protégé Kenneth Copeland instructed listeners: "Your faith is in direct relation to the level of the
Word in you. Get your Word-level up."[98] Affirmations became common

practice as churchgoers frequently displayed faith-building scriptures in cars, homes, and workplaces to remind them to confess multiple times a day. The ascent to higher levels of faith could only take place with careful attention to the spiritual act of hearing.

Yet for God's Word to be heard, it had to be spoken. Faith bound itself to the spoken word. As Hagin opined, "A spiritual law too few of us realize is: Our confessions rule us."[99] Speaking positive things became a spiritual discipline. Believers expected their affirmations to release power (faith) to bring these assertions into reality. The first confession, which Hagin called The Great Confession, began with a confession of Jesus as Lord:

> Confession: I believe in my heart Jesus Christ is the Son of God. I believe He was raised from the dead for my justification. I confess Him as my Lord and Savior. Jesus is my Lord. He is dominating my life. He is guiding me. He is leading me.[100]

This emphasis on a declaration of faith put faith teachers squarely in the company of evangelicals, who had made verbal confession a hallmark of the conversion experience.[101] Yet while evangelicals focused on the personal relationship with God that such a declaration implied, faith believers expected to share in God's power. As Kenneth Copeland explained, "God's power is in direct relationship with His Word. He has used His Word to release His power. He has sent His Word to us so that we may be in contact with His great power."[102] Believers tap into God's power through the spoken word, which "works" when speakers possess the faith to set God's Word in motion. A significant body of literature explained how Jesus' words and actions echoed God's Word, positively confessing realities into being.[103] Consider that the term *confession* referred to every spoken word. Words uttered in prayer or anger, privately or publicly, not only tested character but also defined spiritual success or failure. Jesus himself said as much, Hagin insisted, according to Mark 11:23, "Whosoever shall say . . . and shall not doubt in his heart, but shall believe that those things which he saith shall come to pass; he shall have whatsoever he saith." Hagin's Bible brimmed with promises, and Jesus' comment that "you shall have what you say" offered a guarantee. Faith became the force that would actuate believers' very words.

A theological tradition of the power of speech-acts heavily leaned on Proverbs 18:21: "Death and life are in the power of the tongue: and they that love it shall eat the fruit thereof." Hagin and his followers affirmed that speech creates power and "Faith's confessions create realities."[104] Some of the popular catchphrases from the movement focused on this unique characteristic, as people could "name it and claim it." Oral Roberts' term "seed faith," an idiom that infused the present with potential and purpose, named a similar logic. Faith teachers subsequently dubbed each prayer, tithe, word, emotion, or action a "seed" whose spiritual consequences—good or bad—had not come into season. (Unlike tithes given after income, seed faith money added an element of risk by donating money on the hope of receiving more in return.)

Kenneth Copeland emerged as one of the new stars of the movement. Kenneth and Gloria Copeland moved to Oklahoma in the fall of 1966, eager to attend Oral Roberts University, where Kenneth soon came to the ministry's attention. As a pilot and former pop singer, his talents suited his new employment as Roberts's pilot, chauffeur, and touring singer with the ministry. As Copeland worked and studied under the auspices of Oral Roberts's famous healing ministry, he also became a follower of another faith giant: Kenneth Hagin. Starting in 1967, Hagin's denominational prosperity teaching, Word of Faith, taught Copeland a new vocabulary to describe the relationship between belief and materiality. Copeland adopted Hagin's understanding of "positive confession," the spoken word bringing circumstances into reality, with such conviction that he offered to trade his car to Hagin's ministry for another set of Hagin's taped teachings.[105] With Hagin's teachings on positive confession, Oral Roberts's healing ministry, and a developing theology of finances, Copeland's distinctive brand of faith theology took shape. On September 7, 1967, the couple founded Kenneth Copeland Ministries (KCM).

Orbiting just outside of this Word of Faith circle, another prophet combined the metaphysical and pentecostal threads into a single prosperity gospel. The Reverend Frederick J. Eikerenkoetter (1935–2009), known as Reverend Ike, gave the prosperity gospel its first black spokesman with a national platform. A southerner who had migrated to the urban North and blended pentecostal and spiritualist traditions, Reverend Ike echoed many of the metaphysical prosperity theologies of the first half of the twentieth century. Reverend Ike's flashy jewelry, conked hair, and tailored suits reinforced his expansive message of abundance, summed up in catchphrases like "you can't lose with the stuff I use," and "the lack of money is the root of all evil."[106] In 1969, Reverend Ike moved his United Church of Jesus Christ for All People to the New York City neighborhood of Washington Heights, where he refurbished a theater into a 3,500-seat, gilded worship facility capable of broadcasting his services to national television and radio audiences.

His evolving theology took on new metaphysical fervor, setting aside pentecostal messages for a New Thought-inspired "Science of Living." Reverend Ike heated up the genteel reassurances of Norman Vincent Peale's positive thinking into glittering promises of material wealth, channeling mind-power toward tangible rewards. He implored believers to change their circumstances for the better rather than rely on a heavenly reward, aptly summarized in his famous saying, "Don't wait for your pie in the sky by and by; have it now with ice cream and a cherry on top."[107] Yet Reverend Ike also patterned his ministry and message after Oral Roberts, whose denominational independence, financial focus, and creative fundraising techniques he admired.[108]

Reverend Ike's emphasis on the mechanism of faith likely resulted from the stronger measure of metaphysical mind-power he injected into the prosperity gospel. Although other faith teachers, black and white, rejected any metaphysical legacy and distanced themselves from the flamboyant Reverend Ike, no one forgot his dramatic promises of material wealth for the right-thinking Christian. Reverend Ike's popular message served as a sturdy bridge, across which subsequent preachers and participants carried a metaphysical—and heavily instrumental—Christianity into the future.

A. A. Allen seemed less than pleased with so many evangelistic pretenders to his throne: "Humbly I tell you this, as reports are reaching my headquarters that ministers all over the country are preaching about the blessing of prosperity. . . . God told me he had given me power to bestow power to get wealth. He did not say it was given to Tom, Dick and Harry, or to just anyone who says 'Lord, Lord.'"[109] But it was too late. The secret was out.

Charismatic Faith: 1960–1975

It is a bizarre twist of history that this flowering of the prosperity gospel arrived in a season of withering anti-institutionalism. Its preachers valued clean living and future thinking among a generation in the grips of rebellion, when the first wave of baby boomers became teenagers, arriving in those years of anxiety and hormones in such numbers as to warp the fabric of American society itself. Prosperous beyond the dreams of their forebears and possessing enormous buying clout, young people changed music, clothing, hairstyles, leisure, technology, and sexual morality. They chewed through fads and fashions at a bewildering rate. They made musical millionaires out of buttoned-down folksingers, sun-bleached hymnodists of the joys of surfboards, girl groups bewailing boyfriends their parents didn't understand, mop-topped Liverpudlians, and shaggy, drug-addled guitar kings. They sported miniskirts, midiskirts, maxiskirts and granny gowns, crew-cuts, Beatle cuts, or no cuts at all. They took to the streets in the hundreds of thousands to protest war and racism; they took to the record stores in the millions to buy songs of romance, freedom, and hedonism. Love was in the air and so was the reek of patchouli and cannabis.

Though God was rumored to be dead,[110] this generation still continued to seek the divine, though not always in the usual places. In those years, many middle-class Americans began to consider non-Christian approaches to religious life, along with the notion that believers might access supernatural power through nontraditional means. A number of movements, dismissed as "cults" by the media, captured the attention of troubled celebrities and students on campuses across the United States. A pantheon of gurus made appearances promising spiritual gifts through ancient techniques, recent revelations, or modern drugs; figures such as the Maharishi Mahesh Yogi, Baba Ram Dass, the Reverend Moon, Maharj-ji, Timothy Leary, Moses David, and L. Ron Hubbard became widely known. Some new religions—Scientology and Transcendental Meditation, for example—claimed (like the faith movement) to have discovered universal spiritual laws that adepts could access.[111] Soon homemakers were chanting mantras; movie stars were being hooked up to e-meters; and bishops were experimenting with the consciousness-expanding powers of LSD, séances, or peyote.

Christians began to experiment with unfamiliar spiritual highs. In April 1960, Dennis J. Bennett, rector of St. Mark's Episcopal Church in Van Nuys, California, announced to his thriving congregation that he had received Holy Spirit baptism. His public declaration that he had spoken in tongues (*glossolalia*), and the hundreds of his parishioners who soon followed his example, marked the beginning of the "charismatic movement." Though Episcopalians and Lutherans led the pack, Protestant denominations of all kinds—Presbyterian, Mennonite, American Baptist, and the United Methodist—awakened to charismatic influences. In 1967, this revival spilled into the Roman Catholic Church, newly receptive to Vatican II's invitation to open the windows of the church. Denominational conferences devoted to renewal popped up in rapid succession: Catholic (1970), Presbyterian (1972), Mennonite (1972), Lutheran (1972), Episcopalian (1973), Orthodox (1974), and Methodist (1974).[112] Ecumenism flowered through figures such as David du Plessis, otherwise known as "Mr. Pentecost." He informally represented pentecostalism on a global stage as an observer of Vatican II, member of the National Council of Churches (NCC), and chair of the Roman Catholic–pentecostal dialogue team.[113] The freshly pentecostalized gravitated toward a new batch of periodicals, workshops, tapes, conferences, and prayer groups to hear up-to-the-minute reports of tongues, prophecy, and healing.

The charismatic renewal was a powerful reaction to American disillusionment with institutions and marked the genesis of the sanctified counterculture. By the late 1960s, people spoke of "Jesus Freaks" and noted a wave of barefoot enthusiasts often armed with a 1966 New Testament translation called *Good News for Modern Man*. Tradition was out; authenticity was in. As one evangelist observed, "I don't know what; there's something happening. . . . But people . . . they're more interested in pentecostalism and the occult, mysticism, Buddhism, eastern religions. There's a tremendous interest in the unknown."[114] It was a season of metaphysical curiosity. Breezy summer gatherings, known as the Camps Furthest Out, gathered thousands of the newly spirit-baptized into playful charismatic sessions for healing, prophecy, and deliverance led by an ecumenical assembly of speakers, including faith teachers.[115] The Episcopalian bestselling author Agnes Sanford famously captured the whimsical and metaphysical mood there as she guided Christians into mental and physical alignment with God's healing light.[116]

Glossolalia became the gateway drug for other gifts of the spirit. Healing and deliverance were of particular interest in a sex-, drug-, and alcohol-addicted age. Derek Prince, British scholar and member of the infamous Fort Lauderdale Five, became a charismatic favorite for his teachings on demonology. He, like many, saw himself as cleaning up the spiritual debris of the age, delivering people from a legion of evil forces such as the "spirit of petting," the "spirit of anger," Asian religions, psychedelic drugs, and demons. Christians tried desperately to engage with the counterculture in relevant ways. Streetwise religious folk tried to imitate the example of Dave Wilkerson whose *The Cross and the Switchblade* documented his sanctified approach to youth violence.

The charismatic movement found its voice in song. The acoustic ballads of groups such as the Fisherfolk, a folk ensemble from the charismatic

Episcopalian Church of the Redeemer, could be heard in the popular new Christian coffeehouses and communes that sprang up across America, Canada, and western Europe. Every church seemed to launch its own musical act. Broadway musicals such as *Godspell* (1969) and *Jesus Christ Superstar* (1971), penned in the midst of the Vietnam War, found in the man from Galilee a long-haired, peace-loving avatar who could also sing about important things like love. Jesus festivals called "Fishnet" or "Jesus 1977" belted out music and teaching in giant outdoor events, featuring famous draws like the apocalyptical Hal Lindsey; evangelical Ruth Carter Stapleton; and TV-favorites Father John Bertolucci, Pat Robertson, and Jim Bakker. Roy Hathern, the future father-in-law of evangelist Benny Hinn and famous faith teacher in his own right, pastored an Assemblies of God megachuch in Winter Park, Florida, whose musical festivals attracted up to 30,000 attendees. Positive confession evangelist Kenneth Gaub toured the country with his family band, Eternity Express, in a bus whose destination read: "Heaven." The former Assemblies of God preacher Ralph Wilkerson raised one of the nation's largest charismatic congregations, Melodyland Christian Center, with his musically minded ministry. Young people flocked to its hip atmosphere and "modern" emphasis on Holy Ghost preaching in step with Christian therapy, drug rehabilitation, ethnic diversity, and contemporary music.[117] Even pop crooner Pat Boone, raised in the Church of Christ, found himself caught up in the charismatic movement. His swimming pool baptisms for Hollywood stars were famous for introducing Christianity to the entertainment Babylon. The movement attracted not just Zsa Zsa Gabor, Bob Dylan, and Priscilla Presley but also upstarts like John Osteen and Fred Price who would go on to become integral parts of the prosperity gospel. In song or spoken word, the movement became a fleet of churches, conferences, concerts, and Bible studies devoted to the pursuit of the Spirit.

Pentecostals were confounded. The use of holy tongues that was once the official language of pentecostalism suddenly had made Catholics and Protestants into native speakers. Pentecostals reared to worry about the state of Methodist, Presbyterian, and especially Catholic souls now witnessed their embrace of the one marker—tongues—that had made their faith a spectacle.[118] Classic pentecostal denominations proceeded with interest and caution. Charismatic Protestants and Catholics were equally ambivalent about inheriting pentecostal citizenship with the Southern Baptist Convention and the Missouri Synod Lutherans in vigorous opposition to the movement. Pamphlets produced by these

anti-charismatic denominations tried to assure their members that that
they did not have "incomplete faith."[119] Those open to charismatic influences tried to keep up; Lutheran charismatics, for example, commissioned new reports on the Holy Spirit but decried faith healers as
religious quacks and mass hypnotists who exploited the "desperate, dis-
turbed, and credulous."[120]

Interest in the Holy Spirit flowed like water through congregations.
The charismatic movement's diverse leadership and participants prevented any one person or idea from claiming to represent the center. In
this climate, the prosperity gospel cropped up as one of many spirit-filled
solutions for a curious and experimental generation. It was a rare moment
of ecumenical unity. As Vinson Synan observed, "It was not unusual to see
a Catholic priest, an Episcopal pastor, and a pentecostal evangelist sharing
the same platform at Full Gospel Business Men's dinners or the thousands of other conferences, revivals, crusades, and missions sponsored by
a multitude of churches and para-church organizations."[121] By 1975, the
charismatic revival claimed five million souls belonging to Catholic, mainline, and pentecostal churches.[122]

The prosperity gospel profited from the ecumenism that propped open
doors once shut. Oral Roberts University alumnus Charles Green credited
the growth of his 2,500-member Word of Faith Temple in Catholic New
Orleans to the start of the charismatic movement, when Catholic "people
who had listened to us on the radio for years began to realize they could
now visit us. Many of them came, and some of them stayed. So the church
began to grow."[123] Though the Assemblies of God pastor Tommy Reid initially balked at the hippies and Catholics attending his FGBMFI-sponsored
events, his West Seneca, New York, congregation grew from 150 to 1,000
in the charismatic heyday.[124] Some even allowed "those hippies" to change
the name on the door. In 1961, Wally Hickey founded the Full Gospel
Chapel, an Assemblies of God congregation and active participant in the
expanding circle of faith churches. When newly spirit-filled Catholics who
joined nicknamed it the Happy Church, Wally and his wife Marilyn let it
stick. Before long, Marilyn Hickey rose to fame as one of the most
prominent prosperity televangelists of her time.

How did the prosperity gospel win over a movement of middle-class
white folks who tried to live footloose in the spirit and unencumbered by
material possessions? It worked in part because its preachers were adept
at keeping pace with what felt "modern." As the momentum of the postwar pentecostal healing revivals crested in the charismatic movement,

old-time deliverance evangelists had discovered that the qualities that endeared them to boisterous outdoor spectacles did not suit the new charismatic temperament.[125] If healing evangelism was "outdoor" religion, the charismatic movement was surely made to stay indoors. These unvarnished crusaders of the 1940s and 1950s polished their look and their message, and those like Kenneth Copeland or Kenneth Hagin were better suited for conference centers than sawdust trails. For all the guitars and tambourines that surfaced to rouse new choruses and old camp meeting songs, the charismatic movement ushered in changes that reflected the taste of an educated, middle-class clientele. Teachers, rather than healers, led the growing revival with a focus on spiritual finances and institution building. Many leaders no longer required the platform skills that once kept pentecostal audiences spellbound, as the staid settings of auditoriums and hotel ballrooms favored careful exposition over improvisation. In this new climate, prosperity teachers thrived as audiences sought pentecostal ideas with modern sensibilities.

These prosperity preachers, largely outside of denominational oversight, proved successful at standing in the gap between pentecostalism and the wider charismatic world. Oral Roberts spent the decade winning pentecostals to the vision of a *charismatic* (as opposed to merely pentecostal) university and translating Holy Ghost religion for the wider evangelical world. He soon counted David du Plessis, Ralph Wilkerson, Billy Graham, and kingpins of the World Congress on Evangelism (1966) as friends. In 1968, he cemented his ecumenical aspirations with his own conversion to Methodism.[126] Over two million households of pentecostals and charismatics alike received old-time revivalist W. V. Grant's *The Voice of Deliverance*.[127] Lester Sumrall left the Assemblies of God to found his own evangelistic ministry, producing *World Harvest Magazine* (1962), a 24-hour Christian radio program (1968), one of the first Christian television stations (1972), and the 2,000-member Cathedral of Praise. His media presence helped focus the budding renewal on prophecy, prosperity, and dramatic deliverance. Kenneth Copeland, Kenneth Hagin and John Osteen earned their stripes speaking to suits and ties gathered in nearly 2,000 FGBMFI chapters around the country.[128] FGBMFI had become one of the most important outlets for the charismatic renewal as a whole and a perpetual theology of prosperity in action. The crowded meetings featured sanctified actors, football players, Catholic priests, and successful merchant princes and became the primary place for businessmen to share testimonies and submit their workday to God's credit and scrutiny. The Full Gospel Business Men's Fellowship International appreciated Derek Prince for his unemotional and systematic approach, which contrasted favorably with the "loud, sentimental preaching" of the average charismatic minister.[129] By the early 1970s, the fellowship boasted a membership of 300,000 and an annual budget of more than one million dollars. (The female counterpart to FGBMFI, the Women's Aglow Fellowship, spoke little of health or wealth and did not feature faith teachers prominently. Prosperity theology, in this sense, adopted a masculine cast as the "business" of men.[130]) Neither charismatic dogma nor old-time religion, the faith message became another way of saying that God still moves, bidden or unbidden, in all aspects of Christian life.

Even before the golden years of televangelism, the prosperity gospel's spread and its uniformity owed much to television. Faith preachers joined the spiking number of syndicated programs (those appearing on five or more stations), appearing on more stations with greater frequency. Technological developments eased the cost and speed of television production and allowed programs to broadcast simultaneously, blanketing the airwaves with an increasingly familiar message of prosperity.[131] Oral Roberts, Robert Schuller, and Rex Humbard, reigned as the leading lights of inspirational television, gradually displacing Roman Catholic, mainline, and even denominational evangelical shows as the most-watched religious programs.[132] In 1971, a cluster of independent preachers (predominately prosperity folk) comprised 42 percent of the top syndicated religious programs on television. In 1981, the total jumped to 83 percent. The scope of religious broadcasting narrowed, giving the prosperity gospel a market share that came close to a theological monopoly.[133] Flipping from channel to channel on Sunday morning, viewers might think they were watching endless reruns.

Religious television transported the drama of tent revivalism to American living rooms. "In a sense," noted the historian Edith Blumhofer, "deliverance evangelism never died; rather, it remade itself into the electronic church."[134] A. A. Allen, Kenneth Copeland, and Morris Cerullo's television programs continued to earn respectable ratings and nationwide exposure.[135] The possibilities seemed limitless. In 1970, Rex Humbard's broadcast, *The Cathedral of Tomorrow*, shot on location in his multimillion dollar church of the same name, appeared on more television stations than any other American program.[136] (He grew so popular that even Elvis Presley considered himself a fan; Humbard presided over the king of rock and roll's 1977 funeral.) Twenty-five million people watched Oral Roberts's 1975

Thanksgiving television special. By the decade's end, American religious broadcasting earned an estimated $1 billion in total revenue.[137] Faith ministers did not simply add to television programming: they transformed it.

A handful of the nation's largest Protestant churches stood out as strongholds of prosperity teaching. Lester Sumrall's Cathedral of Praise (South Bend, Indiana), John Osteen's Lakewood Church (Houston), Karl Strader's First Assembly (Lakeland, Florida), Waymon Rodgers's Evangel Christian Life Center (Louisville), Tommy Reid's Full Gospel Tabernacle (Orchard Park, NY), Anne and John Gimenez's Rock Church (Virginia Beach, Virginia), Marilyn and Wally Hickey's The Happy Church (Denver), Dick Iverson's Bible Temple (later City Bible Church in Portland), Roy and Pauline Harthern's Calvary Assembly (Orlando), and Charles and Barbara Green's Word of Faith Temple (New Orleans) gained national recognition as vital congregations and popular settings for radio and television broadcasts of their services.

The 1970s saw an explosion of Christian television as a host of innovators founded networks that soon became electronic empires. Pat Robertson's Christian Broadcasting Network (CBN) built up its fledgling enterprise with popular programs like *The 700 Club* and *The Jim and Tammy Show*, featuring the young Jim and Tammy Faye Bakker. From 1970 to 1975, their estimated viewership climbed from 10 to 110 million worldwide.[138] CBN quickly distinguished itself as one of the most important networks in the industry for its pioneering use of satellite technology and 24-hour programming.[139] In 1973, Paul and Jan Crouch founded Trinity Broadcasting Network, a sprawling enterprise that, within a few short years, acquired Lester Sumrall's modest television network.[140] Not to be outdone, the Bakkers founded the PTL Television Network to become two of televangelism's brightest stars. With prosperity preachers at the helm of expansive television enterprises, they effectively seated hundreds of thousands of new audience members. Faith believers moved from being a side act in pentecostal revivalism to center stage.

BY THE CLOSE of the 1970s, the ecumenical dream that washed over the charismatic movement was receding from its high water mark.[141] Mainline and Catholic interest in pentecostal worship waned, diluted by diminishing curiosity and official denominational attempts to regulate its practice. Historic denominations were less eager to build theological and institutional unity with pentecostals. Even Oral Roberts, who had left his Pentecostal Holiness denomination for the United Methodist

Church in the heat of the charismatic revival, returned to pentecostal circles chagrined. Attempts at imposing unity on this boisterous movement had failed. The "Seattle Presbytery," led by Dennis Bennett, and the "Charismatic Concerns Committee" of Oklahoma City had failed to deal with tensions between pentecostal and charismatic mainliners over such controversial practices as rebaptism or mass exorcisms.[142] The wildly successful 1977 Kansas City charismatic conference that drew 45,000 registrants was forced to accommodate two warring factions of pentecostals. When the preachers known as the Fort Lauderdale Five organized hundreds of ministers in a hierarchy of submission and obedience they were derided as the "Charismatic Vatican."[143] Fears were expressed that the vigorous independence of the movement was being usurped by a few, maverick, more powerful church leaders. The momentum of the charismatic movement was carrying it further from the mainline and back toward the independence and unruliness of stand-alone pentecostalism. And as it did, unfettered pentecostalism found new homes in the rise of evangelical hybrids like John Wimber's Vineyard movement and Chuck Smith's Calvary Chapel.

In the years after the charismatic movement, the prosperity gospel continued to be shaped by the revival's deep imprint on the religious landscape. It was as if a door between pentecostal and traditional churches had been opened, and the prosperity gospel entered in with the rest. Churchgoing Lutherans, Presbyterians, Episcopalians, and Catholics, to name only a few, looked at Holy Spirit-filled teachers with new interest. These nonpentecostal supporters—even those who remained in their own denominations—proved to be an unexpected boon to the swelling ranks of prosperity teachers. Over the years, this demographic would continue to generate many Monday-through-Saturday followers for prosperity conferences, publications, and media, despite their Sunday attendance at traditional congregations. The prosperity movement expanded further as it gathered up charismatic wanderers without a denominational home. After breathing the rarefied air of the Spirit, many did not want to go back.

3

Wealth

Jehovah Jireh (my provider)

TELEVANGELISTS JIM AND Tammy Faye Bakker needed to look no further than their own backyard to see how far the prosperity gospel had come. By the early 1980s, their 2,200-acre Christian resort and theme park in South Carolina, Heritage USA, had become the nation's third most-visited attraction. Tourists could wander from the pricey Heritage Grand Mansion, vacation houses, and restaurants to the roller rink, sprawling water park, and family-friendly campgrounds. It was a Christian playground for believers, who, flushed with their own successes, caught the vision of the charismatic couple who made the abundant life seem possible. The Bakkers presided over the electric church as television royalty, attracting audiences with their campy banter and theatrical delivery. Their high-roller lifestyle—complete with mansion, designer apparel, and twin Mercedes cars—made the couple icons of the billion-dollar televangelism industry and living examples of the power of faith to produce results. Both successful and controversial, Tammy and Jim, an Assemblies of God preacher, embodied the financial heights to which pentecostals had climbed and invited the rest to join the action. "The gospel to the poor," concluded Kenneth Copeland, "is that Jesus has come and they don't have to be poor anymore!"[1]

The most controversial aspect of the movement was its radical claim to transform invisible faith into financial rewards. Its prophets proclaimed a palpable gospel, one that could be clearly seen and measured in the financial well-being of its participants. We miss an important part of the story if we detach divine finance from the larger promise of *demonstrable* faith. Believers accepted what the theologian Miroslav Volf dubbed the *materiality of salvation*, that the work of redemption begins in the here and now. Historically, pentecostals set themselves apart by their expectation that "signs and wonders" accompanied evangelism as anticipations of God's reign. Authentic Christianity bore witness to itself not only by the truth of its teachings but also by the supernatural trail following in its wake. The prosperity gospel elaborated on this doctrine by teaching that these wonders manifested themselves in the life of every individual, and that faith-filled individuals should expect signs and wonders in their lives as evidence of the truth of their convictions. Further, financial abundance and good health stood as public and perpetual demonstrations of Christians' spiritual progress. Prosperity and health were two sides of the same coin. Gloria Copeland marveled that she "had been looking at finances and prosperity in a different way from other things, such as divine health . . . If a symptom of sickness came on my body, I would not stand for it. . . . You should refuse lack just as quickly as you refuse sickness."[2]

This chapter follows the explosion of the prosperity gospel in the late 1970s and how it convinced believers to calculate their conviction according to their wallets. The movement thrived and survived a decadent decade ruled by supersized churches and televangelists with big hair and bigger promises. Success followed those ministers who learned how to combine media mastery, church-growth formulas, and openness to independent pentecostalism. Faith for finances had hit its stride. Its flashy reputation became a public relations nightmare in the late 1980s when the moral failures of a few tarnished the very idea of a glamorous minister. But the movement deftly refashioned itself for the postmodern 1990s as therapeutic and down-to-earth Christian self-improvement, tempering its *hard prosperity* with a *soft prosperity* image. The prosperity gospel had become the foremost Christian theology of modern living. In the movement's peaks and valleys, followers persisted in seeking a God of abundance in scripture, in the example of leaders, but most often, in the twists and turns of their own lives. Prosperity was a gospel of weights and measures. As preachers heaped promise after promise of monetary gain, supporters sought out scales by which to weigh their own rewards.

A Prosperous Movement

By the late 1970s, prosperity preachers could survey the charismatic landscape with satisfaction. The old guard among them had once been a tent-toting assembly of independent revivalists who envisioned pentecostalism as the "child of rejection and poverty."[3] Now, they stood at the helm of the sprawling movement that remade much of pentecostalism in its image. The prosperity movement's tightly knit network—television personalities, senior pastors, media moguls, traveling speakers, and miracle workers alike—shared a vision of universal spiritual laws that drew blessings from the spiritual plane for earthly use. Though the language varied, the movement could be identified by its heavily instrumental definition of faith that, as Kenneth Copeland stated, "can be controlled. . . . You can turn it off, or turn it on."[4] Though the finer points of prosperity theology mattered, faith was faith only because it *worked*.

The prosperity gospel was unhindered—and untested. Miss America winners had become hosts on its television networks, and city mayors heaped accolades upon their hometown heroes.[5] Oral Roberts, Pat Robertson, and Kenneth Copeland were becoming household names while hundreds of lesser known ministries pumped out books plastered with rainbows, waterfalls, and waving wheat that reminded people that, as one title extolled, *There's Plenty For You*. Christian bookstores advertised their manuals for everything from the uses of faith, the reality of healing, and overflowing finances, to the looming end times, and the Christian family. Its authors had a kitschy charm, posing for cover photos shaking their fists at the devil or waiting for a shower of blessings under prop umbrellas. People didn't seem to mind a little corniness as long as it caught nonbelievers' attention. The preaching duo Brenda and Mack Timberlake, for example, bathed their 80,000-square foot church of steel and concrete in the cornflower blue of Mack's trademark suits. (Brenda's characteristic sequins never found architectural expression.) Borrowing a term previously used only to describe the ideas of Kenneth Hagin, a new subculture of believers calling themselves Faith, Word, or sometimes Word of Faith people boldly professed positive words as if to shake down heaven's treasures.[6] The message so captivated and even scandalized co-laborers of this gospel that, by 1981, worried colleagues called a meeting with Kenneth Hagin to express concerns that his graduates were "confessing Cadillacs."[7]

The prosperity gospel's newfound prominence in the pentecostal-charismatic world was written in the headlines of every major conference advertisement. In the 1970s, a prosperity preacher was just one of many Jesus freaks in sideburns and bell-bottoms, but in the 1980s the movement rose up to dominate the stage. Figure 3.2 visually represents all conference participation in the 1980s as advertised in *Charisma* magazine, the era's most widely read charismatic periodical with 100,000 readers.[8] (For more on how to interpret the prosperity movement's network, see appendix B.) Clearly the two most striking features of this picture are the frequency of these pastors' interactions and the centrality of prosperity

FIGURE 3.1 **Kenneth Hagin and Friends** T. L. Osborn, Kenneth Hagin, and Oral
Roberts share the stage at Hagin's 1983 camp meeting.
Source: Used by permission of the Holy Spirit Research Center, Oral Roberts University.

preachers in the pentecostal domain. Names such as Oral Roberts, Kenneth Hagin, Kenneth Copeland, Robert Tilton, Benny Hinn, and Marilyn
Hickey—whose reputations were inseparable from Christian teaching on
divine money—became the most frequently featured speakers of the
1980s. The simple fact was that spirit-filled American churches advertised
prosperity preachers more than any other kind of speaker.

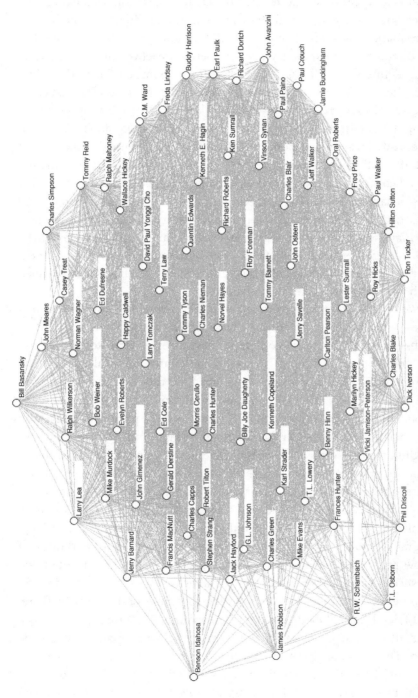

FIGURE 3.2 1980s Conference Participation Advertised in *Charisma* The golden age of televangelism was also the peak of the Word of Faith movement's influence over the pentecostal conference circuit. Anyone associated with Oral Roberts and Kenneth Hagin was a conference mainstay.

Prosperity preachers dominated the conference circuit as the must-see superstars of the pentecostal-charismatic world. Leaders from the bygone charismatic movement, like Francis McNutt and Larry Tomczak, still lingered, but it was clear as day that prosperity preachers stood at the forefront. Kenneth and Gloria Copeland's "Victory Seminars" took them in a yearly circuit of almost two-dozen major cities for a total audience of 80,000. Francis and Charles Hunter, known as the Happy Hunters, brought their healing revivals and prosperity theology to hundreds of American cities. Oral Roberts, Pat Robertson, and Kenneth Hagin could pack the Full Gospel Business Men's Fellowship International's bustling annual conventions. By the late 1980s, the organization had spearheaded 2,646 chapters worldwide, gathering monthly attendance of 600,000 to 700,000.[9] Those with modest reputations—Jerry Savelle, John Gimenez, Vicki Jamison Peterson—used conferences as opportunities to hone their skills and garner wider audiences. Connection was the lifeblood of independent ministries, and conferences, television, and magazines pumped fresh faces and crowds into circulation.

We can see the rough parameters of the prosperity movement at this time—what observers traditionally associate with the term Word of Faith—by focusing on the conference associates of Oral Roberts (figure 3.4) and Kenneth Hagin (figure 3.5). The nearly identical connections shared by Roberts and Hagin illustrate how the movement was both diverse and united. Diverse, as the prosperity gospel gained its vast reach through multiple pillars of support. United, as these preachers' dense web of association allows us to regard them as a single entity.

Until the mid-1970s, the message had never been a full-fledged movement. The prosperity gospel had always been a minor theme in a larger revival or a major theme in a smaller revival.[10] Now, the prosperity movement could claim not only a shared theological platform, but also a newly stabilized base of publications, conferences, associations, and television programs through which pastors promoted their ministries and those of fellow prosperity teachers. In many respects, the movement duplicated the successes of the healing and charismatic revivals that preceded it and in some ways even enveloped it.[11] While magazines of the charismatic revival folded, Oral Roberts, Kenneth Hagin, and T. L. Osborn ramped up their efforts and made their own glossy magazines major evangelistic tools. The personal connections that invigorated postwar independent pentecostalism still coursed through the faith movement, but an observer might have to look in different places. Favored friends not only could

Coming Together

Dominion's "John 17:21" DBS

Dominion is very high power Direct Broadcast Satellites will be capable of transmitting up to eight separate channels of television and 24 channels of radio directly to a small, inexpensive 24 inch dish shaped antenna placed on any home, business or apartment. The cost of local television and cable system access is completely eliminated, and there is no regular fee.

Channel and A Great Deal More.

Seven some 24 hour Dominion DBS channels will feature family entertainment, movies, news, public affairs, children's programs, sports, Christian programming and a host of other services such as stereo radio, weather, stock and commodity quotation, travel guides; video catalog shopping; personal computer programming and a unique personal messaging service, and a great deal more.

Send in the RESPONSE CARD or write DOMINION NETWORK, P.O. Box 9060, Farmington Hills, Michigan 48018 for more information on how you can become a Dominion DBS "Charter Home Affiliate."

These men and women, and many others, have elected to come together under the mandate of unity expressed in "John 17:21" to provide one complete 24 hour TV channel of anointed teaching and ministry each day, including prime time.

Tim and Beverly LaHaye
"We pray earnestly that God will commit this very important work with his richest blessing."

Chuck Smith
"I feel direct satellite broadcasting is the thing of the future and I am extremely interested in participating."

Marilyn Hickey
"Satellite is how Christian television is most exciting. Thank you for your great vision."

John Osteen
"Thank you for the gift of time on the Dominion Network. You are in our prayers."

James Robinson
"Praying that God will richly bless Dominion DBS as we share to gather the Good News of New Life through Jesus Christ."

Jerry Falwell
"I believe one of the greatest breakthroughs for our ministry will be direct broadcasting."

Fr. John Bertolucci
"We applaud your effort to use the latest technology to present the Gospel of Jesus Christ to the Nation."

D. James Kennedy
"We are pleased and grateful to be a part of Dominion satellite to home television and radio."

John and Ann Gimenez
"We accept your gift of DBS. Thank you for your hearts and look forward to working together with you."

Robert Schuller
"Dominion has my blessing and support. We look forward to sharing in this dynamic new technology."

Fred Price
"I look forward to reaching the cities of America with direct broadcast satellites."

Jim Bakker
"We pray that by being a godly channel for the Gospel through your efforts."

Mother Angelica
"I am excited about extending our satellite ministry directly into homes. We are thankful for the gift of you."

Oral Roberts
"I sincerely pray that God supply every needs for his tremendous endeavor for Him."

Karl Strader
"Through Dominion DBS, God is giving us an opportunity to minister to the entire Body of Christ, for which we are grateful."

Kenneth and Gloria Copeland
"We set ourselves in agreement with you for the total success of Dominion satellite."

Charles Stanley
"I will do all that I can to cooperate with other ministries in sharing your vision of Christian DBS fulfilled."

Jerry Barnard
"I am excited about being a part of this great work for the Kingdom."

Louis Kaplan
"DBS will allow us to give unrestrained voice to the salvation message."

Lester Sumrall
"I believe with you that our destiny is in the way we are flowing with you."

Bill Bright
"Dominion DBS can help make an impact on this Nation and the world within any present effort of which I am aware."

David Mainse
"Dominion DBS has Jesus Christ, and the Dominion plan is the best we have ever heard of."

FIGURE 3.3 **1980s Drawing of Televangelists ("Coming Together")** Advertisement for the Dominion Network featuring televangelism's biggest attractions on its Direct Broadcast Satellite services, circa 1988. Prosperity preachers in their heyday still shared the spotlight with a diverse and ecumenical crowd.

Source: Sky Angel U.S., LLC, www.skyangel.com.

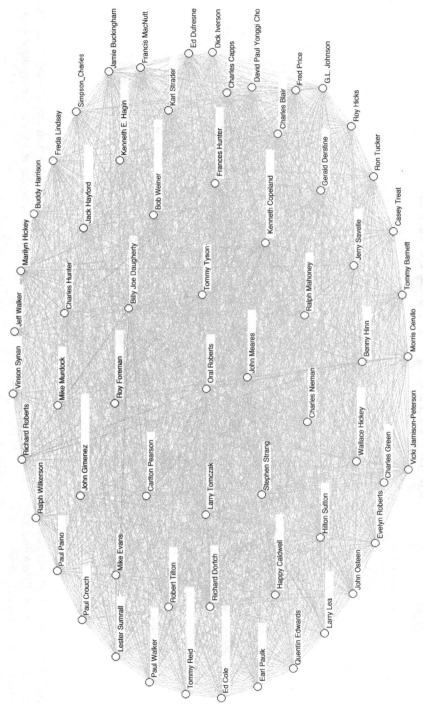

FIGURE 3.4 Oral Roberts's Conferences Oral Roberts conference participation as advertised in *Charisma* magazine, 1980–2009. Roberts was certainly the most influential pentecostal of the 1980s, with institutional muscle and charm to spare. His centrality in the network gives this image the appearance of a circle.

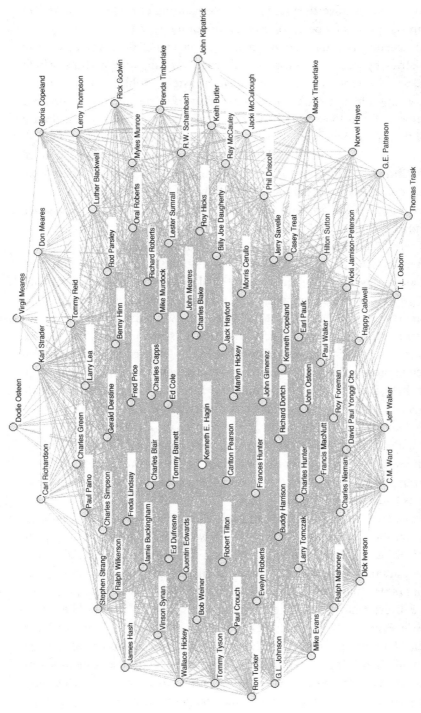

FIGURE 3.5 Kenneth Hagin's Conferences Kenneth Hagin's conference participation as advertised in *Charisma* magazine, 1980–2003. Hagin's sphere of conference associates is a Who's Who of those willing to be linked over time to the Word of Faith movement. Almost all considered themselves ecclesial independents and theological pentecostals.

expect an added advertisement for their upcoming crusades, but a seat on a university advisory board or even an honorary degree.

Its teachers began to cement their informal connections among diverse ministries by joining associations, alternatively called fellowships, which acted as voluntary societies of ordained ministers. Unlike denominations, fellowships did not ordain ministers or oversee the ministries of their members; these loose-knit networks typically shared little more than a brief faith statement, an annual conference, and the company of fine colleagues. In 1978, Jim and Kathleen Kaseman founded the Association of Faith Churches and Ministers (AFCM) "to promote fellowship among the ministers who shared their vision of taking the 'Word of Faith' message to the world."[12] With growing numbers of new churches and ministries founded in the name of faith, Jim Kaseman, a graduate of the charter class of Rhema Bible Training Center, sought to bring much-needed resources to their growing ranks. The following year, Buddy Harrison, Kenneth Hagin's son-in-law, organized the International Convention of Faith Ministries (ICFM) as a voluntary organization of ministers bound by their commitment to the Haginite theology. More would follow. Louisiana pastor Charles Green founded the Network of Christian Ministries in 1984. The Rhema Ministerial Association International (RMAI), founded in 1985, soon followed to provide Rhema graduates with the benefits of official alumni support. In 1986, Oral Roberts formed the International Charismatic Bible Ministries (ICBM), whose annual conference became one of the most publicized and best-attended events in the pentecostal-charismatic world. The vast majority of its founding members were confident spokespersons for divine wealth.[13] The proliferation of faith associations meant more choice, but not necessarily more competition. Many teachers joined more than one, as badges of belonging.

Flushed with enthusiasm, ministers flooded the market with publications on the many uses of faith.[14] There were manuals for the basics like *Say-It-Faith, Power of Agreement, Healing the Sick,* and *Successful Living.* Others attempted to cultivate new niche markets with how-to guides such as *Guarantee Your Child's Success* and *Positive Childbirth* ("Could pregnancy and delivery really be exciting and fun?") and children's books like *Adventures in Faith.* A string of cowboy movies, with titles like *Covenant Rider,* applied faith principles to the Wild West. These starred Tulsa youth evangelist Willie George as a U.S. marshal backed up by fellow televangelists Kenneth Copeland (as Wichita Slim), Jesse Duplantis (as evil Saul Gillespie), and Jerry Savelle as the down-home evangelist. Amidst the shootings, lynchings, and chase scenes, there was always time for a reassuring chat around the fire about covenant principles. Entrepreneurial to the bone, few opportunities eluded the prosperity preachers. Even the aerobics craze of the 1980s found a spiritual home in one evangelist's godly exercise regime, "Confession Calisthenics."[15] (Ten minutes a day, the author claimed, and "you can achieve more! You can experience more prosperity in your life! More success! More victory!") This expansion came easily for most major ministers, who already devoted an arm of their organizations to media and publishing. In 1975, Buddy Harrison founded Harrison House as a general publishing house for Word of Faith literature. Christian bookstores across the country began to feature a display near the cash register filled with pocketsize "classics" of the prosperity gospel. Prosperity books, much like early twentieth-century success literature, swelled the ocean of cheap paperbacks.

Doctrinally speaking, it was the heyday of Hagin's Word of Faith theology and its mechanistic account of spoken prayer. But as indebted as many were to Hagin's teachings, celebrity prosperity preachers made remarkably similar claims in large part because they were so often in each other's presence. The highest-attended conferences featured the same roster of speakers, mixed and matched from only a few dozen names. The largest independent ministries sponsored annual conferences that became a steady evangelistic circuit for other popular ministers, forging strong connections between far-flung preachers. The movement had enough institutional muscle to support big-time celebrities, convert the ambivalent, and nurture the next generation of up-and-comers to this new way of thinking. Junior versions of their famous parents, like Kenneth Hagin Jr. and Richard Roberts, had come of age with all the conviction of youth. The movement teemed with pastors preaching, praying, singing, prophesying, and invoking miracles side-by-side. And though they might grumble that so-and-so stole their ideas about vows or unfairly got top billing, they seemed grateful to have each other. There was power in numbers.

The movement, though expansive, still had room to grow. Ministers educated by Oral Roberts University, Rhema Bible Training Center, Christ for the Nations (CFN), and other like-minded schools were still green. Commissioned as missionaries, the first graduating classes set out to experience the thrilling demonstrations of faith at work. These eager novices fanned out across the United States and Canada to found hundreds of congregations. Gene and Sue Lingerfelt, protégés of Lester Sumrall, founded what would be the Overcoming Faith Christian Center in a dingy

FIGURE 3.6 **Rhema Bible Training Center** Entrance to Rhema Bible Training Center. Founded by Kenneth Hagin in 1974, the school became the institutional center of the Word of Faith movement.

Source: Author's photo.

Ramada Inn, preaching about the significance of words for success, healing, and prosperity.[16] Many graduates struggled through lean years of small-time ministry, but the success of the few sweetened the medicine. Billy Joe and Sharon Daugherty were instant hits, winning national audiences with their down-home charm and organizational savvy.

These former students of both Christ for the Nations and Oral Roberts University planted their own towering congregation and Bible school in the shadow of the 60-foot bronze statue of praying hands marking the entrance to Oral Roberts' campus, a permanent reminder of their entwined fortunes. Even preachers with a small but stable platform rolled out their own schools. Tennessee businessman Norvel Hayes, for example, founded New Life Bible College with students he accumulated on his speaking tours. Rhema Bible Training Center produced an armada of evangelists and church planters. (See table 3.1) Vicki and David Shearin founded Word of Life Christian Center in Nevada as a holy alternative to Vegas' goddess, Lady Luck, while Rick and Sharon Ciaramitaro began Canada's first Rhema success story in the secular climes of southern Ontario.

African American leaders, nurtured by this tight circle of white prosperity ministries, grew in number and stature. Keith Butler, one of Rhema's first graduates, built Detroit's Word of Faith Christian Center from a pocket-sized congregation to a megachurch so large that he took the title of bishop. The turn toward faith ministries meant leaving other influences behind. When James Hash and his sister Francene inherited their parents' apostolic congregation in the 1980s, they used what they had learned at Rhema Bible Training Center and Victory Bible Institute to modernize their legacy. Their parents had railed against ecclesial habits accrued in slavery and pentecostal "legalism," while the new generation quoted prosperity preachers and corporate coaches to push their growing congregation toward becoming a "ministry of excellence." The Hashes watched their church grow from a few hundred to a few thousand as they opened the doors to Kenneth Copeland, Fred Price, Kenneth Hagin, Tommy Barnett, and (later) T. D. Jakes, and Myles Munroe.[17]

Frederick K. C. Price, who counted himself the theological heir of Kenneth Hagin and Oral Roberts, became the preeminent African American educator about God's money. In 1970, Price's experience of the Holy Spirit pulled him away from traditional black denominations and toward the white prosperity circles of Hagin, Roberts, and Copeland.[18] His crusades, publications, sprawling Los Angeles congregation, and nationwide television program broke new ground in black churches, which would turn increasingly toward prosperity preachers in the 1980s and 1990s.[19] Price's prosperity manuals like *High Finance: God's Financial Plan, Name It and Claim It!* and *Prosperity on God's Terms* were always in season.

The only prosperity preacher who could rival Price's fame among black audiences was the charismatic singer Carlton Pearson. Pearson, reared

Table 3.1 Contemporary Prosperity Megachurches Founded in
Church-Planting Heyday

Founder	Megachurch	Year
Kenneth E. Hagin	Rhema Bible Church (Broken Arrow, OK)	1974
Mike and Kathy Hayes	Covenant Church (Carrollton, TX)	1976
Rick Thomas	Abundant Life Christian Center (Margate, FL)	1977
Charles Nieman	Abundant Living Faith Center (El Paso, TX)	1977
Randy Morrison	Speak the Word International (Golden Valley, MN)	1977
Jimmy Evans	Trinity Fellowship (Amarillo, TX)	1977
Rod Parsley	World Harvest Church (Columbus, OH)	1977
Lawrence and Darlene Bishop	Solid Rock Church (Monroe, OH)	1978
Andrew and Viveca Merritt	Straight Gate International Church (Detroit, MI)	1978
Keith and Deborah Butler	Word of Faith Christian Center (Detroit, MI)	1979
Casey and Wendy Treat	Christian Faith Center (Seattle, WA)	1980
David and Roxanne Swann	Faith Christian Family Church (Clovis, NM)	1980
Jim and Marguerite Reeve	Faith Community Church (West Covina, CA)	1980
David Demola	Faith Fellowship Ministries (Sayreville, NJ)	1980
Dick Bernal	Jubilee Christian Center (San Jose, CA)	1980
Mac and Lynne Hammond	Living Word Christian Center (Minneapolis, MN)	1980
Phillip and Holly Wagner	Oasis Christian Center (Los Angeles, CA)	1980
Tommy Barnett	Phoenix First Assembly of God (Phoenix, AZ)	1980
Sharon and Billy Daugherty	Victory Christian Center (Tulsa, OK)	1981
Jason and Gale Alvarez	The Love of Jesus Family Church (Orange, NJ)	1982
David and Vicki Shearin	Word of Life Christian Center (Las Vegas, NV)	1982
Gene and Sue Lingerfelt	Overcoming Faith Christian Center (Arlington, TX)	1984

Table 3.1 *(continued)*

Founder	Megachurch	Year
Walter and Cindy Hallam	Abundant Life Christian Center (La Marque, TX)	1985
Robb Thompson	Family Harvest Church (Tinley Park, IL)	1985
Kevin and Sheila Gerald	Champions Centre (Tacoma, WA)	1986
Thomas Anderson	The Living Word Bible Church (Mesa, AZ)	1986

Though Tulsa remained the institutional heartland, prosperity churches spread widely across the suburban Midwest, Pacific Northwest, and Mid-Atlantic with a heavy concentration in the Sun Belt.

within the Church of God in Christ, became the darling of the movement for his powerful voice in song and in sermon. As his conference participation demonstrates (see figure 3.7), Pearson was a protégé of Oral Roberts and boldly asserted a like-minded message: "God will increase thirty-, sixty-, and a hundred-fold return on the tithe . . . The *giving* starts *after* we've tithed, or as Oral Roberts used to say so often, 'Giving is not a debt you owe; it's a seed you *sow*.'"[20] He was an early ambassador of racial reconciliation, touring with Oral Roberts's son Richard and the ORU World Action Singers to promote the university's interracial character. In 1977, Pearson struck out on his own as a traveling evangelist and founding pastor of Higher Dimensions Evangelistic Center in Tulsa. In 1988, he founded the famous Azusa conference, which quickly became the staging ground for up-and-coming African American singers and preachers to gain recognition. Pearson would go on to launch many careers in the following decade, including an undiscovered pastor from West Virginia named T. D. Jakes.

A flood of black teachers, nurtured inside faith institutions, began to spread their message of divine prosperity to African American audiences. Some saw their message as an end-run around structural barriers. Ed Montgomery built up his 7,000-member Abundant Life Cathedral with the belief that "in God's economy there were no cultural, ethnic, or racial barriers. God responds to faith, anyone's faith."[21] Others walked the tightrope between a social and a supernatural gospel. Like their mentor, Kenneth Hagin, Charles and Carolyn Harrell, pastors of the 1,800-member Full Gospel Christian Center in Pomona, California, preached positive confession but added "education and economics" as equally necessary for

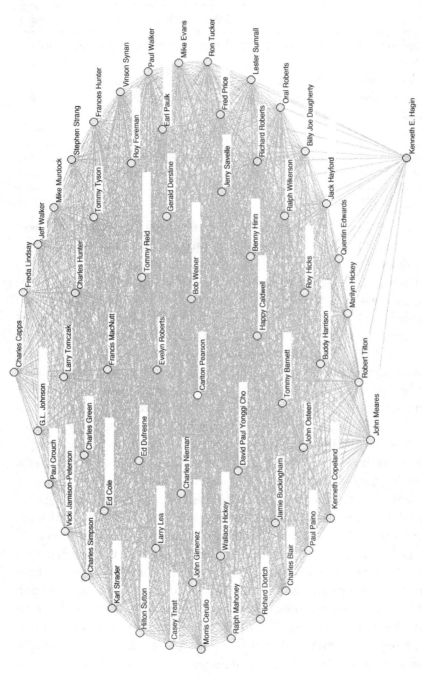

FIGURE 3.7 **Carlton Pearson's Conferences** Carlton Pearson's conference participation in the 1980s. Pearson remained largely within his mentor Oral Roberts' sphere of influence until he branched out on his own in the late 1980s.

transforming the inner city. They taught faith-filled words, financial miracles, vocational skills, career counseling, and black heritage classes to "help black men shake the welfare mentality and help rebuild the collapsed family structure among the poor."[22] Rhema's Keith Butler added a nonprofit foundation to his 5,000-member congregation, dedicated to finding economic solutions for Detroit's disenfranchised. Rising African American stars like Mack and Brenda Timberlake, Phillip and Brenda Goudeaux, and Lamont and Connie McLean joined a host of prosperity preachers founding "Christian centers" (not "churches") in an effort to strip ecclesial forms of false "religious" idioms and uncover the raw power of God. They put phrases like "More Than Conquerors" above their doors and sported tailored suits befitting the executive roles they had assumed.

The prosperity gospel was becoming increasingly influential among Latino Americans. It is difficult to identify precisely when the faith message crystallized in Latino churches, but pervasive media exposure certainly sped its early formation. Radio broadcasts, television programs, paperback volumes, and regular conferences reached out to scattered audiences long before church membership reflected the movement's impact. Ministries, for their part, responded quickly to significance of Spanish-speaking believers. Kenneth Hagin's *La Autoridad del Creyente*, for example, appeared in 1974. And, beginning in the 1970s, Latino pentecostals had begun to leave their denominations for prosperity-preaching churches.[23] Though Spanish-speaking faith churches lacked the large numbers and well-known personalities that earned national attention, the examples of a few thriving congregations made clear that their importance was only a matter of time. These congregations grew from a variety of sources. Massive churches like Iglesia el Calvario began as offshoots of existing Anglo congregations with an emphasis on faith teaching and evangelism. Church planting by Mexican-American graduates of any number of prosperity Bible schools brought many small- to medium-sized congregations to life. By the mid-1980s, waves of immigrant prosperity churches led by immigrant pastors had hit Spanish-speaking populations in Miami, Houston, Los Angeles and across North America. Toronto's Faithful Remnant Spanish Church, served by Puerto Rican pastors Abel Casillas and his wife Apostle Mayra Casillas, began in 1985 and would grow to be one of Canada's largest Spanish-speaking congregations.[24]

Classic pentecostals, squared away in their historic denominations, were lukewarm about the success of the prosperity gospel. The International Church of the Foursquare Gospel published a curt rebuke in their monthly magazine, even while their own General Supervisor Roy Hicks's friendship with Kenneth Hagin and Gordon Lindsay was written all over his publications, *The Word of Faith: Use It or Lose It*, and *Praying Beyond God's Abilities*.[25] The Assemblies of God looked askance at teachers within their fold who preached on divine wealth, as ministers like Karl Strader and Jim Bakker tested the limits of denominational bounds. The leading Assemblies of God evangelist Jimmy Swaggart publicly denounced them as more "charismatic" than "pentecostal" for their prosperity leanings. "Pentecostals and charismatics are two different worlds, " he declared. "It is my feeling they should be one way or the other."[26] Jack Hayford, at the helm of the 6,000-member Church on the Way, cautioned humility and patience to the throngs of those "claiming authority." He could continue to act as father, then grandfather, to a movement centered on a familiar account of a God who "deals in words."[27]

Most overlooked the rift between the two, while supporters protested that their gospel was simply that old-time religion. "Pentecostal historians have told me that the very same things my father teaches today were taught by the pioneers and founders of the Pentecostal movement, and I know this is so," said Kenneth W. Hagin Jr., who called his father's work a "distillation of all that was good in the great movements in the past."[28] Certainly a number of faith teachers saw themselves as grounded in the work of a previous generation. T. L. Osborn's apprentice Don Gossett published *The Power of Your Words* and *Words that Move Mountains* with alternating chapters by himself and E. W. Kenyon. Gordon Lindsay edited a collection of the writings of John G. Lake, while Watchman Nee was resurrected as a like-minded preacher for his thoughts on the spiritual man.[29] The purified truth centered on faith, the unseen force that turned the spoken word into reality. With the structures of the movement firmly established, secured by educational, ministerial, and promotional platforms, followers set out to convince subsequent generations that "without faith it is impossible to please God" (Hebrews 11:6). As the ranks of the faith-filled ballooned, believers smiled at the newfound prosperity of their homegrown gospel.

Jehovah Jireh

Daisy and T. L. Osborn raised their flutes of orange juice in a toast for the camera under the caption "GO FOR IT!"[30] The 1983 photo book featured a day in the life of the two wealthy evangelists enjoying the latest, greatest fads of the decade. They jogged through suburbia in sweatbands, cruised to the mall in a shiny Chevrolet, and lounged in their florid home on over-stuffed couches. Interspersed with footage from their lifetime of overseas crusades, Daisy marveled about the life that a true believer could aspire to. "Can you imagine, honey," she gushed, "they'll be able to get material success, pay their debts, get out of poverty!!! It will be easy with the 7 SECRETS and the 60 SECONDS a day for just 7 days!" The free booklet, advertised in the *National Enquirer*, was a testimony to celebratory con-sumption. To followers of the prosperity gospel, God revealed himself as *Jehovah Jireh*, God the Provider.

God lavished on believers not only spiritual blessings but also the ma-terial comforts that lightened the load of everyday living. "The Lord shall provide all my needs," ran the lyrics of Benny Hinn's favored crusade anthem, "*Jehovah Jireh* takes care of me."[31] The Christian way offered more than subsistence living. Tradition-bound Christians scraped by with barely enough while true believers drilled deeper to tap into the abundant lives that God promised. "He is *Jehovah-Jireh*," explained up-and-coming Rod Parsley, "the God of more than enough. He gives us the ability to plant, to harvest, and to gather the abundance into the storehouse."[32] (According to Genesis 22:14, Jehovah Jireh referred to the place where God provided a ram for Abraham to sacrifice instead of his son Isaac.) Everyone possessed the God-given potential to sow and reap their financial harvest with plenty to spare. Poverty marked a spiritual shortage. Faith believers claimed the promise from Jesus' lips that he came "that they might have life, and that they might have it more abundantly."[33] Outsiders called it baptized mate-rialism. Followers called it living in the overflow.

Three arguments grounded the movement's defense of biblical wealth. First, prosperity theology turned to the cross as the solution to all human needs. Jesus' death and resurrection abolished not only sin and disease but also poverty. In order to understand this financial provision of the atonement, we must recall the priority placed on spirit by the movement. Poverty took on spiritual dimensions as a demonic force that separated people from their godly inheritance. Poverty—as an evil spirit—required a spiritual solution. Jesus reclaimed dominion over the earth from Satan when he took on the spiritual debt of poverty on the cross. "He took your place in *poverty*," argued the African American pastor Leroy Thompson of Word of Life Christian Center in Darrow, Louisiana, "so you could take His place in *prosperity*."[34] As a result, believers could claim wealth as one of their rights and privileges in Jesus' name.

Some teachers found it more difficult to explain wealth than they did health. Jesus' crucifixion tied the atonement to suffering as a corollary of sickness, but there was no moment teachers could point to that signaled Christ's defeat over poverty. Only those who specialized in divine finance approached the subject with much gusto. Pastor Thompson described Jesus' resurrection as the moment when "He couldn't stand being broke any longer! He came up on the third day! He said, in effect, 'Enough of this!'"[35] Jesus rose from the grave as the redeemer of poverty's curse.

Second, believers argued that they followed in the Master's steps. Jesus himself possessed great wealth, and it followed that his devotees should also. Snippets from Jesus' life offered a few clues. "As soon as Jesus arrived, that anointing to prosper acted like a magnet, drawing wise men with gifts of gold, frankincense, and myrrh," argued the Kenneth Copeland-protégé Creflo Dollar. "Those were not cheap gifts, either. Prosperity attached itself to baby Jesus immediately, and that same gift to prosper has been given to us as heirs of Christ."[36] That the guards divided Jesus' cloak among them at his crucifixion suggested that his belongings were valuable.[37] *Heart of a Billionaire* author Thomas Anderson, pastor of the Living Word Bible Church in Mesa, Arizona, counted Mary and Joseph's donkey ride to Bethlehem as proof of their wealth, arguing that the animal was the contemporary equivalent of a Cadillac.[38] *Rich God, Poor God* author John Avanzini detailed Jesus' designer clothes and expensive anointing oils as further evidence. To be sure, the matter caused some disagreement. Kenneth Hagin Sr. and Oral Roberts established a strong precedent for the argument that Jesus lived a wealthy life but defeated poverty on the cross, while others seemed to be content that Jesus' lifetime of poverty was part of his messianic purpose.[39] Further examples of righteous people of wealth sprang readily from the pages of the Old Testament. Preachers understood the high stakes of proving that their savior could be an economic exemplar, much as a late medieval debate about the poverty preached by the mendicant orders had caused a defense of Jesus and his disciples as members of the landed gentry with their own coats of arms. So, too, televangelists continued to scour Jesus' life for signs that he had paved the way for prosperous living.

Third, believers rooted prosperity in covenant theology as an extension of the ancient promises God made to Abraham.[40] Favor and riches sprang from faithfulness to the Abrahamic covenant. "In the Old Testament, according to Deuteronomy," Kenneth Hagin explained, "poverty was to come upon God's people if they disobeyed Him."[41] The scriptures were shot through with the Deuteronomic imperative that blessings accompanied the keeping of the Law (and curses greeted its disobedience). Christians were beneficiaries of Abraham's "spiritual promissory note," explained the Denver evangelist Marilyn Hickey.[42] Pre-Fall humanity once enjoyed unimpeded access to wealth in the Garden of Eden, "when He surrounded Adam and Eve with every material blessing they could possibly need."[43] Their sin transferred legal dominion of the earth to Satan, who kept humanity in want of health, provision, and God's power. Jesus' death and resurrection flooded the world with new victory and financial reminders of believers' redeemed status as God's children. As the gospel-singer Donald Lawrence sang in "Back to Eden":

Our families blessed; finances blessed . . .
. . . Jesus came now all is well.

The saints claimed a rich inheritance as their own.

The surprising gains of prosperity theology in pulpits, publications, conferences, and television airtime strengthened its leaders' resolve to raise their ministries to ever-increasing heights. Teachers, invigorated by constant growth, confidently confessed brighter futures. They concluded that nature yielded to the proper use of divine principles. Mechanistic accounts of giving and receiving dominated. Faith teachers differed in their interpretations of the exact relationship between the spoken word and its coming into being. This was a decade of *hard prosperity*.

Hard prosperity drew a straight line between life circumstances and a believer's faith. Faith operated as a perfect law, and any irregularities meant that the believer did not play by the rules. Specificity was the key to successful prayer. Participants were instructed to name their pleas, their wishes, and even their dollar amounts to command spiritual forces to their desired ends.

Charles Capps stood as one hard prosperity preacher among many. Capps, an ordained minister and popular guest on Gloria and Kenneth Copeland's television program, systematized faith theology into an iron-clad system of causality. The spoken word, by activating faith, bound God to the individual's proclamation. When the one-time farmer built a housing subdivision north of England, Arkansas, he took on a mountain of debt to finance his project. Convinced that faith could remedy the situation, he arranged the numerous mortgages for the development properties on the kitchen table. "Notes," he said, "listen to me. I'm talking to you. Jesus said you would obey me. In the name of the Lord Jesus Christ, I command you, I say to you, BE PAID IN FULL . . . DEMATERIALIZE . . . DEPART . . . BE GONE . . . IN JESUS' NAME, YOU WILL OBEY ME!"[44] When asked if this seemed "silly," Capps confidently replied that the Bible was more practical than believers realized. After all, the proof of the pudding is in the eating: the mortgages were paid, the properties sold, and his subdivision became a success. Capps's major work, *The Tongue: A Creative Force*, sold more than three million copies.[45]

Hard prosperity hammered giving and receiving into rigid rules. First, pay tithes. Though all faith teachers preached about the significance of tithing, hard prosperity found God in the details. Some churches kept detailed financial reports on their members, even asking them to submit tax records to verify that they paid their full tithes. Finance teacher John Avanzini spoke for all when he cited failure to tithe as the primary reason that God failed to return money to believers. Second, hard prosperity made financial miracles an everyday prospect. Positive confessions tailored to "supernatural debt-cancellation" or blessed billfolds that automatically multiplied its contents, arrived in believers' mailboxes.[46] Testimonies of sudden infusions of cash dominated the discussion.

Third, the process was largely epistemic. "Proper thinking produces finances," Avanzini stated simply.[47] Positive confession seemed so powerful that considerable debate arose within the faith movement about the degree to which anyone could use it, regardless of holiness. More than a few suggested that perhaps wealthy people unconsciously lived out the truth. The first lady of one North Carolina congregation argued that anyone could tap into it without personal faith, as she had begun "naming it and claiming it" before she understood its implications.[48] The finer theological points mattered less than the conclusion: divine wealth came with an easy trigger.

Formulas for wealth grew increasingly precise. Tithes alone did not guarantee that the windows of heaven stayed open. The doctrine of "first fruits," first introduced in the 1960s, became a standard classification of donation. For example, the person who received a $50 raise had to donate the first $50 to God. Positive confessors began to affix their tithes and offerings with specific wishes, a practice Oral Roberts had dubbed "naming your seed." Some whispered their desires as they placed their envelope in the offertory. Others took it a step further, taking pains to inscribe the donation itself with their confession. Believers with checking accounts might have their checks printed with scripture about blessing or write verses in the memo line. One wrote, "Money cometh unto you," on the check, hoping that the bank teller would repeat it and positively confess on her behalf. Believers occasionally scribbled their confessions on dollar bills. It was an inventory of ordinary hopes that required small miracles. "For a new car." "For a promotion." "For new school clothes." When needs were met, believers proudly put them on display. Automobiles were marked as heaven-sent with vanity plates boasting PRAYED 4, BLESSED, 100 FOLD, and LUKE 12:31 ("But seek ye first the kingdom of God, and all these things shall be added unto you").

The "hundredfold blessing" (last mentioned in our discussion of the midcentury healing revivals) served as the most common calculus of God's "money-back guarantee." It was often said that God rewarded givers a hundred times their original donation.[49] Gloria Copeland, a famous evangelist in her own right, calculated the returns: "You give $1 for the Gospel's sake and $100 belongs to you; give $10 and receive $1000; give $1000 and receive $100,000. . . . Give one airplane and receive one hundred times the value of the airplane. Give one car and the return would furnish you a lifetime of cars. In short, Mark 10:30 is a very good deal."[50] Hard prosperity emphasized its contractual nature, describing God as unable to "multiply back" blessings except to those who give correctly.[51] The laws of the harvest formed an exact science. Televangelist Jimmy Swaggart decried the hundredfold blessing as "outright fraud."[52] Kenneth Hagin later repented of his own teaching on the matter: "I no longer tell people to expect the hundredfold return on their offerings. I just stay with what the Word of God says: *'Give and it shall be given unto you; good measure, pressed down, and shaken together, and running over'* (Luke 6:38). I always claim the 'running over' blessing."[53] Though other faith teachers protested that the world could not contain enough riches to reward everyone with a hundredfold return, popularity favored the literal minded.

The extravagant promises of the hundredfold blessing became increasingly popular during the troubled 1970s. Money-multiplication strategies seemed credible in light of the broad cultural shifts concerning credit that left Americans with greater faith in an invisible economy. In the mid-1970s, growing inflation and stagnation, dubbed "stagflation," were hallmarks of a sluggish economy. Unemployment and the price of consumer goods continued to rise.[54] Credit and debt—previously stigmatized as marks of moral weakness—became a strategy to cope with soaring inflation.[55] Consumers who paid for goods on credit could expect to pay less in real terms, as inflation devalued the amount they owed. Money became

FIGURE 3.8 100 Fold Car This vanity plate, seen outside a Joel Osteen event, suggests the driver's confidence that God rewards with mid-sized family sedans.
Source: Author's photo.

increasingly theoretical, as the connection between the value of one's labor and one's income grew increasingly unpredictable. From the creation of the Visa card in 1973, credit card spending grew at a rate of $3.5 billion a year as more shoppers began to put their faith in the value of dollars they did not yet see. These economic conditions boosted consumer confidence in unseen multipliers. For many, faith in supernatural hundredfold returns appeared a reasonable economic strategy. It was a movement that treasured the God of checks and balances, whose financial formulas and principles ensured that, when all was tallied, God was more than fair.

Megaministry

In 1983, the Bakkers opened their Praise the Lord (PTL) television studio at Heritage USA to fanfare and a personal note from the equally sunny President Ronald Reagan, who congratulated the duo on their efforts to help "many Americans endure and triumph."[56] This was an America of renewed confidence. It had ditched the president associated with national malaise and humiliation in the Iran hostage affair and replaced him with one whose campaign slogan was "It's Morning Again in America."[57] In foreign policy the nation finally felt able to forget the debacle of Vietnam and flex its muscles once more as first Grenada and then Panama were invaded and bent to the American will. A new generation of medium-range missiles was installed in Europe despite massive protests and Soviet opposition. The diffident Carteresque approach to the Soviet Union gave way to an uncompromising vision of the USSR as an "evil empire." Popular culture reveled in glitter and extravagance: disco, the drug-soaked club scene, big hair, shoulder pads, glam rock, and designer fashions. The decade's economic expansion accompanied a market-oriented viewpoint and an ethic of excess memorialized in the film *Wall Street* as "greed is good." By 1989, the unlooked-for fall of Eastern European communism produced a triumphalist aura surrounding all things capitalist. The galloping optimism and individualism fit well with a decade of growth by the faith movement.

Ministry took on larger-than-life proportions. Megachurches (with 2,000 plus members) loomed large on the religious landscape as innovative centers of revival. In 1970, megachurches numbered 50. By 1990, the total swelled to 310.[58] Of these, roughly three dozen congregations orbited within the prosperity network, a modest but vital minority. Celebrities like Jimmy Swaggart, the Bakkers, and the Crouches headed multimillion-dollar media conglomerates supported by hundreds of thousands of viewers. Oral Roberts alone commanded an annual budget of $125 million.[59] By 1980, his eponymous university had graduated its thirteenth and largest graduating class at 781 students. A. A. Allen's Miracle Revival Fellowship headquartered in Dallas claimed 500 affiliated churches and approximately 10,000 members.[60]

Prosperity megachurches were comparatively late bloomers in the church growth movement that believed that bigger was always better. In the 1970s, the broader conservative Christian culture—fundamentalist, charismatic, evangelical, and pentecostal camps alike—had fallen in love with church growth as an end in itself. Los Angeles pastor Frederick Price spoke for them all when he said: "Every church should be a big church."[61] In their enthusiasm for the great commission, American evangelicals discovered the possibilities for expansion embedded in the work of Donald McGavran, his successor C. Peter Wagner, and their institutional home, Fuller Theological Seminary's School of World Mission. This seedbed and its resulting conferences, seminary classes, literature, and knock-off institutes formed the framework of the church growth movement. In the early 1980s, prosperity preachers joined its interdenominational leadership as natural experts in increase. The intersection between the two movements was like a meeting between old friends. The faith movement's emphasis on results and the materiality of salvation easily absorbed the goal of church growth as a sign of its own faithfulness. Thus in 1985, the Chicago Church Growth and Leadership Conference advertised the expertise of

Word of Faith star Billy Joe Daugherty, *Your Church Can Grow* author
C. Peter Wagner, positive thinker Robert Schuller, and the Korean pastor
of the world's largest church, David Yonggi Cho. All shared a vision of the
God who wanted to bless them abundantly.

The prosperity movement rapidly cultivated transnational connections.
By the mid-1980s, Christ for the Nations Institute could claim an astounding overseas legacy. The small school had helped build 4,074
churches in 100 countries and translated 25 million books into 50 languages.[62] David Yonggi Cho became the patron of American prosperity
preachers and a wildly popular conference speaker in his own right. His
influential book *The Fourth Dimension* (1979) featured a dense theological
exposition of the unseen forces of faith and a foreword by church-growth
expert Robert Schuller. The success of these native megaministries
cemented the international dimensions of the prosperity movement.

During the larger-than-life 1980s, America's largest churches were
growing—not from a flood of the unchurched—but from the increasing
concentration of seasoned churchgoers under one roof. Some theorists
predicted that these baby boomers were spiritual wanderers whose comfort in big box establishments—university classrooms, corporate cubicles,
and Walmart aisles—predisposed them to church models that resembled
these large institutional forms. Others, such as sociologist Mark Chaves,
argued that there was an economy of scale at work; small churches simply
could not compete with the range of services larger churches could provide.[63] Church growth strategists hoped to capitalize on this by making
contemporary churchgoing feel as comfortable as trips to the mall. Continuing in this commercial vein, experts recommended that churches im-
plement marketing strategies and view their church as a product and their
worshippers as consumers. As populations drifted from city centers to the
suburbs, and later to "edge cities" growing near metropolitan hubs, pastors and congregations built sprawling church campuses near freeways
and interstates, hoping to capture the largest market share. Each congregation tailored their product to capitalize on their target audience, demographic preferences, and selling features.[64] Nondenominational evangelical
churches that adopted market-driven features to make their services visitor friendly won recognition as "seeker sensitive" churches.[65]

Prosperity megachurches embodied the entrepreneurial logic of this
movement to the utmost, and included the corporate models that seeker-
sensitive megachurches were willing to employ in both theology and practice. Many prosperity megachurches built in this decade minimized

"churchlike" features such as crosses, steeples, or stained glass in favor of the bricks, steel, and glass of a corporate headquarters. Predominantly white prosperity churches with strong evangelical connections cultivated the atmosphere of an unbuttoned workplace. Women and men could forgo dressy Sunday fashions in favor of the attire of casual Fridays. (Not that polo shirts, khakis, and artfully distressed loafers—the uniform of the average suburban man—did much to disguise their comfortable economic status.) African American megachurch fashion tilted in the opposite direction; custom monograms on the inside of a man's jacket cuff or the gleaming buckle of a woman's designer purse displayed a more overt indication of personal wealth.[66] Yet the same logic prevailed: for faith worshippers there was never a clear distinction between church and the marketplace. Senior pastors took on the title chief executive officer (CEO), frequently splitting their ministries into "for profit" and "not for profit" branches. Successful pastors considered themselves true entrepreneurs, arguing that kingdom principles were, in fact, business principles.[67] They called it kingdom business.

California televangelist Robert H. Schuller, *The Hour of Power* broadcaster and church-growth guru, was one of the ministers most in the public eye.[68] Ordained in the Reformed Church in America like his positive thinking predecessor Norman Vincent Peale, Schuller exhibited an early flair for advertising and church growth. For example, when he could not find property for his church plant in Garden Grove, California, he rented a drive-in theater and preached to the 50 assembled cars while perched on the roof of the refreshment stand. His advertising jingle said it all: "Come as you are in a family car." Drive-in church services (later with sermons piped in through the car radio) remained a fixture of his ministry and a tribute to his interest in making religion appealing to the unchurched. This consumerist model paid off handsomely, allowing Schuller to undertake a hugely expensive building project dubbed the Crystal Cathedral, a church of glass large enough to house a river. The Tower of Hope, with a 90-foot glowing cross, soon followed. Schuller's expansive vision won the day. His church ministry sprawled and added a school, retirement home, call center, and local outreach programs. He topped the *New York Times* bestseller list with a reconfiguration of "positive thinking" into "possibility thinking." His books, which included *Move Ahead with Possibility Thinking* (1967), *Peace of Mind through Possibility Thinking* (1977), *Self-Esteem: The New Reformation* (1982), *Tough Times Never Last But Tough People Do* (1983), and *The Be Happy Attitudes* (1985), established Schuller as the self-help authority of his generation. He founded the Robert H. Schuller Institute for Successful Church Leadership to show others the path he had trod. Schuller's career shows how the earlier trends of positive thinking had grown intertwined with the pentecostal prosperity crowd. At the end of his career, when Schuller sat down with Paul Crouch on Praise the Lord, the two old friends marveled at their personal discoveries of God's abundance, albeit using different language.[69]

Televangelism

This was the golden age of televangelism and prosperity preachers ruled the decade as stars of the small screen. The "Electronic Church" ballooned from five million in the late 1960s to 25 million by the mid-1980s, giving numerous faith teachers top-billing in living rooms across the country (see table 3.2).

In 1983, Jimmy Swaggart, Oral Roberts, Robert Schuller, and Rex Humbard were the most watched of the religious programs nationwide. Schuller's *The Hour of Power* repackaged the church's worship services for mass viewing, an unlikely idea that by 1983 garnered 2.5 million viewers.[70] Three religious networks—the Bakkers' Praise the Lord (PTL), the Crouch's Trinity Broadcasting Network (TBN), and Robertson's Christian Broadcasting Network (CBN)—pumped out religious programming 24 hours a day, seven days a week. As these ministries could produce no more than a few hours of programming per day, they desperately needed other material to fill the time. This offered a golden opportunity for up-and-comers to gain exposure, albeit for small audiences. Sociologist Jeffrey Hadden noted that "for a while, almost anyone who could produce a videotaped program could send it to one of these new networks and be

Table 3.2 **Top Syndicated Television Ministries (1981)**

Television Ministry	Number of Viewers
Oral Roberts	2,351,000
Jimmy Swaggart	1,780,000
PTL Club	1,050,000
700 Club	705,000
Kenneth Copeland	381,000

Source: Margaret M. Poloma, *The Charismatic Movement: Is There a New Pentecost?* (Boston: Twayne, 1982), 175.

accepted for satellite broadcast."[71] The focus on money that characterized the televangelist decade owed some of its reputation to these cowboy preachers who jockeyed for attention with their low-budget shows saturating the airwaves.

Through the 1980s, prosperity preachers squeezed television for every last emotional drop. The frequent use of direct appeals to the camera—teaching, arguing, cajoling, or even pleading with at-home audiences—defined the era as the high drama of tent revivalism brought to prime-time television. Emotion ebbed and flowed through every broadcast, and those who taped their programs before live audiences learned to ride the current. Nothing tested the financial resolve of viewers (and the mettle of leaders) like telethons. Their marathon programming was a feat of organization and improvisation as preachers scrambled to fill the time with education, entertainment, and financial pleas. Jim Bakker made fundraising history when the fledgling CBN failed to meet its telethon goal and he burst into tears. The boards lit up with incoming calls, flooding the station with pledges as viewers frantically responded to his emotional entreaties.[72] Subsequent telethons tried to duplicate Bakker's magic, with varying results. TBN founder Paul Crouch credited his first telethon, side-by-side with Jim Bakker, as the beginning of his experimentation with the prosperity gospel. "Without really realizing it at the time," Crouch recounted, "I had put into motion one of God's most powerful laws—the laws of giving and receiving—sowing and reaping."[73] Close-up camera shots and roller-coaster emotions made telethons the favored fundraising tool of the decade and a perpetual demonstration of the power of sentimentality. Bakker proved to be one of the most successful fundraisers in television history, perennially demonstrating his ability to connect to audiences with his maudlin charm.

Television and prosperity theology were a natural fit; spiritual programming proved not only an effective tool of evangelism but also one of generating income. Outsiders commonly reduced all prosperity theology to fundraising, a cliché that had some merit. Faith televangelists dominated religious programming as masters of persuasion, able to inspire the continuous financial donations required to maintain their electric churches. Appeals for donations came in many forms. The Bakkers kept a loose lid on their emotions, weeping or rejoicing openly as financial goals were missed or met.[74] Televangelist and church planter Don Stewart mastered the hard-sell tactics of his predecessor A. A. Allen, promising viewers miraculous returns on their donations. Faith pledges became a fundraising basic with audiences phoning in their promised donation. Yet the networks' dependence on faith pledges repeatedly left them in the lurch. A Trinity Broadcasting Network telethon went awry when it turned out that a fourth of its pledges had come from prank callers.[75] Teachers threatened that "unpaid vows" constituted a terrible sin, but they could do little.[76] They too had to live by faith.

Faith televangelists memorably went to great lengths to cultivate intimacy with their television audiences. Teachers presented themselves foremost as family, inviting viewers into stage sets imitating the preacher's own home. Constant declarations by teachers that "I love you . . . I pray for you each day" assured viewers that they were known and loved.[77] Studios trimmed their stages to mirror conventional notions of gender. Male preachers sat at a desk or living room chair with few accessories, while women were perched among flower arrangements or at the kitchen table itself. Husband and wife teams were popular, referring to one another by first names, and often revealing personal information and anecdotes about their married life. Couples such as Jim and Tammy Bakker and Jan and Paul Crouch lived out their married life on camera, teasing, flirting, and even arguing before live studio audiences. Children and extended family popped in, introducing viewers to the cast as a family and inviting listeners to be part of the family. The staff of volunteers answering phones in the backdrop of the Bakkers' shows reminded audiences that they were only a call away. The steady stream of footage of faces in the audience—joyful, concerned, inspired, or chastened—further connected viewers to a preacher who almost seemed as close as the television screen.

Televangelism soaked up the glamour and conspicuous consumption of the decade. Though hemlines might be a tad longer and suit jackets a little stiffer, on-screen preachers wanted to be counted every bit as fashionable as any other wealthy celebrity in the public eye. The prosperity gospel made modest inroads in men's fashion, as its star preachers updated their designer apparel with the width of their ties or the length of their sideburns. The young Jim Bakker made a splash with his gold chains and blue and green suits. T. L. Osborn took the greatest fashion risks, as he surprised his suit-and-tie colleagues by alternating between native costumes from his crusades and bell-bottoms, open shirts, and leisure suits. On the controversial terrain of women's bodies—especially female *preachers'* bodies—the prosperity gospel made a lasting impression. Teachers like Tammy Faye Bakker and Jan Crouch became media icons for their conspicuous displays of wealth, earning them the constant criticism (or shy admiration) of viewing audiences for their "worldliness." Their radical departure from pentecostal-holiness standards of dress dismayed traditionalist supporters. Jan Crouch's infamous beehives were piled high with cotton-candy pink and purple tufts of hair. Tammy Bakker faced constant opprobrium for her heavy mascara, blond bouffant, and country-girl sex appeal. "Painted hussy, that's all I can see, like Jezebel," huffed an elderly male viewer.[78] But when Tammy Faye peeked out at the camera from under her white fur hat, she embodied (as well as sang) the title of her musical album: *We're Blest.*[79]

Testing Televangelism

Before the scandals. After the scandals. The prosperity gospel can be divided into these two distinct eras, separated by a gulf of suspicion. The exponential growth of prosperity TV sputtered in 1987 when a series of outrages tested audiences' faith in its leaders. In February, the City of Faith hospital founder Oral Roberts faced national ridicule when he fell short of his eight million dollar fundraising goal and wrote to followers that he would retreat to Oral Roberts University's prayer tower to fast and pray until the stated goal was met or "God calls me home." Richard Roberts confirmed his father's dire situation in a follow-up letter, stating that without the funds earmarked for medical missions, "God will not extend Dad's life."[80] The media derided Roberts's emotional blackmail, while the sympathetic observed that prophecy was a lonely profession.[81]

The following month the fresh-faced Jim Bakker shocked the nation when reporters revealed that he had committed adultery in 1980 with a 21-year-old church secretary named Jessica Hahn. *The Charlotte Observer* broke the news that Bakker used PTL funds as hush money. Rival televangelist Jimmy Swaggart led the charge against his fellow Assemblies of God minister, denouncing him as "a cancer that needed to be excised from the body of Christ."[82] John Ankerberg, a Christian talk-show host, further accused Bakker of homosexual encounters. Bakker resigned his presidency of PTL and attempted to salvage his faltering empire by giving temporary control to the *Old Time Gospel Hour* preacher Jerry Falwell. Yet the damage had been done. Shortly thereafter, the Assemblies of God defrocked Bakker for sexual misconduct.

Bakker's trouble had only begun. Falwell discovered the full extent of the Bakkers' financial mismanagement and denounced them in a news conference as unrepentant frauds. A firestorm of controversy ensued as

FIGURE 3.9 **Jim and Tammy Faye Bakker** Jim and Tammy Faye Bakker inter-
viewed by reporters at U.S. Bankruptcy Court, June 29, 1988.
Source: Copyright © Don Sturkey 1988, North Carolina Collection, University of North
Carolina at Chapel Hill Library.

the public learned about the Bakkers' lavish living while their ministry
had floundered in debt, and cover stories in *Time* and *Newsweek* gave
details of the Bakkers' annual salaries and bonuses in excess of a million
dollars. Reports emerged that a few years prior, the Bakkers' question-
able spending had narrowly escaped charges from a Federal Communications Commission investigation of their purchases of a Corvette, mink
coat, and 42-foot houseboat. PTL ministries filed for bankruptcy and, in
1989, Jim Bakker stood trial for fraud and conspiracy. A jury convicted
him for defrauding viewers by overselling lifetime "partnerships" that
entitled members to stay at the Heritage Grand Mansion, raking in payment for thousands of time-shares that the property could not accommodate. Long lines of picketers protested the court's mistreatment of
Bakker who, they argued, was a man of God. To many insiders, these
faith teachers loomed as spiritual giants beyond reproach because they
had transformed believers' lives. Bakker went to prison for five years,
and Tammy filed for divorce.

PTL's downfall exposed the uncomfortable disparity between rich leaders and traditional views of Christian stewardship. The extravagant lifestyle that once testified to the Bakkers' piety now sealed their condemnation as reports of their gold-plated bathroom fixtures and air-conditioned doghouses emerged. In many ways, the couple's convictions accelerated their downfall. Audiences loved them for their demonstrative faith—yet the burden of their gospel was it always had to be *proven* in an endless cycle of bigger and better. Only scant days before their disgrace, the debt-plagued ministry broke ground on what was to be the world's largest church, a 1.25 million square foot complex with a $100 million price tag.[83] Heritage USA alone cost an exorbitant amount to build, and Jim's illegal attempts to keep it afloat landed him in deeper waters. As Tammy later reflected, the financial pressure was suffocating. Tammy developed an addiction to anti-anxiety medication, while Jim turned to romantic affairs. They skated the "thin ice of monthly contributions."[84] Soon they fell through.

At the close of the 1980s, the American televangelist seemed like an unredeemable figure. Audiences dropped from 15.1 million in 1986 to under 10 million. The career of Jimmy Swaggart (who by this time had abandoned the prosperity gospel) fell to pieces when he exposed the adultery of a fellow preacher, Marvin Gorman. Gorman, himself a proponent of prosperity teaching, retaliated by producing evidence of Swaggart's sexual misconduct.[85] The Assemblies of God suspended and defrocked Swaggart. An estimated 100 million people worldwide tuned in to watch Swaggart's tearful apology. Televangelists and their humiliation was fodder for popular derision. In 1990, even NBC's furry extraterrestrial ALF openly parodied the recent scandals by mortifying his sitcom family with his attempts to open a Christian theme park and become a faith healer.[86] Television viewership plummeted as the widespread support for celebrity preachers soured. The grins, tears, and fundraising pleas that had defined the decade no longer won popular support for this upwardly mobile message, and few observers, academic or otherwise, predicted its return.

What appeared to be a theological and ethical crisis of confidence had multiple causes. The declining viewership of religious television in the late 1980s partly reflected market forces. The expanding opportunities that fueled televangelism in the early 1980s—from 24-hour religious networks to ballooning television syndication—tapered off by mid-decade, leaving too many big fish in a shrinking pond. The crowd of preachers that had filled up round-the-clock programming now saturated the market, driving up prices for airtime. In 1975, the televangelism pioneer, Rex Humbard, appeared on 175 stations with an average audience of almost 10,000 households per station. Increased competition and airtime costs forced Humbard to cut back, his losses barely mitigated by aggressive mass mailing and telemarketing solicitations. In 1985, the Ohio evangelist had lost 36 percent of his stations. By the year's end, the *Cathedral of Tomorrow* broadcast tumbled off the air.[87]

The disgrace of financial mismanagement continued to haunt faith networks. Larry Lea, dean of the seminary at Oral Roberts University, called it a "chasm of mistrust."[88] Earlier attempts to subject televangelists to financial oversight had failed. The 1979 formation of the Evangelical Council for Financial Accountability (ECFA) had been a much-publicized lame duck. The National Religious Broadcaster's Ethics and Financial Integrity Commission was scarcely more effective. Though it expelled Jimmy Swaggart, the commission refused to fully investigate charges brought against TBN founder Paul Crouch.[89] Broadcast ministries continued to fill their boards with family members who reaped rewards from the ministry, further obscuring financial transparency. "God is shaking his church," warned *Charisma* editor Jamie Buckingham. "Today's shaking is forcing leaders to turn to one another."[90]

When prosperity teachers returned to the spotlight, some things had changed significantly. In a media environment that had learned to mistrust overwrought emotional preaching and beseeching figures, new faces like Joel Osteen, Joyce Meyer, T. D. Jakes, Creflo Dollar, and Eddie Long replaced flamboyant stereotypes with a suave, businesslike image. By the mid-1990s, these postmodern prophets would not beg but rather focus on the returns. They would offer "tools" in the form of relationship guides, financial principles, or family reconciliation. The new generation of teachers set aside much of the hard prosperity that had characterized the decade in favor of the therapeutic inspiration of *soft prosperity*. They were now preaching to a less credulous, more cynical generation, who tended to put little faith in institutions but were willing to invest heavily in relationships and personal emotion. They elected a president who could "feel their pain." It was a wired generation, linked by e-mail and search engines, exploring all that the World Wide Web could do for them. But for all that audiences had become media-savvy and accustomed to high-tech solutions to daily inconveniences there were still millions who sought the now old-fashioned and supernatural working of the prosperity gospel.

The New Overcomers

The decline of white televangelist empires did little to dampen many black churches' enthusiasm for faith, wealth, and victory. In the same year that Jim Bakker was sentenced to federal prison and Oral Roberts's City of Faith hospital shut its doors because of lack of funds, Frederick Price opened the 10,000-seat Faith Dome in Los Angeles, which would become the nation's largest worship center. The prosperity gospel thrived in numerous black churches with all the innocence and delight of youth. The faith message is only a newborn, warned Pastor Ed Montgomery in 1988, "and we must get that baby through childhood and adolescence and into adulthood."[91] More and more African Americans, undeterred by the scandalous dalliances of a few white television preachers, shared Montgomery's desire to raise up the message in their own churches.

Throughout the 1980s, prosperity theology rose with new vitality in African American churches and enormous prosperity churches sprang up like daisies (see table 3.3). The largest black congregations in the country were swept up in a larger charismatic revival of their own, a turn toward

Table 3.3 African American Prosperity Megachurches Founded Before and After the Televangelism Scandals

Senior Pastor	Church (Location)	Founded
I. V. Hilliard	New Light Christian Center (Houston, TX)	1983
Eddie Long	New Birth Missionary Baptist Church (Lithonia, GA)	1983
Lamont McLean	Living Faith Christian Center (Pennsauken, NJ)	1985
Creflo Dollar	World Changers Ministries (College Park, GA)	1986
William Winston	Living Word Christian Center (Forest Park, IL)	1988
Marvin Winans	Perfecting Church (Detroit, MI)	1989
David Evans	Bethany Baptist Church (Lindenwold, NJ)	1990
Rickie Rush	Inspiring Body of Christ Church (Dallas, TX)	1990
Dale Bronner	Word of Faith Family Worship Center (Austell, GA)	1991

Note: Ron Gibson's Church of God in Christ congregation was effectively reborn in 1987 when he took charge. It grew from nine members to more than 4,500 under his guidance.

enthusiastic worship and gifts of the spirit. The majority were massive, one-off start-ups, led by magnetic and well-educated pentecostalized preachers across denominational lines.[92] Scholars have parsed this phenomenon in various ways. Jonathan Walton divided these spirit-filled churches into ecclesial categories, each with its own aesthetic and culture: neopentecostal (both denominational and independent), charismatic mainline (historic black denominations), and Word of Faith (nondenominational prosperity churches.)[93] Tamelyn Tucker-Worgs's illuminating sociological survey found pentecostal influences common to virtually all black megachurches, though they exhibited diverse theological orientations (prophetic, black theology, nondenominational, and prosperity gospel).[94] But the lines between these categories often blurred. The prosperity movement had nurtured black preachers inside their predominantly white independent networks, but now the message had outgrown its original structures. African American leaders from classic pentecostal, neopentecostal, and historic black denominations not only began to join faith preachers onstage, but tailored the message of wealth for their own audiences.[95]

The influence of the prosperity gospel spread far beyond the faith movement we have mapped so far, for at least four reasons. First, the message suited the economic mood. An emerging generation of black prosperity preachers spoke to a rising black middle class and those hungry for spiritual gifts that fed daily life. As African Americans entered the middle class in greater numbers, becoming more prosperous, mobile, and aware of a hard-won higher status, many flocked to the churches that reified their hopefulness and ambition. Observers worried that black churches were no longer able to seat the middle class and the poor under the same steeple.[96] The this-worldly focus of African American megachuches in general (and prosperity-preaching megachurches in particular) reflected believers' yearning to extend the economic, social, and political gains of the civil rights movement into limitless possibilities.[97]

The second (and related) reason centers on African American migration. In the Reverse Great Migration, as it is sometimes known, African American populations drifted away from Northern cities and settled in the South and Southwest.[98] Further, African American city-dwellers everywhere were leaving for the suburbs. These uprooted people (much like white pentecostals before them) sought out prosperity churches to make sense of their new social location. Their burgeoning churches predictably settled in urban black centers like Houston, Dallas, Los Angeles,

Atlanta, Chicago, Washington D.C., and Detroit, home to the highest number of megachurches and African Americans.[99] As Tucker-Worgs argued, the new black megachurches functioned like prewar storefront churches—migrant churches for a transplanted people.[100]

Third, interaction among megachurch leaders led to theological cross-pollination. The prosperity movement was growing increasingly top-heavy, captivating many of the country's largest white and black churches. Prosperity preachers were fast becoming the gatekeepers to the most coveted pulpits, and those who joined them onstage could expect exciting and lucrative opportunities to follow. As black churches of all ecclesial and doctrinal varieties grew larger and more successful in the 1980s, their leaders enjoyed friendlier relationships and often found more in common with each other than with their denominational kin or headquarters. Megachurch pastors were orbiting in a postdenominational sphere of shared platforms and concerns. Multimillion dollar institutions had saddled these pastors with common burdens and elevated them to similar heights. Further interaction bred familiarity (and often similarity). Pastors in close physical and relational proximity often found themselves speaking two languages—one reflecting their theological and educational training and another better suited to address postdenominational popular audiences.

Fourth, African American congregations have historically been the institutional epicenter of mutual aid, what W. E. B. Du Bois called "the central organ of organized life," and the place to debate and work out questions of political action, spiritual solace, and community meaning.[101] Black churches forged a long tradition of self-help. As C. Eric Lincoln and Lawrence Mamiya observed, this survivalist practice began in "the crucible of the slave quarters" and carried through the country's barbed history of racial inequality.[102] Black religious communities, barred from the luxury of separating spiritual and socioeconomic spheres, not only shouldered social services but assumed the tasks of fostering economic mobility.[103] In this context, the spiritual solutions proposed by the prosperity gospel joined timeworn debates about the relationship between the so-called black church and forms of social and economic liberation.[104] The materialism and hyper-individualism of the prosperity gospel—what scholars have identified variously as "thaumaturgical" or "positive thought materialism"—was tempered by other emancipatory visions.[105] As diverse denominational streams poured into the prosperity gospel, these newcomers allowed a blurring of roles not seen before: the prophetic could merge with the priestly or the social gospel with the empowering of individuals. In African American churches (particularly denominational churches) the prosperity gospel emerged as a concordant theme that blended with other long-standing concerns.

Consider these four factors—class, migration, cross-pollination, and mutual aid—in the rise of one black megachurch in suburban Atlanta. In 1986, the Disciples of Christ called one of their rising stars, Cynthia Hale, to found a congregation in Decatur, Georgia. This bedroom community of Atlanta was the new home of thousands of wealthy black migrants looking for religious experiences that mirrored their growing ambitions.[106] The city was fast becoming a hotbed of the prosperity gospel, and Hale's growing reputation drew her outside of her predominately white mainline denomination and toward pentecostalized audiences, more plugged into televangelism than seminary disputes.[107] The constant interaction with prosperity preachers, observed Hale, began to influence her theology to the point where her sound technician casually remarked that she was "finally starting to sound like everyone else." The comment stopped her in her tracks. "I had to check myself," recalled Hale candidly. She maintained her conviction in divine economic empowerment (as well as her respect for thoroughgoing prosperity preachers) but made a concerted effort to balance her message of "whole life prosperity" with her theological and exegetical roots. The result was a hybrid pentecostal-mainline identity and a revolving door of guest preachers with similarly varied commitments.[108] She did not mind being called a prosperity preacher as she promoted tithing, seed-faith, and "more-than-enoughness," but flatly rejected mechanistic accounts of divine formulas as "Reverend Ike-ish." The church bought her a Mercedes ("people don't want to see their pastor looking broke") but also established a nonprofit ministry to fulfill their "social mandate from God" to provide far-reaching healthcare, education, and affordable housing for the community's poor.[109] The prosperity gospel was breaking new ground.

Holy Ghost Prosperity

Holy Ghost denominations—black and white—handled the prosperity gospel like quicksilver. Most proceeded cautiously and trusted only the most experienced hands. And yet who could resist the chance to transform spiritual mettle into something more? Throughout the 1980s and 1990s, the prosperity gospel appeared as a common resolution to the problem of modernizing the pentecostal legacy. The Church of God in Christ and the Pentecostal Assemblies of the World, the two largest denominations, stood astride black pentecostalism with questions to resolve. Should they follow the well-trod way of television ministries? Should their annual conferences remain a dignified assembly of bishops or show an openness to the wider pentecostal world? All denominations had begun to face the slow hemorrhaging of church attendance and aging demographics. The inherent conservatism of denominational headquarters tested the patience of the senior pastors of their largest churches who searched for ways to stay young, fresh, and on the pulse of cultural trends. The famed televangelist Clarence McClendon put his small (and historically white) Foursquare denomination on the map with his vast television ministry and bustling 12,000-member church. His buoyant prosperity preaching and youthful good looks (said to draw so much attention that he was forced to file restraining orders against women in his congregation) charmed audiences with such success that his denomination hesitated to rein in his extravagant lifestyle.[110]

The Church of God in Christ (COGIC) cracked open their doors to the prosperity movement under the leadership of Bishop G. E. Patterson and his era of media expansion, shining a spotlight on COGIC through radio and television expansion.[111] He and Charles Blake, the future head of the denomination and pastor of one of the country's largest churches, ruled as denominational royalty on the pentecostal conference circuit.[112] They wore the priestly collar, robes, the stoles of consecrated men and the slight frown of administrators. Patterson embraced a televangelist career on Black Entertainment Television and the Trinity Broadcasting Network, but with none of the glitz of television mainstays like Frederick Price. Blake was foremost a pastor and ambassador of the largest African American denomination. In a decade marked by cutbacks in social services, his West Angeles Church of God in Christ earned a reputation for community outreach with programs addressing unemployment, homelessness, small business development, and neighborhood revitalization.[113] Both thrived within the high walls of classical pentecostalism as esteemed bearers of its traditions. Here they adopted forms of the prosperity gospel altered to familiar aesthetic forms, with the red carpets, dark wood pews, rich choir gowns, lively praise, and the breathy cadence of hooping (sermonic song) so at home in black pentecostalism. Blake and Patterson became decorated speakers at Oral Roberts's International Charismatic Bible Ministries' Conference. (Blake would go on to join the Board of Directors for both the ministry and university.) They appeared frequently beside Word of Faith favorites, often seeming more at home with the wider prosperity network than shut up in denominational circuits. For example, in 1993, Blake joined Frederick Price and Joyce Meyers as the headliners at the West Coast Azusa Conference, and, in 1994, Patterson appeared with R. W. Schambach, T. L. Osborn, John Osteen, Rod Parsley, Daisy Osborn, and David Nunn under a canvas cathedral.[114] The annual COGIC Holy Ghost conference began to feature not only a robed assortment of in-house leaders but also visiting faith celebrities.

Charles Blake's message, for example, demonstrates the diverse forms of "prosperity preaching" inside denominational pentecostalism. His preaching lacked the instrumentalism of classic Word of Faith theology: while he spoke little of positive confession, he promised listeners their faith would transform their economic and physical health situations. Rather than the story of Abraham's covenant, Blake preferred the biblical tale of the slave-turned-ruler named Joseph, who "kept faith in the dream no matter what his circumstances. He made the best of the situation and God caused him to prosper."[115] It modeled the entrepreneurialism and sweat equity of a prosperity gospel but also communal and institutional transformation of a social gospel.[116]

The prosperity gospel became a common language within classic pentecostalism to talk about a religion of solutions. Apostle Otis Lockett of Evangel Fellowship Church of God in Christ billed his church as "Providing Biblical Solutions for Life, Family, and Work."[117] The chief apostle of COOLJC (Church of Our Lord Jesus Christ), William Lee Bonner, son of a Southern sharecropper, gloried in his discovery of prosperity teaching through its nineteenth-century roots in Ralph Waldo Emerson and showed his flock how their thoughts could take them to financial levels they never dreamed possible.[118] Pentecostals, black or white, who could preach prosperity and grow their churches found that they had their uses to denominational headquarters. Despite the ambivalent legacy of the prosperity gospel inside denominational structures, successful prosperity teachers always seemed to land on their feet and be called to serve at the highest levels. After his church reached 2,000 members, *Anointing for Acceleration* author Otis Lockett was appointed the National Director of Church Growth and Development for the Church of God in Christ.

Charles H. Ellis III, later chosen as the leader of the 1.5 million-member Pentecostal Assemblies of the World, blended prosperity theology into a densely pentecostal form. His recent predecessors in the presiding bishop's seat, Norman Wagner and Horace Smith, had been old hands on the conference circuit that brought prosperity preachers into their churches and confidences.[119] Ellis continued this tradition in his sacramental vestments befitting a pentecostal bishop, clergy jackets embroidered with his Greater Grace Temple logo at his breast pocket and a clerical collar bobbing at his neck. He preached with the fervor of a Holy Ghost minister rather than the didactic manner of most prosperity teachers, an exclamation of "Hya!" serving as the metronome of his melodic phrases. He stuck to the fundamentals—salvation, prayer, praise, healing—but returned to the inevitability of victory and blessing. As Ellis made clear in a Sunday sermon about living abundantly in the face of dire economic circumstances:

> [God] said "Whatsoever he doeth shall prosper."
> And that's where I'm trying to move to in my walk with God.
> I'm trying to get to the place, where *everything* I do,
> according to the Word and will of God,
> it comes to fruition.
> It's got to prosper.
> It's got to come to pass . . .
> But if you *plug in,*
> to the Word of God—
> like the blessed man of Psalm One—
> If you *plug in* to the source of the power . . .
> if you stay connected to the vine,
> then you will produce and you will bring forth.
> And it will not matter what's going on in the world,
> people will look at you and have to call you blessed.
> People will look at you and have to call you delivered.
> People will look at you and have to call you the righteousness
> of God.
> Am I talking to anybody in here?
> I'm trying to get to the place, where everything I touch
> it turns to gold.
> I'm trying to get to the place, where everything I touch
> it's got to come forth.
> Where everyone around me
> They've got to be blessed.[120]

To grasp hold of these blessings, he continued, believers must delight in the Lord. Read the scriptures. Speak words of praise and wait until the appointed (but fast approaching) time when God will bring forth "their season" of provision. Like Blake's, his was not a hard prosperity. Ellis evoked the images of harvest without the laws of sowing and reaping; he implored listeners to dwell on the upbeat without the mechanism of positive confession. Yet the gilded guarantee of the prosperity gospel remained: God brings adherents to that place where dust turns to gold.[121]

Prosperity and Black Neopentecostalism

One of the most striking sources of growth in the prosperity movement was the rise of African American neopentecostalism unmoored by denominations. A wave of independent ministries brought an emphasis on spiritual gifts and ecstatic worship to some of the nation's largest congregations. The New Black Charismatics, as the historian Scott Billingsley has called them, shared the earlier charismatic movement's playful wonder at the Spirit and classic pentecostalism's investment in its power. But unlike the charismatic movement's nostalgic and alternative vibe, neopentecostal congregations positioned themselves as modern, media literate, and expansionist. As Jonathan Walton argued, these churches adopted a contemporary aesthetic and a flexible attitude to popular culture, jettisoning traditionalism as a barrier to the spread of the gospel. Efforts to engage contemporary audiences ranged from the entertaining (senior pastors and their first ladies dressed like drill sergeants to host spiritual bootcamps) to the mildly scandalous (like R. A. Vernon's church-growth manual entitled *Size Does Matter*). Many neopentecostal churches developed into natural allies of prosperity theology as they sought to become relevant in a highly consumerist culture. They engrossed audiences with the latest in video projection; theater seating; and sermons on sex, work, and children that addressed the pressures of a fast-paced world. The typical neopentecostal male pastor had two uniforms, an untucked tailored shirt with designer jeans and a fitted three-button suit-and-vest combination. Pastors found that parishioners wanted leaders who looked and preached like an ambassador for unrelenting progress.

The prosperity movement grew so pervasive that it captured the imagination of even the most preeminent African American preacher of his generation and one of the most sought-after speakers in the country, Thomas Dexter (T. D.) Jakes.[122] Jakes, founder of the nation's eleventh largest church, the Potter's House, ruled the American media as one of the nation's leading preachers. He solemnly stared out from the cover of *Time* magazine under the heading, "Is This Man the Next Billy Graham?" and was a *New York Times* bestseller, a Hollywood film producer, Grammy nominee, and an advisor to presidents. His fame had not come easily. Reared a Baptist, he converted to pentecostalism as a teenager, pounded the preaching circuit in West Virginia, and, in 1979, began Greater Emmanuel Temple of Faith, a small congregation in the mining town of Montgomery. His first evangelistic efforts in the early 1980s yielded a short-lived radio ministry, *The Master's Plan*, and a fledgling Bible conference. In the 1990s, Jakes moved his ministry to Charleston, where it grew from a hundred members to more than a thousand. His message centered on emotional healing, a theme that struck market gold with his series *Woman, Thou Art Loosed!* Jakes's focus on psychological healing for women addressed domestic violence, discrimination, rape, and divorce, issues he explored in his 1993 book and conference of the same name. *Woman, Thou Art Loosed!* became a phenomenon, with two million copies in print, record-breaking conference attendance, a play, a gospel album, and a film adaptation. It also began a long stream of media exposure. In 1993, Jakes began a weekly television program, *Get Ready with T. D. Jakes*, and, a year later, an accompanying radio program. By 1995, his national success brought increased scrutiny, as West Virginia newspapers drew attention to Jakes's lavish living. In 1996, Jakes decided to forget winning them over and transplanted his ministry to Dallas, Texas. He founded The Potter's House Church, headquarters of T. D. Jakes Ministries, his nonprofit outreach, and T. D. Jakes Enterprises, his for-profit wing. Potter's House flourished in its new locale, attracting predominately African American audiences with white and Hispanic minorities. His church claimed over 50 outreach programs, intent on raising the economic status of believers and nonbelievers alike. He earned a reputation as a preacher who taught "the formula of faith" but knew its limits: "Do I believe in supernatural return on your giving? Yes, sir! Do I believe God blesses tithes and offerings? Yes, I do. But why should we teach you to claim a car without teaching you about the car payment and interest rates on the loan?"[123] His tempered messages did not prevent him from "sowing into" the ministries of hard prosperity preachers. Ron Carpenter Jr., for example, claimed that T. D. Jakes had helped buy his megachurch for him.[124] At one time, Jakes both counted Paula White and Juanita Bynum as his spiritual progeny.

Though fellow neopentecostals could never match Jakes's fame, they exhibited a similar flair for sanctified commerce. These churches embraced luxury and personal blessings as an extension of their stylish, contemporary aesthetic.[125] In 1990, Pastor Rickie Rush founded the Inspiring Body of Christ Church in Dallas with a reputation for frenetic sermons and a megawatt smile. Over the cheers of worshippers, he preached about a God who, like a fast-food chain, worked tirelessly behind the scenes to "fill your special orders." First, however, the believer has to pay for what they want. "God never said you couldn't have it," he chastised, "only that you had to pay for it first."[126] In 1989, Marvin Winans of the Grammy-winning musical Winans family founded The Perfecting Church in a Detroit, Michigan, basement with a congregation of eight people. Outgrowing location after location, the church came to build a performing arts charter school, a transitional home for women, a television studio, and 30 ministries serving a range of needs. These neopentecostal churches were densely networked to each other but also to the larger prosperity movement. Marvin Winans's annual conferences, for example, regularly assembled Word of Faith stalwarts R. W. Schambach, Charles Capps, Kenneth Copeland, and Creflo Dollar with neopentecostals like T. D. Jakes, Paul Morton, and Noel Jones. (See figure 3.10 for Marvin Winans's neopentecostal conference associations.) Neopentecostal preachers adeptly wove the prosperity gospel into a modern message of Christian adaptation to an ever-changing digital world.

Historic Black Denominational Prosperity

The prosperity gospel followed in the wake of neopentecostalism and its surprising revival of charismatic influences within mainstream African American churches. Pentecostal-flavored preaching, emotional worship, emphasis on the Spirit, and an interest in supernatural gifts enlivened these old-line churches and opened their doors to a new perspective on holiness. High-spirited talk of wealth and health found its way into some of the largest churches in the dominant Baptist and Methodist culture. The aesthetics of these churches remained mostly unchanged: pastors in clerical collars, prominently displayed crosses, and sanctuaries fashioned in the age-old style rather than as television studios. There was little of the didactic atmosphere found in worship spaces of independent prosperity churches, where parishioners were wont to bring pens and notepaper to take down the teaching;[127] rather congregants could be found waving their

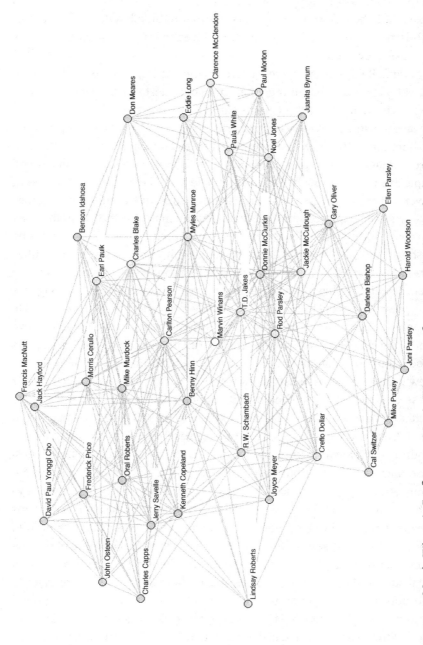

FIGURE 3.10 Marvin Winans's Conferences Marvin Winans's conference participation as advertised in *Charisma* magazine. Winans's sphere of associates offers a snapshot of shared Word of Faith and neopentecostal influences like Noel Jones and T. D. Jakes.

arms, shouting "Amen!" and taking off uncomfortable shoes to dance in the Spirit. Those pastors who began traveling in prosperity circles tended to be media-savvy, entrepreneurial, and trend-setting mavericks willing to take a little heat from headquarters in order to broaden the scope of their ministries. Their parishioners, in turn, loved them for lingering on topics so close to everyday life.

Frank Reid, pastor of the historic Bethel African Methodist Episcopal (A.M.E.) church in Baltimore, Maryland (and guest star on the gritty crime show *The Wire* set in the Charm City), hoped to steer his denomination toward a distinctly Wesleyan prosperity gospel. In the 1980s, his presiding bishop, John Bryant, was instrumental in reclaiming Methodism's sanctified heritage and opening the denomination to pentecostal influences and explosive church growth. Educated at Yale and Harvard, Reid was one of several Bryant protégés with the talent, media savvy, and administrative ability to raise up megachurches that would remake the A.M.E. in this new image.[128] Young guns, like Baltimore megachurch pastor Jamal Bryant (the bishop's son), followed in these footsteps with eye-catching sermon titles like "I Just Want to Be Successful" and seminars on "How to Create Wealth."[129] Reid understood his role as a mediator between those attempting to ignore the prosperity gospel and those too easily persuaded by its extremes. He sought to reclaim the prosperity gospel as a Methodist idea with a liberative end—the wholesale economic empowerment of black America. Just as God's promise of abundant life had once fostered upward mobility for the newly discipled Methodists drawn from slavery and the English lower classes, Reid argued, so should contemporary believers be counseled to be better managers of their time, talent, and treasure.[130] This, he warned would be a "costly" prosperity gospel, while an easy prosperity gospel required nothing but a hustling preacher. He decried abuses of practices, like confession and visualization, but cautioned believers not to ignore the scriptural foundations of 30-, 60-, 100-fold blessings and Mark 11:24's "I shall have what I say." He preferred to be called an "empowerment preacher" as his sermons unveiled God's "biblical keys to abundant living" and the need to "put on the winning ways of Christ-like champions."[131] He spoke of generational "strongholds" rather than curses that bound Christians who used fatalistic words (others might have spoken here of "negative confession"). He hoped that the denomination could offer a reasoned middle ground between independent pentecostalism and historic black churches. "The survival of the African Methodist denomination," warned Reid, "hinges on how well we engage and embrace this debate."

Kirbyjon Caldwell headed the second-largest congregation in the largely white United Methodist Church and traveled in the nation's highest circles. Caldwell was well known for his role as a spiritual advisor on the national political scene and a pioneer in community development as the founder of the Power Center—a cluster of services including a bank; an AIDS outreach center; Women, Infants, and Children (WIC) center; and the Memorial Hermann Hospital health clinic. His book, *The Gospel of Good Success*, promoted "God's mathematics" and common-sense wisdom for creating financial abundance; he could be found on the rosters of national conferences dominated by prosperity teaching.[132] Nary a Methodist book could be found in his ministry's bookstore, stuffed with the glossy inspiration of neopentecostals like Eddie Long and Myles Monroe. Caldwell promised readers a sure path to God-given prosperity and the miracles wrought by the divine "multiplication process" of tithing. He plotted a slow (but measurable) trajectory toward Christian victory proven by his own example. Even so, many of the familiar ingredients of prosperity messages were absent. He preferred to speak of praise over positive confession, no longer attributing to words the properties of quick cement. He downplayed the instantaneousness of health and wealth; nonetheless, faith yielded rewards. "God has promised you power, abundance, and good success," Caldwell argued, "God did not make provisions—whether it's stocks and bonds, nice cars and nice homes, or peace of mind, joy, and healthy self-esteem—for Satan's kids. God's provisions are for His children, if they're for anybody!"

Pentecostalized Baptists (playfully called "Bapticostals") seemed to find a natural place for the prosperity gospel. A dozen of the largest black Baptist congregations responded quickly to the growing interest in divine health and wealth (see table 3.4). These churches, some independent and some denominationally tied, began to incorporate faith teachers and theology into their Baptist identity. In 1992, Paul Morton of New Orleans' St. Stephen's Baptist church accepted spiritual gifts as central to his ministry. Saying that he knew too much about the Holy Spirit to ignore it, he added Full Gospel to the church's name (along with 10,000 more members) and embarked on a more independent ecclesial path that would see him presiding over the Full Gospel Baptist Church Fellowship with more than 5,000 affiliates. He "covenanted" other black leaders, like Kenneth Ulmer, Clarence McClendon, and Eddie Long, with the dream of synthesizing black Baptist and pentecostal traditions.[133] The fellowship was diverse, but among many things it soon became a hotspot for prosperity megachurch pastors aspiring to bishoprics.[134]

A new pentecostalized realm had been opened. Many of the most successful African American pastors had forged a postdenominational world of densely networked churches and leaders. Publishers and Bible colleges clamored to share in their reputations, and new opportunities arose for conferences, speaking tours, and accolades. Friends International Christian University, a distance-learning institute centered in Florida, granted honorary doctorates to the highest rung of African American celebrity pastors, including prosperity preachers like T. D. Jakes (Dallas), Clarence McClendon (Los Angeles), Paul Morton (New Orleans), and Ira Hilliard (Houston). Small networks of local black prosperity churches thrived by corporate worship, sponsoring trips to nearby crusades, and mixing and matching their preachers as visiting speakers. In the 1980s and 1990s, the movement had far outreached its largely white foundations. African American churches baptized in the prosperity gospel were like the Grammy-award-winning Clark Sisters—they went from singing "Nothing to Lose" to "Name It, Claim It."

Table 3.4 African American Baptist Megachurches Participating in the Prosperity Movement

Church	Senior Pastor	Numbers	Location
Mount Zion Baptist Church	Joseph Walker III	25,000	Nashville, TN
New Birth Missionary Baptist Church	Eddie Long	25,000	Lithonia, GA
Bethany Baptist Church	David Evans	23,000	Lindenwold, NJ
The Fountain of Praise	Remus Wright	16,000	Houston, TX
Jericho City of Praise	[In Transition]	15,000	Landover, MD
Faithful Central Bible Church	Kenneth Ulmer	13,000	Inglewood, CA
St. John Church	Denny Davis	12,000	Grand Prairie, TX
First Cathedral	Leroy Bailey Jr.	11,000	Bloomfield, CT
Greater St. Stephen Full Gospel Baptist Church	Debra Morton	10,000	New Orleans, LA
The Park Church	Claude Alexander Jr.	8,000	Charlotte, NC
Elevation Baptist Church	T. L. Carmichael Sr.	3,000	Raleigh, NC

Soft Prosperity

The prosperity movement that emerged in full health and vigor in the early 1990s was more diverse than ever before. It had survived the disgrace of many of its standard-bearers and outgrown its denominational boundaries. It appealed both to white Americans and those of color. It was no longer a child from the wrong side of the tracks but a powerful movement with boundless confidence. It claimed many of the nation's largest churches, and others like the Victorious Faith Center in Durham, North Carolina, one of hundreds of small congregations swept up in the heterogeneous prosperity movement. Nationally, prosperity theology coursed through popular television, radio, books, seminars, conferences, and many of the country's largest congregations. Locally, the message wound its way into hundreds of independent pentecostal churches, loosely associated with other like-minded churches, sharing ministers, church programs, worship events, and healing services, offering the saints a host of solutions for their particular spiritual and physical needs. In churches large and small, the movement had developed a smooth new language and style of persuasion that admirably fit the times. It was therapeutic and emotive, a way of speaking that shed its pentecostal accent for a sweeter and secular tone that I call "soft prosperity."

Teachers like Joel Osteen, John Osteen's son and successor at Houston's Lakewood Church, softened the hard causality between the spoken word and reality. Prophets of soft prosperity tied psychological to fiscal success, believing that a rightly ordered mind led to rightly ordered finances. Osteen chose mainstream language over Christian jargon, changing the term "positive confession" to "positive declarations." Yet the principle remained the same: change your words, change your life. He wrote: "Every day, we should make positive declarations over our lives. We should say things such as, 'I am blessed. I am prosperous. I am healthy. I am talented. I am creative. I am wise.'" For Osteen, the transformative power of positive confession could be demonstrated psychologically, rather than appealing to the forces of faith. The words build self-image, Osteen taught, for "as those words permeate your heart and mind, and especially your subconscious mind, eventually they will begin to change the way you see yourself." A healthy mind became an important indicator of good spiritual health and a vibrant conduit of faith. Life's circumstances still depended on a believer's use of faith. Divine wealth eventually came to good people, he reasoned, for a chain of causality-linked thought, the spiritual self, and life's circumstances. "As you speak affirmatively, you will develop a new image on the inside, and things will begin to change in your favor." God rewarded the faithful with wealth, though believers typically earned it indirectly. Perhaps a careful budget tamed household over-spending or the boss noticed the believers' cheerful attitude and tapped them for promotion. "If you'll do your part, God will do His," promised Osteen. "He will promote you; He'll give you increase, but first you must be a good caretaker of what you have." Promotion and increase arrived as an assortment of ordinary and supernatural opportunities. A believer should simply rely on God's promises of an abundant life. "Call in what God has promised you," Osteen urged readers.[135]

African American prosperity preachers, in particular those with de-nominational ties, often added an entrepreneurial twist in emphasizing the slow work of upward mobility. Debt counseling. Tax write-offs. Job banks. Small business loans. Pragmatic and bootstrapping methods charted the long journey to prosperity. Bishop Noel Jones, pastor of the 10,000-member City of Refuge church, demonstrated this dual mental and tactical commitment in *Vow of Prosperity*. His soft prosperity defined success as the net result of right thinking because "your spirit will either attract negatively or positively," but he also lent equal weight to the gritty details of financial management.[136] He warned readers of the dangers of overnight success, urging them to embrace the process of receiving God's blessings.

Paula White embodied the therapeutic spirit of the times as the every-day woman who offered biblical solutions to poverty and a broken spirit. This televangelist and megachurch pastor preferred to call herself a life-coach and motivational speaker. Her books, *You're All That; Deal With It!; Simple Suggestions for a Sensational Life; Birthing Your Dreams*; and *He Loves Me, He Loves Me Not* promised to deliver readers, especially women, from pain that might prevent victory. As Phil Sinitiere and Shayne Lee observed, it was a spiritual climate that favored confessional tones.[137] Believers wanted their pastors to have tell-all journeys to share and minds they had to master along the way. White introduced readers to a thought-world that was potent, where the successful would learn to get their minds to "work for them."[138] She traced the relationship between these thoughts, positive or negative, and life's circumstances.

Your thoughts become your words.
Your words become your actions.

Your actions become your habits.
Your habits become your character.
Your character becomes your destiny.[139]

In a sense, therapeutic language replaced sentimentality as the preferred medium of religious advice giving. Healing revivalists before them had worried that it hovered too closely to positive thinking. The new generation had converted to a new way of thinking, in which spirituality doubled as mental warfare and mental health.

Sunday Prosperity

Most Sunday services passed without a word from the first lady of the Victorious Faith Center in Durham, North Carolina, who appeared calmly to accept her husband's fiery prose, nodding or fanning herself. Her stillness may have been mistaken for mildness, but she too had a stubborn fire. Other worshippers seemed to draw their enthusiasm from the crescendoing piano or the pastor's admonitions, rather than the stolid presence of the first lady. Yet one Sunday, the first lady rose unexpectedly from her seat in the first row, turning toward the congregation.

Faith requires action, she declared with surprising volume. Faith requires that believers resist signs of Satan's power—disease, poverty, and lack—and reclaim God's abundance. Her small figure seemed to grow as the room grew more excited when she led believers in a measure to put poverty in check. She urged everyone to stand and prepare to receive. She explained that after she called, "Money cometh unto me, NOW!" each congregant must proclaim this faith and reach out for God's blessings. They must act as if God's financial blessings poured out, and money fell from the sky to meet every need. "MONEY!" she shouted, the congregation calling out with her. "Cometh unto me . . ."—she paused in anticipation— "NOW!" With that, the first lady began to dance. Her legs bounced in place, high-heeled shoes kicked under a chair, and her short arms pumped as she reached high and plucked invisible dollar bills from the sky. The room danced, as some 80 believers, young and old, threw off their inhibitions and joined her. The murmur rose to a din as people began to call out their needs. Most of them fervently reached out for the money visible to their spiritual eyes. Young mothers jostled their babies as they jumped, while elderly women waved their arms to catch what fell. Tears streamed down as people remembered what they desired or the losses that they hoped to replace. "Money cometh unto me NOW!" voices called again, echoing the first lady's refrain. When the moment faded, feet slowed and hands clutched their invisible findings. The first lady sank into her seat and resumed her quiet authority, the silent demonstration of what invisible faith, when made visible, could accomplish.[140]

Prosperity congregations, unable to find sufficient precedent in pentecostal and Holiness church practices, developed modern rites to celebrate divine wealth on Sunday morning. Although, there was little uniformity across the movement's diverse congregations, several trends emerged. Tithing eclipsed the sermon, worship, and communion as the emotional peak of the service, as pastors pushed their audiences to envision greater financial miracles. Soft prosperity churches commonly kept the mood light as the ushers took the offering, reminding audiences "God loves a cheerful giver" (2 Corinthians 9:7). Hard prosperity congregations adopted stronger measures, dwelling on the negative consequences that befell the uncharitable. In the book of Malachi, teachers found ample evidence that Christians cursed themselves when they "robbed God."[141]

Financial themes surfaced throughout the service. Congregations might open the worship service with positive confessions tailored to wealth, such as, "I am out of debt. I am healthy and wealthy. I'm having good success." Testimony found new purpose as churches made liturgical space to glorify the financial and physical improvements in their members. Small churches allowed members to pipe up with news of a newly acquired car, promotion, or home, while megachurch pastors read them aloud in a segment for prayer and praise. St. Peter's Church and World Outreach Center placed tall glass coffers labeled "Answered Prayers" at the foot of the pulpit. One might be forgiven for thinking that at a prosperity gospel service speech and ceremonies would be about receiving, but, in fact, the emphasis is often on giving—to the ministry. There seemed to be as many ways to separate the faithful from their money as there were pastors. Giving was turned into a public spectacle, the new liturgy.

Innovative tithing rituals compelled members to present their donations before curious eyes. Pastor Marvin Winans of Perfecting Church in Detroit separated the givers from the bystanders when he asked those "who give more than $30, but only more than $30" to stand and bring their offerings to the altar. "I want you to give 'cause we need a bigger church," he stated bluntly.[142] Soft prosperity preachers in tune with white evangelical audiences typically offered more subdued requests, sometimes simply announcing what percentage of their congregation was giving their full tithes. Numerous black prosperity churches followed sanctified church custom in asking all present to stand and file past the offertory plate or (in the case of megachurches) bucket.[143] Empty-handed believers touched the bucket and prayed that they might soon have something to give. It raised to new heights the old-fashioned custom of placing a wooden tablet at the side of the sanctuary, totaling last week's attendance and offerings. Lynette Hagin, Kenneth E. Hagin's daughter-in-law, introduced an interactive tithing convention adopted by many Rhema churches. Participants raised their tithing envelopes in the air and repeated this offering prayer:

> This is my seed. I sow it into the Kingdom of God. I sow because I love God and want to see [insert name of church] continue to fulfill what God has called us to do.
>
> I believe that as I sow my seed, it shall be given unto me—good measure, pressed down, shaken together, and running over! It shall come back to me in many ways!
>
> I thank You, Lord, for good opportunities coming my way. I thank You that the windows of Heaven are opening because of my obedience to sow my seed.
>
> I thank You, Lord, for the favor of God upon my life and the grace to prosper, as You have promised me in Your Word.[144]

At the mention of "good measure, pressed down, shaken together, and running over," Rhema Bible Training Center graduates even added their own playful actions.

Tithing, in part, was about show and tell. People were called to stand, dance, wave, or parade their donations before the congregation and television cameras. In Orlando, Florida, Faith World placed transparent buckets emblazoned with the word "release" on the stage at the end of every aisle for parishioners to "sow into" a moment in the sermon. At Paula White's Without Walls church, a feminine aesthetic pervaded the sanctuary and encouraged giving through the provision of floppy pink envelopes which tithers were encouraged to wave during the service. Solicitations for tithes to her church offered concrete guidelines:

> *I'm enclosing my best offering of:*
> ☐ One month's pay
> ☐ One day's pay

☐ One week's pay
☐ My best First Fruits offering

The Minneapolis megachurch Speak the Word Church International suggested to its mostly immigrant congregation that they could donate fine jewelry and foreign currency in lieu of dollars. "The silver is mine and the gold is mine,' declares the Lord Almighty" (Haggai 2:8) read the handout, explaining that treasures placed in the offering bin would be liquidated for resale.[145] (Tiny print at the bottom allowed that the vendors used may include businesses that church board members have an interest in.) Other churches laid the bare bills on the platform as the preacher paced a stage littered with cash and checks.

The significance of divine wealth led churches to publicize tithing and to set givers apart from the crowd. Pressure was often unsubtle. Pastors might ask congregants to turn to their neighbors in the pew and inquire: "Did you give what you were supposed to?" and to tell any reluctant givers, "I'm not going to sit by you if you're not here for victory!" At a megachurch in a destitute area of Maryland the speaker breathlessly recounted how the previous week for the culmination of Pastor's Appreciation Month many givers had promised donations of $1,000, even $50,000. What would be given this week? Those who had been absent last Sunday and missed out on this opportunity were told to stand and to "name their seed" of no less than $1,000. The first man to stand coughed and looked around as the video camera closed in on his face. With his shirt untucked and his cautious expression, he seemed like a man out of step with the polish and confidence of the congregation. When the speaker asked him to announce what he was "sowing," he stunned the audience by saying: "I'll sow what I got." This news was received with silence and muttering, as the preacher surmised that he could not have been at this church very long to think that those with a small or vague offering would prosper.[146]

Seminars to teach pastors these financial techniques became a cottage industry. Bishop Don Meares of the 5,000-member Evangel Cathedral and Michael Chitwood, creator of the *Building and Accumulating Wealth* system, toured the United States for months with their "Church Financial Seminars." Hyped by a theological cross-section of the prosperity movement (including Shirley Caesar, Kenneth Ulmer, Dennis Leonard, Clarence McClendon, and John Avanzini), it promised to teach pastors the basics:

- How to Prove Tithing is in the New Testament
- How to Deal with Delinquent Tithers
- How to Double the Pastor's Salary
- How to Complete Your Pledges in 120 Days
- How to Prove that Non-Tithers are Robbers

Seminar topics like "How to Setup a Love Offering Program LEGALLY" allowed pastors to receive gifts without violating their tax exemption status as charities.[147] The advertisement featured Bishop Jimmie Ellis of the Victory Christian Center raving, "I did not realize how underpaid I was on my salary and housing allowance. I am now making 3 times what I was making." Divine finances came as a lesson to all.

The megachurch pastor Clint Brown stressed the significance of touch, urging those in the audience who would not or could not tithe to "Just get something in your hand. If you are not tithing then at least give an offering, have something in your hand!" James Hash, an African American graduate of Rhema Bible, paraded with his wife on the stage of his St Peter's Church and World Outreach Center in Winston-Salem, telling his congregation, "You're looking at Mr. and Mrs. Favor!" One of the deacons was asked to join them, followed by a dozen more representing the different ministries of the church, holding hands to create a long chain that would allow the pastor's favor to rub off on them and spread to the whole church.[148]

Small churches claimed an equal share of prosperity. Bishop Edward Peecher's Chicago storefront church, the New Heritage Cathedral, printed their "Personal Confession" in the bulletin:

> I am under Divine Decree of Increase. God has spoken Increase to me. I am destined to Increase, my anointing is Increasing, my wisdom is Increasing, my health is improving–EVERY DAY is a day of Increase for me and my family.[149]

A banner near the altar of the Memorial Baptist Church of Newark read: "Are you giving God a tip or a tithe?"[150] Large churches proclaimed victory over their own financial woes. The conference organizer of "Would Thou Be Made Whole?"—in celebration of the singer-preacher Shirley Caesar—attempted to meet the conference's diminishing budget by praying over the offerings asking God that the small bills be transformed into larger denominations. It was a frequent joke at prosperity gatherings that the audience be given more time to write out their checks because it was time consuming to write all those zeros at the end of the amount.

Some prosperity preachers earned their reputations as biblical mathematicians. Earlier pentecostals and fundamentalists, like many before them, had mined apocalyptic literature for the raw data of prophecy, unearthing fragments from Daniel or Revelation for clues that foretold the unraveling of time. This was exacting work, a tangle of dates counted backward and forward through the reigns of kings and stretches of exile. A handful of prosperity evangelists including faith healer Benny Hinn and Millionaire University™ creator John Avanzini approached scripture as a treasure trove of covenants, agreements cut between God and ancient Israel. The obsession with numerical precision often influenced the ways they encouraged Sunday giving. Televangelist Mike Murdock, a staple on *Paula White Today* and Benny Hinn's *This Is Your Day*, saturated his messages with numbers: *365 Wisdom Keys, 31 Reasons People Do Not Receive Their Financial Harvest,* and *7 Ingredients In Every Miracle.* Symmetry was encouraged. Ministers might ask for $3,500 for a 35th anniversary in the ministry. George Bloomer, spiritual son of Eddie Long, divided his Durham-based Bethel Family Worship Center into lines come tithing time: a $10 line, a $50 line, a $100 line, etc. Grammy-winning Shirley Caesar preferred marches: marches of men, marches of women, with a preordained amount in their hands. Sometimes mathematics worked in favor of the congregation. Pastor Mike Freeman of Spirit of Faith Christian Center in Temple Hill, Maryland, celebrated the 17th anniversary of his church by giving away envelopes full of money to 17 people born on the 17th. (Pastor Mike was not born yesterday—he spent fifteen minutes of his sermon checking the IDs of those claiming to be born on the auspicious day.)

Sometimes preachers abandoned smooth persuasion for old-fashioned hell-fire. The mild-mannered Jim Hammond of Minneapolis' Living Word Christian Center played the part of a financial exorcist, releasing his audience from satanic control over their money. "Devil, take your hands off my $9,500!" he shouted, asking his white congregation filled with lapsed Lutherans to substitute their own number and demand that the Devil release it. It was a low-flying theology, hovering just above people's daily needs and desires.

Give and get. Divine prosperity rested on a simple exchange. To be sure, careful preachers warned believers against giving *to* get, but all agreed that openhearted givers should expect to see significant returns. Money served as a common and practical means of assessing one's faith.

Yet the actual calculation of gains and losses in a believer's life proved more difficult. Whether donations appeared in the heat of a crusade or the cool of a casual Sunday, believers often struggled to account for precisely how much the prosperity gospel yielded.

Every now and again, divine wealth came as miraculously as a sudden bank transfer or a mysterious envelope of cash in the mailbox. Joan, a visiting prophetess to the Victorious Faith Center, testified that her $255 tithe was recompensed by following God's instructions to find the same amount in the parking lot of a particular store.[151] Most often, however, calculations demanded a roundabout arithmetic. One of Kenneth Hagin's favorite stories of financial obedience illustrates this calculus at work. A poor widow in his congregation scarcely had enough to eat but faithfully paid her tithes. One night during a revival, the woman's mentally ill daughter accepted the gospel and was miraculously restored to near-perfect mental health. She soon married. Hagin later discovered that the young woman's husband died in a truck accident, and that his ample insurance left her several hundred thousand dollars. "I was so glad, praise God," wrote Hagin, "that I had obeyed God and had taken her mother's tithes. This girl had learned to pay tithes, too. . . . Would she ever have gotten to that place if she hadn't been obedient in her finances?"[152] To the casual observer, the connection between a mother's donation and her daughter's tragic loss seemed a distant one. Yet the faithful saw providence, not coincidence, at work. As Paula White explained of God, "He is the master puppeteer who is making all the right moves, orchestrating each event that comes your way, preparing your blessing . . . and He is doing everything that concerns you in His perfect time."[153] No circumstance fell outside God's purview. Believers did what they did best: they found God in the particulars of their lives. Members of VFC told me of God's providence in securing a loan, a company car, or winning a bidding war over a new home. God provided for them as faithfully as He did for Moses, parting the seas that they might pass through.

The flip side of this same coin was the veiled threat of misfortune for those who tried to escape God's consequences. Evangelist Joyce Meyer recalled that her attempts to avoid tithing caused all her household appliances to malfunction, exacting from her the amount that her tithes would have been. Because she did not have her "seed" in the ground, she explained, Satan stole her money.[154] Pastor Walton warned parishioners that robbing God might bring a curse on their houses. Their appliances and cars would break down. "Money gets away from you," he said, shaking his head.[155] Followers repented of withholding their tithes, but then worried about the residual debt they owed God. "How can I 'clear my account' with Him?" fretted a reader of Marilyn Hickey's *Charisma* column.[156] The world of prosperity was a closed spiritual system, encompassing all aspects of everyday life. "Spiritual currency works the same as natural currency," explained Gloria Copeland. "If you have an abundance in your natural bank account, you can enjoy plenty of material things. If you have an abundance of faith in your spiritual account, you can enjoy plenty of *everything*—wealth, health, good relationships, peace, success."[157] Believers treated faith as a loose Christian equivalent to Hinduism's karma, an explanation for causality in which all actions brought good or ill consequences. It was both the carrot and the stick, as *"whatsoever* we sow, whether good or bad, is coming up again!"[158]

For those who could not yet see prosperity in their own lives, patience became the highest virtue. "Patience! The power twin of faith!" exclaimed Kenneth Copeland.[159] Virtually every book on the subject of prosperity addressed the issue of God's timing. Brother John Avanzini listed "No Patience" as one of the 25 major obstructions to blessing. "Everything God does is scheduled. . . . Just hold on," urged Paula White.[160] Juanita Bynum's popular song encouraged believers to rest in the gap between asking and receiving with the single, repeated refrain: "I don't mind waiting for you, Lord."[161]

Leading by Example

Leaders proved to be the most powerful demonstrators of divine wealth, and the living testimony and continued revelation of successful prosperity teachers presented an idealized portrait of what it meant to live victoriously. Their chauffeured cars and private jets served as tangible reminders of their blessedness, as Creflo Dollar reminded his congregation: "I own two Rolls-Royces and didn't pay a dime for them. Why? Because while I'm pursuing the Lord those cars are pursuing me."[162] As embodiments of prosperity, these pastors offered tangible reminders of God's goodness and the abundant provisions in store for all who believed. Frederick Price, pioneer of African American prosperity theology, made his financial success a perennial theme with a theological bottom line: "I'm only doing it so that you can see that there's somebody the same color that you are, breathing the same contaminated air, paying the same outrageous prices for everything else, and I'm prospering because of the Book."[163] In short, they served as "proof-producers," divining rods for the community to understand the work of the Lord.

Dollar's rise to fame demonstrated this desired career trajectory. When Atlanta singer and rap-phenomenon, Ludacris, starred in the music video, "Welcome to Atlanta," a faux-tour of his city's hip-hop landmarks, Pastor Dollar was the first stop. Between footage of a raunchy tour guide and Ludacris's camera-close rapping, the senior pastor of World Changers Church International stood solemnly in front of the 30,000-member facility that had made him an urban black sensation. As pastor of the 15th-largest church in America, an African American congregation, Dollar's popularity reached into unlikely spheres. As the spiritual son of Kenneth Copeland, an older generation of pentecostals respected Dollar's exuberant traits. Handsome and quick-witted, he commanded a female fan base that crossed racial lines and ensured frequent invitations to women's conferences. In 2008, for example, Joyce Meyer's Women's Convention slated Dollar as the sole male speaker. A popular presenter across diverse sectors of the American Christian landscape, Dollar succeeded in bringing an urban black ministry to national acclaim.

Dollar's reputation was born and bred in Atlanta. A native of College Park, Dollar grew up in the Methodist church, converting to pentecostalism as a teenager. His first pastoral efforts came in West Georgia College, where he and a roommate started a "World Changers Bible Study." Under his guidance, the group grew to 300 attendees.[164] Dollar's subsequent graduate work in counseling, though unrelated to theology, equipped him as a teacher and self-help advisor. In 1986, Dollar founded a church in College Park, Georgia, with eight members. Their numbers grew steadily, though not meteorically, despite Dollar's ambitions.[165] In the early 1990s, however, the church's growth increased exponentially. In 1991, Dollar began construction on an $18 million facility, the World Dome. While large-scale building projects formed the rule, not the exception, in faith ministries, Dollar's projects facilitated both his growing ministry and a spiritual symbolism. In keeping with his teachings against debt, Dollar refused any bank financing, gradually paying for the facility himself. By December 24, 1995, World Changers Ministry International began services in the new 8,500-seat sanctuary and Dollar proved his theological point. As his church biographers stated, "The construction of the World Dome is a testament to the miracle-working power of God and remains a model of debt-freedom that ministries all over the world emulate."[166]

Dollar majored in spiritual finances. His television program, *Changing Your World*, launched in 1990, was syndicated on almost 200 television stations and cemented his reputation as God's financier. Each broadcast offered strategies to achieve Christian victory, largely through the "supernatural method of finance."[167] The close of his November 24, 2004, broadcast explained things clearly. As Dollar sat comfortably beside his wife, Taffi, they summarized the findings of their series, "Becoming Financially Fit." "God is the one giving us the power to get wealth," he explained, quoting Psalm 66:10, that "we went through the fire but thou brought us to a *wealthy place*." He smiled jubilantly as he arrived at the punch line: "We've been bought out! And brought out!" God saved and rewarded, a lavish promise to every believer. His dozen popular titles like *Total Life Prosperity* (1999), *No More Debt!: God's Debt Cancellation Strategy* (2001), and *Claim Your Victory Today* (2006) detailed his financial promises from God. Dollar's consistent focus on godly acquisition made financial empowerment seminars a hallmark of his ministry.

Fellow faith teachers hailed Dollar as one of the youngest success stories of the American prosperity movement. In 1998, Oral Roberts confirmed his achievement with an honorary doctor of divinity degree, and a host of like-minded preachers, black and white, counted him as an ally. His was an unlikely accomplishment: a multimillion dollar ministry in an Atlanta neighborhood where 20 percent of citizens lived below the poverty line. Yet the ministry itself seemed proof that Dollar's optimistic brand of self-help delivered concrete results.

Believers, for the most part, wanted their leaders to live well. Yet these examples of lavish living rarely escaped the criticism that they exploited their followers by profiting from their donations. Media pundits relentlessly cataloged televangelists' assets and expenses as evidence of greed and probable corruption. Insiders protested that heaven's windows stood wide open, and pastors hardly could be faulted for acting on a divine prescription for prosperity. In truth, believers rarely acknowledged the line between manipulation and abundant living until it had been crossed. In 2007, the publication of images of Dollar's mansion provoked heated criticism, as did reports of Ohio evangelist Joyce Meyer's $23,000 toilet seat.[168] Yet, on the face of it, these displays of wealth were not a *theological* problem. Their divine economy operated on the principle that they lived in a world of more-than-enough. It was when pastors mishandled funds that believers typically lost faith. When Jim Bakker defrauded shareholders of Heritage USA, the problem at first was not that he profited. That he resorted to deception undermined the grounding logic of his gospel: wealth comes to any and all who ask. If accumulation was easy, why do it secretly? And why must he do it at the expense of others? Bakker, by his actions, had seemed to live in a world of not-enough.

The mighty fell hard. Famed faith teacher Robert Tilton made national news when reporters showed him dumping thousands of prayer requests into the dumpster after removing the money from the envelopes. In 2007, a lawsuit alleging the illegal use of university funds led Richard Roberts to resign his presidency of Oral Roberts University.[169] (The university survived with an infusion of cash from Pat Robertson and Christian retail mogul Mart Green, as well as the interim presidency of Billy Joe Daugherty of Victory Christian Center.) The same year, Senator Chuck Grassley of Iowa opened an investigation into the finances of many of the most famous names in prosperity theology: Benny Hinn, Eddie Long, Joyce Meyer, Kenneth and Gloria Copeland, Creflo and Taffi Dollar, and Randy and Paula White. It was a narrow road, and few managed to walk it without rebuke.

Some gave up the prosperity gospel altogether. Jimmy Swaggart was one of the first. In 1982, in his *The Balanced Faith Life*, Swaggart excoriated his fellow Assemblies of God televangelists for preaching prosperity theology, retracting the message that he himself had espoused in *The Confession Principle and the Course of Nature*, published earlier that year.[170] Jim Bakker's post-prison biography *I Was Wrong* denounced the faith message as false. The globetrotting healer Benny Hinn waffled. The celebrity T. D. Jakes played both sides of the prosperity debate. Though he closely associated himself with prosperity preachers, promoting the ministries of up-and-coming faith teachers like Paula White, he avoided the "P-word" for fear of "being positioned in a camp of preachers who some say have marginalized the Gospel and relegated it in favor of capitalist ideals." He rejected the "so-called Prosperity Gospel" as a confused attempt to reach a "capitalistic, tax-sheltered heaven."[171] The elderly Kenneth Hagin penned *The Midas Touch* to correct some of the abuses of the movement he helped shape, forbidding ministers to "lead people to believe that prosperity means conspicuous, lavish wealth. It simply is not true that everyone who has faith for prosperity will live in a palace, drive a luxurious car, and dress in expensive designer-label clothes."[172] Before his death, he assembled a meeting of some of the leading prosperity preachers (including Kenneth Copeland) and castigated preachers who sought financial gain, corrupting spiritual truths with wrong motivations at the expense of the Body of Christ. Yet the

message that faith works had proved so successful that no one, not even
Hagin, could take it back.

Tammy Faye Bakker later recalled that the impetus behind Heritage
USA was that they wanted a place where followers could catch the vision
of PTL. Most preachers undoubtedly would have built a church. That the
Bakkers built a Christian wonderland testified to the joyful and enter-
prising spirit of the movement. They had wanted believers to meet Jehovah Jireh, the God of more-than-enough.

4

Health

Jehovah Rapha (my healer)

THE VICTORIOUS FAITH CENTER (VFC) in Durham, North Carolina, was lit up like a jack-o'-lantern, its orange-tinted fluorescent lights illuminating the bustling sanctuary as seen from the street outside. Sandwiched between a nail salon and a payday loan office in a mini-mall, the storefront church rang with shouts of praise and prayer on this and every Wednesday night. A dozen or so women—elders, deacons, and mothers of the church—bantered and laughed as they prepared for the service. The din of chatter ceased when a woman stumbled through the doors and stood teetering there, her eyes scanning the room and her face twisting as if she were in pain. A mother of the church sprang from her seat, crossed the room, and pulled the newcomer, a fellow church member, into a tight hug.[1] "Praise God!" Shouts of encouragement erupted from all corners. The woman's face brightened and ran with tears as people clustered around her in a spontaneous praise circle.

"I'm going to praise His name!" sang the church mother, beginning the familiar tune of a VFC favorite. "Each day is just the same!" joined another. The stomping of tennis shoes on the beige-carpeted floor anchored the chorus:

He healed my body, He touched my mind,
He saved me JUST IN TIME.[2]

The woman, whose name was Essence, I soon learned, had just taken her first unaided steps after a sudden illness had left her paralyzed. The VFC members celebrated her healing as a triumph over Satan, who robs believers of the health, prosperity, and abundant life that God grants to all the faithful.

As one of thousands of U.S. congregations belonging to the prosperity movement, the Victorious Faith Center practices healing as part of a broader prosperity theology, claiming divine health as a fundamental demonstration of the power of faith.

The drama of healing and health is a defining feature of the American prosperity movement, as believers use their bodies, and not just their finances, as a testing ground for their faith. Almost two-thirds of American pentecostals report that they have been healed or have seen another person healed, and it is clear that divine healing lays at the core of what captured prosperity believers' hearts.[3] Most faith teachers grew to accept a positive attitude toward medicine, leaving behind the antimedical rhetoric that characterized the postwar healing revivals. A minority, however, shunned hospitals and doctors and nurtured divine health only by spiritual disciplines such as prayer, fasting, and deliverance. Whether they accepted, or, like VFC, rejected biomedical solutions, believers ultimately put their confidence in the power of a divine prescription: faith.

Spiritual Promises and the Laws of Faith

Pastor John Walton, the senior pastor of the Victorious Faith Center, relished remembering the moment he realized that "traditional" Christianity was dead. Reared in a black Baptist church in Durham, North Carolina, he had known nothing of miracles and spiritual gifts—just lively preaching and the boisterous praise of the assembled. One Sunday, a man interrupted the Baptist service, approaching the altar with the shrill repetition of "Praise Jesus! Praise Jesus!" Walton, though a layperson at the time, approached the pastor with a warning from God. "God said, 'That's not my spirit in him,'" Walton told the pastor. The Baptist pastor, Walton remembered, turned to him sharply.[4] "*You* do something!" he retorted.

"I ran up to the man, put my hands on him, and I declared 'In the name of the Lord Jesus, come OUT of this man!'" The man dropped to the ground, shrieking. Walton's eyes widened in the telling. "He moved across the floor like a snake. Like he had not a bone in his body." Walton grabbed the slithering demoniac by the leg as the man vomited up the spirit, which lay like a green, glistening sac on the church floor. In the chaos of the altar scene, Walton glanced back at his pastor. There he was, said Walton, hiding behind the pulpit. Traditional Christianity, for all its Bible reading, praising, and community support, had failed. It was dead without the one thing Walton claimed that day, a word he repeated in his deep baritone: power.

Prosperity theology claims a power rooted in the operation of faith. Believers conceptualize faith as a causal agent, a power that actualizes events and objects in the real world. Faith acts as a force that reaches through the boundaries of materiality and into the spiritual realm, as if plucking objects from there and drawing them back into space and time. As Kenneth Hagin explained, "It is already real in the spirit realm. But we want it to become real in this physical realm where we live in the flesh."[5] Faith makes things "real," transcending the separation between two universes for the sake of each believer.

Grounded in the thought of E. W. Kenyon, and following well-established pentecostal precedents, the prosperity gospel promises divine health as a provision of the atonement, connecting Jesus' crucifixion with believers' physical healing. The words of Isaiah sealed the promise: "But he was wounded for our transgressions, he was bruised for our iniquities: the chastisement of our peace was upon him; and with his stripes we are healed" (Isaiah 53:5).[6] Prosperity teachers, though varying widely in interpretation and focus, agreed on three fundamental ideas. First, healing is God's divine intention for humanity. Second, Jesus' work on the cross earned not only redemption from sin but also deliverance from its penalties: namely, poverty, demonic interference, and sickness. Third, God set up the laws of faith so that believers could access the power of the cross. Believers' primary task was to live into the power of the resurrected Christ by applying faith to their circumstances, measuring their lives and bodies for evidence of spiritual power.

Leaders perform divine health in its idealized form every Sunday. Many faith celebrities have made their own healing the centerpieces of their ministries, embodying God's healing power and the ability of believers to tap into that power. Oral Roberts, David Yonggi Cho, Nasir Siddiki, and Benny Hinn are but a few examples.[7] As the figurehead of the contemporary faith movement, Kenneth Hagin's own healing became the standard for all subsequent healing narratives. Stricken with tuberculosis and bedridden, a teenaged Hagin believed he was no longer sick after reading Mark 11:24: "Therefore I say unto you, What things soever ye desire, when ye pray, believe that ye receive them, and ye shall have them." As a result of Hagin's faith, he said: "I have not had one sick day in 45 years. I did not say that the devil hasn't attacked me. But before the day is out, I am healed."[8] Prosperity televangelists and megachurch pastors frequently cite their own divine health as the gold standard of faith, encouraging congregants to reflect prosperous living in their own bodies, minds, and circumstances.

Practices of Healing

"Does anyone need healing today?" Pastor John Walton, senior pastor of the Victorious Faith Center, called out to the 80 assembled before the close of the service. During my time at VFC, I had seen dozens of people respond to his calls for healing. A middle-aged man I recognized as new to the congregation approached the altar, and the two quietly discussed his symptoms. "Get this man a chair," Walton said. "Sit down!" The congregation sat expectantly as Walton knelt before the seated man, holding one outstretched leg in his hands. He diagnosed the problem easily. "One leg is shorter than the other!" he exclaimed and implored God to lengthen the other leg to match. "Oooh!" Walton exclaimed in surprise. "It jumped when I touched it just now!" We waited. Some moved quickly into prayer, both for the pastor and for the patient. Pastor Walton prayed heartily, but not exuberantly, as he asked for God's healing touch. When he finished, the brief expected show of agility followed, as Pastor Walton asked the man to touch his toes several times, like an athlete warming up for a sprint. Everyone burst into applause. Walton smiled. "Praise Jesus!" someone called out.

From the pulpit, VFC preached a clear route to healing. Right standing with the divine focused on sacred alignment, a mystical connection that harmonized the believer with God. Prosperity theology asserted that people shared in God's healing power by activating their faith and tapping into God's spiritual laws. For the sick congregants of the Victorious Faith Center, healing restored both mental and physical wholeness and aligned believers with God's divine intentions. These public acts of healing consistently exhibited a moment of spiritual fulfillment when believers succeeded in reinvigorating their spiritual authority over the demonic causes of their illnesses. Psychological, social, behavioral, emotional, and physical causes could be rooted out and identified as spiritual realities: a spirit of cancer, a spirit of laziness, a spirit of jealousy, etc. As Pastor Walton argued, "It's all spiritual! It's all spiritual. It is! Because it deals with spirits." What outsiders categorized as distinct etiologies, VFC churchgoers attributed to a single spiritual cause subject to an epistemic cure.

Within this Holy Spirit framework, healing required that belief and practice mutually reinforce one another. Rather than accepting illness with passive resignation, prosperity believers understood the will as the master of the body.[9] Believers understood their senses to be deceptive, ruled by what E. W. Kenyon called "sense knowledge"; they did not simply wait for their bodies to assure them that healing had occurred. They believed and *acted as if* it had. A few examples will illustrate the centrality of performances of faith. A respected elder taught Sunday school, where he urged believers to avoid negative confession by keeping their troubles to themselves. "If anyone asks," he said, mimicking a hobbled walk with a crutch, "Just say 'I'm blessed! I'm going on in Christ!'" Rather than asking for prayer again and again, the believer must ignore "sense knowledge" and trust that God has already healed because enacted faith would not be limited by circumstances. "On your deathbed you'd better be saying 'By His stripes, I am healed!'"[10] The elder's instruction to mimic health was not an invitation to fakery, but rather to imitate the desired outcome, entwining action and belief. Going through the motions of divine health, similar to the nineteenth-century faith cure practice of "acting faith," put performance on an equal footing with reality. Take the common occurrence of a VFC believer, who, after receiving a revelation from Pastor Walton that they were healed, began a "shout" (an ecstatic dance of praise). Published guides for positive confession of healing and health ended with the prompt, "Now praise Him for it!" as if it were already so.[11] Or, to return to the case of the VFC member's public healing from a stunted leg, the man was not asked how he *felt* but rather to perform exercises enacting a healed body. Performance and belief were linked so that believers acted out their healing before they identified symptoms to confirm it.

This application of healing power remained virtually unchanged from its inception in the cradle of the postwar pentecostal healing revivals. Divine healing stood on certainty. "Your healing," argued Creflo Dollar, "is not based on whether the doctor can heal you; it's based on the Word and your covenant with God for the healing of your spirit, soul, and body."[12] After all, God revealed himself as Jehovah Rapha—the Lord who healeth thee.[13] Even the tumult over the HIV/AIDS epidemic in the mid-1980s did little to dampen prosperity teachers' enthusiasm for God's medicine; healers like Don Stewart and Kenneth Copeland took on seemingly impossible cases with the assurance of the cross. "Receive your healing," Copeland told AIDS victims at his 1987 West Coast Believer's Convention as he embraced them, "for Jesus Christ of Nazareth now makes you whole."[14] Pastor Walton counted the healing of a man in the final stages of AIDS as one of the most meaningful miracles he had seen. God restored the man, said Walton, when he was delivered of the spirit of homosexuality. Illness, after all, indicated a spiritual problem that required a spiritual solution.

In the 1980s and 1990s, the healing ministries of Morris Cerullo, Benny Hinn, Don Stewart, Frances and Charles Hunter, and Kenneth and Gloria Copeland drew hundreds of thousands of American believers to urban healing conferences. Some stressed the metaphysical underpinnings of the practice. Cleansing Stream Ministries offered heavily endorsed retreats that guided participants into "spiritual alignment" with the "flow of blessing and anointing."[15] Others reconciled with medical sciences, placing doctors and preachers at the podium together. Though promising an alternative (or supplement) to medical intervention, faith healers appropriated medical rhetoric for their own use. In the late 1980s, Larry Lea, former dean of the Signs and Wonders Seminary at Oral Roberts University, rekindled widespread interest in the power of prayer for healing. He hosted "prayer clinics" with the purpose of unlocking the "secrets of prayer."[16] Teachers often referred to positive confession as "taking your medication," recommending daily doses of healing-related scripture to tend to any need.[17]

As before, believers shared faith in the power of religious objects to prevent, diagnose, and treat illness. Many faith teachers followed the widespread pentecostal use of handkerchiefs, cloths, or ribbons to convey healing. For example, Oral Roberts, Marilyn Hickey, and Benny Hinn made such "points of contact" a staple of their divine healing ministries, asking believers to place an object that had been specially "blessed" on the afflicted area. At times, preachers chose objects with symbolic as well as talismanic value. Creflo Dollar advised the saints to cure poverty with dollar bills hidden in their shoes.[18] The widowed Evelyn Wyatt sent a golden key to every *Wings of Healing* donor to open the windows of heaven. Oral Roberts, though one of the era's most influential Christian leaders, cultivated the impression that he was only an arm's length away. He mailed out thousands of handkerchiefs with an imprint of his anointed right hand so that believers might receive a special blessing by laying their hand upon his.[19]

An anointed ribbon or a handkerchief mailed by a famous evangelist was not simply a reminder of faith, but a vehicle for it. A letter to Baltimore evangelist R. G. Hardy illustrates the personalized significance of these objects:

Dear Radio Pastor, I've been reading about your good works and faith you have in Christ. . . . I was having black spots coming over my eyes. I couldn't see good, and it just worried me. I was so worried and weak in my body. I placed your magazine under my head, and the next morning the spots were gone! Thank God for you and your books![20]

Smaller ministries like Hardy's typically traded on more experimental forms of the miraculous than the well-established teachers. Those who relied exclusively on mass mailings typically offered the most unusual tokens, promises, and prophecies. California revivalist Peter Popoff regularly included pages of instructions on how to use his miracle oil, pennies, or handkerchiefs at ominous moments in the day or night so that believers might exact the greatest result. Victorious Faith Center churchgoers fondly remembered Pastor Walton's use of an anointed handkerchief as a symbol of a powerful spiritual era. Yet Walton had eventually set aside the handkerchief so as not to seem to rely on it, for the movement maintained a deep ambivalence to the sacred and profane uses of objects. The ritual uses of any item stood in tension with an emphasis on the sufficiency of positive confession, as prosperity theology taught that the spiritual required no material medium. Further, to those drawing on voodoo, hoodoo, or black spiritualist understandings of sacred relics, it might also signal that congregants began to see the object as invested with its own power. The term "contact" itself reflected an intentional distancing from undesirable spiritual corollaries—icon, relic, sacrament—all which pointed to Catholicism and perceived superstitions.

A spiritually healthy mind provided the only true immunity. Sickness was a mental contagion and wrong thinkers spread their diseases. "You know God heals," argued Word of Faith teacher John Avanzini. "You may experience symptoms of a sickness. They may manifest themselves in pain or in some inability. Your mind will want to reason from these symptoms that you are sick and may even become sicker."[21] Healing began with an epistemic change, a mind turned toward God's divine precepts. What the sick required most was *knowledge*. Quoting Hosea 4:6, divine healers typically warned that God's people "perished for lack of knowledge."[22] Believers needed to ferret out the lying symptoms from the gospel truth— the faithful were healed the moment they believed. It pitted the mind against the body, whose painful symptoms seemingly contradicted God's promises. In Frederick Price's healing manual, *Is Healing For All?*, only two short steps separated believers from divine health: (1) Prayer claiming God's promise of health; (2) thanksgiving and positive confession to be prayed "until the physical manifestations of the healing takes place."[23]

The book coached sufferers on how to maintain a godly state of mind, including a warning to keep silent about how they felt since it would only privilege sense knowledge. However rampant prosperity theology's materialism may have been, its priority on mind and spirit ran bone-deep.

Sunday Healing

In the arched sanctuary of the First Cathedral of Bloomfield, Connecticut, a rich pageantry of spiritual performances unfolded. One hundred choir members filled the loft above the pulpit, along with sharply dressed musicians on electric guitar, bass, drums, and electric organ, swaying and belting out their praises to God. On the platform below, at the right of the pulpit, stood a small detachment of white-collared pastors who paced and nodded, while at the left sat the spiritual dignitaries on throne-like chairs. There, Bishop LeRoy Bailey, First Lady Reathie Bailey, and the preacher for the morning presided over a thousand predominately African American worshippers whose waving, singing, and shouting filled the space with rousing praise. Performers and audience alternated in the call-response style service, and worship built 45 minutes of spiritual momentum, from the welcome and announcements to the climactic call for "seed money." In the afterglow of the offertory, the bishop began the celebration of communion by elevating the bread: "This is my body, broken for you, do this in remembrance of me." To this customary rite, he added a brief reminder that prosperity would follow as the fruit of Jesus' suffering. At this, many cheered. Raising the cup he said: "This is the blood of Christ, shed for you . . . but he was pierced for our transgressions, he was bruised for our iniquities, the punishment that brought us peace was upon him."[24] Here the congregation joined in with the pastor: "And by his wounds *we are healed!*" Triumphant shouts rippled through the crowd, joyful that the cross had snuffed out any further need for sickness in God's kingdom. Though the high drama of an evangelist's Miracle Crusade may have seemed the right setting for divine healing, most believers were given the opportunity to reach out for the miraculous in their local congregational worship.

In the bustle of Sunday services, believers found a multitude of entry points to divine health. Church services provided several significant opportunities for worshippers to silence sense knowledge and (so the saying went) to take God at his word. The first step, of course, was getting through the door. At VFC, Pastor Walton preached almost weekly about how poor church attendance led to failed health. Once inside church walls, participants could sink into the familiar rhythms of corporate spiritual performances intended to draw them into mental and physical restoration. Through confession, worship, and communion, the saints enlivened their spirits and acted as those whom God had favored.

Worship was a powerful catalyst for healing. As in most Protestant worship services, music set the rhythm and tone of the meeting, from congregational singing to the barely there chords accompanying the closing prayer. Within African American faith congregations of all denominational stripes, music further punctuated the sermons with emotional crescendos. In a spiritual world dominated by right-mindedness, song prepared the heart to receive God's truth. As verbal confession set faith in motion, song offered opportunities for believers to activate the spiritual laws to effect divine healing. Most Sunday faith services devoted as much time to song as to preaching, and music served as a lengthy and guided form of positive confession. Keeping in mind the two steps to healing— one request followed by perpetual praise—the meaning and forms of right worship become clearer. In the simple and repetitive musical phrases of most prosperity hymnody, worshippers found the right words to accelerate the work of faith.

At the close of an evening service at World Harvest Church in Greensboro, North Carolina, visiting preacher Kenneth Hagin Jr., the heir and acting head of Rhema Bible Training Center, demonstrated the tight connection between worship and healing.[25] As his confident alto tapered to a whisper, he reminded the 500 assembled that "God's cure is the praise cure, and it doesn't cost a dime. So let's start now! Lift your voices!"[26] The backup trio of vocalists began to sing softly. "What do you want?" he called out. "What do you want!?" He urged the crowd to call out their deepest desires. Only a few voices began at first, but more followed until Hagin had to shout above the din. After a minute or so, Hagin and the praise team sweetened the clamor into song with the familiar tune of "Shout unto God." The lyrics gloried in Satan's defeat, Christ's victory over death, and the Christian need to "lift our voice in victory."[27]

As the song closed, Hagin paced the low stage. "What are you going to do when you are alone? Praise! What are you doing to do when you need healing? Shout! Praise is the cure!" Hagin looked out at the crowd with satisfaction, and removed his suit jacket. "I was going to close but . . . is anyone having back pain?" A dozen people pressed into the aisle and streamed to the front where Hagin prayed with them, one by one, as a new song promising divine healing rippled through the auditorium. In Hagin's praise cure, music not only provided a theological script but also acted as a trigger for divine healing. It cultivated the atmosphere in which people could name their desires, then offered them the words required to set the principles of divine healing in motion. Worshippers could benefit from the cyclical language of the oft-repeated choruses, repeating positive confessions that ideally allowed participants to "release" their faith. Finally, Hagin stepped in to complete what the music had begun.

Healing and communion accompanied one another with unnoticed harmony. Though the Lord's Supper did not receive the theological and liturgical attention of tithing rituals, it nonetheless served as the most powerful signifier of Christ's resurrection power. For believers, the power was indelibly personal. Receiving the bread and wine (juice), believers often personalized Jesus' agony as their own. As one of Kenneth Hagin's standard confessions for health specified, "He took *my* infirmities, He bore *my* sickness By His stripes *I* am healed."[28] Some VFC members surmised that each lash Jesus received in his Passion corresponded to every known disease, ensuring that God knew precisely what the sick endured. Winnipeg megachurch pastor Leon Fontaine went so far as to say that when Jesus bore humanity's sin on the cross, he physically embodied all diseases. This message designed for first-time visitors enumerated Jesus' many illnesses, the multiplication of cancer cells, the bacterial spread of tuberculosis, and even swelling limbs of elephantiasis. The comfort lay in the specificity, the knowledge that Jesus' pain and victory embraced one's own. In this way, Jesus became a deeply personal savior, whose body experienced and conquered each ache and pain.

Communion carried powerful healing properties. Some followed evangelical Protestants in treating the Lord's Supper as a symbol and token of remembrance. "We take communion to remember what Christ already accomplished for us," remarked Mark Brazee, pastor of World Outreach Church in Tulsa. If what people lacked was *knowledge*, a reminder would suffice to effect divine health: "Communion services should be some of the biggest healing rallies around because we should partake of the emblems, saying, 'Thank You, Jesus, by Your shed blood my sins are washed away. By Your broken body, I'm healed."[29] For others, when traditional means of healing failed, people held out hope that bread and wine might contain an extra measure of resurrection power. Benny Hinn offered the elements as a means of transmitting God's healing power, arguing that the bread and wine were much more than symbols. "They are spirit!" he argued fervently, "The body is spirit. The blood is spirit. We take it into our bodies as spirit."[30] Communion was the ritual by which believers ingested God's spirit in order to restore their own to health, a practice that held deep resonances with Catholic notions of the sacraments as a material vehicle of grace. In his adaptation of the Words of Institution (the narrative of the Last Supper), Hinn asked the crowd to repeat: "As I partake of this bread, heal my body. As I partake of this wine, heal my body. Make my body whole." Communion brought healing power out of the spiritual realm and allowed participants to make it indelibly their own. Miraculous testimonies abounded. Faith evangelist Marilyn Hickey avowed that a wheelchair-bound woman, though "no one laid hands upon her, and no one prayed for her" got out of her wheelchair and walked after having received communion.[31]

Destiny Christian Center, a nondenominational African American megachurch in Greensboro, North Carolina, made communion a weekly ritual of healing faith.[32] After almost an hour of playful dance-in-the-aisles worship, Senior Pastor Lee Stokes—a former employee of both Rod Parsley and Benny Hinn—encouraged the assembled to "grab your sacraments!"— a double-sealed juice and wafer set handed out by the greeters upon arrival. As we peeled open our communion wafers, Stokes explained the healing significance of the familiar verses of 1 Corinthians 11:17–34 instructing the disciples to celebrate the Lord's Supper. "The whole purpose of communion," Stokes argued, "is to bring healing to your body . . . This is one of the biggest secrets of the Kingdom to combat the aging process! To combat sickness and decay!" Believers grow weak and die when they do not understand what Jesus did on the cross.[33] "This might not mean that much to you yet," he acknowledged to the congregation of mostly twenty- and thirty-somethings, "but every birthday that passes this will mean more to you. We should be living until a hundred and twenty years old!" He raised his communion cup in the air. "It is the will of God for you to be healed one hundred percent of the time. Jesus paid too great a price for you not to be. We can have blessed bodies, blessed children, blessed marriages, blessed riches, blessed . . ."

A signal from an usher in the back brought the proceedings to a halt. A mother of the church wanted prayer for healing, and three husky ushers half-carried her to the front where Stokes labored in prayer for her for ten minutes, often pausing to encourage the congregation to pray on her behalf. "Does anyone else need healing today?" Stokes called out finally, foregoing his sermon entirely for an unscripted healing service. A dozen people approached the stairs to the wide platform, where Stokes moved between petitioners at a dizzying pace. The congregation swayed, sang, and prayed intermittently for the next half hour as Stokes ministered to the sick and the worship band led a familiar call-and-response tune.[34]

"I'm blessed," crooned the praise leader.

"Blessed," echoed the congregation again and again, as their voices merged in the verse. They sang about the "fresh anointing" of the spirit that granted them power and prosperity in the here and now. The young congregation, encouraged to have as much fun in church as at a night club, danced and threw their hands up in the air as they sang "I'm living in the overflow! I'm living in the overflow!" Children twirled in the aisles and couples shared affectionate glances as they hit the refrain: "I've got more than *enough*. I'm coming to get my *stuff*." Prosperity, health, body, and spirit all came together in the new sacramentalism of the American prosperity gospel.

In word, song, and communion, Sunday gatherings offered worshippers a familiar and supportive atmosphere in which to align their minds to God's truths and experience the fruits of divine healing.

Keeping Your Healing

Good health required full participation in the liturgical and sacramental life of the church. Devout believers spent the week in spiritual preparation for their corporate worship, often fasting, praying, and preparing themselves for what God might have in store. A sense of heightened spiritual intensity electrified Sunday mornings, particularly for those waiting for answers to their prayers. Suspended confirmation—a healing believed but not yet experienced—required believers to position themselves to be blessed. Though followers frequently described God's provision as a direct channel, some language suggested a circuitous route between the waiting believer and their personal miracle. The saints left room for answers to prayer that did not always arrive on schedule. "Some lessons can't be taught," so the saying went, "they can only be caught." Often, believers held out for a word of revelation from the pastor or a visiting evangelist. Prophetic revelations frequently manifested as visual cues; one visiting pastor, for example, described seeing clouds above the heads of those for whom he had a message. Angels, doves, dragons, and clouds of light leapt out of the realm of metaphor and danced around the sanctuary. Pastor Walton's acute spiritual sensitivities allowed him to see and hear things "in the spirit," an ability that allowed him to monitor his congregants' faith lives.

Those with chronic pain or problems did not revisit the altar. As healing had unfolded once-and-for-all, church life did not make liturgical space for those whose prayers had not yet manifested. Ruth, a pillar of VFC, lived in the not-yet. She did not yet experience the benefits of her faith, and she struggled with an ailment she would not speak aloud. Although Ruth had become one of my closest consultants and someone I considered a friend, she avoided being interviewed. Concerned, I asked Ruth's best friend and another close consultant, Anita.

"Is she worried about having to talk about the fact that she . . ." I stumbled for words, "hasn't been healed?"

"No. No," Anita countered quickly. "She has been healed. She is just claiming her healing. No, I think she's worried about negatively confessing." Saints who had "claimed their healing" must maintain their faith until the physical evidence corresponded to the mind's assent, a process known as "keeping their healing." Spiritual vigilance was essential during this period, as believers had to be careful not to speak or act in any way that might hinder their blessing.

God's healing promise was that all who ask *will* receive healing, but few who received God's blessings "keep" them. As Benny Hinn explained, "We know that in the presence of God there is healing, and I would give all that I have to see people healed, so I really believe it is the fault of the person. They have failed to enter into God's presence and allow Him to touch them."[35] On returning from a Creflo Dollar conference in Atlanta, a VFC elder described his disappointment that, though every attendee had received healing, few maintained their divine health. Careless words were the common culprit. Pastor Walton recalled a healing service where he had seen a woman cured of arthritis, but then only a short while later that same woman was clearly not healed. "I know you delivered this lady," he told the Lord hesitantly, to which God replied: "Listen to what she's saying." When Pastor Walton approached the woman about her healing, she told him that she had arthritis. "She was claiming it!" Walton said incredulously. "And when I tried to talk to her about changing her confession, it was a losing battle. You could confess your faults, or you can confess your faith. Many times Christians say the wrong thing," he concluded. To be sure, not every avid participant lived up to this requirement all the time. For example, Alisha, who grew up in the church, wandered into church one Sunday long after the sermon had begun and plunked down loudly in the back row beside me. She had been sitting in the car for most of the service, she told me in a congested voice. After blowing her nose loudly a few times, she abruptly stood up again. "I'm sick! I'm going home!" she half-whispered, loud enough for most to hear. Come Sunday morning, however, most VFC members attempted to live by these guidelines, limiting their small talk to positive subjects and spiritual topics.

Divine health, at times, was a difficult pill to swallow. Prosperity theology promised once-and-for-all healing, a mechanism that immediately released God's power in people's lives. The saints asked and received healing in a single moment. Yet in the long stretches between the spiritual peaks of the Christian life, believers had to make sense of the waiting without the comforts of soliciting prayer. "If you pray and you believe that you have received you can never pray about it again," argued Frederick Price. "Only to the extent of thanking the Lord that you believe you have it . . . but you sure can't ask for it again. Because if you ask for it again, you've just said by asking that you didn't believe you received it. And therefore the system is short-circuited. And it can't work! Because if you did have it, why would you ask for it again?"[36] For some, this enforced silence led to new isolation. One interviewee described his father's place of prominence within a faith church until he was stricken with cancer. Weekly, his father would go up to the altar for prayer. The church leaders stopped him at the altar one day and instructed him to stop coming for prayer. "There's nothing else anyone can do for you," they said. "You have to heal yourself." In the certainty of prayer and healing, sufferers struggled to keep their healing by means of right confession and thanksgiving, waiting for one spiritual season to change into the next.

Deliverance

It was our northern-most stop on Benny Hinn's 2008 Holy Land Tour, and 900 spiritual tourists were checking into the Nazareth Plaza Hotel to see Benny Hinn perform miracles in Jesus' backyard. I had joined this two-week excursion as a traveling ethnographer, hoping to learn more about the spiritual expectations of these pilgrims who invested time and money on a modern prophet of healing and finance.

We were all hot and tired, waiting for the peppy tour guides to call our room assignments while we combed the sea of bags to retrieve our luggage. Even over the loud hum of activity, I could hear a familiar shrill voice clear across the lobby. It was Miyu, a fashionable young Japanese woman who sat in the first row of my bus, alone and usually in the grip of emotion. Here under the bright lights of the lobby, her tear-stained face and disheveled hair made her look as if she were coming undone. On the first day, my bus mates had marveled at Miyu's intense spirituality as she wept openly over her first glimpse of the Holy City. But by the fourth day, they had begun to mutter with concern and some suspicion when she burst into tears at a diamond refinery where Benny Hinn's tour organizers had deposited us for an afternoon. And today, before a crowded assembly, her face twitched as she paced and shouted at the staff. She had been the first to get a room key, but her face registered dismay at being assigned a roommate when she had paid for a single room. Dismay turned to tears and then to yelling. At first, she shouted short bursts of Japanese, while hotel staff brought her a chair, then some water, though they were refused. As fellow members of the tour attempted to intervene, her body was wracked with the same trembling that had earlier been interpreted as a spiritual manifestation. With her glassy eyes, grimaces, and trembling frame, Miyu was quickly becoming a spectacle. In this heightened atmosphere, the spiritual verdict was soon read. A woman approached her with concern and a little trepidation, raising a hand out toward her:

"Father, in your name, I rebuke this demon! I call out this . . ."

"You can't talk to me that way!" Miyu shouted back.

"Let her alone," said an elderly woman quietly, watching from a distance. "She was fine earlier, just let her calm down." The hotel wait staff and a tour guide came to intervene, brushing the exorcist away as they asked Miyu to retake her seat. The bus matriarchs, waiting with me for their luggage, debated the matter.

"She is unwell," murmured one. "I knew it on the first day."

"But she was manifesting!" said another, "You just can't talk to someone when they're in the spirit like that." The others shook their heads.

"Maybe it's medical, but this isn't the time. She needs testing first," observed one sister carefully.

In the meantime, Jim had taken notice of Miyu. I had met Jim in the lobby for only a moment, though in that time he had offered his spiritual resume to those assembled. Tall and graying, Jim spoke with his hands on his hips as he looked around. He had just written a book and would someday, he believed, be traveling with Benny Hinn ministries. "I have the office of a prophet," he announced. (He felt this confirmed because he had muscled his way onto the crusade stage the night before and been prayed for by Hinn himself.[37]) Passing through the lobby, Jim noticed

FIGURE 4.1 **Touching Benny** Participants of Benny Hinn's Holy Land Tour jostle one another to touch the divine healer on the set of his *This Is Your Day!* program on location in Jerusalem, 2008.

Source: Author's photo.

Miyu's condition and immediately launched into his own spontaneous exorcism. I looked up to see Jacob, our Jewish tour guide, shooing away Jim and his outstretched hands.

Exhausted, I was soon lined up for dinner. Then I saw a familiar face. Jim was coming toward me. He caught sight of my serious expression, stopped dead, and raised his hands over the buffet table where I was scooping up some hummus. "Father God, I ask that you pray for that girl. Pray that she may come to know you." Unsure of how to respond, I paused to reply. But Jim did not notice. His eyes were already squeezed tightly as he prayed loudly for another miracle.

Prosperity believers were vigilant interpreters of the body. Signs of favor. Signs of decline. Signs of spiritual interference made fellow Christians into battlegrounds. Believers expected to counteract even the most intractable foes. Demonic forces, manifested in any state of mental or physical distress such as anxiety, cancer, or paralysis, were no match for the spiritual weapons prosperity believers had at hand. "Deliverance," the process of breaking spiritual strongholds, was chief among them. Unlike exorcism, which referred specifically to the ejection of a demonic personality, deliverance included a range of practices. Although the church drew techniques for deliverance from a variety of sources, VFC members largely practiced methods popularized in charismatic circles in the 1970s and 1980s and in prosperity groups in the 1980s and 1990s.[38] Using a popular deliverance manual as a guide, the church began a ministry that earned it a local reputation as a deliverance specialist.[39] The deliverance team, men and women trained for spiritual warfare, would first privately question the patient about their sins, asking a comprehensive list of questions designed to inventory the person's spiritual history. In a process that often took hours, the participant pored over the past and present to shine a light on demonic manifestations embedded in habits, generational curses, and emotional distress. The team, through prayer and the laying on of hands, commanded the devils in Jesus' name to be gone. In a spiritual practice referred to as "purging," the believer was coached to cough up the demons by vomiting.[40] This preliminary deliverance required total disclosure by the patient and sincere repentance, as an incomplete deliverance brought about the return of multiplied demonic forces. Once delivered, believers were encouraged to "take themselves through deliverance," purging the spirits in their bathrooms at home and praying the blood of Christ upon themselves (to invoke Jesus' atonement as salvation and protection).[41]

Deliverance ministries remained an important specialty among strongly spirit-centered prosperity teachers. While soft prosperity intuited emotional states with sensitivity, hard prosperity folk tested the atmosphere for the presence of angels and demons. Evangelists like Benny Hinn, Reinhard Bonnke, and Benson Idahosa identified and combated spiritual interference through a range of practices, from the targeted repentance and purging practiced by VFC, to prayer walks, spiritual mapping, public exorcisms, and deliverance seminars.[42] Overseas crusades were still the largest public gatherings devoted to deliverance, so it is no surprise that in American churches these practices were especially popular with Christian immigrants, especially Africans and Latin Americans.

Smaller networks sprang up devoted to the art of deliverance. Typically, they were hard prosperity preachers, adept at following the circumstances of people's lives back to their spiritual origin. Apostle Ernest Leonard, whose logo read "You Don't Have to Take the Devil's Junk," led a black apostolic network of conferences, churches, and ministers devoted to deliverance. His weekly appearances on Black Entertainment Television and well-publicized conferences made him a familiar figure. Always dressed in a uniform befitting a field marshal, he was a spiritual general ready to do combat with spirits of "fear, barrenness, self-inflicted curses, poverty, witchcraft, anxiety, suicide, rejection, the Occult and hundreds more!"[43]

These new apostolic churches, stacked with "fivefold" offices like apostle and prophet, were links in vast transnational networks that intertwined healing, deliverance, and divine money.[44] Healing networks like Randy Clark's Global Awakening purposely set themselves apart from prosperity ministries by downplaying promises of financial blessings. But others simply added prosperity to the long list of miracles. In pentecostal magazines, a typical advertisement—for example one for a 2008 deliverance convention on the topic of the "12 Streams of Increase"—was illustrated with photos of assorted apostles, bishops, prophets, and prophetesses under a shower of $20 bills. By the 1990s, the church-growth guru Peter Wagner had turned his attention to the global surge of apostolic ministries. His Global Harvest Ministries made clear the connection between deliverance from demonic forces and financial prosperity in a 2006 "Apostolic Decree" that read:

> I hereby take the apostolic authority that I have been given by God as an ambassador for the kingdom of God. . . . I declare this to the principalities and powers who have been agents of Satan to obstruct this transfer of wealth for too long: Your time is up! Your evil powers are broken! . . . Let go of the wealth of the nations! I loose this wealth for the kingdom of God. What has been loosed on earth will be loosed in heaven!
>
> I decree that vast amounts of wealth will be released supernaturally, even from godless and pagan sources. I decree that large numbers of God's chosen people will be empowered in fresh and creative ways to gain wealth according to Deuteronomy 8:18. New inventions will multiply. Disruptive technologies will change the life patterns of the whole human race. The earth will disgorge vast riches of hidden resources. These will be entrusted to God's agents. Profits will increase exponentially.[45]

My second encounter with deliverance came as a surprise. On route to our second encounter with Benny Hinn (a sermon delivered on the shores of the Sea of Galilee) an unscholarly thing occurred. I got sick. Our concerned guide quickly identified it as heat exhaustion, common among tourists in Israel. My symptoms met with general dismay. I soon realized that being even mildly ill among people who searched their bodies for evidence of spiritual power was an occasion for drama.

I was too sick to hear most of the crusade. My seatmate on the bus, Sarah, tried to escort me to the event, but I had to turn back.

"Actually, I think I might have to meet you later. Could you save me a seat?" I asked.

"Sure," she said and stopped, looking at me more intently. "I can see that it's not out of you yet."

It. What was inside of me suddenly took not only shape but also character. I found refuge in a nearby hotel and soon fell asleep on a lobby couch. I awoke to Sarah's concerned face as she kneeled beside me.

"Kate, I came back because I needed to tell you something. I didn't want you to be afraid. What's inside of you is trying to come out," she continued. "What are your symptoms?"

I hedged. A polite Canadian never talks about such things. "My stomach. My head hurts." She frowned.

"Your head hurts because you've been forcing it down by thinking too much. You're too much up here," she said, gesturing to her head. "Okay? You can't reason your way out of this. This is spiritual. What's inside of you is a spirit trying to get out." She pressed on. "Have you thrown up just now?"

"No," I said. She frowned again.

"You need to vomit this out." She paused. Perhaps she sensed my distress or fatigue, because her forehead crinkled and she smiled reassuringly. "Don't worry! There is no sense trying to figure out why this happened. It could be any number of things. You said that you talk a lot so maybe it was something you said. Or something you did. But it doesn't matter. Now is not the time and the Holy Spirit will reveal it to you when you're ready. And don't be embarrassed! This happens to everyone. I just want you to know what to do about it. I want you to go into the bathroom and try to throw up. And if you can't, just go like this," she said, mimicking gagging. "You'll be doing it by faith." With that, she stood up abruptly. She flashed a brilliant smile. "You'll be fine." And she left.

Sarah had just advised me to exorcise myself of a spiritual demon. Indeed, purging as a spiritual discipline was part of the teaching set forth by Don Basham and Derek Prince, who argued that Christians could be targets for demonic activity and that "in most cases the spirits seem to leave through the mouth."[46] This practice illumined the importance of reading signs and acting on them for healing. In a spiritual cosmos oriented by materiality, believers found the body to be an unruly but reliable marker of faith. Illness became evidence, causally indeterminate, but evidence nonetheless. Purging the spirit provided the counter-evidence, proof that demonic forces had fled.

Deliverance required action and faith in lock step. Thought without speech or healing without deliverance rendered faith impotent or, rather, proved its absence since believers understood their senses to be deceptive. Sarah's instruction to go through the motions of deliverance—or, earlier, the VFC elder's teaching on mimicking health—placed performance and belief on equal footing.

Observers who focused on public displays of healing—the high drama of a miracle crusade—might forget that behind these demonstrations, an individualistic ethos was at work. To return to my case, though I *got sick* at a Benny Hinn Miracle Crusade, no one encouraged me to seek out Pastor Hinn. Rather, I was offered an American prescription: do it yourself.

Spiritual Competitors: Hoodoo

Across the faith movement, believers envisioned a spiritual cosmos dominated by unseen forces, divine and demonic, which steered the course of people's lives. Through Christ, believers commanded the authority to declare, as VFC members did in their Sunday confession, "Jesus lives in me. In Jesus' Name, I will cast out all devils. In Jesus' Name, I will lay hands on the sick and they shall recover." Though all the saints equipped themselves to "come up against" demonic interference, not all communities battled the same foe. For the parishioners of VFC, hoodoo and other African American folk practices contended for the saints' allegiances. Although largely invisible to outsiders, hoodoo (known also as "conjure" or "rootwork") has survived as a viable religious tradition in African American communities in the heavily Protestant South. Church members at the Victorious Faith Center spoke openly about its unwelcome presence, either as a supplement to Christianity or as an alternative.

Hoodoo persisted as a religion of utility. It came to the Anglo-Protestant South through African slaves whose descendents, despite large-scale conversions to Christianity during the Second Great Awakening, retained elements of their indigenous religious traditions.[47] The African-based traditions that survived the Christianization of slaves bore few of the markers of an "organized religion" that were found in its Catholic Voodoo or African Caribbean Santeria counterparts. Hoodoo boasted no priests or priestesses, sacrificial offerings, gathered community, or even devotion to ancestral spirits and de-ities.[48] Hoodoo functioned as a healing practice, not a cosmology. It was "a system of magic by which individual 'workers' serve their clients."[49] Most often, believers who hired a hoodoo "doctor" or "worker" sought to protect themselves from harm, particularly the evil intentions of others. Charms, composed of symbolic substances (such as hair, roots, or bones) were potent spiritual agents. Clients sought charms that could work for them; for ex-ample, a woman might purchase a love charm to induce a man to marry her. Clients also turned to hoodoo doctors to diagnose spiritual maladies. Hoo-doo workers discerned which illnesses were "unnatural," caused by the "hex" or "trick" of a human enemy. A hoodoo worker might identify a charm buried near a client's house as the cause of their disease. Some believed that the specialists' abilities came from Satan and others that they came from God, but most churchgoers agreed that hoodoo held the power to heal or harm.[50]

For the sanctified believers of the Victorious Faith Center, hoodoo equaled only one thing: witchcraft.[51] Although people joked about des-perate women who put "roots" in a man's food to work as love potions, the matter was treated with deadly seriousness. African Americans who emphasized the instrumentality of faith saw strong parallels between faith's and hoodoo's power to effect change, and believers drew thick theo-logical lines between them. In the prosperity gospel, negative conse-quences visited those who failed to live by faith. Believers sedulously sought out the cause of any personal misfortune, from trivial matters like the common cold to major ones like cancer or a car accident. They often settled upon two answers. First, in most cases, they assumed that their own actions had failed them. The cause and effect were commensurate; small mistakes warranted small difficulties. A negative word spoken at home may have led to a headache. Second, believers frequently concluded that Satan had launched a direct attack on their lives. A car accident on the way home from church, for example, may have been a sign that the Devil hated faithful worship. In interpreting misfortune as an answer to either sin or righteousness, believers exhibited some flexibility, as the rigidity and certainty of prosperity theology was molded to meet the spiritual needs of individual believers. Many of the larger and more enduring prob-lems believers faced were attributed to evil forces. Hoodoo workers' use of hidden charms, secret attacks, and defenses were seen in this light, as Satan's clandestine attacks. God's faithful must be alert to the spiritual forces working against them. Believers exchanged stories of men who fell under the spell of witches and married them, unaware of Satan's shadow over their lives. Pastor Walton warned his congregants against "roots" secretly placed in their food or drink.

Although Satan's attacks might come from anywhere, hoodoo influences did not. Churchgoers pointed the finger at South Carolina. As several members reported, North Carolinians drove down to the Palmetto State to do rootwork or buy charms. Yet as historian Carolyn Long has shown, this centuries-old healing tradition flourished up and down the southeastern coast, from northern Florida to southern North Carolina.[52] The South Carolina native Reverend Ike tailored his 1980s mass mailings for readers steeped in hoodoo, who worried that "secret enemies" worked against them. Just as Jesus had won victory over Judas, his secret enemy, Ike assured generous donors that they could likewise expect a spiritual solution (his promised "ENEMY-FIXER") to "get rid of my SECRET enemies BEFORE THEY GET RID OF ME!"[53] Some churches, large and small, simply acknowledged hoodoo and voodoo as among the many sinister forces pulling believers down. The small storefront Ebony Missionary Baptist Church acknowledged rootwork's pervasive power by adding it to a laundry list of prayer concerns with boxes to check on their prayer request form.[54]

Hoodoo stood as the evil twin to the Victorious Faith Center's triumphant faith. On a community level, it was an ugly reminder of pain. Pastor Walton, during a Sunday school lesson for committed members, characterized their African religious past, "the religion of our ancestors," as witchcraft and satanic worship. He interpreted African American history as one not only of hardship but also of failure. Slavery, poverty, and suffering must be, in part, God's judgment on their African witchcraft. Walton's conclusion that to some extent black Africans had merited the horrors of slavery tempered his belief that all suffering was temporary. God would have rescued all who called out for him.

Hoodoo workers and VFC believers share a faith in the power of religious objects to prevent, diagnose, and cure illness. Hoodoo workers' reliance upon symbolic agents—objects representative of or invested with spiritual power—resembles the widespread pentecostal use of handkerchiefs, cloths, or ribbons to effect healing. Many prosperity teachers, black and white, borrow freely from this pentecostal heritage in the sacred use of commonplace objects, particularly handkerchiefs, as one divine healing practice among many. Hoodoo and the prosperity gospel speak with an overlapping spiritual grammar, ruled by unseen forces, spiritual power, and supernatural beings, and expressed by ritual objects.[55]

Those who relied on hoodoo and those who did not reached similar conclusions: evil attacks were a constant threat. Secret sources of spiritual evil must be excised to restore emotional and physical wellbeing.

Spiritual Competitors: Medicine

In 1984, Hobart Freeman, a once-renowned leader in prosperity circles, died of heart failure caused by an ulcerated leg. The coroner concluded that the Freeman's ill-fitting orthopedic shoe had caused the ulcers, and Freeman's opposition to medical intervention had prevented him from seeking the help he needed. The celebrated teacher, who throughout the 1970s had appeared alongside John Osteen and T. L. Osborn, by the early 1980s, had rotted away before the eyes of his followers at Faith Assembly in Wilmot, Indiana—a macabre test of his own faith. On Freeman's watch, as many as a dozen members of the Faith Assembly died of medically treatable illnesses.[56] The faith movement, as a religion of proofs, always found some partisans willing to be tested to the extreme, though few would follow Freeman to such lengths.

The faith movement mirrored the wider pentecostal acceptance of medicine, holistic remedies, and, to a limited degree, psychology, as methods of divine healing.[57] Most teachers, black and white, were increasingly comfortable with medicine as *part* of God's divine plan for human health.[58] A minority, however, railed against medical science as a threat to faith.

Spiritual healing may have been the only treatment available to some believers. Benny Hinn's Miracle Crusades drew many attendees from minority and immigrant communities, and they crowded the stage for Hinn's healing touch. As theologian Tammy Williams observed, "In a country in which forty-two million persons lack health insurance, twenty percent of whom are African American, Jesus may be the only doctor that some African Americans encounter on a regular basis."[59] But not so in Durham, known as the City of Medicine. Unlike many underinsured African American communities, VFC exhibited familiarity with, knowledge of, and access to the health care system. Many of the members worked for Duke University Hospital as health care providers—nurses, laboratory technicians, phlebotomists, pharmacy assistants, etc.—and knew the medical options available to them. Their mistrust of the health care system stemmed from broader cultural sources, including past and present failures to provide African Americans with colorblind treatment. Racism dressed as impartial science, seen clearly in intelligence theories, Social Darwinism, and eugenics, has cataloged the supposed biological, social, and intellectual inferiority of the black population.[60] The majority of African Americans, unlike their white counterparts, distrusted both biological and social explanations for the causes of mental illness; the former implied black genetic inferiority, while the latter characterized the black family as dysfunctional.[61] African American faith churches simply reflected the popular denial of the authority of the health care system to restore black bodies to health.

Theological differences further refined these cultural sources of alienation from the medical establishment. Believers protested that doctors, hospitals, and pharmaceutical companies promised materialistic solutions to what were actually spiritual problems. Unlike Christian Scientists, faith believers did not deny the physical reality of illness. Prosperity theology drew on its metaphysical (particularly New Thought) heritage and denied that the causes of illness resided outside the spiritual mind. Victoria, a head nurse at a major medical facility, explained the distinction during a discussion about how to live by faith while simultaneously working as a medical professional. I had wondered aloud how she and others could diagnose illness without negatively confessing, since labeling the disease *as such* would speak it into existence or confirm its reality to the believer. Instead of saying "This is what it *is*," she explained, a believing doctor could say, "This is what we *found*." Illness as material reality was not an illusion or the mind's projection. It was a physical manifestation of a spiritual problem. Victorious Faith Center members did not contest biomedical accounts of the symptoms of illness but disagreed on the nature of its causes and cure.

Members of VFC accepted medical intervention at different levels. At the level of diagnosis, most accepted biomedical science's authority to name the disease. Although they were warned by the pastor not to repeat the diagnosis and to whisper it only in prayer, no one questioned the effects of medical intervention. Most believers accepted medical treatment as a supplement to divine healing. This was known as practicing "according to your faith." This allowed the saints to accept treatment for more serious illnesses while leaving smaller problems to the power of faith. From the pulpit, Victorious Faith Christian churchgoers were encouraged to start with a small ailment—a headache—and find faith commensurate to overcome it. Walton himself had overcome his reliance on glasses that way, as he fought through the initial headaches and impairment to his sight before gradually regaining his vision. Members frequently reminded each other to "start with a headache," using positive confession and the efficacy of faith to overcome small tests before moving to larger ones. The testimony of one VFC member provides a helpful illustration. Advised that her gallbladder was about to burst, the believer underwent an ultrasound, but leapt off the examination table when the preliminary screening seemed positive. (She counted it a success that she did not need surgery, though occasional pain continued to bother her.) Medicine, for many saints, proved diagnostic but not curative.[62] Most VFC believers accepted some heath intervention as an unwanted necessity, as vaccinations were prerequisites for children to attend school or for them to travel abroad. Preventive medicine such as flu shots or regular doctor visits created significant dilemmas for many adherents. Even the notion of "flu season" articulated a negative confession that, for those toeing a strict line, required reimagining as "health season."[63] Kenneth Hagin Sr. used caution in this matter and was not definitive regarding vaccinations as a test of faith. "It's pretty well up to the individual," he concluded.[64] Others avoided preventive care as a marker of spiritual honor. "My children have not been to the doctor in years!" boasted a VFC elder. With access to excellent health care if they wanted it, believers argued that they already had true "preventive medicine" in a spiritual "bottle," through fasting, tithing, prayer, and worship.

Medical treatment posed a direct threat to the logic of faith. Medicine relied upon the diagnosis of symptoms, signs that believers called "lying symptoms" because they relied upon "sense knowledge" rather than "revelation." Headaches were a useful and frequently cited example. Just as Tylenol could not cure a headache but simply numbed the pain, believers indicted medicine as incapable of attacking the root of the problem. Medical reliance on materialistic solutions contributed to believers' untimely demise, the saints argued, as people yielded to their sense knowledge and would not develop the faith required to subdue their disease. Pastor Walton claimed that most believers with advanced illnesses did not recover because their symptoms had grown stronger than their faith. Medical science bolstered confidence in the material over the spiritual realm, thus undermining true faith.

New etiquette arose to handle public displays of illness. For example, rather than answer a sneeze with "Bless you," churchgoers might reply, "I curse that sneeze in Jesus' name!" countering demonic interference with a positive confession. On a congregational visit to a local megachurch, participants instructed me to say, "I'm catching a blessing," in reply to any questions concerning my obvious cold symptoms. The ethnographer Milmon Harrison found that his acknowledgement of his thinning hair received a stern redirection: "Oh, no, don't confess that. We're believing for you a full head of hair. You're *not* going to lose your hair, in Jesus' name!"[65] Believers disagreed about the degree to which they should ignore symptoms. Kenneth Hagin Jr. eventually attempted to counter this preoccupation with denying illness, arguing that those who refused to admit they were sick were not being faithful—they were liars. Regardless, believers continued to view disease as having spiritual elements as they examined their own bodies for proof of God's blessings.

Harmonizing Health

Throughout the twentieth century, preachers of the prosperity gospel followed the religious current flowing closer to acceptance of medicine, holistic solutions, and, to some extent, psychology, as divine healing techniques.[66] Most teachers, black, white, and Latino, displayed increasing comfort with medicine as *part* of God's divine plan for human health.

Oral Roberts paved the way for the broader prosperity gospel's acceptance of traditional medicine. Prosperity teachers had shared early pentecostalism's rejection of medical solutions. Though most evangelists roughly equated sickness with demonic interference, Oral Roberts expressed the first stirrings of interest in medical solutions in the late 1940s, when he suggested that doctors might be able to "assist nature" in nurturing bodies to health, though he also cautioned that nothing could be done for those whose "spiritual channels are blocked."[67] By the early 1960s, influenced by Dr. William Standish Reed, founder of the Christian Medical Foundation International, Roberts began to formulate a plan to merge traditional medicine and divine healing into one comprehensive cure.[68] In 1977, he unveiled the blueprints of his City of Faith, a medical complex complete with a towering clinic, hospital, and research center heralded by that 60-foot bronze sculpture of hands folded in prayer (figure 4.2). He envisioned it as a preeminent research facility, where Holy Spirit-filled doctors could surpass secular scientists by rooting out both spiritual and physical causes. A photo essay of Richard Roberts being prayed over, getting blood drawn, and receiving prescriptions printed with biblical verses was intended to show readers the difference that faith-filled medicine could make.[69] Roberts's dual commitment to science and divine healing emerged clearly in his understanding of cancer, which he said had a distinct "spiritual origin" with a relationship to demonic powers so strong that he could smell its odorous presence.[70] Roberts believed whole-heartedly that a breakthrough in cancer research would come through the City of Faith, whose doctors, seeing spiritual and physical causes simultaneously, would be uniquely equipped to cure the disease. In 1989, the City of Faith closed under financial duress. Roberts bravely labeled the expensive collapse a completed assignment from God; he was not entirely mistaken, for the endeavor had signaled the broader shifts of the prosperity gospel and pentecostal culture more generally.

FIGURE 4.2 **Oral Roberts University Praying Hands** A 6o-foot bronze statue of praying hands marks the entrance of both Oral Roberts University and the City of Faith hospital across the street.

Source: Kari Sullivan

Some groups found the acceptance of scientific medicine more difficult than others. The faith movement took some time to overcome their suspicions, as they tried to reconcile their belief in the power of faith with the demonstrable power of medicine. Mainline charismatics (whose leadership tended to be well educated, less sectarian, and more cosmopolitan) never adopted the over-and-against attitudes of their pentecostal brethren. Pentecostals faced a choice, explained historian Joseph Williams, between maintaining their antimedical stance or choosing "to adapt their methods to fit with the increasingly persuasive evidence of medical efficacy."[71] Most chose the latter. Gradually, trust in medical intervention became standard, and it became unremarkable for believers to contribute to ministries that used modern medicine. Most faith celebrities, including T. D. Jakes, Eddie Long, Creflo Dollar, Joel Osteen, Paul Morton, Keith Butler, and Joyce Meyer, made medical assistance a significant part of their charitable outreach. In March 2009, for instance, the Spirituality and Medicine Recognition Banquet celebrated Pentecostal Assemblies of the World Bishop Noel Jones's efforts to eradicate HIV/AIDS.

Naturalistic healing, naturopathy, occupied a convenient middle ground between noninvasive physical treatment and healing by faith. Throughout the 1960s and 1970s, as the faith movement warmed to the benefits of science, believers shared the wider culture's growing interest in naturalistic healing, favoring the herbs, dietary supplements, and nonsurgical methods of alternative medicine.[72] Faith practitioners took up naturopathic healing as a reflection of their confidence in the healing power of God's creation. Some doctors rose to prominence on major Christian networks as naturopathic experts on diet and health. Dr. Don Colbert, author of *The Bible Cure* and *What Would Jesus Eat?* graduated from Oral Roberts University School of Medicine and Christ for the Nations to meet with great success in the prosperity movement. Colbert offered detailed biblical exegesis that uncovered "God's nutritional laws," scriptural truths that foreshadowed (and confirmed) modern scientific breakthroughs. Dr. Reginald Cherry, another Trinity Broadcasting Network favorite, touted natural herbs and remedies to help believers live "God's best." Dr. Jordan Rubin's *The Maker's Diet* and Benny Hinn's *Fruits, Vegetables & Herbs for Energy, Wellness, and Power* focused on the healing properties of foods mentioned in scripture. Crisscrossing between divine and secular authorities, these healers applied biblical remedies to restore followers to spiritual and physical health.

The biblical diets and bottled cures of faith celebrities presented a welcome alternative to traditional medicine for followers anxious to see God's work inherent in the natural world. In many ways, these interests brought the prosperity movement back to its nineteenth-century roots. Alternative medicine—naturopathy, chiropractics, acupuncture, homeopathy, and osteopathy, among others—had appeared in America as rivals to traditional medicine, and these practices were incorporated into a medley of metaphysical, scientific, and evangelical healing practices. Pentecostalism and metaphysical religion, as twin gospels of health, shared an affinity for spiritual alignment with God and a rejection of the heavy materialism of traditional medicine.[73] When the 1960s counterculture and the 1970s "holistic" health care movement urged natural medicine and its metaphysical assumptions to the fore, prosperity believers rediscovered naturalistic medicine as a like-minded reflection of their own mandate.

In this climate, fasting regained its position as a biblical means of attaining divine health and a stronger measure of spiritual power. The evangelist Franklin Hall first popularized the health benefits of fasting in the late 1940s with his bestselling manual, *Atomic Power with God thru Fasting and Prayer*. After Hall, every major figure of the postwar healing revivals, including Oral Roberts, Kenneth Hagin, and T. L. Osborn, took up Hall's method of ridding the body of spiritual and physical toxins by limiting food intake.[74] In fasting, believers found a porthole to blessings, as the process promised a leaner, healthier body, as well as new supernatural opportunities.[75] Marilyn Hickey made fasting a centerpiece of her ministry with *The Power of Prayer and Fasting*, a 21-day model to release protection, plenty, health, and happiness. By 2009, Jentezen Franklin of Atlanta's Free Chapel had become the foremost authority on fasting. His *New York Times* bestseller *Fasting* promoted the "Daniel Fast," a wholegrain partial fast guaranteed to multiply the return on believers' prayers from thirtyfold to hundredfold.[76] Testimonials of healing, job promotion, and supernatural favor filled his website as evidence of the material and heavenly potency of fasting. As an extension of his "first fruits" theology, Franklin proclaimed the heightened effectiveness of corporate fasting if it was reserved for January. He explained, "If we will pray and seek God and give Him our best at the first of the year, He will bless our ENTIRE year!"[77] Sacred time compounded power upon power.

Ever entrepreneurial, some celebrities promoted health products of their own, pointing to their own health and fitness as inspiration. Pat Robertson developed "Pat's Diet Shake," a nutritional supplement and accompanying weight loss program that reportedly 720,000 ordered for its promise to "lose weight, never feel hungry, improve your health, gain confidence, and brighten your outlook."[78] In 2006, Randy and Paula White, then married co-pastors of Tampa's Without Walls International megachurch, marketed Omega XL as a life-changing dietary supplement.[79] Similarly, James Robison, author of *True Prosperity*, promoted Tri-Vita vitamins in infomercials and on his popular television program *Life Today*.[80] Bishop Jack Wallace of the 9,000-member Detroit World Outreach, along with fitness competitor Randy Woody, founded Prosperity Nutrition, a line of muscle-building and meal-replacement merchandise.[81] Promoted with spiritual language, their "Inferno" products promised to help body fat meet an untimely end. For the Holy Spirit-filled doctors featured on TBN, INSP, CBN, and other major Christian networks, these entrepreneurial ventures followed as naturally as prescriptions. Dr. Reginald Cherry, host of *Doctor and the Word*, founded Abundant Nutrition to sell a host of weight- and health-management pills, billed to improve memory, weight, sleep, menopause, and even virility.[82] Though immersed in the science of healthy living, prosperity teachers maintained that what people truly needed was mental change. In promoting his diet shake, Pat Robertson reminded readers, "There's no reason to 'perish for lack of knowledge.' My hope and prayer is that you'll find a healthier and more joyful life, fit for the Kingdom and the Master's use." As Bishop Wallace aptly summarized, these prosperity health products offered "science integrated with wisdom."

America's diet and fitness culture captured the religious imagination of conservative Christians of all stripes, but the faith movement seemed most prepared to evaluate obesity on spiritual terms. As believers looked to their own bodies for evidence of faith, modern fitness ideals set a new standard against which people could measure their spiritual progress. Teachings on food and exercise dripped with judgment as they piled up the sins of obesity: gluttony, bondage, idolatry, and moral weakness. Frances Hunter put the problem starkly: "God spoke very loud and clear and I almost fell off the rostrum. He said, 'Fat Christians are the biggest liars of them all—and you're a FAT Christian.'"[83] Body fat advertised moral dysfunction. Some of the boldest attempted to banish fat with the immediacy of miraculous healing. A. A. Allen, for example, famously claimed that a "fat sister" lost 200 pounds before his eyes at a healing crusade.[84] Most limited their interventionist claims to sudden changes in appetite, as Frances Hunter explained: "HE COMPLETELY TOOK AWAY MY DESIRE

FOR FOOD!"[85] But because all physical imbalances could be traced to demonic influences, for prosperity teachers deliverance—the binding and loosing of spiritual forces—was the most useful interpretive framework. Numerous manuals sought to isolate the demonic cause of fat. T. D. Jakes's *Lay Aside the Weight* encouraged believers to unburden themselves of the generational curses that kept families fat and unsatisfied, offering his own 100-pound weight loss as inspiration.[86] Frances Hunter warned that Satan might tempt believers in the guise of a cake, pudding, or a candy bar, arousing sinful desires of the flesh that people must "loose" in order to "lose."[87] Joyce Meyer's *Eat & Stay Thin* encouraged people to listen closely to the Holy Spirit guiding them daily to rewarding food choices.[88] "Toss out the tempters!" declared the second commandment of Paula White's *Ten Commandments for Health and Wellness*, as she implored readers to repent of their sins and empty their pantries of sweets.[89]

Positive confession served at deliverance's right hand. Confessions tailor-made for weight loss were found in every detail of nutrition, exercise, and healthy living, promising to strip away demonic interference. Creflo Dollar prompted followers to repeat "Jesus is Lord over my eating habits!" Bill Winston, pastor of the 19,000-member Living Word Christian Center in Forest Park, Illinois, published a detailed confession:

> I come out from among foods that deplete my body of essential nutrients. . . . I exercise regularly and my body is strong and limber, has excellent muscle tone and endurance. . . . I keep my body under and do not allow my flesh to control me. I cancel all destructive cravings for food and substances that threaten my health and well being. I speak to all junk food that comes into my presence. I decree that you have no power to control my desires or my appetite. I am free from bondage to unhealthy food products.[90]

By the late 1990s, most celebrities balanced the language of deliverance with nutritional and fitness advice. White co-wrote her weight-loss guide with personal trainer Dodd Romero, dividing each chapter between practical and spiritual recommendations. Joel Osteen's *Healthy Living* series devoted as much attention to his fitness regimen as to his divine principles of weight loss.[91]

Many blended this physical, rather than metaphysical, approach with institutional solutions. In 1976, Oral Roberts imposed stern measures at Oral Roberts University to ensure that students overcame sinful gluttony and shed unwanted weight.[92] Students who failed to keep their body fat percentage below the university's standards (20 percent for women, 15 percent for men) would face disciplinary measures. Other institutions simply opened their own fitness centers. While T. D. Jakes, Willie George, and others promoted their state-of-the-art facilities as another opportunity for parishioners to become involved, some touted their gyms as places to pursue spiritual excellence. Eddie Long played with images of biblical strength with his Sampson's Health and Fitness center, advertised with a sculpted Sampson breaking the temple columns (despite the fact that Sampson died in the attempt).[93] Creflo Dollar's World Changers Ministries Body Sculpting Center promised to assist people in "achieving a body that is fit for the Master's use."[94] Pastors commonly detailed their own weight and fitness successes. Joel Osteen appeared on the June 2008 cover of *Health & Fitness Sports Magazine* as a featured "fit father" with his son Jonathan. Paula White's *Ten Commandments for Health and Wellness* included a personal workout video, featuring the pastor in a spandex top and pants leading a full-body strength and cardiovascular workout. Bishop Jack Wallace advertised his ability to bench press 500 pounds with photos showing his peak physical condition. Only a decade earlier, prosperity believers would have objected to seeing pastors in scanty tops and shorts, bouncing across the television screen with dumbbells or perspiring in the midst of jumping jacks. In the 1980s, aerobics expert Pamela Cole had starred in TBN's *Get in Shape* in a full-body leotard modestly covered with a conservative blouse and skirt.[95] But modern prosperity believers knew the power of living examples, those whose Midas Touch encouraged them to reimagine their lives (and bodies) as God's worthy temples. Apart from the sanctuary, the largest building found on the megachurch campuses of hard prosperity preachers across the country was usually not an outreach center. It was a for-profit gym.[96]

(Super)natural Health Care

After the eleven-o'clock Sunday service, I picked up a Starbucks latte in the wide-mouthed lobby of a 3,000-member congregation nestled in an exurban industrial complex and wandered into the reception area designated for first-time visitors. Jake and Linda, an affable middle-aged couple, greeted me warmly. As we chatted about my project, Linda began to explain how they had applied the church's teachings on divine health to their own family's difficulties. Their daughter had suffered six miscarriages before the family decided to switch spiritual strategies. Rather than pray for their daughter's ability to carry the children, they decided to pray instead for the "seed" inside her; meanwhile, the would-be mother scoured the Bible for verses about children as a basis for positive confession. After another miscarriage, the doctors discovered that a genetic incompatibility caused her body to reject her pregnancies. With new treatment, she bore three children in a row. Linda smiled triumphantly as she declared it a miracle, brought about by the renewed focus of their prayer. For Linda, her daughter's medically based diagnosis and recovery did not undermine the spiritual causes and cures at play.

Testimonies like these demonstrate not only the persistence of underlying spiritual readings of health and sickness events but also the kind of *bilingualism* that frames these accounts as believers acknowledge that two intersecting processes—medical and miraculous—were simultaneously at work. A churchgoer recovers in the hospital from a car accident, and the church declares it a miracle. Lindsay Roberts, Oral Roberts's daughter, claimed miraculous healing from a tumor in her breast but also went on to publicize breast cancer on her television show *Make Your Day Count.*[97] Did this admission dilute the concept of the miraculous? "We're faith people," said VFC's first lady with an upturned chin. "We look at the doctor and say 'You do your thing, and I'll do mine.'"

At a live taping of Benny Hinn's *This Is Your Day!* television program, I watched this bilingualism at work. Dr. Braverman, author of *Younger You*, sat comfortably beside Hinn on the open-air platform and lectured on weight loss, reminding listeners with a wry expression that "fat is for the Lord, not for our buttocks." He smoothly alternated between describing his approach as "holistic medicine" and "Holy Spirit medicine" as he prophesied that people will soon live much longer, more abundant lives: "For it is written, death will flee from us!" Braverman's naturalistic health program, Hinn explained, had been so successful that Braverman canceled all of his patients' bypass surgeries. "A hundred of them, not all," Braverman quickly corrected, but Hinn pressed on in recounting the miraculous effects of everyday foods and spices. The next guest cut an imposing figure as he perched his large frame on the stool beside Hinn. The audience took a moment to recognize the internationally renowned Reinhard Bonnke, faith healer and evangelist to Africa. The rough edges of his German accent resonated like a low growl as he dove into a sermon on Pentecost. "Your body is the residential address of the Holy Spirit," he exclaimed to rousing cheers from the audience. "If you desire your fire, then you'd

FIGURE 4.3 **Reinhard Bonnke** German evangelist Reinhard Bonnke joins Benny Hinn on the set of his *This Is Your Day!* program on location in Jerusalem, 2008. *Source:* Author's photo.

better claim your flame!" The audience that had sat in quiet interest for Dr. Braverman now swayed with enthusiasm. "The best pill is the gospel! Any miracle is possible! I'm going to pray and the fire is going to come down now!" he shouted before the tenuous calm of the crowd was broken. People pressed forward to the stage and dozens crowded up the steps, eager to be one of the few that Reinhard Bonnke clutched with his large hands before they fell to the ground in spiritual ecstasy. People spoke of faith and medicine in the same breath, accepting divine health as from a spiritual buffet. They took what they liked.

And the Life Everlasting, Amen

At the onset of a healing revival, the Texan evangelist Gordon Lindsay warned audiences not to demand youth from their healers. "The purpose of the gifts of healing is not to restore youth to old age," he chided.[98] But many in the prosperity movement were reluctant to accept that teaching as the last word. The generation that grew up in the abundance of postwar America had never really known suffering and showed little desire to restrain their expectations. They longed for triumph over sickness, decay, and even death. The always controversial A. A. Allen published the first of the prosperity gospel's anti-aging manuals, *How to Renew Your Youth*, asking, "Are your eyes growing dim? Are you losing your natural force? Would you like to feel younger than you feel?" The movement's obsession with youth grew with the preachers' age, as baby boomer ministries now had legions of followers entering the stage to face "end of life" issues. If the outside world could invest in research on prolonging life or storing bodies cryogenically for future reanimation, why shouldn't the faithful demand at least as much? By 2010, the stylish Gloria Copeland not only modeled mature beauty but also sought to spread her secret to "the Bible-based fountain of youth." In *Live Long, Finish Strong,* she urged readers to die a glorious death at the age of 120 by "divine appointment."[99] She called it "unlimited life."[100]

"Death by divine appointment"? This was the notion that faith-filled Christians could choose the time of their own home-going, that death would await their consent to be transported to the heavenlies. These claims transformed the way that prosperity teachers narrated the deaths of the significant expositors of their message. Kenneth Copeland, for instance, claimed that E. W. Kenyon and Smith Wigglesworth had announced their own deaths and passed away on their own terms. Contrary to Kenyon's daughter's eyewitness account that Kenyon died from cancer, teachers continue to renarrate his death as his last act of faith. Similarly, Hagin was later described as dying peacefully at age 86, having simply put his head down one morning after eating breakfast; critics note that Hagin claimed to have been healed of heart problems at age 16, yet he was repeatedly hospitalized for cardiovascular failures—including on the day of his death. As in life so in death, the will must consent. "You can live life and when the time comes to depart from this life, you will leave your physical body *on purpose*," argued Kenneth Copeland. "You and God can make the choice together about where and when you lay your body down."[101] When a leader's life was cut short, believers struggled to make sense of the evidence. When the much-loved pastor of City Bible Church, Wendell Smith, died at 60, his church family published a memorial pamphlet honoring his life and explaining his death. "Some may ask why Wendell died and was not healed," it acknowledged, and cataloged the spiritual and physical lengths to which Smith had gone to exhaust "every means available to strengthen and enrich his body."[102] He had just completed his own healing treatise, *Faith for Healing, Wisdom for Health,* before his passing. Among the tender accolades of fellow preachers like David Yonggi Cho and Reinhard Bonnke, Smith's family took comfort in the rewards of heaven and his good fight in faith. Yet his bestselling "Rhema cards"—personalized note cards scribbled with paraphrased scriptures, his drawings, and prayer requests that became used worldwide—told a sadder story. His card entitled

"WHAT I WANT" asked God for restored bones, a full measure of days, and a last request highlighted in green:

DIE OLD + HEALTHY
in
SWEET SLEEP

When giants of the faith succumbed to their mortality, a cloud of doubt seemed to descend. When Billy Joe Daugherty passed away suddenly in the prime of his ministry, the unspoken question lingered during his funeral. How could a great man of faith not fulfill the divine destiny he preached? In his eulogy, Kenneth Copeland attacked the question itself with the fury and love of grief. He rebuked the audiences for thinking such a thing of a beloved minister whom scandal and dishonor had never diminished. It seemed unimaginable that those loved and lost were just that—ones who had lost the test of faith.

Explanations for Suffering

How did believers within the faith movement reconcile their beliefs with the persistence of disease and, worst of all, death? Funerals served as a perpetual reminder to believers of the limitations of faith. For the duration of an illness, however intractable, congregants and leaders traded testimonies of sudden recoveries, miraculous cures, and God's interventions. Expectations ran high. Pastor Walton, like teachers dating back to the healing revivals, frequently reminded believers that God had promised them 70 to 80 years of divine health.[103] (Long life had always been such a staple in the movement that when the evangelist Jack Coe died in his prime, followers tried to resurrect him.[104]) Still, tragedy visited the Victorious Faith Center, although church members would protest that it happened less frequently there than in other communities. Spouses died unexpectedly, children succumbed to diseases, members perished in accidents. Although hardship could be deemed a test, the finality of death revoked any license for retrospective blessing. In a spiritual cosmos dominated by possibility thinking, funerals marked a true ending.

During my time at VFC, Judy, a longtime member in her 60s, was diagnosed with a brain tumor, failed to respond to chemotherapy, and died. Her participation in church life had grown limited, and as her health waned her visibility also diminished. Privately, the church rallied around

Judy's grieving widower, providing him with meals, assistance, and comfort. Publicly—in sermon, song, tithing, and prayer requests—the church passed over her illness and subsequent death in silence. While sickness and death were constant topics in church life, her death, other than an announcement of her funeral, received neither positive nor negative acknowledgment.[105]

Four categories of interpreting "failure" emerged from my interviews with members and my ethnographic observations that may contextualize the silence surrounding Judy's death. First, and most commonly discussed among believers, was suspension of judgment. Believers frequently declared themselves unable or unwilling to draw conclusions regarding another person's difficult circumstances. Though the physical evidence appeared to confirm a member's spiritual distress, observers chose not to, in their words, "judge." When a soloist's congested voice cracked on the high notes, or a speaker sniffled into the microphone, shouts of encouragement rose from the pews. Believers continued to cite their unfailing certainty in God's blessings but refused to apply their conclusions to their neighbor's plight. Victoria, a medical professional in her 50s, described seeing another church member exiting a discount department store with purchases that included cold medication. Embarrassed, the member immediately confessed to Victoria. Victoria remembered thinking to herself, "I don't care what you have in the bag! I can't see what you have in the bag!" Yet she replied: "I'm not God!" Victoria's silence over her fellow believer's spiritual misstep was rooted in a cultivated humility. As she explained:

> I've learned not to judge people. When I see people prostituting, drug addicts, I see it like this: there but for the grace of God go I. It could be me. So I don't judge people. I don't judge people when they're sick. If they're in the hospital, I wouldn't say, "OH, YOU DON'T HAVE ANY FAITH." I always say, you don't know what you're going to do if you're put in that person's position.

Victoria's work in the medical field frequently put her in a position to see fellow churchgoers as they sought out medical (and therefore less spiritual) solutions, and still she declared herself unable, as "not God," to pronounce a critical verdict. In the difficult months that followed the congregation's loss of Judy, the silence implied a similar attitude of charity and suspension of judgment.

Second, however, silence may have betokened lingering condemnation. In the Holy Spirit-centered demonization of disease, bodies charted a spiritual territory. Preachers encouraged the saints to examine their own bodies for signs of Satan's triumph over divine health. Any other conclusion appeared to mitigate death's harsh lessons. "A baby dies and a pastor says 'God has a plan,'" Walton said, shaking his head. "No! That baby was stolen [by Satan]." Death meant failure, the failure of the believer to win the spiritual battle against illness. "Your biggest enemy is not Satan! It's yourself," Walton preached weekly.[106] Further, since prosperity theology taught that healing was granted once-and-for-all, some saints when ill avoided or were discouraged from asking for continued help because it might identify them as faithless. For example, members typically asked for public prayer for others or waited until a triumphant testimony before acknowledging their own illness and its healing. In contrast to the black church's historical position of solidarity with a suffering Christ, believers chose a once-and-for-all Savior and silence in illness rather than face public shame.[107]

Third, contrary to church teaching, some believers quietly concluded that illness could portend righteous suffering. Although the saints expected that their faith would be measured in their bodies as reflected in their personal health, some would not accept blame for the evidence stacked against them. Suffering believers referred often to Job, where they found a righteous man who suffered without blame. Ruth, who taught Sunday school from a wheelchair, described her predicament as a "Job moment." Setting aside the hard causality between faith and health, Ruth argued confidently, though not publicly, that her suffering was a difficult test of faithfulness. As her reference to Job implied, her misfortune would eventually dissolve to reveal only empty accusations and a righteous sufferer.

Fourth, some members of VFC questioned the church's teachings that tragedy implicated any individual in failure. In whispers, mutters, or private conversations, some believers struggled with the theodicy attached to personal loss. How could a good God allow suffering? Or, in this case, how could any church heap condemnation on tragedy? Public silence muzzled public grief, creating friction between some churchgoers and the church itself. I often heard these complaints framed as examples of overcoming the negative confession of others, as members recalled their dealings with fellow believers who expressed doubt, anger, or frustration. In an environment where speech acts were closely monitored and controlled, parishioners rarely disagreed openly with the church's teachings.

Within faith communities, the multiple interpretations of the meaning of suffering often found expression in silence. The silence may have reflected a breakdown in spiritual vocabulary to express the inexpressible, that God had somehow failed or that a loved one had. In the intimate and totalizing spiritual environment of a faith church, where each member's health, wealth, and circumstances stood on display, the ambivalent silence might simply have allowed for a deep breath, a little space that mitigated the anxiety of revealing both the good and bad that unfolded in each person's life.

Sitting between the grieving widower and Ruth's wheelchair on a regular Sunday morning, I listened to Pastor Walton preach against resigning oneself to death. As the sermon detailed God's promises to provide perpetual health, Pastor Walton seemed convinced that believers could never meet precisely the same end as nonbelievers. After all, famous faith healers like A. A. Allen and Smith Wigglesworth, Walton reminded listeners, raised the faithful from the dead. (Allen eventually abandoned his vigorous preaching on raising the dead when too many followers sent the bodies of their deceased to his Miracle Valley headquarters in Arizona.[108]) In the everyday healing practices of the prosperity movement, faith operated as a spiritual guarantee, drawing health and finances into the lives of people willing to suspend naturalistic explanations in favor of supernatural, Holy Spirit causality. From where I sat, divine health did not always seem plausible. Yet through God, the saints reminded me, all things were possible.

5

Victory

Jehovah Nissi (my victory)

AN ELECTRIC GUITAR was improvising a drawn-out solo of "Amazing Grace" that reverberated throughout the Greensboro Coliseum, as hundreds of latecomers took their seats for the Joel Osteen meeting. Ten thousand worshippers were packed into the stacked oval tiers of the arena, many of them visitors to the burgeoning urban center of North Carolina's third-largest city. This stadium seemed not so different from Osteen's home church, Lakewood, in the refurbished Houston Rockets arena. Churchgoers longing for steeples and peaked roofs would have to make their peace with rippling neon light displays, projected lyrics two stories high, and Lakewood's symbol: a towering golden globe in slow rotation.

A whirl of clicks and blinding flashes from a thousand cameras lit Osteen's entrance, which he rewarded with a squinting smile. "Good evening!" He thanked the audience for sacrificing their Friday night to join him for a Night of Hope, his 2008 international speaking tour. He surveyed the dark expanse of his audience: "You guys look like *victors*, not *victims*, to me!" A rush of applause followed. He implored them to stop dwelling on the negative aspects of their lives, because "our lives follow our thoughts." Those who notice the rainy days or the difficult circumstances will only "draw more negativity into your life. . . . It's a decision that we have to make. Don't wait for happiness to fall on you. Just make a decision that you're going to enjoy your life to the fullest. Every day you're going to live that abundant life." A cascading piano accompaniment softened Osteen's drawling message into a gentle reminder, as if from friend to friend. Osteen offered to open the floodgates of the victorious life, explaining how everyday people could escape the everyday grind. It would begin, as the brochure promised, with hope. "We love you guys. I've just been telling our congregation back home, and I'm going to declare it over you that 2008 is going to be your best year so far." He paused for the applause to die down. "Well, Joel, what does that mean? You're just up there saying that," he teased, with mock skepticism and a wide smile. "It doesn't mean anything unless you take it into your heart. This is a *seed* God's trying to deposit on the inside! Why don't you let God birth some new dreams tonight? Why don't you enlarge your vision? . . . It's going to be a year of promotion, a year of increase, a year of favor, a year of supernatural opportunities!"[1] This was Osteen's vision of the victorious life, in which positive thinking became Christian currency.

Here we take up the third and last characteristic of the American prosperity gospel: victory. The movement preached a gospel of triumph, holding that no circumstance could stop followers from living in total victory here on earth. Leaders inscribed this indomitable spirit in church names such as World Changers (Atlanta), Victory World Church (Norcross, Georgia), and Champions Centre (Tacoma, Washington). The byline of Fred Shipman's multiracial megachurch in West Palm Beach, Florida, said it all—"Winners Church: Where Winning Is a Lifestyle."[2]

According to historian Dale Simmons, Keswick Higher Life followers of the late nineteenth century recognized only three types of people: "the unsaved, the merely saved (who live lives of constant defeat), and the victorious Christian."[3] We might say much the same about the modern faith movement, which set triumph as the perpetual goal of the Christian life. Traditional Christians survived, while faith-filled believers thrived. "I reign as a king in my domain in this life through Jesus Christ," declared Kenneth Hagin.[4] The soaring anthropology of early pentecostals like John G. Lake and his "God-men" theology pumped confidence into the veins of faith believers who called each other "overcomers," "dominators," and "little gods." The atonement had raised humanity to a higher spiritual plane and sealed their destiny as victors.[5] "When these truths really gain the ascendancy in us," argued E. W. Kenyon, "they will make us spiritual supermen, masters of demons and disease."[6] Contemporary prosperity preachers expected nothing short of spiritual dominion. Creflo Dollar surmised that the Devil has trouble distinguishing triumphant believers from Jesus "because we look so much alike!"[7] The slogan for Impacting Your World Christian Center in Philadelphia aptly summarized the prosperity gospel's startling pledge: "Creating People That Cannot Be Destroyed."[8] The prosperity gospel promised total victory over crushing circumstances, guaranteeing believers the tools to become true conquerors.

FIGURE 5. 1 Joel Osteen Joel Osteen praying before the start of his weekly sermon at America's largest church, Lakewood Church, Houston, 2010.

Source: Nick De La Torre, © 2010 *Houston Chronicle.*

FIGURE 5.2 **Success Chapel** The front view of Success Chapel, Durham, North Carolina. Their tagline "The Church Where Your Success is Guaranteed!! Relationships, Business, Career, Family, Spirit, Marriage, Profession."
Source: Author's photo.

An Overcoming Movement

The prosperity movement had every reason to be confident. By the early twenty-first century their pastors were national figures and their churches occupied a significant place in the American Protestant landscape. The prosperity gospel exerted tremendous influence on the country's religious life. Its largest congregations had captured a significant share of the spiritual market. In 2011, approximately 1,400 American churches attracted 2,000 or more weekly attendees, earning the title of "megachurch," and faith churches crowded the upper reaches of this phenomenon. Prosperity giants like Joel Osteen and T. D. Jakes led the first and eleventh largest churches, respectively, with Osteen's Lakewood Church towering over its nearest competitors. Almost half of all churches with more than 10,000 members preached prosperity from the pulpit.[9] By 2011, a tally of self-reported membership showed that one million people were attending American prosperity megachurches.

The prosperity movement's place at the top gave it astounding reach. The sociologist Mark Chaves of the National Congregations Study demonstrated that roughly 45 percent of all worshippers in the United States

Table 5.1 Prosperity Megachurch Distribution by Size Compared with
Megachurches Nationally

Number of Attendees	Percentage of Prosperity Megachurches	Percentage of All Megachurches
2,000–2,999	14.8	53.8
3,000–3,999	17.4	19.1
4,000–4,999	7.8	11.1
5,000–9,999	23.5	12.0
10,000 or more	36.5	4.00
Total	100.0	100.0

Source: National megachurch data used for comparison is drawn from Thumma and Travis, *Beyond Megachurch Myths*, 8 (table 1.2).

attended the largest 10 percent of churches.[10] Since the 1970s, Americans have gravitated toward the biggest churches, concentrating more worshippers and financial contributions in fewer houses of worship. The top 1 percent claimed 15 percent of America's churchgoers.[11] As seen in table 5.1, prosperity megachurches dominated the upper tiers of megachurches nationally. Almost 60 percent had more than 5,000 members, as compared with 16 percent of all megachurches. As seen in figure 5.3, the average prosperity megachurch hovered around 8,500 members. As the smallest 50 percent of congregations drew only 11 percent of all American churchgoers, the majority of the resources accrued to super-sized congregations.[12] With a combined annual income of seven billion dollars and vast electronic audiences, megachurches rivaled whole traditional denominations, historic seminaries, and religious publishers in their influence on American religious life.[13]

Most of those attending prosperity megachurches considered themselves nondenominational. Those who kept their denominational affiliations, broadly speaking, had been won to the prosperity gospel in two waves: from white pentecostal denominations in the 1970s and 1980s (see chapter 2) and African American denominations of all varieties (see chapter 3) in the late 1980s and 1990s. Regardless of any formal affiliation, these megachurches were orbiting in a virtually postdenominational world of their making (see figure 5.4). Mammoth organizations that were almost denominations in themselves, they had the popularity and institutional backbone to make and break allegiances at will.

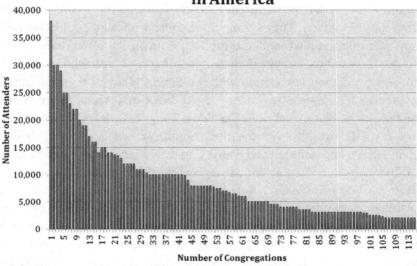

FIGURE 5.3 The Largest 115 Prosperity Churches in America, 2011 Prosperity megachurches by size. The average congregation contained 8,577 members.

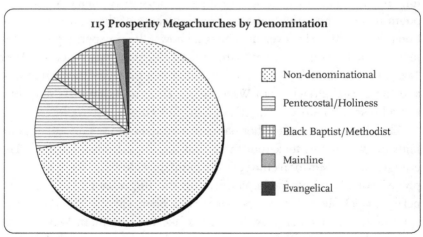

FIGURE 5.4 115 Prosperity Megachurches by Denomination Almost three-quarters of all prosperity megachurches were nondenominational. Those retaining their pentecostal and Baptist or Methodist denominational ties formed two significant minority traditions.

The prosperity gospel thrived in cityscapes across the nation, in a towering testimony to the urban religious imagination. As seen in map 5.1, faith megachurches popped up across the country. For the most part, in this the prosperity megachurches loosely followed the trends of megachurches in general. They sprang up in areas with high population density, suburban sprawl, and the highway infrastructure to draw people from a large radius. Despite their geographic spread, megachurches never fully escaped their association with the South. Many of the best-known prosperity televangelists, young and old, black and white, spoke with a telltale drawl. Black celebrities like Eddie Long, T. D. Jakes, Creflo Dollar, and I. V. Hilliard ruled over the urban South. White favorites Joel Osteen, John Hagee, and Kenneth and Gloria Copeland made Texas home to some of the country's largest ministries, while Oklahoma's Rhema Bible Training Center and Oral Roberts University had made the southern plains the institutional epicenter of the movement for over four decades. The faith movement followed the broader trends of megachurch growth when, in the 1980s, prosperity congregations began to show signs of rapid growth outside of the Sunbelt.[14] Map 5.2 shows the regional distribution of megachurches. As can be seen, prosperity megachurches were found in higher numbers in the South and Southeast (with slightly lower numbers in the Deep South). Michigan, California, Florida, and Washington in particular became new centers of prosperity theology, as their booming churches supplied an increasing share of the movement's national leadership. However, as table 5.2 shows, the prosperity gospel was just as much an Eastern seaboard and Californian phenomenon. After Texas, California held the highest number of prosperity megachurches, and the coastal stretch from Washington, D.C., to Baltimore, Maryland, was a hotspot for African American faith churches.

The Northeast, on the other hand, proved to be stony ground. Smaller faith megachurches took root there, but the largest ones did not.[15] The evangelical and Mormon ethos of the mountain states and western prairies proved equally inhospitable, confirming the impression that the prosperity gospel favored cityscapes over wide-open spaces. This failure in spite of strong popular growth in areas like the mountain West can be explained only in part by the region's general resistance to megachurches. While the movement's regional successes showed it to be a national phenomenon, prosperity churches sprouted less quickly outside the Sunbelt.

Whether in Dallas, Texas, Minneapolis, Minnesota, or Sayreville, New Jersey, church leaders were generally homegrown celebrities, locals able to

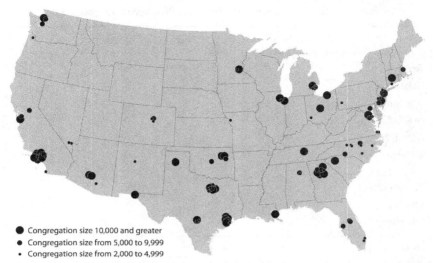

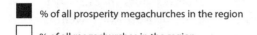

MAP 5.1 **Prosperity Megachurch Locations in Mainland United States, 2011** The largest prosperity megachurches were located most frequently in Houston, Dallas, Atlanta, and Los Angeles.

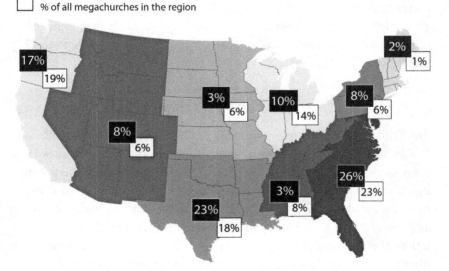

MAP 5.2 **Regional Distribution of Prosperity Megachurches Compared to Megachurches Nationally** Prosperity megachurches are concentrated in the West, South, and Southeast.

Source: The regional distribution of national megachurch data, used for comparison, comes from Thumma and Travis, *Beyond Megachurch Myths*, 9.

Table 5.2 Top Ten States with the Most Prosperity Megachurches

State	Number of Megachurches
Texas	21
California	18
Georgia	8
North Carolina	9
New Jersey	6
Oklahoma	6
Michigan	5
Pennsylvania	5
Florida	5
Maryland	4

meet the particular needs of their religious marketplace. In 1980, Casey and Wendy Treat, for instance, founded the Christian Faith Center of Seattle in largely unchurched Washington state. The Treats provided a fashionable and media-savvy service attuned to the area's secular ethos and its deeper evangelical vein, becoming able participants in what sociologist James Wellman calls the "new churching" of the Northwest. Wellman estimates that "sectarian entrepreneurs" like the Treats garnered believers at rates higher than the population growth, and much higher than fellow religious conservatives.[16] These local heroes seemed better able to keep their ears to the ground.

Techniques of Triumph

The faith movement's many varieties of churches, large and small, were theologically unified by far more than an inventory of health and wealth. They were bound by a sense of the inevitability of victory after victory based on the proper use of principles. Believers lived in a closed spiritual universe ruled by consistent cosmic laws. Yet beyond the basics of sowing and reaping and giving and getting, there were additional rules that calibrated the sacred universe. Responsibility lay at the feet of believers to discover them. Markus Bishop, author of *Our Covenant of Prosperity*, urged readers to devote their lives to discovering how God's kingdom worked. As he explained, God "is saying: 'You have to discover the operation of My kingdom. Learn how to apply its principles in specific areas of your life. Work the principles and laws of My kingdom and obey My instructions.

FIGURE 5.5 Highway Sign A billboard on Highway 70 advertises Durham, North Carolina's local prosperity celebrity, George Bloomer.
Source: Author's photo.

Then all these things will be added unto you."[17] In the last decades of the twentieth century, four techniques of binding and loosing spiritual power—agreement, names of God, angels, and directional prayer— became popular as means to open the windows of heaven. Having developed a consistent language of faith in the late 1970s, proponents now concentrated on developing techniques of power, often borrowing from other preachers in their network.

First, prayers of agreement proved one of the most enduring techniques for tapping into the victorious life. "The prayer of agreement is joining your faith with two or three others before God," explained T. D. Jakes's protégé Juanita Bynum.[18] This idea echoed the post–World War II revivals in which evangelists rested on the promise of Matthew 18:19: "Again I say unto you, that if two of you shall agree on earth as touching any thing that they shall ask, it shall be done for them of my Father which is in heaven." Revivals could not be scheduled or building foundations laid without the power of agreement. Lay people gathered around to "agree" for a fellow Christian hoping to secure a promotion, car loan, divine healing, or family unity. The development of satellite ministries in the early 1980s lent weight to these unity prayers, as leaders orchestrated satellite conferences to join the greatest number of supporters in prayer. These new technologies allowed teachers to harness maximum spiritual momentum in a single moment. In 1982, Kenneth and Gloria Copeland's broadcast beamed into 137 American cities at once, so that a projected 500,000 people could pray and take communion together. Robert Tilton's Word of Faith Satellite Network imagined the spiritual power of thousands of tiny congregations channeled though his monthly Success-N-Life seminars and Bible school "live via satellite" featuring leaders such as Charles Capps, John Osteen, Fred Price, T. L. Osborn, Marilyn Hickey, David Yonggi Cho, Kenneth Copeland, and Norvel Hayes.[19] This practice added a communal aspect to an otherwise individualized movement, as followers learned to rely on one another to bring their spiritual plans to completion. Of course, the presence of others brought a new set of problems, as adherents worried that their own prayers might be undercut by another's disbelief. If the best-laid plans failed, prayers of agreement sometimes soured believers' faith in one another. A Christian satire entitled "Couple Claims Opposing Promises" about a husband and wife purposefully canceling out each other's agreement prayers made the point in jest.[20] You cannot simply agree with anyone, warned Jay, an avid Victorious Faith Center churchgoer and a retail owner whose good looks attracted female would-be prayer partners.[21] Protocol (and common sense) dictated that members should choose same-sex allies whose spiritual lives were above reproach.

Second, the names of God provided a consistent source of strength and safety. As ever, the name of Jesus remained paramount. A popular lyric by Lakewood singer Martha Munizzi repeated "Jesus" again and again, reminding worshippers of its ability to "make a way when you say . . . the name of Jesus."[22] Drawing from Oneness pentecostal practices, followers typically used Jesus' name as a breaking power, to sever demonic ties and fasten believers to the power of the cross. In using Jesus' authority over demonic powers, believers retained the pentecostal practice of "pleading the blood."[23] It referred to the blood of Jesus (shed on the cross) as commensurate with atonement power. Yet adherents also relied on other names of God in their quest to live the victorious life. Creflo Dollar's multivolume series on the names of God introduced readers to Jehovah M'Kaddesh (my sanctifier), Jehovah Nissi (my banner), Jehovah Rophe (my healer), Jehovah Tsidkenu (my righteousness), and Jehovah Shammah (my ever-present one). These names stressed different aspects of God and, through positive confession, allowed believers to bring God's power to bear on their unique circumstances. Bridget Hilliard, co-pastor of Houston's New Light Christian Center, advertised that her book, *My Strong Tower: Power in Knowing the Names of God*, enabled readers to "achieve victory through applying the names of God to work in your situations."[24]

Third, like the millions of other North Americans who succumbed to the "angel craze" of the late 1980s and 1990s, adherents of the prosperity gospel discovered angels to be necessary companions on the road to a life of total victory. "I found this secret several years ago," confided *Angels* author Charles Capps, "The Angels are waiting for you to say things that will loose them!"[25] In a tightly bound system of cause and effect, the presence of ministering angels, assigned to each person, seemed an unusual twist. Faith, after all, operated as a power without personality, as impersonal as gravity. Even so, the prosperity gospel retained a thoroughly pentecostal cosmos peopled with demons, angels, and spiritual forces caught up in worldly affairs. Angels, bound to faith-filled words, moved about in the material world to bring believers' words to fulfillment. Teachers heavily influenced by Word of Faith agreed that God assigns every Christian an angel to "watch you and your family,"[26] a view commonplace to a medieval theologian. Angels assisted believers in mundane matters such as finding lost car keys and not-so-mundane matters such as life-threatening emergencies. Pastor Walton of the Victorious Faith Center remembered an angel lifting him in his wrecked car from the train tracks, moments before the oncoming train would have crushed him.[27] Angels were especially seen as harbingers of prosperity. They crossed the bridge separating heavenly and earthly realms, able to bring money from spoken words to a believer's pocketbook. Creflo Dollar's "Angel Power Confession" urged readers to loose angels to "bring my prosperity in my spirit, in my home, in my body, in my family, and in my finances."[28] Misfortune visited the careless or doubtful, as angels could not protect those who gave negative confession. These cosmic personalities were additional cogs on the wheel of things that turned faith to reality.

Fourth, thanks to this densely populated cosmology and sense of principalities and powers of darkness, believers often conceived their prayers as directional, possessing geographical and dimensional properties. In this, the prosperity movement was overlapping with pentecostal networks wholly devoted to the cartographical dimensions of spiritual warfare. Prayer could be "over" or "toward" landscapes, horizons, or whole continents. St. Peter's Church and World Outreach Center, for example, hung banners of North, East, South, and West in their sanctuary as a prayer tool to bring the outdoors indoors, thus combining two distinctive features of this strain of Protestantism: a love of banners and "spiritual mapping."[29] Physical locations took on personal characteristics and spiritual values, viewed as "evil" or "blessed." Michael Pitts's 2005 book *Power Shifters: Atmospheres, Climates and How You Can Influence Them* helped believers identify spiritual zones that were dense as fog but invisible as ether.

These techniques could bring the user into the realm of "favor." Florida evangelist Paula White explained favor as the feeling that "He is 'on your side,' that He is making a way for you."[30] It was that intangible quality that outsiders might simply call "luck." Favor attached itself to those doing God's will and transformed their lives for the better. Testimonies at the

FIGURE 5.6 Directional Prayer Benny Hinn's Holy Land Tour participants pray over the Jerusalem cityscape, 2008.
Source: Author's photo.

close of VFC services brimmed with accounts of favor as churchgoers credited God for the blessings of the week. When a middle-aged man testified that his boss had given him a gas card and the company car to visit his ill father, whoops and cries of "favor!" broke out across the sanctuary.[31] The world, it seemed, stepped aside for the triumphal parade of believers. In the words of a song made famous by the Clark Sisters' gospel ensemble, the extraordinary good fortune of believers can only be explained this way: "Just know that we're blessed and highly favored."[32] Seasoned faith believers would respond to "How are you?" with "I'm blessed and highly favored." Jacqueline Jakes, the first lady of the nation's eleventh largest church, penned *God's Trophy Women: You Are Blessed and Highly Favored* to inspire women to reach for extraordinary goals[33] and explain why some prospered while others languished. Favor, believers testified, spun the straw of their lives into gold.

From the few endowed with favor, God expected excellence. Joel Osteen, handsome and charismatic, was a natural prophet of achieving "God's Best." "God didn't create any of us to be average," explained Osteen from America's leading pulpit, "we were created to excel."[34] He hoped to inspire followers to climb to great spiritual heights rather than live out the middling lives of those "condemned to mediocrity."[35] Excellence was the watchword of prosperity megachurches, each claiming to be ruled by a "spirit of excellence." T. D. Jakes called mediocrity a Christian "addiction" and a "terrorist threat" that demanded a spiritual recovery.[36] Without a cure, Christians would remain tragically ordinary. Books such as John Avanzini's *Financial Excellence*, Paula White's *Move On, Move Up*, and Eddie Long's *Called to Conquer* testified to the movement's call to press toward perfection. Children at Joel Osteen's Lakewood Church learned the gospel from the ministry mascot Champ. Depicted with four arms, antennae sprouting from his head, and tennis shoes, he served as a friendly reminder of the church's message: "Discover the Champion in You."

The prosperity gospel was hard work. Two-and-a-half hours into a Sunday service at Robyn Gool's Victory Christian Center in Charlotte, North Carolina, I heard the chilling words: "Does anyone have more announcements?" The preliminaries were scarcely over; the sermon had not yet begun. The high calling of the prosperity gospel frequently translated into heavy church commitments. It fostered a culture of learning that demanded eagerness and attention. Much like New England congregational churches, whose straight-backed pews brought the classroom to the meeting house, faith churches encouraged attendees to approach church with the seriousness of seminars and workplace evaluations. Creflo Dollar's World Changers Church required members to become "spiritually employed" and accept volunteer positions inside church walls. From traffic attendants to choir members to "bathroom ministers," church offices required diligence.[37] The ambitious visions of most prosperity congregations placed strong demands on believers' time, money, skills, and attention. Members, observed Milmon Harrison, often found it difficult to make time for activities outside church walls in a religious culture whose demands might seem "all-consuming and overwhelming."[38] This requirement was a natural corollary of the "Full Service Church," a congregation teeming with opportunities for music, dance, counseling, education, sports, fellowship, and social services.[39] More programs meant a greater need for volunteers.

The prosperity movement's culture of expected excellence also extended to small churches like the Victorious Faith Center. Total victory required total commitment. Joan, a well-dressed teacher in her forties, told me that her sister was also a VFC church member, adding regretfully: "But she only comes every Sunday."[40] To Joan and other dedicated prosperity churchgoers, the victorious life required more. Sunday morning attendance met the lowest standard of participation. Few excuses warranted absence from church. Sickness signaled an attack from the devil that must be met with more church. Working folks should know that further prayer and discipline generated the divine wealth required to give up working double shifts. "We try to be here whenever the doors are open," explained Brenda, bouncing her grandchild on her lap, "Nothing else to do but serve the Lord!"[41] Brenda seemed to have plenty of other things to do. She sat beside me in scrubs from her shift at the hospital, because she had no time to change between work, dinner, and babysitting. My ethnographic journals were dotted with exasperated notes such as "All I do is go to church!" as church attendance engulfed 10 to 15 hours per week. I pressed consultants for answers. "How do you manage to fit it all in?" I wondered and heard their firm reply: I had it backward. Everyday life fit in the margins of church participation, and God intended it that way. Ruth, seated beside me in her wheelchair, explained how she approached every service with anticipation for the spiritual breakthroughs awaiting her. For her, every moment of preparation was time spent wisely.

To be sure, not all churchgoers approached worship with such vigor. Some came late, left early, or stuck to the back pews. Prosperity churches, like most American congregations, worried about the preponderance of women, the absence of men (especially African American men), and the eye-rolling of teenagers. The problem ran deeper than demographics. The infectious positivity of Sunday morning could be downright exhausting. And some grew immune. Seldom did I attend a prosperity church without numerous greeters telling me that today would be life changing or asking if I had my dancing shoes on. Most churches spelled out their high hopes before the close of the first song. "We should be the happiest people on earth!" exclaimed Pastor Lee Stokes in his opening address, "We're the freest! The richest! The healthiest!"[42]

Sunday services that doubled as television broadcasts demanded even more. Worshippers anticipated observation, as cameras trolled for expressions of praise, prayer, or penitence. Attendees were hustled to the front to make the sanctuary seem full. Fidgeting made bad television, but also mortified those who saw their bored faces projected on to large screens flanking the pulpit. These were people who were asked to master their own affect. The prosperity gospel had for decades demanded a performance of victory. During the Great Depression of the 1930s, Elder Lightfoot Solomon Michaux and his Happy Am I Choir had shown the way. Throughout the offerings, men in tuxedos and women in choir robes and jaunty hats would clap to the accompaniment of a harmonica singing, "Happy am I! Singing along the way."

Now believers had to act their emotions for the benefit of televised worship.[43] These congregations, particularly hard prosperity churches, were the happiest I ever attended. Dancing, singing, hugging, and crying with joy were common behavior—happiness was performed at every meeting by people whose life circumstances might warrant gloom.

This emphasis on the positive could produce some jarring notes. Central events in the liturgical calendar were passed over as being too gloomy. Of the many prosperity churches in Houston, Texas, only Lakewood Church even held a Good Friday service. Their Good Friday service, a time of sober reflection and sorrow throughout Christendom, began with a chipper greeting of "HAPPY GOOD FRIDAY!" from at least six different hosts as I made my way from the cavernous parking garage, up the escalator, and into the sanctuary. The setting was meant to be heavenly. Swirling artificial fog had been pumped in, pierced by hundreds of overhead lights tinted azure, imitating the sun breaking through the clouds. At the front, huge screens showed a similar scene with gemstone skies and fluffy white clouds, from which emerged their symbolic spinning golden globe. On the screens flickered advertisements for Victoria Osteen's book *Happy,*

Healthy and Whole and calls to join their army of volunteers. This com-memoration of Jesus' death opened with our singing the classic hymn, "When I Survey the Wondrous Cross." By the second song, Jesus had been resurrected and glorified in the Hillsong chorus, "This is Our God." In it, Jesus is "lifted on high" and reigns as sovereign Lord.[44]

Pumping her arm in the air, Victoria, blond and exuberant, took the stage.

"Isn't it great we serve a Risen Lord?" she shouted, preempting Easter by two days. Even Lakewood Church's chemical dependency and sexual abuse support groups operated under the sunny title Celebrate Recovery.

Milmon Harrison observed that the high expectations of prosperity be-lievers led people to adopt coping strategies, "exhaust valves" in an envi-ronment that tightly monitored speech and behavior. Some filtered the faith message (selectively accepting or rejecting aspects of church teaching), vented to trusted associates, took a break from involvement, or left the congregation altogether.[45] Disillusioned participants complained that the emphasis on spiritual excellence led to a competitive atmosphere, as people struggled to live up to the rigorous standards set for them. The prosperity movement never really abandoned the strictures that defined holiness and pentecostal culture. Adherents adorned their bodies with jewelry and clothing that would have turned heads in Holy Ghost circles, but prosperity folk pursued holiness with the same single-mindedness. Faith cost.

Conventional Triumph

In the heart of Winston-Salem, North Carolina, perfume sweetened the air in the Lawrence Coliseum as a sea of middle-aged white women filled the arena, eager to hear Joyce Meyer speak. It was a vision of pastels and turtle-neck sweaters, and the 90-percent-plus female audience was cheerfully raucous, some taking pictures with friends, cheering, or attempting to start the wave, in anticipation of the conference commencement. Meyer's popularity extended far beyond charismatic circles. Mainliners, evangeli-cals, and charismatics of all stripes supported her ministry. My patience had been tested by this ecumenism in the parking lot when my car was blocked by a busload of elderly Moravians followed by two vans of Baptists and Lutherans. Once inside, as the women around me chatted, their diverse denominational backgrounds emerged: one a Baptist, another a pentecostal, and a Lutheran who "just loved to listen to Joyce on podcast at work." A pair of emcees took the stage to applause, nurturing the crowd's enthusiasm and preparing them for the day's television broadcast. Take out your gum, don't fidget, and try to remember that this would be broadcast to 145 countries in 39 different languages and more than 260 American stations, they advised cheerfully. The nearly 200,000 households viewing Meyer's program *Enjoying Everyday Life*, formerly *The Life in the Word*, would come to see this single March 13, 2008 event broken into segments and repackaged for television audiences globally. With more than a million monthly podcast downloads and hits on joycemeyer.org, combined with a potential broadcast audience of more than 4.5 billion, Meyer could be sure that her reputation preceded her.[46] Excited murmurs crescendoed as Meyer took the stage, her projected image flanking the platform for the thousands assembled to see her every eyebrow twitch. With her rough mannerisms and self-confessed short temper, the St. Louis native was not the picture of midwestern nicety. Audiences loved her candid admission that her experiences with divorce, sexual abuse, and emotional trauma could be overcome in a born-again victory.

Not one for theatrics, Meyer entered without fanfare as the background music faded. "I'm here to tell you that God is not mad at you," she announced matter-of-factly. Too many Christians live "under condemnation," she preached, the grim certainty that their lives are not pleasing to God and that circumstances cannot improve. Life in Christ would bring a fuller life and deeper joy, while negative circumstances were the "tricks of Satan." As she transitioned into her call for contributions, she voiced the awkwardness of asking for money. But a deeper spiritual logic was at work, she said, for God left believers in the position of having to ask for what they needed. "Why?" she wondered aloud. "So God can bless us," breathed a seatmate, closely tracking Meyer's argument. "Nothing works if we sit back and do nothing but take, take, take," Meyer continued, "but if we sow, there will be a harvest in our lives." Meyer's promised "harvest" meant financial blessing, though her focus was often elsewhere. Her eighty titles, including *Look Great and Feel Great*, *The Secret Power of Speaking God's Word*, and *Me and My Big Mouth*, encompassed emotional healing, Christian living, and the importance of positive thinking.

Meyer's lasting appeal lay in her ability to balance the victory of the prosperity message with the reality of emotional hardships.[47] She represented the everywoman who suffered like the rest but modeled the ability to obtain God's blessings. Her opulent lifestyle, though consistent with her message, did not escape the notice of critics. In 2003, the *St. Louis*

Post-Dispatch itemized her abundant assets, including millions invested in real estate, cars, and a corporate jet. Her tax-exempt status seemed precarious in 2003 as groups like MinistryWatch, a parachurch Christian watchdog association, enjoined the Internal Revenue Service to examine Meyer's spending. Later that year, Joyce Meyer Ministries implemented a series of measures to increase financial transparency and assure supporters that, though her success was God-sent, their dollars were spent wisely. In 2007, Senator Chuck Grassley of the United States Senate Committee on Finance raised similar concerns against the ministry, though the accusations were later rescinded. But Meyer's down-to-earth reputation continued to invite listeners to identify with her, superseding negative media attention. She joked easily about her only obvious indulgence, clothing, when her trademark boxy blazers, sparkled tops, and bobbles caused an envious stir. "If you want to know how many blazers I have," she retorted, "I'm not telling. It's a lot!" As the favored evangelist of middle-aged American women, Meyer continued to be relatable among her own demographic. She urged them to *Enjoy Everyday Life* and supplied commonsense methods to make it a reality.

One of the most popular offerings of the prosperity gospel was its treadmill of conferences promising to improve attendees' lives and fix their marriages, finances, and emotions. The faithful could choose from a variety of gatherings, some focusing on leadership, others on finances, prophecy, church growth, or healing. Men's conferences surged in the 1990s as faith preachers teamed up with Promise Keepers to refocus missionary efforts on the man of the household. It was muscular Christianity renewed. Most of the best-known prosperity teachers thrived not only as senior pastors but also as popular conference speakers. The convention circuit catered to much wider audiences in a multitude of denominations and not just dyed-in-the-wool prosperity churchgoers. The sheer number of faith teachers in religious primetime allowed believers to pick and choose, sifting appealing messages from their less palatable neighbors. Anthropologist Marla Frederick's *Between Sundays* documented the cafeteria approach to sundry aspects of the prosperity gospel among African American Baptist women in Halifax County, North Carolina, who were adept at picking and choosing the lessons they thought they needed and ignoring the rest.[48] Ministers were adept at cross-promotion. A church might advertise a Rod Parsley conference and in return receive an endorsement from the evangelist for their website. Attendees at a T.D. Jakes convention might receive a copy of Juanita Bynum's latest book. The world of prosperity fostered a dizzying global economy of self-help that seemed uncomplicated. All believers needed to know was that there was help right around the corner.

Aesthetics of Triumph

I wound my way through the suburbs of Charlotte, North Carolina, slowing the car for the last few blocks to read the signs: Victory Christian Center Daycare, Victory Christian Center After School Program, Victory Christian Church Office, and finally, the Victory Christian Center. The white peaked roof suggested a large sanctuary, but I fixated morosely on the empty parking lot. After three hours of driving, my normally sunny personality was a tad clouded. I grouched my way to the door, knocked on the glass, and an usher with a toothy smile appeared with an explanation:

"No, no, you're looking for the Dome. This is just the children's building. Better hurry before the parking lot is full." Another half mile away I found the 4,000-seat sanctuary and its 236-foot high ceilings towering over its suburban neighborhood.

The victorious life began on Sunday mornings, as churches sought to give believers a foretaste of wealth divine. The faith movement joined fellow church-growth enthusiasts in abiding by Jerry Falwell's maxim that "a cheap church makes God look cheap."[49] As the megachurch scholars Otis Wheeler and Anne Loveland put it, "believing that 'God deserves our very best' led many evangelicals to underwrite costly facilities featuring luxurious appointments such as plush carpeting and upholstered theater seats, gleaming tile restrooms, expensive woodwork, and the like."[50] Many achieved spectacular results. Archbishop Earl Paulk's Cathedral of the Holy Spirit employed rich hues and neo-Gothic elements to create old-world drama, while Rod Parsley's World Harvest Church revamped a squat brick-and-glass structure with state-of-the-art sound and light displays. The Inspiring Body of Christ Church in Dallas installed a 70,000-gallon walk-through aquarium under the banner "Follow Me, And I Will Make You Fishers of Men." Church sanctuaries, logos, and websites frequently evoked a princely heritage with the unstinting deployment of royal colors: red, gold, and purple. Ministries without lavish accommodations occasionally settled for the superficial appearance of wealth. When religious studies scholar Stephanie Mitchem visited televangelist Leroy Thompson's congregation in Darrow, Louisiana, she found the sanctuary decked in contact paper and plastic that mimicked marble and gold.[51] Participants might easily have pointed out that it was simply a form of positive confession. God rewards those who proclaim (and enact) what cannot yet be seen. "Fake it until you make it" had long been a catchphrase among faith preachers.

The globe replaced the cross as the most common symbol of the prosperity gospel.[52] It communicated two important aspects of their message. First, it alluded to the Great Commission's missionary imperative to make disciples of all nations. Kenneth and Gloria Copeland's logo showed a planet wrapped in the banner, "Jesus is Lord." Second, the globe signified spiritual dominion and the quest for an international ministry. Hungry for expansion, prosperity megachurches often affixed the label "international" or "world" to their titles.[53] This aspiring internationalism was as old as the prosperity gospel. Even the smallest theological contenders like Theodore Fitch, a Oneness evangelist from Iowa, hoped for global domination. His globe logo was wrapped in a banner proclaiming "My Books Are Read in Many Countries." Keith Butler's Word of Faith International Christian Center (Detroit, Michigan) and Jim and Deborah Cobrae's The Rock and World Outreach Center (San Bernardino, California) flaunted their global outreach by displaying in their sanctuaries the flag of every nation that was home to their ministry. Each was a trophy. (An exception to this rule was the Lone Star State where typically only the Texan flag was allowed to fly beside the Stars and Stripes.)

The sheer size of America's leading prosperity churches spoke of an expansive faith. The cultural analyst Robbie Goh, writing about Australia's 20,000-member Hillsong Church, observed that the megachurch experience reinforced the "performance of the mega."[54] Prosperity megacongregations placed their size in the foreground of their public image, reasoning that a bigger church pointed believers to a bigger God. Vaulted ceilings, cavernous sanctuaries, and expansive video monitors defined the space. Pastors appeared to churchgoers as larger-than-life figures. Most prosperity megachurch attendees saw their senior pastor on a huge media screen, knowing him as a public persona rather than a "real person."[55] Generally, leaders of mid-to-large-sized congregations appeared on television and/or radio, which amplified their reach.[56] These churches typically found even larger audiences through blogs, podcasts, streaming media, and social networking such as Facebook and Twitter. The conference experience showed the same tendency. T.D. Jakes fused his wildly popular conferences—Woman Thou Art Loosed, Manpower, Mega Youth Experience, and MegaKidz—into Megafest, which in 2004 hosted 140,000 attendees for a marathon of preaching, worship, and entertainment.

The twenty-first century saw a trend toward multiple campuses. This served as a demonstration of the growth of the organization but also presented technological and theological challenges. My survey of 115 prosperity megachurches found that 40 percent of all megachurches were split into multiple campuses.

The prosperity gospel centered on the personality and biography of the leader. How was one pastor to be present in several places at once? Some pastors refused to announce where they would be appearing on any given Sunday lest attendance suffer at the other campuses. Steve Kelly of the Wave Church tried a helicopter shuttle whipping him from congregation to congregation until a noise-abatement lawsuit shut down the whirlybird. Some used their grown-up children to solve the problem, passing on smaller churches to members of the up-and-coming generation. These multisite churches were often linked by complicated technology that did not always function as required. Like evangelists since the invention of radio, prosperity movement practitioners were great enthusiasts of the latest in electronic communication devices. Using Twitter, iPads, and streaming video was not only an attempt at the broadest possible outreach but also a sign of their willingness to engage with modernity. The megachurch experience reinforced prosperity theology's evidentiary faith and introduced worshippers to an immanent God—seen, heard, and felt in this "'materialization' of the invisible God."[57]

The victorious life presented a thoroughgoing imperative; we underestimate the movement if we ignore the totality of its promised triumph. The prosperity movement tackled not only individual issues but also larger social and cultural impediments that stood between believers and ultimate victory. We turn now to the prosperity gospel's response to racism and sexism, as adherents oscillated between collective and individual solutions to institutional barriers.

Triumph and Racism

On a sunny November Saturday, I took my seat in The Park Church, Charlotte, and prepared to hear T. D. Jakes, the famous African American evangelist, in a rare guest appearance.[58] This was to be no crusade or revival. The church greeter had been an Allstate insurance agent, and the conference was entitled the B.E.S.T. Leadership and Empowerment

Seminar. Hundreds of African American entrepreneurs crowded the church to get the B.E.S.T.—Black Economic Success Training—and hear a parade of successful black businesspeople share their stories. Speakers included Max Siegal, the first black president of a NASCAR franchise, Glinda Bridgforth, an Oprah-endorsed financial consultant, and Bishop T. D. Jakes, billed as "a beloved pastor, a successful entrepreneur, a global advocate and philanthropist."[59]

Christianity and business acumen twined as the gospel became interchangeable with the business virtues required to get the job done. From the ornate pulpit, the NASCAR entrepreneur credited loving God as his leg-up on the competitors, while the financial expert argued that godly self-esteem could be the foundation for a solid economic footing. The Park Church Pastor Claude Alexander Jr.'s short address drew a stronger correlation: God's laws and the laws of business were one and same, as sowing and reaping yielded financial as well as spiritual harvests. Those who placed money in the offering "know we're going to receive" and so must give accordingly. "Plant a seed of faith!" he shouted, and "put away the Washingtons,"—dollar bills would not suffice. As the offertory music swelled, Alexander urged everyone to file past transparent bins the size of garbage cans, so all could see generosity (or stinginess) as it happened.

In spite of the buzz of a thousand eager listeners in a half-full auditorium, Jakes clucked with disappointment as he took the stage. If this were a worship service, he surmised, this place would be packed. Black people want to "dance and shout, but not to learn," he concluded. The fault was not entirely theirs. Traditional Christianity, as it was taught "by slave masters to pacify their slaves," sapped the gospel of its liberating qualities. Jakes enumerated the consequences: only 48 percent of African Americans owned homes, 58 percent enrolled in college, and 25 percent lived in poverty. God promised more. Listeners could seize the Deuteronomic promise that God "giveth thee power to get wealth," so long as they would learn, as his latest book was titled, to *Reposition Yourself.*[60] His imperative to change *yourself*, redirect your *own* thoughts and actions, was a model of individual spiritual and psychological change that opposed the dominant voices of a century of African American thought. As part of the legacy of slavery, the black church had long recognized the sway of institutional sin, corporate evil, and preached with an eye toward macrolevel injustice and oppression. Jakes promised largely microlevel solutions: a changed heart, better job, and renewed marriage. "You're an overcomer! Get rid of cancerous thoughts! Don't get sick in your attitudes! Every day is a new day!" he declared and received a deafening response.

As the B.E.S.T. conference illustrated, African American faith teachers adopted a range of strategies for black empowerment. Some assured black believers that they required primarily spiritual tools. The Atlanta preacher Creflo Dollar's *The Color of Love: Understanding God's Answer to Racism, Separation and Division* argued this position as he diagnosed racism as a demonic force dividing the church.[61] "The only way to defeat racism," argued Dollar, "is by discovering the foundation for unshakable faith."[62] Dollar rallied believers around the supernatural power of faith that made each adherent, regardless of color, a son or daughter of acquisition. African Americans should not dwell on the past or seek government restitution for slavery: "You ought to say, 'No I don't want payment from the government. I don't want to say that a man made me rich. I want God to pay me back.'"[63] God restored faith-filled black people to their rightful place by spiritual means. The lingering racism of black and white churchgoers, warned Dollar, blocked God's spirit of increase and broke their power of agreement. Dollar promoted a one-on-one model of racial reconciliation; white people must repent of their racism to a black believer, and vice versa. He took his own advice when he and his fiancé, Taffi, adopted a white child.[64] These microsolutions to racial reconciliation mirrored the thinking of white churchgoers in a study of evangelical responses to racism. Sociologists Christian Smith and Michael Emerson found that white evangelicals' emphasis on individualism and free will led them to see racism as a problem that stemmed from individuals' prejudices, not structural disadvantages.[65] So too the dogged individualism of the prosperity gospel predisposed many African American teachers to adopt personal solutions to racism. Rather than dismantle social structures or call for political change, adherents formed cross-cultural friendships or attended a multicultural Sunday service, or, in Dollar's case, embraced a multiracial family as a perpetual testimony to the power of racial unity.

Teachers like T. D. Jakes offered an entrepreneurial prescription.[66] Following a robust tradition in African American thought that gave priority to black economic advancement, Jakes attempted to dismantle racism through financial empowerment. He joined many black charismatic leaders who, beginning in the mid-1980s, developed programs to encourage African Americans to own and run their own businesses.[67] Jakes's B.E.S.T. conferences stood as one of many attempts to rear a generation of black entrepreneurs. Unlike Dollar, Jakes focused on the social and environmental causes of inequality, advocating mentorship, education, and opportunity as "great emancipators in the fight for equality."[68] He questioned the prosperity gospel's rough equation between individualism and victory as he counseled people to seek environments conducive to living a winning lifestyle. Though he stood apart from many prosperity teachers in his indictment of structural sin, Jakes shared their theme of self-reliance.

Frederick Price, centered in Los Angeles' inner city, earned national acclaim as an authority on race and poverty. His message to black America promised spiritual empowerment and debt reduction, a message that spoke directly to people's needs. Price first reached black audiences across America in 1978 when he bought airtime in four of the largest black urban populations: Washington, D.C., Detroit, Chicago, and New York City.[69] His ministry began to flourish. Newcomers overflowed his 1,400-seat facility and by 1981 the church had acquired Pepperdine University's downtown campus for $14 million. Price, with his unique style, broke the mold of 1980 televangelism: he taught for an hour without musical flourishes or appeals for money. Explained historian Scott Billingsley, "Price believed that if people were taught what the Bible said about finances, divine health, and other practical aspects of daily life, they would be inspired to change their lifestyles."[70] Price's gamble paid off, and his heavily instructional program claimed one-third of the audience for all Sunday morning religious programs. New achievements followed in short order. In 1986, Price's 10,000-seat worship facility—the Faith Dome—became the new home of the Ever Increasing Faith program and its millions of television viewers. His conferences, begun in 1982, drew thousands to his urban crusades, with one event boasting 42,000 in attendance.[71] A prolific author, Price published more than 50 titles, totaling more than two million copies sold since 1976. He founded the Fellowship of Inner City Word of Faith Ministries in 1990 as a parachurch ministry designed to support urban faith ministers, a network that swelled to 300 pastors and 150,000 parishioners in 35 states.[72] His own congregation launched an extensive inner-city mission to urban Los Angeles, including Christian education from preschool through high school.

The prosperity movement had seemed a bright spot of interracial unity in the fractured pentecostal–charismatic domain, where the persistence of separate black denominations was a testimony to the bitter segregation that had carved up the early pentecostal community.[73] Sweeping attempts at racial reconciliation intensified during the 1990s, from Promise Keepers rallies to the 1994 "Memphis Miracle," the Pentecostal Fellowship of North

America's attempt to unite black and white pentecostal denominations.[74] The faith movement had managed to create an easy alliance of diverse preachers, facilitating a high degree of racial mixing at conferences and at home without ever having to surrender a pulpit to another's lasting control. Frederick Price was its darling, the protégé of a white preacher and commander of vast black television audiences. His spiritual father was none other than Kenneth E. Hagin, who had given Price his first charismatic audiences and fiercely promoted him among the largely white Word of Faith network.[75] "I am Brother Hagin's black child," joked Price and set his admiration in stone, naming a building in the Crenshaw Christian Center campus after the elderly Hagin.[76]

Then, an ugly incident seemed to give the lie to the movement's promise of equal divine opportunity. Kenneth Hagin's son and ministerial heir, Kenneth Hagin Jr. was discovered to have preached a sermon condemning interracial dating and marriage.[77] Price was incensed, and though Hagin Jr. claimed to have apologized, Price felt that the Hagin family and Rhema Bible Training Center had failed to speak out against racism. Price responded with a theme for the upcoming television year: Race, Religion, and Racism.[78] This series and accompanying books represented Price's most developed thought. His three volumes on the subject, *A Bold Encounter with Division in the Church*, *Perverting the Gospel to Subjugate a People*, and *Jesus, Christianity and Islam*, challenged white leadership to repent of inaction and injustice, and described faith theology as the consummation of Christian liberation. He did not mince words: "Don't shake my hand and give a charismatic hug and act as if you love me when you really see me as a nigger."[79] Racism, he continued, thrived in America with the church's tacit permission.[80] Black Christians had been denied their God-given power to determine their own destinies: holiness, wisdom, and increase. Price embraced the controversy as a prophetic confirmation: "I believe that the Lord has raised me up for a time like this: to be, as it were, a catalyst to find the solution to what I consider to be America's biggest challenge."[81] Price successfully linked social injustice to structural racism in the context of a highly individualistic gospel. He gained countless admirers and inspired a new generation of black charismatic preachers.

Controversy simmered in many black churches over the popularity of the prosperity gospel and whether it could ever have liberative ends. Opponents complained that it had abandoned the path to sociopolitical reform exemplified by Martin Luther King Jr. and replaced it with promises that were facile at best and reprehensible at worst.[82] Much of the 126th

annual conference of the 7.5-million member National Baptist Convention
USA was spent railing against the prosperity movement, which President
William Shaw dismissed as "a capitalistic devotion to personal privilege."[83]
"Black communities are suffering," argued Baptist megachurch leader
Frederick Haynes, "while this prosperity-pimping gospel is emotionally
charging people who are watching their communities just literally dissolve."[84]
Others, however, saw the prosperity gospel as compatible with the recognized American path to success. The Reverend Floyd Flake, an African
Methodist Episcopal megachurch leader and former Democratic con-
gressman from New York, dubbed it "The Way of the Bootstrapper."[85] But
for others, it was a matter of dire consequences for African Americans. As
the ministerial icon T. D. Jakes argued, "economic empowerment and
family prosperity are crucial to our survival."[86] The economic gap for racial
minorities had to be addressed from the pulpit before it was too late.

The swelling ranks of Latino faith churches demonstrated the potency
of the prosperity gospel as a new liberation theology. In this reconfiguration of the Catholic "option for the poor," Maranatha World Revival Ministries in Chicago, Illinois, and other Latino churches promised to deliver
members from the roots of their oppression, a vision summed up in the
motto: *Santidad, Salvación, Sanidad, Liberación* (Sanctification, Salvation,
Healing, Deliverance).[87] As historian Arlene Sánchez Walsh describes, the
adoption of the prosperity gospel by Latino believers happened in two
waves. The first wave of Latino congregations, beginning in the 1970s,
comprised recent departures from classic pentecostals denominations
who were attempting to carve out a distinct "faith" theological identity.
"Those initial Word of Faith expressions," says Sánchez Walsh, "did not
include much in the way of cultural markers that allowed Latina/os to
maintain their ethnic identity."[88] The second wave began to reimagine
prosperity theology as having a special message for Hispanic believers and
encouraged churchgoers to hold on to their linguistic and cultural heritage. It was an era of renewed cultural confidence. By the 1990s, Latinos
had become the most desirable demographic for their extraordinary promise of new church growth. Anglo churches seeking to expand frequently
brought in a Spanish-speaking pastor to expand their reach into newly
immigrated or second-generation Latino communities. Twenty-two percent of prosperity megachurches ran Spanish-speaking ministries as part
of their outreach efforts, not only in states like Texas, Florida, and California, but up the Eastern seaboard and across the Midwest.[89] Religious
broadcasters considered Spanish-language programming to be one of the

industry's hottest markets. Religious programming for the Hispanic community began in the 1980s and 1990s, when CBN, TBN, and the Catholic EWTN (Eternal Word Television Network) began operations in Latin America. Networks like EWTN and Mexico's Maria Vision served the 27 million Catholic Hispanics, while prosperity televangelists successfully targeted pentecostal Latinos. CBN's *Club 700 Hoy* was launched in 2004. TBN's *TBN Enlace* produced 70 percent of its programming in Spanish, with the rest offered dubbed. It constructed a new studio in Mexico to create programming specifically for Mexican immigrants.[90]

The prosperity gospel offered a compelling alternative to competing visions of race and the victorious life. Black leaders exulted when they snatched followers from Nation of Islam.[91] Frederick Price devoted an entire volume to Nation of Islam's rival theology of the divine high life; as scholar Kirk MacGregor asserted, Word of Faith and Nation of Islam offered similar narratives of God-like believers, robbed of legal dominion of the earth.[92] Latino celebrities like Miami-based Apostle Guillermo Maldonado of King Jesus Ministry (El Rey Jesus); Bishop Jay and Jeannine Ramirez, founding pastors of Kingdom Life Christian Church in Milford, Connecticut; and Pastors Diego and Cindy Mesa of the 5,000-member Abundant Living Family Church in Rancho Cucamonga, California, hoped to pluck parishioners from their Catholic competition. The message was simple: God offers more. "Back in Mexico," remembered Billy Gonzales, his church gave him a gospel of "Jesus and heaven and being good." But at Casa del Padre in Charlottesville, Virginia, his new pastor offered a clear path to victorious life beyond subsistence living: "It doesn't matter what country you're from, what degree you have, or what money you have in the bank . . . The blessings will come! The blessings are looking for you! God will take care of you. God will not let you be without a house!"[93]

The prosperity gospel's results-driven approach effectively competed for believers' hearts and minds against the available alternatives. A 2008 Pew survey found that 83 percent of Spanish speakers surveyed agreed that God granted financial success and good health to believers, compared with 54 percent of English-dominant Latinos.[94]

Multicultural megachurches demonstrated—at least on the surface— that the prosperity gospel could triumph over racism and the isolation of segregation. For the most part, the prosperity movement followed the well-established American pattern of racial segregation in worship. Separate congregations for black, white, and Latino churchgoers remained the norm.

But a new form of multiracial ministry arose in the 1980s and 1990s, as prosperity megachurches placed a premium on bridging differences among ethnic groups and attracting potential converts from growing immigrant populations.[95] Dennis Leonard, former head of Heritage Christian Center, inspired fellow pastors when he looked out on his all-white congregation in Denver, Colorado, and decided to make a change. Leonard replaced their usual music with a gospel choir and implored members to invite Latino and African American acquaintances. "I don't think it's our natural thing to integrate. But I believe it's God's will," argued Leonard.[96] In 1999, the Full Gospel Baptist Church Fellowship (FGBCF) ordained Leonard as the first white bishop in their fellowship to oversee multiracial ministries. Lakewood Church also served as a national model. In 2010, Joel Osteen reported that his congregation had equal numbers of members of European, African, and Latin descent. Marcos Witt, winner of four Latin Grammys, joined the congregation in 2002 to lead Lakewood's Hispanic ministry, a popular draw for Texas's burgeoning Latino/a population. His Spanish services, comprising first- and second-generation immigrants from Mexico and Central America, were among America's largest Hispanic congregations.[97] Israel Houghton, worship pastor at Lakewood, bridged the black-white divide as a Grammy-winning biracial Christian performer, bringing a fusion of gospel, rock, and jazz to Sunday services.

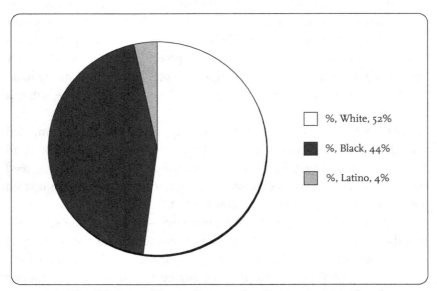

FIGURE 5.7 The Ethnicity of Senior Pastors of 115 Prosperity Megachurches

By 2011, prosperity megachurches claimed some of the highest rates of multicultural congregations. Forty-three percent of prosperity megachurches boasted a multiethnic or multicultural congregation, far exceeding the national rate of 7 percent and even higher than the results of a 2005 survey of megachurches, which found that 31 percent of all megachurches considered themselves multicultural.[98] These claims can be parsed in several ways. Multicultural churches, by definition, were those where no single racial group exceeded 80 percent.[99] Paula White's Without Walls church, for example, successfully appealed to black and white audiences. Others counted diversity by national origin or ancestry. Mike Freeman's megachurch in suburban Washington, D.C., for example, looked at its all black congregation as multicultural because of its international members. For others, multiculturalism may simply have been an aspirational goal, not a lived reality, but one of the many positive confessions that prophesied the future of the ministry. But looking back to map 5.1, with its map of prosperity megachurches, it seems highly probable that many churches achieved racial diversity in part because they were concentrated in those areas of the country with multiethnic populations.[100]

In the heavily spiritualized world of prosperity theology, race and racism might not have been deemed problems worth addressing.[101] But the profound economic consequences of ethnicity in America made the needs of minorities a perennial test for the prosperity gospel. Could the message solve a problem as old as the nation itself? Prosperity preachers were determined to present concrete solutions, for it was not the gospel, after all, unless it took every force captive in Jesus' name.

Triumph and Women

Gloria Copeland commanded the pulpit with Texas gentility—tough spiritual talk draped with a little lace. Her sermon at the March 2008 Branson Victory Campaign extolled the blessings of a godly life. The early years of her marriage to Kenneth Copeland had brought nothing but poverty, she remembered, and she turned to the Bible for a solution. Jesus' imperative to "Seek ye first the kingdom of God, and all these things shall be added unto you," struck her as significant. "*Things!*" she exclaimed, "I was *very* interested . . . I needed some *things!*"[102] In 1962, she converted to Christianity, with her husband soon to follow, and found their material circumstances radically changed. They had experienced the life abundant, and her Branson message promised it to others: "Get in on the good life!"

Gloria Copeland proclaimed what experience and prosperity theology confirmed: the laws of faith worked for her no less than for anyone else because "God is no respecter of persons."[103] The careers of Maria Woodworth-Etter, Aimee Semple McPherson, and, later, Kathryn Kuhlman, Freda Lindsay, and Daisy Osborn had made inroads in pentecostal culture for the acceptance of female evangelists, but progress came inch-by-inch.[104] Few churches called a woman to the position of senior pastor or boasted of female spiritual oversight. Like many famous female preachers in the prosperity movement, Gloria's career began as a supporting role in her husband's ministry. Much like Freda Lindsay and Daisy Osborn, whose full partnership in their husband's work often went unnoticed, Gloria took on spiritual responsibilities with limited public exposure. She was, after all, a founding member of Kenneth Copeland Ministries.

In the 1970s, female faith teachers gained greater—albeit still limited—acceptance in an atmosphere hostile to encroaching feminism. The political and cultural upheavals of the late 1960s and the 1970s ended the resolute evangelical and pentecostal consensus with American culture. A political and social maelstrom was underway, including African American civil rights, women's rights, and the Vietnam War, as well as the rise of non-marital sex, abortion, divorce, and open homosexual activity. Concurrently, women gained better access to health care, birth control, fair wages, and legal rights, changing the social, economic, and legal context of marriage. The divorce rate more than doubled during this period, eroding the centrality of the traditional male-as-breadwinner family.

Perceiving the authority and esteem of the family to be on the decline, many religious conservatives clung to time-honored attitudes to gender roles. A pink training manual for women attending a Full Gospel Business Men's Fellowship International meeting instructed wives to play a supportive role for their minister husbands and ensure that their clothes were neatly pressed. At heart, churches balked at women in leadership positions. Daisy and T. L. Osborn returned from their successful international crusades to discover that conservative audiences did not accept the egalitarianism that characterized their ministry. In 1948, Daisy said "my husband and I have walked together, prayed, fasted and read together, taught and preached together, enjoying the supreme privilege of leading broken, bleeding, and suffering humanity to the feet of Jesus."[105] Though Daisy was a seasoned speaker, American churches sat her in the front row rather than onstage with her husband. Daisy vowed that she would not attend speaking engagements for her husband that did not specifically include her.[106]

In the 1980s, Daisy organized the hugely successful International Women's Conferences, while her husband taught the accompanying workshop: "How to Assist a Woman in Ministry." Yet traditional views of femininity could not be completely overridden. An early photo essay about Daisy Osborn entitled "How to stay young and grow more beautiful" explained to American women that ministry itself was the key to her youthful attractiveness.[107]

So too Gloria Copeland emerged from her husband's shadow. In 1973, the couple founded their ministerial magazine, *The Believer's Voice of Victory*, and Gloria wrote her first book, *God's Will for You*. A year later she appeared onstage at crusades. In 1975, their ministry took to the airwaves, and, in 1979, they debuted the *Believer's Voice of Victory* television show, the engine of the ministry's outreach. The same year construction began on KCM's new headquarters on Eagle Mountain Lake, the 1,516-acre property housing their television studio, production center, and staff offices.[108] She spoke for the first time at their inaugural Believers' Convention, their six-day conference series and ministerial trademark. Though Kenneth initially took the sole pastoral role, by the decade's close, Gloria's popularity with audiences gave her a ministry of her own.[109]

Some women gained leadership the old-fashioned way: spousal death. In 1973, Freda Lindsay took over Christ For the Nations after her husband, Gordon, passed to glory. Adherents had revered Gordon for his central role in the postwar healing revival but soon realized that Freda's behind-the-scenes role had been larger than they imagined. Freda's shrewd business sense and forthright management steered the ministry from shaky financial ground, and she secured her status as a significant leader in her own right.[110] Whereas in times past, a widow might have been expected to fade into obscurity, the status now became a badge of honor. Conferences such as PTL's 1987 "Widows Indeed" boasted that it had assembled "the greatest gathering of widows ever!"

There were potential problems in a widow's succession. When Brenda Timberlake's husband Mack died in 2002 she replaced her youthful husband as senior pastor of the empire they had built together. She had been among the first to join her husband onstage, then in the pulpit, as co-experts in strong marriages and debt-free living. However she found it difficult to establish her own authority and continually had to refer to the past life they had shared. Her influence seemed to rest on his legacy and her cultivation of their son Tim as heir apparent to the ministry.

When the prosperity movement became more confident in the 1980s, the women within it became bolder as well and seized opportunities for greater visibility. Daisy Osborn wrote *Five Choices for Women Who Win* and asserted "You Can Do It." In the introduction to another of his wife's books, T. L. Osborn claimed: "Every woman on earth has unlimited possibilities in God. Redemption cannot be qualified sexually any more than it can be qualified economically, racially or socially."[111] A string of autobiographies of powerful women preachers appeared, among them Freda Lindsay's *Freda: The Widow Who Took Up the Mantle.*[112] Celebrated faith teachers used their influence and popularity to promote women's concerns in pentecostal churches. By the mid-1980s, women's leadership conferences had become a fixture of the largest ministries.[113] Marilyn Hickey, Vicki Jamison Peterson, Tammy Bakker, Evelyn Roberts, Freda Lindsay, Gloria Copeland, Dodie Osteen, Sandy Brown, and Marte Tilton received top billing. In the 1990s, Joyce Meyer, Paula White, Juanita Bynum, and Billye Brim joined them at the top.

In the 1990s, the faith movement's acceptance of therapeutic paradigms opened up new avenues to address women's mental health. T. D. Jakes was famed for his attention to women's emotional healing, a theme that struck market gold with his series, *Woman, Thou Art Loosed!* His book and his 1993 conferences of the same name addressed the hushed issues of domestic violence, discrimination, rape, and divorce and focused on women's psychological healing. *Woman, Thou Art Loosed!* became a selling phenomenon, with two million printed copies, record-breaking conference attendance, a play, a gospel album, and a 2004 film adaptation.

Not only did audiences hear more about women, adherents turned to female evangelists as guides into the spiritual realm of emotion. Women made emotional topics not simply acceptable but significant avenues of spiritual growth. Paula White, a self-described "messed-up Mississippi girl," told how the gospel healed her from the wounds of her childhood sexual and physical abuse.[114] Joyce Meyer told a similar story. Her early life was full of hardship; she suffered sexual abuse at the hands of her father and struggled through a failing marriage and a divorce in her early 20s. Her tale of spiritual recovery, retold in the novel *The Penny*, followed the rags-to-riches trajectory of the faith message. She preached a gospel of prosperous sanctification, a life improved financially, spiritually, and socially through God's blessings. The victorious life for women was said to be at hand.

Female teachers struggled to maintain their images as both authoritative leaders and submissive wives. When a reader questioned the 1980s evangelist Marilyn Hickey on this issue, Hickey assured audiences that she unflinchingly obeyed her husband. If her husband forbade her traveling ministry, she would stop immediately because "he clearly hears the voice of the Spirit."[115] Years after the women's liberation movement, women evangelists continued to make the same pledge. Their ministries, observed Scott Billingsley, mirrored the wider American culture's growing commitment to sexual equality while retaining the traditional conservative mores of mother and wife. When their marriages failed, female evangelists often faced stronger opprobrium than males. After Paula White's marriage to her co-pastor Randy fell apart, disapproval dogged her every step. During her interview with Larry King, an e-mail question from a San Antonio viewer stated it bluntly: "How can you preach from the pulpit regarding marriage when yours failed?" White replied that she was committed "never to waste my trials in life, to find purpose in all things." Critics were not convinced.[116] Even when the public blame for divorce fell on the husband, it was the wife's ministry that suffered. Juanita Bynum received heated criticism for divorcing her husband and fellow prosperity pastor Thomas Weeks III even after he was jailed on charges that he had assaulted her in an Atlanta parking lot.[117] The ministerial duo Zachary and Riva Tims parted ways after reports surfaced that he maintained a yearlong affair with an exotic dancer. Even so, it was Zachary who retained the bulk of their spiritual assets: the leadership of their 7,500-member New Destiny Christian Center.[118] It was Riva who had to begin again.

Many independent female teachers, whether for reasons of principle or pragmatism, placed themselves under male spiritual leadership. To be sure, evangelists commonly chose the spiritual oversight of respected peers and most pastors were, of course, men. But it was the rhetoric of that oversight that underscored not only spiritual gratitude but a greater inequality. Some women arranged their spiritual houses like their domestic ones, deferring to a spiritual father. Paula White referred to T. D. Jakes not only as her mentor but her "spiritual daddy," while Juanita Bynum called Jakes, Rod Parsley, and I. V. Hilliard her "fathers-in-the-Lord."[119] When Bynum and Jakes clashed, she publicly apologized before the thousands gathered at his Woman Thou Art Loosed conference by kneeling before him barefoot and tearfully saying: "You are my spiritual father. I submit to you."[120] Kenneth E. Hagin in *The Woman Question* agreed that it was "usually best" to keep gifted men at the helm of churches, but if they could not be found then "let us call the sisters into action." Those women laboring as pastors and evangelists must endeavor to "be content with whatever place the Lord opens" and remain humble, sweet, and faithful.[121] Anne Gimenez, co-pastor of Virginia's Rock Church and author of the book *The Emerging Christian Woman*, deplored Christian women's aggression, "arguing for their 'rights,' displacing men, grasping for leadership."[122] Audiences wanted women to be anointed not aggressive, experienced but not proud. It was a tall order.

From the 1980s onward, most major ministries felt that the best of both worlds lay in husband-and-wife teams. With its obvious advantages, it became ministry's new gold standard. Married leaders typically duplicated the traditional model of conservative households, upholding the husband's spiritual oversight but also encouraging women to exercise their own expertise. Joel and Victoria Osteen raised their interlaced fingers in a triumphant salute at the close of every conference. But women typically were delegated authority over stereotypically feminine domains such as marriage, relationships, child rearing, and emotional turbulence. Creflo Dollar headlined national tours while Taffi Dollar focused on her own women's conferences. These married teams assured audiences that the

FIGURE 5.8 **Joel and Victoria Osteen** Victoria Osteen, pictured beside her famous husband, at the front row of their Lakewood Church, Houston. She was the consummate co-pastor: beautiful, supportive, and a regular preacher on tithing before Joel's sermon began. 2010.

Source: Nick De La Torre/© 2010 *Houston Chronicle.*

ministry reflected family values, even when wives outshone their husbands. In Joyce Meyer's 2008 speaking tour, she painstakingly defended her husband's authority and support of her ministry, though it was clear who wore the pants in their ministry—Dave was always relegated to the unlucky breakfast slot on the conference circuit.[123] In time, there were prosperity duos in which the female came to eclipse her male partner. Frances Hunter became more prominent than Charles; Marilyn Hickey overshadowed Wally; and Joyce Meyer outshone Dave. The prosperity movement had learned to accept women's contributions to the victorious life, albeit with mixed results.

A husband's promotion was an alternative route to the top for some women. Paul Morton, head of the expansive Full Gospel Baptist Church Fellowship, renounced his negative views on women in ministry. In May of 2008, having gathered more and more churches under his authority, he appointed his wife Debra the senior pastor of his own St. Stephen congregation in New Orleans, lowering himself to the role of co-pastor. Said Morton: "For her to come in and initially serve as 'first lady' in our church, then head up our ministry in New Orleans, then in 1993 become my co-pastor and now become my senior pastor in New Orleans—that's wonderful."[124] Granted, he now oversaw a much larger spiritual realm as the bishop of bishops.

For all the egalitarianism among the leadership of some prosperity churches, there remained clear gender roles for many of the participants. In a movement that preached abundance, not just in money but in family life, singlehood was perceived as a problem: marriage was the desired state for women. Single females were often called to the altar to be prayed over in order that they might be soon blessed with a husband. In churches where the majority of the congregants were women, who already shouldered the heaviest burdens in supporting the work of the church, being without a loyal man was an additional cross to bear.

Triumph and Recession

In 2009, seven prophets crowded the narrow table, their starched clerical collars and black suits the dark backdrop to the gold instruments before them. Master Prophet E. Bernard Jordan, his coiled dreadlocks pulled back from an impassive face, narrated the proceedings for the at-home Internet viewers. The tabletop tree with slips of paper as leaves was, in fact, a money tree, garnished with the names of $10,000 donors. One thousand dollar pledges earned people a spot at the base of the tree in the burled wooden bowl, where their names would be manually agitated with coins to "stir up faith."

"Now I want you to put your hands in here," Jordan said, as the ministers slipped their hands, heavy with gleaming rings and watches, into the bowl.

"Money, money, money, money, money, MONEY, MONEY, WEALTH!" intoned the master prophet, growing louder. "Come now, let every yoke be broke. In JESUS' name." He paused at length as he rubbed the coins and paper together. "And the question is, is your name in the base of this tree? Your name needs to be there . . . How long will we do this?" Jordon asked his fellow ministers.

"Until the recession is over," they replied in unison.

The economic disaster that struck North America and Europe in 2008 and came to be known as the "great recession" posed a sharp challenge to preachers of the prosperity gospel. How could a movement predicated on abundance possibly thrive in an era of unemployment, cutbacks, restricted credit, and home foreclosures? A number of prosperity ministries were, in fact, hard hit as revenues plummeted. Robert Schuller's Crystal Cathedral and Dewey Friedel's Shore Christian Center in New Jersey filed for bankruptcy. However, most prosperity churches met the challenges with an air of confidence and a number of coping strategies. Rather than behaving defensively in the face of the recession, preachers used it as an even-stronger selling point for what they were offering. "A worldwide financial crisis is here," crowed a Morris Cerullo advertisement, "Are you prepared?" Cerullo helpfully offered his "Financial Breakthrough Spiritual Warfare Bible" for $69.95. ("As seen on worldwide TV. Regularly valued at over $120.") The prosperity gospel was universally touted as God's "ultimate bailout plan" by preachers looking for a snappy tagline.[125]

Master Prophet Jordan himself had risen from straitened circumstances and survived a scandalous reputation in the 1990s for selling personal prophecies.[126] Adopting an Afrocentric aesthetic rich in Egyptian and diasporic imagery, he followed in the metaphysical footsteps of Reverend Ike. He conceived of a course in cosmic economics that promised to help followers "recession-proof" their lives. His son, nicknamed "Young Prophet," appeared alongside Benny Hinn delivering miracle words and dramatic healing touches. Prophet Manasseh Jordan's ministry might be at the margins of the movement, but even those more conventional ministers with a message of soft prosperity, such as Latino megachurch pastor

Benny Perez, saw the need to continue to make promises of wealth despite the gloom. His *Kingdom Finances* CD set was decorated with a shower of currency—all large denominations.

Prosperity preachers steamrolled through the tough economic times with brash promises and taught believers to look past the grim evidence in the newscasts and hearken instead to otherworldly cues. Church of God evangelist T. L. Lowery's *Living in God's Economy* encouraged readers to take shelter from the financial meltdown "in the safety of God's economy where His provision of blessing is flowing continually to meet your needs."[127] Berin Gilfillan, a former television producer for the German revivalist Reinhard Bonnke, sold the keys to financial multiplication, backed by "the highest oath in the universe."[128]

Some evangelists showed remarkable ingenuity in adapting their ministries to match the newly restrained economic climate. Catherine Eagan and her husband Victor were touted by prosperity heavyweights Paula White, Myles Munroe, and Keith Butler as "kingdom multimillionaires" anointed by God to help believers realize their financial potential. Finding the roles of pastor, millionaire, and entrepreneur to be mutually reinforcing, Eagan hosted Wealthy Women seminars. Before the recession, their product was the hope for opulence. In advertisements featuring mountains, palm trees, private jets, mansions, yachts, and sports cars, readers were urged to pay steep prices to join Kingdom Millionaire seminars in Boca Raton, Florida. After the economic downturn, the message changed. Realities were acknowledged—seminars offered instruction on "what to do when your company is downsized"—and emphasis was placed on trusting the techniques of faith that had been proven effective in countering the market slide.

If those on the podium exuded confidence, what of their listeners? Were they blind to the reality of the worst economic slump since the 1930s? An incident in Winston-Salem in 2008 showed the passive and direct ways in which, at times, the sheep resisted the shepherd.

On a muggy July evening, I joined churchgoers from across North Carolina to celebrate the 36th ministerial anniversary of the gospel music legend Shirley Caesar. The featured guest was Florida evangelist Paula White, whose sudden rise to stardom had made her a popular attraction.[129] White, mired in divorce proceedings against her co-pastor husband, had attracted a smaller crowd to this conference than expected by the organizers, and the sweet chords of the preliminary worship raised hollow echoes off the arena walls. Members drawn from Caesar's 1,500-member Mount Calvary

Word of Faith church, located in North Carolina's Research Triangle, were scattered like leaves throughout the cavernous space. The emcee, a polished member of Caesar's church staff, transitioned from worship to the offertory with a sharp admonition. The cost of this event, she warned, would burden Pastor Shirley if people were not generous in their offerings. In fact, God had given Pastor Shirley a vision of 100 women marching, each with $100 to place on the stage. With them, she believed, seven business people were being called by God to march with $1,000 in hand. As the emcee elaborated on where the women would stand and in what formation, an uncomfortable realization dawned. No one moved. The crowd was as silent as 300 people in a tin-can arena could be.

The emcee persisted through more silence, urging the women to stand and prepare to march for God. "One hundred dollars! How many will stand with one hundred dollars?" The crowd answered with silence. "Seventy-five?" Rustling. "Fifty?"

"We don't have it!" a woman's voice called from the crowd. A few peals of laughter reverberated through the crowd, followed by more silence. The economic recession and rising gas prices had struck average Americans hard, and the anonymous voice had named the uncomfortable truth.

The emcee, a willowy middle-aged woman in a tweed suit, tugged on her pearl necklace, visibly flustered. "Because you said that, you'll NEVER have it! The Bible says that death and life are in the power of the tongue," she shot back. The crowd answered with brief applause. "You've lost the opportunity of a lifetime!" She continued with a lengthy reprimand. Three women stood in their seats, and the announcer jubilantly gave them their marching orders. More followed when she implied that credit cards would be accepted. "You charge a vacation! Why not charge a miracle?" Though the emcee declared that she would not beg, she continued to squeeze the crowd for donations that, in the end, failed to match Pastor Shirley's hopeful vision. In every prosperity church I attended I heard the message: "This isn't *our* depression!" But sometimes for the people in the pews, those on whom the prosperity of the prosperity preachers ultimately rested, it *was* their depression.

Triumph and Time

Benny Hinn leaned into the podium and rolled his eyes. "I don't have to even say it because we are thinking the same thing!" he said, shaking his head. The call to prayer from the Dome of the Rock's could be heard in the background of Benny Hinn's first address on his Holy Land tour, an unwelcome reminder that thousands of Muslims knelt in Ramadan worship just over Jerusalem's city wall where we had assembled. Not far away, the cheers of hundreds of Israeli soldiers, dressed in fatigues, yarmulkes, and casually slung assault rifles, marked the commencement of the Soldier's Oaths festivities at the Western Wall. Unbelievers besieged the Holy City itself, no matter how loudly the Christian crowd sang "The Old Rugged Cross."

"It won't be like this for long, because Jesus will take care of all of this!" Hinn shouted. Jesus would return to this very place, Hinn assured us, and we would not have to wait long. Israel's miraculous rebirth as a nation in 1948 marked an explosion of prophecy, truths that God would reveal in 100 years. Unwilling to bait the crowd with generalities, he named the date: 2048. Jesus would gather up the faithful, the true seekers who were present this night.[130]

As we straggled back to the hotel, a few labored over the implications. "Everything is just coming together!" a man in a Hawaiian shirt exclaimed, while an elderly woman appeared more concerned. She carefully counted and recounted the years between now and then and tallied it to her age. It would be too late for her.

FIGURE 5.9 **Benny Hinn Crusade** Benny Hinn in his trademark all-white Nehru suit at his crusade in Anaheim, California, July 2004.
Source: Brent Peters.

On this first night, "Pastor Benny" proclaimed that this would be a life-changing experience and a profound encounter with God. In his role as a popular prophet, Hinn modeled intimacy with God and history. As the markets fluctuated, the global political climate threatened, and the social mood darkened, believers turned to those who interpreted their faith in the context of changing times. Leaders like Benny Hinn set the grand stage for spiritual expectations by constructing timetables for the end of the world or putting the daily news in cosmic context.

In a general sense, every prosperity leader took on this role. Often, it translated into general assurances that the spiritual laws of sowing and reaping did not shift with the times. Believers would ascend to greater heights, regardless of circumstances. In 2008, while markets collapsed, banks failed, and the housing bubble burst, Joel Osteen proclaimed, "It's going to be a year of promotion, a year of increase, a year of favor, a year of supernatural opportunities!" Faith teachers frequently declared "the Year of..." based on God's revelation for the year to come. Paula White declared 2008 to be the year of new beginnings and a start for new supernatural increase. Kenneth Copeland sent out hundreds of thousands of recorded phone messages declaring 2008 the year of the fullness of God's measure. The Word of Faith Christian Center in Nashville went a step further, declaring 2011 as "A Year When Everything Will Be All Right."[131] Critics dismissed these as gimmicks, but followers expected their leaders to provide this kind of macrolevel eschatological interpretation. It located believers in spiritual time, establishing expectations for how Christians should set their own lives to the cosmic spiritual clock.

A portion of victory lay in the past. The past connected believers to a spiritual bloodline, traceable from the crucified Christ to every child of God. Spiritual lineage superseded natural family background as the new indicator of identity and ability. "You have the DNA of Almighty God," stated Joel Osteen. "You need to know that inside you flows the blood of a winner."[132] Victory came as a birthright. Why then did sin stubbornly persist? Osteen answered simply: "bad blood." The natural bloodlines flowing through grandparents, parents, and children passed down hereditary sin that perpetuated generational curses. Prudent believers cautiously combed through the past to find the residual effects of their natural family's bloodline. All manner of illnesses and behaviors—especially debt, abuse, alcoholism, and depression—fell under the rubric of generational curse. Derek Prince, one of the charismatic movement's experts on the subject, likened curses to a "long, evil arm stretched out from the past."[133] Seven probable indicators of curses were mental breakdown, chronic illness, barrenness, family alienation, financial difficulties, repeated accidents, and untimely deaths. Adherents learned to look for negative patterns in their lives and root out their spiritual cause. Faith believers applied spiritual solutions to what outsiders might see as problems with genetic, social, economic, and environmental causes. Prosperity folk would not concede defeat to genetic or social circumstances. Brenda, a nurse from Durham's Victorious Faith Center, said that, people surrender their God-given victory when they repeat, "I have this because my daddy had this . . ." as if it were inevitable. Take responsibility! Take control![134]

Two conflicting impulses squared off in prosperity theology. The first was the prosperity injunction to do well on this earth by increasing in measure and deepening in faith. Outsiders often depicted the prosperity gospel as so "worldly," so preoccupied with perfecting life on earth, that it lacked the apocalyptic vision that featured so prominently in the theology of many other Christian groups. To Kenneth E. Hagin, this was good common sense: "I'm more concerned about the life that now is than I am about the life that is to come. Because the life that 'now is' is the life I'm living right now." Adherents did not want to jettison the promise of heaven, but they championed the present as a garden of delights. However, as prosperity theology was subsumed under a broader pentecostal cosmology, the prosperity gospel anticipated that this world would come to an end. Human life remained a conditional gift, and time would someday unravel. "We are the end-time generation," warned Kenneth Copeland.[135] How could the same gospel be committed both to prospering on this earth, and to seeing this earth come to an end? Could believing folk maintain a strong stake in the soon-to-be abandoned world and still be committed to the coming apocalypse?

The traditional pentecostal narrative of time was laid out in Premillennial Dispensationalism.[136] This biblical hermeneutic found discrete spiritual principles at work in different historical epochs and commonly saw the present as an era of cultural and spiritual decline that believers must endure until they were "raptured" (physically taken up to heaven while living). Faith preachers affirmed a pentecostal theology of decline but exempted believers from its hardships. Hard prosperity could be deeply apocalyptic. Those prophets peered into the end times and saw a brighter future. Their lives plotted a trajectory of unbroken progress. Texas evangelist John Avanzini promoted an apocalyptic message of "biblical economics" that described an army of saints who "take the wealth of the wicked for the harvesting of the world in these last days!" God promised to transfer the wealth of the wicked into the bank accounts of the righteous. World evangelism remained the goal but Christian imperialism the means: "God is going to take the silver from the wealthy wicked, and He is going to hand that silver, and the monies of the unsaved bankers, and the oil riches of the Arabs, and the money in the International Monetary Fund—*all* over to the 'innocent' for the funding of His final endtime harvest!"[137] But believers must first prove themselves worthy. The Lord scoured the earth for those keeping watch.[138]

"The Lord is watching everything we do for Him today," warned Benny Hinn. "He is looking for a people He can trust, for the day will come when true riches will be committed to believers who are faithful. These true riches not only are the invisible power of God but also the coming wealth transfer on earth that will finance the end-time harvest!" Televangelist Perry Stone of the Church of God (Cleveland, Tennessee) swore that he had unlocked the biblical code for the apocalyptic timetable and that believers were *Entering the Time of Double Portion Blessing.*[139] Money earned theological value as an eschatological and creational marker of God's intent, proof positive that God set Christians aside for special blessings.

Gloria Copeland assured audiences that while crime increased, moral decay flourished, and others suffered, she did not "plan on being with them."[140] She would continue to progress financially and spiritually, moving from "glory to glory to glory." Faith believers redefined the notion of rapture. Traditionally, it was thought that God would rescue believers from their problems by taking them up to heaven. Instead, God took the problems *from* the believers, bringing them a bit of heaven on earth. This notion fortified a theology of upward mobility, for the wicked world, however corrupt, could never prevent believers from living victoriously in the present one. All structural sin—including racism, sexism, and poverty—must be placed in the context of this narrative of sweeping confidence. History rewarded the faithful who stubbornly believed that the earth brimmed with opportunities, a sure field for any believer's harvest.

Three prescriptions for the end times were common. In the first, God called for individual purity and that virtue would ensure a safe haven while the world deteriorated. Some teachers went so far to say that the timing of Jesus' Second Coming hinged on the progress of individual regeneration. In the second reading, Jesus would not return until the church (taken to mean a local, independent congregation) demonstrated a perfected faith.

The Victorious Faith Center labored to be the glorious church described in the book of Ephesians as "not having spot or wrinkle" but "holy and without blemish."[141] Churchgoers should be ready to show the "signs and wonders" accomplished through the prosperity gospel, from paid mortgages, to respectable jobs, strong families, and sustaining faith. Third and last, some prosperity preachers applied the formula at a national level. America's future depended on its wholehearted support of God's original Promised Land: Israel.

Triumph in Zion

Benny Hinn took off his sunglasses and looked out at the gathered crowd. "It's a beautiful view, isn't it?" he asked, gesturing behind him to the sweeping view of the Old City, Jerusalem, gleaming white over the thoroughfare and steep embankment that separated us. "You know," he continued, "Jerusalem needs our help." He claimed that Condoleezza Rice, George W. Bush's Secretary of State, sought to divide the sacred city between Palestinians and Israelis, posing a threat not only to Israel's future but also to God's blessing on America. "Come up here! Gather around!" Several hundred travelers crowded around the platform and stretched out their hands out toward Jerusalem as Hinn began to pray vigorously for Israel's continued survival and prosperity. Its founding 60 years ago had unleashed a prophetic and miraculous season. God blessed Israel as his chosen nation and would continue to bless America so long as it supported Israel. "Israel needs you now more than ever!" he cried. Around him, the murmur of pilgrim prayers rose until it drowned out Hinn's voice altogether.[142]

Some prosperity preachers refused to soft pedal the news. God's provision rested on a national covenant that bound America and Israel to one fate. Pointing to God's promise to Israel that "I will bless those who bless you, and the one who curses you I will curse," they argued that America must bless Israel to claim its own divine wealth.[143] In most respects, they followed the theological framework of Christian Zionism. The founding of the state of Israel signaled Jesus' imminent return and—though the details remained debatable—Israel's history would determine the course of the end of time. Two different forms of Christian Zionism prevailed in pentecostal circles: the apocalyptic and the dispensational. Benny Hinn represented the former. He interpreted Israel's history in light of apocalyptic prophecies but did not attempt to situate the daily news in a rigid

dispensational framework. The famous Christian Zionists (and prosperity preachers) John Hagee and Rod Parsley held the latter position,
seeing history as divided into discrete epochs (dispensations) that defined
God's plans for human salvation. In this last epoch, Israel would be the
staging ground for the final battle of armageddon and Jesus' return.
Benny Hinn's tour split the difference between the two approaches and
included sidebars for end times tourism. We stopped at the Mount of
Olives to consider prayerfully that Jesus would descend from heaven to
this spot. We climbed the heights to survey the valley of Jezreel and
Megiddo, where the final bloody battle will take place. Of my 80-person
tour group, only Trudy, a retired schoolteacher from Wisconsin, picked
through the apocalyptic details with relish. A frequent visitor to the Holy
Land, Trudy rattled off the characteristics of the antichrist and the battle
itself before our bus mates stopped her with skeptical questions. The rest
snapped pictures of the panorama and shuffled down the dusty hill to the
waiting buses.[144]

John Hagee was pastor of the 10,000-member Cornerstone Church
in San Antonio, the nation's 16th-largest prosperity church and one of
the leading centers of Christian Zionism. He popularized a dual commitment to the prosperity gospel and a dispensational theology. In
Financial Armageddon, for example, Hagee detailed the apocalyptic significance of the 2008 economic meltdown and a faith-filled path around
its obstacles.[145] He preferred Jewish prayer shawls "designed by God" to
regular prayer clothes, touting their special "power to energize your
prayer life."[146] Israel's future determined the fate of American success,
as he outlined in *From Daniel to Doomsday* (2000), *Attack on America*
(2001), *The Battle for Jerusalem* (2003), *Jerusalem Countdown* (2006),
and *In Defense of Israel* (2007). Christians United for Israel, which
Hagee founded and Parsley led, hosted a yearly Washington rally where
several thousand participants and a star-studded roster of politicians
and preachers vented Israel's concerns. With its advisory board made
up almost exclusively of the faith movement's top brass, the organization opposed the two-state solution to Israel's political woes and sent
millions of dollars to settle new immigrants there.[147] Pat Robertson famously declared that Yitzhak Rabin was cursed for dividing Israel.[148]
The number of faith congregations actively supporting Zionism
remained small, but some of the prosperity gospel's beloved pastors
applied the logic of faith to this critical international problem. God has
tethered both believers and nations to lasting covenants.

Compassionate Victory

A frequent criticism of the prosperity gospel was that in its concentration on transforming individual lives through the power of faith, it ignored the physical and economic needs of its communities. It is true that one prosperity preacher in Sacramento refused to use the term "poor" to describe those suffering economically, preferring to see them as "people between blessings,"[149] but such language did not preclude a helping attitude to those in need. The Word of Faith International Christian Center operated a nursing home, hospice, halfway house, homeless shelter, and prison ministry. The Abundant Living Faith Center donated toys, food, and clothing to families in their neighborhood. World Changers Ministries offered GED preparation classes, legal resources, and substance abuse programs. Numerous churches opened schools. In Maryland, Bishop James R. Peebles and his wife, Betty, spiritual mother to a generation of neopentecostals, founded the Jericho Christian Academy, followed in 1978 by a four-year accredited college with more than 3,000 students.[150] Outreach to prisoners, addicts, and the homeless were common, especially among churches in impoverished areas. When hundreds of parishioners in Eddie Long's Atlanta New Birth Baptist Church faced foreclosure on their homes, the church responded with financial aid for some, job placement, financial counseling, and aid from real estate professionals for others.[151] Anxious to be seen as "full-service" churches, some ministries offered niche market assistance: Kenneth Copeland reached out to bikers, and Church on the Move supported cowboys on the Oklahoma rodeo circuit.

A few generalizations about the social services of prosperity megachurches can be drawn from my survey of the websites of 115 prosperity megachurches. Most churches were happy to address needs that could be met individually with a plethora of ministries such as clothing drives, food drives, soup kitchens, grocery giveaways, neighborhood pantries, school supplies for children, or car maintenance for senior citizens. The didactic air of the prosperity gospel was always thick. The most common institutional form of ministry was educational, from Christian primary schools through to unaccredited Bible colleges. Affordable housing, job banks, and sustained social services were more difficult to find; most initiatives were geared to immediate relief and not structured for long-term engagement. Tamelyn Tucker-Worgs, in her comprehensive study of the civic engagement of black megachurches, convincingly argued that adherence to the prosperity gospel in nondenominational black prosperity churches inhibited social outreach, particularly those ministries that addressed long-term and organizational change. This characterization, from my preliminary study, mirrors the individualistic and short-term solutions offered by prosperity megachurches overall, dominated as they are by nondenominational churches. Future research must come to terms with the full scale of the prosperity gospel's independent and denominational varieties.[152]

Churches that did attempt to promote structural change on a deeper social level were likely to be among the minority of African American prosperity churches that belonged to denominations. Black Baptists, Methodists, and pentecostals typically preferred community-development organizations as the vehicle for a range of services, from affordable housing to food distribution, health clinics, homelessness programs, and day care. Other than compassion ministries, prosperity churches favored programs that fostered entrepreneurialism and virtues such as thrift, timeliness, and budgeting that were instrumental in achieving financial success. Prayers for new businesses were not only a regular part of many church services but also a privileged form of church support. Job banks,

FIGURE 5.10 **Church Housing** A cluster of brick houses sponsored by a nonde-nominational prosperity megachurch, the Christian Faith Center, sits on the outskirts of Creedmoor, North Carolina. 2012.

Source: Author's photo.

financial counseling, and small business workshops were often features of these churches who hoped that prosperity was just around the corner.

THE PROSPERITY GOSPEL told the Christian narrative as if it were an upward sweep toward ultimate and assured victory. Social, cultural, institutional, or individual barriers crumbled before believers to make way for personal and collective breakthroughs. The Grammy-winning Clark Sisters encapsulated the faith movement's triumphant spirit when they sang what amounted to a primer on how to "grasp" things with your mind and "speak it" with your mouth.

> Just name it and claim it,
> It's yours, it's yours.[153]

From individual victory to national blessings, the movement reasoned that the spiritual universe operated according to fixed principles that true believers could see, plot, and track. Believers would have concurred with the title of eighteenth-century writer John Toland's book *Christianity Not Mysterious*. Their gospel was supernatural, to be sure, but not mysterious. Faith-filled principles guided believers through the minefield of life's obstacles toward greater and greater heights.

Conclusion

An American Blessing

WAS THE PROSPERITY gospel a uniquely American phenomenon? The message certainly resonated with a set of national characteristics deeply embedded in the American social imaginary. At times, the prosperity gospel hovered so closely to its nationalistic alter ego, American civil religion, that it appeared to be its pentecostal twin, each offering an account of transcendent truths at the core of the American character. But rather than sacralizing the founding of the United States or visions of manifest destiny, the prosperity gospel was constituted by the deification and ritualization of the American Dream: upward mobility, accumulation, hard work, and moral fiber. The two shared an unshakably high anthropology, studded with traits that inspire action, urgency, a sense of chosenness, and a desire to shoulder it alone.[1] If the prosperity gospel can be taken as a gauge of the nation's self-perception, this is surely a country soaring with confidence in the possibility of human transformation. The movement's culture of god-men and conquerors rang true to a nation that embraced the mythology of righteous individuals bending circumstances to their vision of the good life.

The prosperity movement did not simply give Americans a gospel worthy of a nation of self-made men. It affirmed the basic economic structures on which individual enterprise stood. Caretakers of any gospel of success trusted the "innate moral equilibrium of the marketplace" to mete out rewards and punishment in fortune or failure.[2] The virtuous would be richly compensated while the wicked would eventually stumble. This was a theology of excess that separated the faith-filled few from the poverty of the masses. It effectively disengaged spiritual purity from cultural separation, allowing adherents to participate fully in the world *as is*. Effectively mythologized in Horatio Alger's dime novels of "rags to riches," the prosperity gospel retold the inevitable triumph of character over an unruly free-market economy. It was a picture-perfect American tale when prosperity celebrity Frederick Price received the 1998 Horatio Alger award for "remarkable achievements accomplished through honesty, hard work, self-reliance, and perseverance over adversity."[3] The movement had not only tapped into a well of imagined traits thought to be inseparable from civic character, but articulated values that were equal parts of spiritual and secular value. In this, modern prosperity believers are not unlike Max Weber's early Puritans, whose religious insecurity about their post-mortem fate transmuted into capitalist virtues. It was the Protestant work ethic resurrected for a breathless nation of multitaskers and entre-preneurs and customer service professionals. Even the creative class could find their ambitions sanctified. Little wonder that Oasis Church, in the heart of Los Angeles' film distinct, commemorated Jesus as Savior by giving him his own Hollywood star.[4]

The prosperity gospel's emphasis on the individual's responsibility for his or her own fate resonated strongly with the American tradition of rugged self-reliance. In a political climate in which socialist was a deadly insult, raw individualism was entrenched as the American way despite the cold truth that, since Franklin Roosevelt's New Deal and Lyndon Johnson's Great Society, government programs had swelled to meet the needs of tens of millions of Americans who required assistance ranging from local welfare to Medicare and Social Security. Love of liberty was a national pas-time and a country music bonanza. Lee Greenwood's 1984 patriotic song, "God Bless the USA," often reprised after 9/11, celebrated the individual freedom for which Americans were willing to die, not socialized medicine or a national pension plan. Freedom was the sacred language of choice. Such an atmosphere oxygenated the words and message of prosperity preachers. Family Harvest Church pastor Robb Thompson's credo, "people can actually bring to themselves what they believe about themselves," spoke to a country steeped in the mythology of individual effort.

The prosperity gospel consecrated America's culture of optimism. "We should always walk with smiles on our faces, our heads held high, our shoulders squared, believing God," said the young Jimmy Swaggart.[5] Americans, for the most part, agreed that they should learn to see the sunny side of life. When television psychologist Dr. Phil introduced a jilted wife, who had written a book titled *My Husband's Affair Became the Best Thing That Ever Happened to Me*, audiences nodded approvingly.[6] A positive outlook transformed personal slumps or tragedies into tests of character and opportunities for growth. Positive by reputation and self-image, Americans preferred to look for the silver lining. As Barbara Ehrenreich argued in *Bright-Sided*, American society cultivated consummate positive thinkers. They learned not simply to anticipate the best but also to rely on their upbeat expectations to change their circumstances.[7] Despite being ranked 150th in happiness among the world's nations, the United States valued preachers, prophets, and authors who taught us how to accent the upbeat. Beginning in the 1980s, life-coaches invaded corporate culture as companies hired speakers to bring "winning" attitudes to America's boardrooms.[8] Corporations considered employees' spirituality as an untapped resource.[9] Psychologists devoted to the new "science of happiness" published their findings in venues like the *Journal of Happiness Studies*, while books such as Tal Ben-Shahar's *Happier* and Martin Seligman's *Learned Optimism* and *Authentic Happiness* brought positive psychology to the mass market. The nation soared so high on good feelings, warned the author of *Never Saw It Coming*, that it lacked the ability to anticipate and prevent worst-case scenarios.[10] American optimism reigned.

Over the last century, bright-sided faith mixed with American conceptions of the self. Numerous evangelical pastors and public speakers saw the virtue of blending Protestantism and the principles of positive thinking. Bruce Wilkinson's bestselling *The Prayer of Jabez* championed an Old Testament prayer as the way to petition God for spiritual and material increase, and its sequel piled on to the growing evangelical consensus that business acumen and Christian virtue were synonymous. Laurie Beth Jones, author of *Jesus, CEO* and *Jesus, Inc.*, described a boardroom savior:

> He didn't work for money
> > He had impeccable market timing.
> > He did sweat the small stuff.
> > He was not a perfectionist.
> > He finished what he started.
> > He knew a business plan wouldn't save him.
> > He was . . . a spiritreneur.[11]

Mediocrity acquired the taint of sin, as authors fretted about the wastefulness of lives not fully lived. "Not long ago and not far away, a Nobody named Ordinary lived in the Land of Familiar," wrote Wilkinson of the everyman. The Tulsa pastor John Mason identified it as *An Enemy Called Average*. The earliest manuals for prosperity provided rough sketches of what this more-than-average believer should look like. The 1957 cover of *Releasing the Power Within* showed a man standing in the open plains with his arms upstretched, electricity radiating from his fingertips and the bearded face of Jesus anchored on his chest. Inside, the same man lifts a mountain as a ghostly apparition of the Savior lends a helping hand. The caption reads: "The faith that takes . . . takes mountains."[12] The sheer impossibility of the task meant little. In fact, it was precisely the point.

Twentieth-century metaphysical gospels made the mind a spiritual playground. Common-sense realism, the bread and butter of American evangelicalism, yielded to religious knowledge that was elusive and, at times, esoteric.[13] Truth was not always apparent; it had to be ferreted out as it emerged from the mind's hidden recesses. American readers hoping to apply this secret knowledge to their advantage made bestsellers of Louise Hay's *You Can Heal Your Life* (1984) and Deepak Chopra's *The Seven Spiritual Laws of Success* (1994). Indeed, the emphasis on practice was irrepressible. Truths were techniques, waiting to be applied. Whether through hypnosis, the use of placebos, or the power of suggestion, positive thinkers cultivated religious practices and techniques to subdue, focus, or activate the mind's hidden powers. This opened the door for popular religion and the mainstream alike to construct an image of the individual as autonomous, and only as powerful as his or her mind. This is not to say these ideas achieved pure individualism. As Courtney Bender showed in *The New Metaphysicals*, the tangle of ideas and practices that constitute modern American mysticism was inextricable from the history and societies of those who lived them out. In 2007, Rhonda Byrne's breakaway hit, *The Secret*, became the latest New Thought-inspired articulation of the idealized self-made American. Endorsed by a host of successful inventors, authors, and metaphysical leaders, the book encouraged people to direct their thoughts toward achieving their desires. Fans like Oprah Winfrey, along with the ever-increasing ranks of those claiming to be "spiritual but not religious," found that *The Secret* ritualized two American sentiments: people rise to the level of their ambition, and there's no such thing as luck.[14]

However, as much as this is an American story, it is also an account of globalization, the rapid compression of economic, social, political, and cultural forces into a complex system of transnational interactions. Dating back to the 1950s (and dependent on a long history of evangelical and pentecostal missions), prosperity preachers were tied into an international circuit of crusades, native schools, host churches, books, magazines, radio broadcasts, television, and satellites. The development of digital media only accelerated the breathtaking pace of transnational communication. The prosperity gospel was obsessed with modernity and delighted in exploiting the latest methods of communication.[15] As congregations, audiences, and leaders in disparate locations became increasingly interactive and integrated, the prosperity gospel rapidly spread as a global phenomenon.

Christianity, as scholars were slowly discovering, had "gone South," as the Christian world slipped its moorings in Europe and North America and shifted toward Africa, Asia, and Latin America.[16] Many of the Global South's best-attended congregations proclaimed a prosperity gospel. The world's largest church, with a million members, was the Yoido Full Gospel Church in Seoul, South Korea, led by Paul Yonggi Cho. The Philippines' El Shaddai movement, a medley of prosperity and Roman Catholic themes, began in the early 1980s, and in three decades grew to a following of roughly nine to eleven million.[17] The Singapore-based City Harvest Church gathered 27,000 believers weekly to hear Dr. Kong Lee and his wife Ho Yeow Sun, the "singing pastor" and pop star. In the same metropolis, Joseph Prince boasted a congregation of 20,000 and his New Creation Church services were broadcast internationally.[18] Australia's largest church, Sydney's Hillsong Church, claimed more than 20,000 attendees and an international faith ministry. Led by pastors Brian and Bobbie Houston, Hillsong's famous worship music earned more than 50 gold and platinum sales awards, becoming some of the world's most popular contemporary Christian songs. Riverview Church in Perth grew out of Rhema Family Church to become one of the largest churches in Australia.[19] Brazil's Universal Church of the Kingdom of God (UCKG) grew to one of the world's largest prosperity-preaching denominations, with 2,000 congregations across its native land alone. Nigeria's Winners Chapel and Faith Tabernacle seated more than 50,000 apiece for prosperity teaching in that nation's capital. International expressions of divine health and wealth had become the testing grounds of God's immutable laws. As Kenneth Hagin argued, "prosperity is not an 'American gospel.' It will work in Africa, India, China, or anywhere else God's people practice the truth of His Word. If it's not true in the poorest place on earth, it's not true at all!"[20]

The prosperity gospel proved readily exportable. While the degree to which these international prosperity churches relied on American faith teaching has not yet been determined, we can see clearly that preachers and ideas bounced back and forth in the global spiritual market.[21] When Brother Mike Velarde searched for a name for his independent Catholic prosperity gospel in the Philippines, he found it in the title of the Kenneth Hagin booklet, *El Shaddai: The God Who is More Than Enough.* Yet when Brother Mike rallied his followers to depose or elect various Filipino officials, few American believers would have recognized this faith message as their own. Though the American prosperity gospel provided some of the theological underpinnings, like all indigenized faiths, it was transformed as it traveled.

So, too, the American gospel was influenced by its global offshoots, and Americans found themselves relying on and importing some of its many international incarnations. As non-European Christianity swelled, the pool of Christian immigrants in America grew with it. Newcomers from the Global South, particularly Central America, Latin America, and Africa, filled American pews and coffers. Sociologist Steven Warner reported that two-thirds of the newcomers to America were Christians.[22] The American prosperity gospel enjoyed the benefits. Korean pastor Paul Yonggi Cho became the world's foremost authority on church growth, touring American churches from the late 1970s onward as a trusted advisor. His Yoido Full Gospel Church's 600 missionaries canvassed the globe, planting churches in over 60 countries, including the United States.[23] In 1986, the Universal Church of the Kingdom of God, a Brazilian denomination with prosperity themes, opened its doors in the United States, with 138 outreach centers scattered across 19 states.[24] Techniques pioneered in Latin America were adopted by prosperity churches in the United States.[25] Prosperity leaders from South and Central America found followers in the United States, often employing a new twist on the cell-group approach to church growth labeled the G12 Vision, whereby believers trained 12 followers to go out and make more converts. Myles Munroe of the Bahamas grew to be one of the most popular leaders in the American faith movement. Armed with an honorary doctorate from Oral Roberts University and a winsome personality, he captivated audiences with his island approach to "kingdom principles."[26] A Nigerian recipe for Christian prosperity also proved especially popular in America. By 2010, the Redeemed Christian Church of God (RCCG), founded in 1952 by Josiah Akindayomi, had established 359 congregations across the country.[27] Their aggressive strategies for church planting and enthusiastic worship enticed new immigrant groups—Asian, African, Latin American, and Caribbean in particular—at a steady rate, and their North American headquarters, a 550-acre compound in Hunt County, Texas, demonstrated their commitment to expansive

American evangelism. Even the gospel from Down Under returned to win American converts. In 1999, Steve Kelly, a former associate pastor at Hillsong Church, left Australia to found the 3,000-member Wave Church in Virginia Beach, Virginia.[28] In all of this transnational migration the key was networking and point-to-point contact—it was not a sea that lapped every shore.[29]

Working Prosperity

What does the prosperity gospel offer to its believers? Why has it become so successful in so many places? We must not think that it is simply the lure of financial success. The prosperity movement offers a comprehensive approach to the human condition. It sees men and women as creatures fallen, but not broken, and it shares with them a "gospel," good news that will set them free from a multitude of oppressions. The promise offered by a Chicago-based Latino congregation—*Santidad, Salvación, Sanidad, Liberación* (Sanctification, Salvation, Healing, Deliverance)—is one that all believers can claim.

On one level, the appeal of prosperity theology is obvious. The faith movement sells a compelling bill of goods: God, wealth, and a healthy body to enjoy it. But it is the enjoyment, the feelings that lift believers' chins and square their shoulders, that is its fundamental achievement. The first step in accessing this good news is the belief that things *can* get better. The prosperity gospel's chief allure is simple optimism. Simple, but not easy. Humans need so much to thrive: not just a sufficiency of goods but happy families, rewarding jobs, exercise, friends, harmony with neighbors, etc. These are so much more difficult to achieve when laboring under negative expectations; when expectations are high, greater things can be achieved. The faith movement perpetually demonstrated the practical effects of its brand of optimism. Members cited such benefits of its emotional resources as a sense of self-worth and escape from personal pain.[30] Throughout services in every prosperity church, the message of cultivated cheerfulness is proclaimed. Don't complain. Everybody's got a sad story. Speak only positively and believe for the best. It was perhaps the movement's greatest gift and heaviest burden. The cheerfulness and optimism which the prosperity gospel called for were *cultivated* habits that had to be worked at but which would lead to success in every realm, including the economic. But the imperative to perform happiness at every turn also prevented the sick, the poor, and the unlucky from taking stock of their circumstances. Believers learned to live with the joy and pain of a spiritual world where no one was considered a victim.

Scholars often portray the prosperity gospel as a poor people's movement, an expression of believers' longing for (and distance from) socioeconomic stability.[31] Certainly some preachers aimed directly at this segment of the population. A. A. Allen's and Rex Humbard's ministries had a blue-collar tinge. John Avanzini's pitch for his Millionaire University reassured his poorly educated readers that more than 25 percent of the Forbes 400 wealthiest Americans had never graduated from college.[32] The most compelling evidence that the prosperity gospel preaches to the lower class comes from a recent study that found pentecostals to be the second poorest in the United States with fewer than 20 percent of followers earning at least $75,000.[33] As a child of pentecostalism, the prosperity gospel may not foretell a sunny financial destiny. In truth, we have not yet accurately measured the income levels of American prosperity believers. Challenges abound for the researcher: the movement's scattered congregations can be hard to find and often just as difficult to study. Its networks are diffuse and fluid. The movement that prided itself on the financial well-being of its constituents resists disclosing pastors' salaries, church budgets, and members' income.

There are some reasons to think that historically many American prosperity believers already enjoyed a comfortable standard of living. The prosperity gospel took shape among post–World War II pentecostals, whose modest wealth made them neither paupers nor princes. The charismatic movement, as we have seen, was preaching prosperity to the prosperous. In 1985, an analysis of 23 top-rated religious programs found that prosperity televangelists catered to the upwardly mobile and middle class, rather than the working class (with the exception of working-class favorite Rex Humbard).[34] Pat Robertson's *The 700 Club* talk show, for example, earned strong ratings from educated, middle-class, and midwestern viewers, making him the prophet of middle America.[35] The gospel's strong presence among America's largest churches over the next three decades reinforced its middle-income status. Though megachurch attendees were drawn from a variety of income levels—from those grazing the poverty line to the upper middle class—the largest pool were educated professionals.[36] Prosperity did not always hover out of reach as the target of inspiration: many people embraced the faith message as a lived reality.

It was clear that the cultivation of optimism for divine recompense worked in different ways for different ethnic groups and socioeconomic classes. For many it provides a religious expression of middle-class confidence in the proper workings of the market economy. For the poor it imbues a sense of determination and a reason to make painful investments of money, time, and effort. Believing that changing your actions will ultimately result in success makes you more likely, for example, to acquire a different set of work habits or a higher level of education. Of course, those attending congregations that preached a prosperity gospel also received the usual benefits of church life. Researchers have long recognized that church attendance has a positive correlation with mental health, family stability, and even longer life. The spiritual succor received on Sunday mornings is complemented by greater socialization, psychological counseling, economic networking, and sometimes social assistance. Prosperity churches were strongholds of social services and resources that gave members a competitive advantage: social connections, educational facilities, and social assistance during times of crisis. These faith churches, as self-supporting entities, relied on the engine of a highly active lay leadership. The assignment to laypeople of all the tasks necessary for a large church to hum along helped them develop skills such as organization, budgeting, and leadership, which translated well into entrepreneurial virtues.[37] Further, the prosperity gospel's strict moral code kept more money in believers' pockets by eliminating alcohol, nicotine, drugs, and promiscuous behavior. Historian and missionary Donald McGavran, author of *Understanding Church Growth* (1970), dubbed these effects "redemption and lift."[38] Faith believers created many of the conditions of their own success.

"I tried poverty," quipped Oral Roberts, "and I didn't like it."[39] The prosperity gospel helped the poor to identify with middle-class values and self-image, but the middle class responded just as eagerly, though in different ways. To be sure, the lure of financial gain was part of it. Though they might have more material goods than the poor, their expectation of what constituted "enough" was correspondingly higher. However, as Christians they also had to confront the words of Jesus about rich men, camels, and the eyes of needles. Were they risking divine judgment by seeking Mammon? Here the prosperity gospel offered help. Their God was not a critic of earthly happiness but rather a God who was *for* humanity. The money that the faithful came to possess was blessed because *they* had it and could do godly things with it, unlike the world's unfaithful who might use it in shameful or destructive ways. At a fundamental level, the gospel cultivated and sanctified desire. It is here that the ostentatious displays of wealth by the movement's leadership may be understood, not as crass or garish exhibitionism, but as inducements to economic virtue on the part of the faithful. The Mercedes parked by the church lobby encourages those who have little toward a longing which, in order to be fulfilled, puts them on a path of prayer, frugality, and hard work.

The prosperity gospel articulated a language of aspiration that spoke of materialism and transcendence in a single breath. "Blessed to be a blessing" was the watchword here. It baptized as it ascribed spiritual meaning to everyday needs. A letter written to Evangelist R. G. Hardy made that point effectively: "I am writing to thank you for your prayer for a cooking stove," penned Mrs. L. G. from Virginia, "God has answered this prayer!" Without specifics, she praised the Baltimore preacher for the $384.75 cash she needed to buy a double oven stove.[40] She wanted, and received, a God of everyday miracles.

This message hit the middle class at an opportune time. The great recession did not spare even those well above the poverty line: job loss, underemployment, loss of benefits, and mortgage difficulties also afflicted the middle class. The domestic technology the middle class had acquired with such zeal—the computers, smart phones, tablets, iPods, stereos, flat-screen TVs, home entertainment systems, game boxes, refrigerators, air-conditioning, stoves, wireless security, heavily computerized automobiles, etc.—had left them dependent on objects they could barely operate without assistance, much less repair. Whereas previous generations could change a fuse, set the spark-plug timing, replace the needle on a record-player, or bang hopefully on the television console, modern homeowners were at the mercy of machinery beyond their understanding or control. Prosperity preachers (whose churches themselves were monuments to techno-lust) found a natural way of teaching relatively wealthy Americans about God's invisible economy. Believers must learn to use spiritual laws to gain more or else lose what they already possess. If God was stinted by refusal to tithe or donate generously, then these precious objects could be lost. I heard countless sermons around the country connecting the importance of giving with the ability to maintain control over a domestic economy dominated by gadgets and unforeseen expenses. In a tithing sermon Pastor Walton of Victorious Faith Center lingered over the implications of Malachi 3:8, "Will a man rob God? Yet ye have robbed me. But ye say, Wherein have we robbed thee? In tithes and offerings." Those who did not give robbed not only God but themselves—there would be a curse on their house, their car might break down, bills might go unpaid. "Money just gets away from you," he said.

By the early twenty-first century the prosperity gospel, like its New Thought predecessor, had lost its sectarian flavor. To many, it now tasted as American as apple pie. Phases such as "favor," "abundant life," "positive confession," and "I'm blessed!" popped up in television sitcoms, reflecting a new style of piety that had become common fare. Whereas the movement's story had once been dominated by pentecostals trying to come to grips with modernity, it was now a suaver, more enculturated tale,[41] and one of great influence in American Protestantism.

White evangelicalism, in particular, had taken onboard the sunnier aspects of the prosperity message. Although megachurch evangelicals like Rick Warren and Bill Hybels continued to denounce the prosperity gospel, others slipped an arm around Joel Osteen and encouraged their members to get blessed. Nondenominational evangelical churches like Living Hope Church in Vancouver, Washington, fortified their call for tithing with references to a "system" set up by God to release blessing.[42] Evangelicals challenged one another to consider the tithe an "opportunity" for divine recompense. Churches, big and small, began to launch tithing challenges that asked for 10 percent of gross income with the assurance that "if you tithe faithfully for 90 days and God doesn't hold true to His promises of blessing, we will refund 100% of the tithe you have during that 90 days. No questions asked."[43] Churches, like Walmart, could now offer money back guarantees on big spiritual purchases. Pastors began to toy with the warranty language of large appliance sales and the risk management advice of investment strategists. Kerry Shook, the evangelical pastor of America's tenth-largest church, appeared on a Christian answer to *The Secret* (appropriately called *The Source of the Secret*) to claim the law of attraction as a biblical principle that created a greater relationship with God. Give and it shall be given unto you.

Prosperity messages echoed in the most unlikely places, reverberating through Mennonite, Moravian, and Lutheran houses of worship. Old foes became friends. Even denominations that strongly condemned the teachings of Oral Roberts, T. L. Osborn, and other early prosperity preachers borrowed a page from their playbook. Kregg Hood of the Church of Christ, an avowedly anticharismatic denomination, authored a tithing manual that might as easily have been written by Benny Hinn: *Take God at His Word: Expect a Harvest*. Business mogul Donald Trump, supermodel Tyra Banks, and the late superstar Michael Jackson called faith teacher Paula

White their personal pastor. T. D. Jakes advised American presidents, past and present, with ease. When the legendary Coretta Scott King died, Bishop Eddie Long presided over the funeral.

Since its inception, the prosperity gospel had known trials and tests. But the faith movement had never died away like the healing revivals from which it emerged. Its dense network spread in fits and starts but had grown so diffuse that no one failure could sap its strength. Energized by the concurrent international growth of charismatic congregations, the movement attained international proportions so quickly as to simultaneously confirm and diminish its American significance. What American prosperity preachers had in institutional resources, international prosperity preachers made up for in scale. These two demonstrations of the prosperity gospel—power and numbers—reinvigorated each other. American preachers craved the vast overseas audiences that confirmed their evangelistic reach, while international celebrities trotted out American leaders to remind audiences that their economic dreams could be fulfilled. The movement had taken on the character of its theology, preaching with an air of invincibility so audacious that it compelled an audience. Though its ministers came and went and its jargon and sanctuaries were updated, its good news had become too powerful an idea to be easily displaced. More and more churches looked and sounded like just another megachurch with a respected pastor and multicultural congregation, enjoying a soft prosperity easily mistaken for optimism. People wanted churches that lifted their gaze, enlivened their spirits, and assured them that help was around the corner.

Gloria Copeland, like all prosperity teachers, preached about a world in which all things were possible. She told listeners at the 2006 Azusa Centennial that when a hurricane threatened her home, she knew that "I can do all things through Christ who strengthens me." She woke up her husband and told him of her plan. They crept down to their back porch in the darkness of the storm and prayed faith to the storm, declaring it unable to cross their property line. For good measure, they protected their neighbor's property as well.[44] The image of two of the world's wealthiest Christians shaking their fists at the sky exemplifies the audacity that characterized the new face of popular religion. A host of American preachers claimed not only to predict the rain and the harvest but also to tell it when to pour.

Prosperity Megachurch Table, 2011

Church	Senior Pastor	Self-Reported Attendance	Location	Founded
Lakewood Church	Joel Osteen	38,000	Houston, TX	1959
World Changers Ministries	Creflo Dollar	30,000	College Park, GA	1986
The Potter's House	T. D. Jakes	30,000	Dallas, TX	1996
New Light Christian Center	I. V. Hilliard	29,000	Houston, TX	1984
Mount Zion Baptist Church	Joseph Walker III	25,000	Nashville, TN	1866
New Birth Missionary Baptist Church	Eddie Long	25,000	Lithonia, GA	1939
Bethany Baptist Church	David Evans	23,000	Lindenwold, NJ	1990
West Angeles Church of God in Christ	Charles Blake	22,000	Los Angeles, CA	1943

(continued)

Prosperity Megachurch Table (*continued*)

Church	Senior Pastor	Self-Reported Attendance	Location	Founded
Crenshaw Christian Center	Fred Price, Jr.	22,000	Los Angeles, CA	1973
Abundant Living Faith Center	Charles Nieman	20,000	El Paso, TX	1977
Gateway Church	Robert Morris	19,000	Southlake, TX	1999
"THE WORD" Church	R. A. Vernon	19,000	Cleveland, OH	2000
Victory Christian Center	Sharon Daugherty	17,000	Tulsa, OK	1981
Phoenix First Assembly of God	Tommy Barnett	16,000	Phoenix, AZ	1980
The Fountain of Praise	Remus Wright	16,000	Houston, TX	1959
Family Christian Center	Steve and Melody Munsey	15,000	Munster, IN	1950
Jericho City of Praise	[in transition]	15,000	Landover, MD	1964
Jubilee Christian Center	Dick Bernal	14,000	San Jose, CA	1980
Redemption World Outreach Center	Ron Carpenter	14,000	Greenville, SC	1991

Prosperity Megachurch Table (*continued*)

Church	Senior Pastor	Self-Reported Attendance	Location	Founded
Windsor Village United Methodist Church	Kirbyjon Caldwell	14,000	Houston, TX	1982
The Rock and World Outreach Center	Jim and Deborah Cobrae	13,750	San Bernardino, CA	1988
Living Word Christian Center	William Winston	13,500	Forest Park, IL	1988
Faithful Central Bible Church	Kenneth Ulmer	13,000	Inglewood, CA	1936
World Harvest Church	Rod Parsley	12,000	Columbus, OH	1977
Free Chapel Worship Center	Jentezen Franklin	12,000	Gainesville, GA	1953
Higher Dimension Church	Terrance Johnson	12,000	Houston, TX	1999
St. John Church	Denny Davis	12,000	Grand Prairie, TX	1921
First Cathedral	Leroy Bailey, Jr.	11,000	Bloomfield, CT	1968
Word of Faith International Christian Center	Andre Butler	11,000	Detroit, MI	1979

(*continued*)

Prosperity Megachurch Table (*continued*)

Church	Senior Pastor	Self-Reported Attendance	Location	Founded
Church on the Move	Willie George	11,000	Tulsa, OK	1987
Faith Fellow-ship Ministries	David Demola	10,300	Sayreville, NJ	1980
Greater St. Stephen Full Gospel Baptist Church	Debra B. Morton	10,000	New Orleans, LA	1937
Crystal Cathedral	Bobby Schuller	10,000	Garden Grove, CA	1955
Cornerstone Church	John Hagee	10,000	San Antonio, TX	1975
Covenant Church	Mike and Kathy Hayes	10,000	Carrollton, TX	1976
Trinity Fellowship	Jimmy Evans	10,000	Amarillo, TX	1977
Christian Faith Center	Casey and Wendy Treat	10,000	Seattle, WA	1980
Faith Commu-nity Church	Jim Reeve	10,000	West Covina, CA	1980
Living Word Christian Center	Mac and Lynne Hammond	10,000	Minneapolis, MN	1980
The Living Word Bible Church	Thomas Anderson	10,000	Mesa, AZ	1986
Word of Faith Family Worship Center	Dale Bronner	10,000	Austell, GA	1991
City of Refuge	Noel Jones	10,000	Gardena, CA	1994

Prosperity Megachurch Table *(continued)*

Church	Senior Pastor	Self-Reported Attendance	Location	Founded
Church on the Way	Dan Hicks	9,869	Van Nuys, CA	1951
Evangel World Prayer Center	Bob and Margaret Rodgers	9,000	Louisville, KY	1950
The Park Church	Claude Alexander, Jr.	8,000	Charlotte, NC	1913
Bethany World Prayer Center	Larry Stockstill	8,000	Baker, LA	1963
Rhema Bible Church	Kenneth W. Hagin	8,000	Broken Arrow, OK	1974
Greater Mt. Calvary Holy Church	Alfred Owens	8,000	Washington, D.C.	1966
Faith Chapel Christian Center	Michael Moore	8,000	Birmingham, AL	1981
Shoreline Church	Rob and Laura Koke	8,000	Austin, TX	1993
Elevation Church	Steven Furtick	8,000	Charlotte, NC	2006
Victory Christian Center	Mark Crow	7,800	Oklahoma City, OK	1994
Acts Full Gospel Church	Bob Jackson	7,500	Oakland, CA	1984
Inspiring Body of Christ Church	Rickie Rush	7,500	Dallas, TX	1990
Jubilee Christian Church	Gideon Thompson	7,000	Boston, MA	1982

(continued)

Prosperity Megachurch Table (*continued*)

Church	Senior Pastor	Self-Reported Attendance	Location	Founded
Living Faith Christian Center	Connie McLean	7,000	Pennsauken, NJ	1985
Empowerment Temple	Jamal Harrison-Bryant	6,750	Baltimore, MD	2000
Turner Chapel AME Church	Kenneth Marcus	6,500	Marietta, GA	1839
Champions Centre	Kevin and Sheila Gerald	6,500	Tacoma, WA	1986
The City Church	Judah and Chelsea Smith	6,085	Kirkland, WA	1992
Greater Grace Temple	Charles Ellis	6,000	Detroit, MI	1927
Victory World Church	Dennis and Colleen Rouse	6,000	Norcross, GA	1990
Calvary Assembly of God	George Cope	5,000	Orlando, FL	1953
Christian Faith Center	Brenda Timberlake	5,000	Creedmoor, NC	1974
Calvary Christian Center	Phillip Goudeaux	5,000	Sacramento, CA	1980
The Potter's House of Denver	Christopher Hill	5,000	Denver, CO	1985
Without Walls International Place	Paula White	5,000	Tampa, FL	1990

Prosperity Megachurch Table (*continued*)

Church	Senior Pastor	Self-Reported Attendance	Location	Founded
Faith World	Clint Brown	5,000	Orlando, FL	1993
Abundant Living Family Church	Diego and Cindy Mesa	5,000	Rancho Cucamonga, CA	1994
Life Church of God in Christ	Ron Gibson	4,500	Riverside, CA	1987
Perfecting Church	Marvin Winans	4,500	Detroit, MI	1989
Kingdom Church	Dharius Daniels	4,500	Trenton, NJ	2005
Deliverance Evangelistic Church	Glen Spaulding	4,000	Philadelphia, PA	1961
Evangel Cathedral	Don Meares	4,000	Upper Marlboro, MD	1968
Rock Church	Anne Gimenez	4,000	Virginia Beach, VA	1968
Straight Gate International Church	Andrew Merritt	4,000	Detroit, MI	1978
Word of Life Church	Brian Zahnd	4,000	St. Joseph, MO	1981
Cornerstone Church	Sergio and Georgina De La Mora	4,000	San Diego, CA	1998
Saint Peters World Outreach Center	James Hash	3,500	Winston-Salem, NC	1940
Detroit World Outreach Center	Ben Gilbert	3,500	Redford, MI	1993

(*continued*)

Prosperity Megachurch Table *(continued)*

Church	Senior Pastor	Self-Reported Attendance	Location	Founded
Elevate Life Church	Keith and Sheila Craft	3,500	Frisco, TX	2000
The Church at South Las Vegas	Benny Perez	3,500	Henderson, NV	2003
Orchard Road Christian Center	Reece and Sarah Bowling	3,000	Denver, CO	1960
Victory Worship Center	Zane Anderson	3,000	Tucson, AZ	1970* [says early 70s]
Abundant Life Christian Centre	Rick Thomas	3,000	Margate, FL	1977
Speak the Word International	Randy Morrison	3,000	Golden Valley, MN	1977
Solid Rock Church	Lawrence and Darlene Bishop	3,000	Monroe, OH	1978
Faith Christian Family Church	David and Roxanne Swann	3,000	Clovis, NM	1980
Oasis Christian Center	Philip and Holly Wagner	3,000	Los Angeles, CA	1984
Greenville Community Christian Church	James Corbett	3,000	Greenville, NC	1982
More Than Conquerors Faith Church	Steve Green	3,000	Birmingham, AL	1982

Prosperity Megachurch Table *(continued)*

Church	Senior Pastor	Self-Reported Attendance	Location	Founded
Word of Life Christian Center	David and Vicki Shearin	3,000	Las Vegas, NV	1982
Abundant Life Christian Center	Walter and Cindy Hallam	3,000	La Marque, TX	1985
Family Harvest Church	Robb Thompson	3,000	Tinley Park, IL	1983
Spirit of Faith Christian Center	Mike Freemen	3,000	Temple Hills, MD	1993
Elevation Baptist Church	T. L. Carmichael Sr.	3,000	Raleigh, NC	1998
Wave Church	Steve Kelly	3,000	Virginia Beach, VA	1999
DFW New Beginnings Church	Larry and Tiz Huch	3,000	Irving, TX	2004
City Bible Church	Frank Damazio	2,900	Portland, OR	1951
Summit Christian Center	Rick and Cindy Godwin	2,834	San Antonio, TX	N/A
Kingdom Life Christian Church	Jay Ramirez	2,500	Milford, CT	1991
Impacting Your World Christian Center	Ray and Tracey Barnard	2,500	Philadelphia, PA	1994
Destiny Christian Center	Lee and Shonia Stokes	2,500	Greensboro, NC	2000

(continued)

Prosperity Megachurch Table (*continued*)

Church	Senior Pastor	Self-Reported Attendance	Location	Founded
Legacy Church	Steve Smothermon	2,400	Albuquerque, NM	1980
Agape Family Worship Center	Lawrence Powell	2,200	Rahway, NJ	1990
Word of Life Christian Center	Tim Bagwell	2,000	Lone Tree, CO	1970
Covenant Church of Pittsburgh	Joseph Garlington Sr.	2,000	Pittsburgh, PA	1971
Evangel Fellowship	Otis Lockett	2,000	Greensboro, NC	1982
The Love of Jesus Family Church	Jason and Gale Alvarez	2,000	Orange, NJ	1982
Overcoming Faith Christian Center	Gene and Sue Lingerfelt	2,000	Arlington, TX	1984
Ray of Hope Christian Church	Cynthia Hale	2,000	Decatur, GA	1986
Covenant Love Family Church	Al Brice	2,000	Fayetteville, NC	1991
Place For Life	Rick Hawkins	2,000	San Antonio, TX	1993
Winners Church	Fred Shipman	2,000	West Palm Beach, FL	1997
Gospel Tabernacle Church	David Martin	2,000	Dallas, TX	N/A

Naming Names

Any account of the American prosperity gospel must first ask: who is a prosperity preacher? To undertake this study, I had to become practiced in the imperfect art of labeling people and congregations, of naming names. To some, this might seem like finger-pointing. I often saw this played out as I lectured on the prosperity gospel. Hearing a familiar name, students would react with vindication ("I knew it!") or frustration ("I really like that preacher . . .").

This question is frustrated by the absence of a shared self-identifying label. Few want to be stereotyped as prosperity preachers. "I'm not one of those who would be called a prosperity preacher," insisted Pastor Carl Stephens of Faith Assembly of God, Orlando, Florida, "I believe in prosperity. I believe in the blessing of God. But typically a prosperity preacher [makes it] their life's message. I don't feel like it's my life message, but it's a part of the Message, the Word of God."[1] This assertion, a prelude to a sermon on divine wealth, illustrates the problem of relying on participants' self-identification. Most deny that they are "faith" or "prosperity" preachers, seeing *prosperity* as a pejorative label for an extreme point of view.

The term *prosperity* is clumsy for two reasons. First, for believers to call their message anything other than "The Gospel" would place it outside the boundaries of orthodox Christianity. In my interviews with participants, the first ten minutes inevitably circled around the question of why I might be calling it the "prosperity" or "faith" movement when the message sprang from the pages of the Bible itself. The act of classification cannot be avoided, but participants naturally bristled at the implication of theological innovation and (as with earlier labels like "Puritan" or "Methodist" or "Shakers") it ran the risk of trivializing specificity. Second, the label "prosperity" conjures up a primarily economic motivation. It suggests the thesis, set forth by Irvin G. Wyllie in *The Self-Made Man in America*, that where religion and self-improvement meet, riches are at the heart of the matter.

Nonetheless, the term "prosperity gospel," however imprecise, has practical value. Insiders agree that (rightly defined) "prosperity" accurately summarizes the focus (or *a* focus) of their churches. Aesthetic, theological, and material validations of prosperity are sure signs that the complete gospel is being preached. There are some who are comfortable using terms such as "faith," "word," or "Word of Faith" to distinguish their church from those they deem "traditional," or "religious," and therefore dead. Believers may avoid labels, but they observe boundaries. Church-goers become adept at identifying precisely who is inside and outside of their theo-logical orbit and take pride in "prosperity" as an indication of a deeper and more committed faith. Likewise, outsiders recognize prosperity gospel as a familiar marker for this movement, and a more respectful equivalent for the less flattering "health and wealth" or "name it, and claim it." The term resists other tempting over-simplifications, for observers often conflate the entire movement with excess ("ma-terialism," "worldliness,") or consider it a subcategory of another religious trend (usually megachurches, pentecostalism, or nondenominational evangelicalism.)

Some scholars have called it the Word of Faith movement, after Kenneth Hagin Sr.'s monthly publication *The Word of Faith*. Word of Faith is often equated with the prosperity gospel as a whole, seeming to imply that Kenneth Hagin's Rhema Bible Training Center was its only wellspring. The prosperity gospel draws from multiple historical and theological streams, while the Word of Faith is a particular movement that came of age in the 1970s as a rarefied form of positive confession to achieve money, health, and victory. In my usage, the term "Word of Faith" refers not only to Kenneth Hagin but also to his entire sphere of associates as represented in the net-work illustration of his most frequent co-presenters (see figure 3.5, p. 85).

The influence of the prosperity message goes much further than independent Word of Faith preachers. For this reason, I prefer the terms "prosperity" and "faith" movement to describe the diverse sources and preachers who have made the mes-sage a national—and international—success.[2] I follow E. W. Kenyon, the theological architect of the movement, in identifying the movement by its understanding of "faith." I try to draw attention to the animating qualities that separate this word from its traditional definition of "hope" or, perhaps, "trust."

This book is not a theological typology. Not everyone who preaches about faith, wealth, health, and victory, can be found in these pages. The prosperity gospel refers not only to a set of shared ideas but also to the network of preachers, churches, schools, conferences, television and radio networks, associations, and publications that circulate these concepts. If a pastor has all the theological earmarks of the pros-perity gospel but is not an active participant in these networks, he or she is not ger-mane to this book. Take, for example, Steve Long of the Toronto Airport Christian Church. He was instrumental in the Toronto Blessing and the transnational net-works that developed from it. Long has espoused a theology of soft prosperity (though he has concerns about an overemphasis on the agency of faith) but does not widely associate with prosperity preachers, choosing to emphasize a ministry of healing inside new apostolic networks. He is, as a result, absent from these pages. He may preach prosperity, but he is not a prosperity preacher by this standard.

To complicate matters, the prosperity gospel refers to multiple transnational ministry networks that intersect with other charismatic crosscurrents. We can see the prosperity gospel in denominational networks, new apostolic networks, prophetic networks, evangelical networks, and neopentecostal networks. It must always be remembered that faith, health, wealth, and victory were a side dish for some and a main course for others. In other words, this cross pollination across networks means that the prosperity gospel rarely dominates other networks into which it crosses. Further, many of the people in this book operate within multiple spheres of influence. For example, each classic pentecostal denomination–historically divided into black and white, Oneness and Trinitarian—operates with its own schools, publications, headquarters, conferences, and century of traditions. Every denomination seems to have someone in its ranks who operates across faith and in-house networks. The Church of God evangelist T. L. Lowery, for example, believes in a fivefold ministry and so operates largely within new apostolic networks. Black pentecostal leaders are more likely to appear beside neopentecostals than Word of Faith types.

Many times the prosperity gospel thrives out of the interests of a senior pastor of a large congregation inside a much broader denominational system. In such cases, the prosperity gospel may be tolerated within the denomination as an eccentricity. But three-quarters of prosperity megachurches are independent, so most of these associations are flexible and voluntary.

Naming Rhetoric

The first step in identifying a church as a part of the prosperity gospel is to examine what sorts of preaching each church favors and the terms each employs. The first piece of evidence is often the name of the congregation. Certain kinds of names offer clues as to whether a given church is part of the prosperity gospel. Those most heavily influenced by Word of Faith in the 1980s almost invariably were called "Christian Centers" (though by 2000 this label had gone out of fashion). Since we have identified "faith, health, wealth, and victory" as the core of the movement's theology it is not surprising to see these words reflected in nomenclature. We find telltale signs in megachurch names such as Jim Reeve's Faith Community Church or David Demola's Faith Fellowship Ministries. Churches with "abundant living" or "harvest" in their name reflect the preoccupation with wealth. The emphasis on positive confession is revealed by "Speak the Word International" or "Living Word." Victory crops up in many churches' names: More Than Conquerors Faith Church, World Changers, Victory World Church, and Champions Centre. Church mottos too are revealing. The slogan for Impacting Your World Christian Center in Philadelphia aptly summarizes the prosperity gospel's pledge: "Creating People That Cannot Be Destroyed."[3]

A church name offers an initial indication, but the real classifier of prosperity affiliation lies in the language used by churchgoers and vocalized in church services. Prosperity believers talk about "releasing their faith," "speaking their faith," and "believing God *for* things," emphasizing the instrumentality of faith itself.

An interview with Senior Pastor David Swann, a little-known pastor with a 3,000-member church in Clovis, New Mexico, serves to illustrate these rhetorical hallmarks. On this May 26, 2010, broadcast of *Praise the Lord*, the flagship program of the Trinity Broadcasting Network, the celebrity host was the silver-haired Word of Faith preacher Jesse Duplantis, whose Louisiana charm had long made him one of the most sought-after speakers in the faith movement. His first guest was Pastor Swann, who looked the part of an unfussy businessman, his tousled hair and unbuttoned pinstriped suit offset by his neatly folded pocket-square. After brief introductions, Swann began to speak about his passion for evangelism and community outreach.

SWANN: If you just keep diligently seeking good for other people, the community will end up loving you. The only people who don't like us in our city are religious people. [laughter] Because our church is growing. They try to figure it out in their mind instead of just saying "It's the love of God!" We're loving people. We're reaching people. We're preaching the gospel. Every week we give people a chance to get saved. And they get saved!

DUPLANTIS: It's amazing how religious people will come against acts of kindness. There is so much envy and jealousy in the body of Christ. I mean . . . I've had the media attack me. Because I'm a blessed man. I can't help it if I'm blessed. It ain't my fault. [laughter] It's the Bible that says "He has given thee power to get wealth!" What do you want me to do? [They both shrug in jest.] I just do what the Lord tells me to do and He just blesses me. . . . See, what you're doing in your church, David, is what God did. God so loved the world that he *gave*. What did he give? His only begotten Son. Now if that's not an act of kindness, I don't know what is.

SWANN: See, you've taught us. You taught the Body of Christ. You've come to our church. You taught us not just to be a giver, man, but just put your heart into it. [Swann begins to tell the story of how his church grew too large for its building, and how God instructed him not to sell the building but to give it away to an up-and-coming African American congregation.] Wouldn't it be great if we were so blessed financially that we wouldn't have to sell it but we could give it away? . . . Then the Lord said, "You've got it backwards. You want to wait till the money comes, and give it away. But you've taught your people to give . . ."

DUPLANTIS: And expect a harvest!

SWANN: And expect a harvest. I'm out in rural America . . . [God] said, "The farmer doesn't wait for the harvest to sow." He sows and he expects a harvest. And not one of my farmers feels bad about harvesting. I don't know why Christians feel bad about harvesting . . . So the Lord said, "Give away your building. And I'll cause the money to come." . . . So we committed this building to them debt free, brand new sound system, brand new carpet, totally remodeled. [audience clapping]

DUPLANTIS: In other words, you didn't give a broke-down church. You gave a totally remodeled church.

SWANN: Yeah. We didn't give a bad seed. I didn't want to reap a bad harvest. We gave our *best*.

Even a cursory glance at this discussion turns up some unusual language particular to the prosperity gospel: sowing financial seeds, reaping harvests, "causing" money, the power to get, and giving one's best to God.

Figure 8.1 summarizes some prominent preachers' use of the prosperity gospel's distinctive language. As figure 8.1 illustrates, some phrases and concepts are particular to the prosperity gospel but not universally employed. Kenneth Hagin, Kenneth Copeland, Benny Hinn, and Fredrick Price all use terms like positive confession, sowing and reaping, seed faith, and "rhema" (a specific prophetic word for a particular moment) commonly found in Word of Faith theology. Given that these four preachers share a similar variation on Haginite theology, this is not surprising. Eddie Long and T.D. Jakes, both neopentecostals, are slightly more hesitant to promise a hundredfold recompense and do not speak of words of knowledge as "rhema." Joyce Meyer and Joel Osteen, both

PREACHER	To Speak Faith	Positive Confession	Divine Wealth	Divine Health	Sowing and Reaping	Divine Favor	Destiny	Rhema	Hundredfold Blessing	Jehovah Jireh	Seed Faith
Kenneth Hagin	●	●	●	●	●	●	●	●	●	●	●
Kenneth Copeland	●	●	●	●	●	●	●	●	●	●	●
Benny Hinn	●	●	●	●	●	●	●	●	●	●	●
Frederick Price	●	●	●	●	●	●	●	●	●	●	●
Creflo Dollar	●	●	●	●	●	●	●	●	●	●	●
Eddie Long	●	●	●	●	●	●	●	○	◑	●	●
Joyce Meyer	●	●	●	●	●	●	●	◑	○	◔	◐
Joel Osteen	●	●	●	●	●	●	●	○	○	●	◐
T. D. Jakes	◐	◑	◐	●	◐	◐	●	○	○	●	○

FIGURE 8.1 **Legend of Prosperity Terms as Used by Prosperity Celebrities from Diverse Backgrounds** Preachers did not always share the same terms and concepts. A range of celebrities from hard prosperity (Benny Hinn) to soft prosperity (Joyce Meyer), Word of Faith (Frederick Price, Kenneth Copeland, and Kenneth Hagin) to neopentecostal (Eddie Long, T.D. Jakes) shows their varied use of hallmark "prosperity gospel" rhetoric.

white pentecostals at home in evangelicalism, use even fewer sectarian words. In this way, preachers' language is indicative of the networks in which they move.

The careful choice of words serves as a spiritual discipline. During my eight years visiting prosperity churches, I learned to avoid self-deprecation, negativity, or sarcasm, which seemed to make churchgoers squirm. The type of humor that other Christians seemed to find appealing flopped in these Sunday morning chats. Consultants and friends I made along the way gently chided any comment that lacked a bright side, steering every conversation with careful positivity. They seemed to wash their own mouths out with sanctified soap. (Here is a neologism that reveals a hard prosperity church: "catching a healing." The pastor can never be "sick" because this would be a negative confession. Only in soft prosperity churches can one admit to "having caught a cold.")

Naming Publications

A further examination of language that reveals the identity of a prosperity church must include its creedal statement, the content of the sermons preached, the hymns or choruses sung, bulletins, church membership manuals, publications by the pastor, CDs and DVDs, websites, podcasts, and even the content of the bookstore. Surprisingly, the topics of wealth and activating faith seldom appear in church belief statements, but they are inevitably discovered in the bookstore. A typical Word of Faith church bookstore will devote much space to the works of Kenneth Hagin, John Osteen, and Charles Capps a soft prosperity church will offer Holly and Philip Wagner, Joel Osteen, and Joyce Meyer; neopentecostal bookstore will have books or videos by Paul Morton, Eddie Long, and Noel Jones. Everyone will have America's preacher, T. D. Jakes.

Naming Personalities

The senior pastor is the heart and soul of a prosperity church's self-image. Take, for example, the church that first inspired my research in my hometown of Winnipeg, Manitoba—Springs Church. The church claims to have no historical antecedents and to have been born out of pastoral inspiration by the Holy Spirit. Springs Church, like most prosperity megachurches, declares to be the result of one man's vision (though in fact the preeminent leader had inherited a smaller, already established congregation). That the overwhelming majority of such congregations are still led by their founding and senior pastors—or their children—demonstrates the connection between pastoral and ecclesial identity.[4] I began to investigate Springs Church under the pastorate of Leon Fontaine. That one must drive down Fontaine Road to get to Leon Fontaine's church was a promising start.[5] Logging on to LeonFontaine.com,

I confronted Fontaine's likeness. He appears in a fitted collared shirt, a few buttons undone, smiling into the glare of a spotlight. The website declares him to be a "world class leader" whose ministry was "spirit contemporary" and "impacting the nations." A link to Springs Church's homepage leads to a photo of the pastor and his wife Sally and an invitation to "Get to know Leon and Sally and the heart of Springs Church." Seemingly, the vision of the church could only be known by becoming acquainted with this pastoral couple. This emphasis on the senior pastor and his spouse was not an anomaly: 71 percent of American prosperity megachurches use the image of the senior pastor as the primary advertisement on the church's homepage.[6]

This emphasis on personality over sanctuary can be seen in common naming practices. As the cultural critic Jonathan Walton observed, "when people speak of a particular congregation they do not say 'the Potters House,' 'New Birth Missionary Baptist Church,' or 'World Changers Church International' but 'T. D. Jakes' church,' 'Eddie Long's church,' or 'Creflo Dollar's church,' respectively."[7] A comparison of the covers of recent books by bestselling prosperity preachers with those of evangelical megachurch leaders makes a similar point. Nonprosperity leaders such as Kerry Shook, Andy Stanley, Craig Groeschel, Rick Warren, and Bill Hybels lead five of the ten largest churches in America. Their book jackets feature sunsets and nature scenes. The latest works by prosperity pastors, by contrast, show the senior pastor's glamour shot.[8]

Naming Spaces

Some characteristic ideas of the movement are not directly stated but rather embodied in the rituals and imagery of the church. As we have seen, many of these churches shun traditional Christian iconography like the crucifix (symbol of suffering), instead presenting images of globes (world triumph) or eagles (soaring victory). In such churches, there is emphasis on and pageantry surrounding healing and financial miracles. Tithing might constitute the peak of the service, with a short sermon and something like an altar call. There are places in the service to showcase healing, testimonies, healing lines, and the laying on of hands. These practices are so important that they must be performed in public. Believers are urged to cultivate private devotional habits such as focusing on positive outcomes, visualization, and repetition of scripture and uplifting phrases.

Naming Education

Another test is to see whether connections exist between a particular pastor or congregation and other prosperity-speaking institutions or leaders. The movement is loosely knit together by educational, denominational, institutional, and performative connections.

Are there common ties to certain educational centers? Has the pastor attended Rhema Bible or Oral Roberts University? If so, this is highly suggestive of prosperity affiliation. Kenneth Hagin's and Oral Roberts's lasting influence on the movement springs in part from the centers of theological education they founded. Hagin founded Rhema Bible Training Center in 1974. By 2008 it claimed to have graduated nearly 30,000 students.[9] Oral Roberts University, founded in 1963, also brought ministerial credentials to the movement. Prosperity televangelists like John Hagee, Marilyn Hickey, Benny Hinn, Creflo Dollar, Kenneth Copeland, and Billy Daughterty dominated its Board of Regents.[10] Alumni associations and their yearly conferences continue to draw pastors back to the source and introduce them to new connections. Honorary degrees from one of a few select universities, bricks-and-mortar or online, have become an even stronger sign of inclusion among the prosperity ranks. Roberts decorated countless fellow ministers with honorary PhDs. Life Christian University was a favorite among white televangelists, and Friends International Christian University honored celebrated black prosperity preachers with doctoral accolades.

Naming Institutions

As we have seen, denominational membership is a weak indicator of prosperity movement involvement. Most participants in a prosperity megachurch, if asked what kind of congregation they belong to, they will likely say that it is nondenominational (see figure 5.4, p. 183). A third attend churches belonging to pentecostal, evangelical, mainline, or African American denominations. Many African American prosperity churches retain denominational markers and are hard to distinguish from churches in their denomination that do not embrace prosperity thinking. In many cases, when prosperity churches stay in denominations it is a sign that the denominational headquarters has become amenable to their theology.

Let's turn now to associational connections that demonstrate prosperity movement ties. New types of ministerial organizations bind faith churches into networks: some offer theological vetting of ministerial candidates and government licenses of ordination. Dozens of these organizations promote prosperity ministries, forming links among hundreds of otherwise independent churches. For example, the Association of Faith Churches and Ministers (AFCM), founded in 1978, provides legal qualifications and spiritual accountability to hundreds of member churches. Another type of ministerial organization is associated with a particular faith teacher and offers inspiration rather than credentials. Most prosperity teachers oversee a collective of smaller churches that turn to them for guidance, theological grist, and institutional support. These informal and voluntary associations gather hundreds of congregations into loose affiliations that rely on the success of a charismatic leader. Creflo Dollar's Ministerial Association (CDMA), for instance, includes several hundred American churches. With few requirements—a shared belief statement and a yearly financial contribution—these structures accommodate numerous participants by providing them with (albeit limited) exposure to their role model.

Naming Performances

Another category of connection among prosperity preachers might be deemed performative—that host of conferences, television programs, speaking tours, book blurbs, podcasts, and DVDs through which pastors promote their own ministries and those of religious allies. Performative ties allow us to see the flexible and changing connections between personalities, institutions, and media platforms.

Pastors thrive on the particularity of their spiritual journeys—the personal revelations that allow them to embody God's message of prosperity—and they tend to downplay their identification with educational and ministerial networks. Pastors build their reputations by the success of their preaching, their ability to connect with audiences, and their track record of publications, accolades, and building projects.[11] In order to confidently link ministers to the movement, one must try to capture snapshots of religion in motion. I took the most widely circulated Pentecostal and charismatic magazine, *Charisma*, and copied the advertisements for every conference in the 30-year period between 1980 and 2010. I wanted to see the conference participation connections between pastors who otherwise claim to be independent. In total I tracked 4,267 separate speakers across 1,637 conferences over three decades.

The connections between preachers shown are performative, as each preacher intersects with another by speaking at the same conference. More intersections between two individuals equates to a stronger graphical relationship (represented by the darker lines). The greater total number of intersections an individual has the more central they are to the network. This is represented by the location of individuals to one another. The layout is based on a graphing algorithm such that the distance between individuals is proportional to the shortest path linking them and the overall length of ties is minimized. For example, in figures 8.2 and 8.3, each dot represents a pastor, and the line between them represents those who have spoken at the same conference. Given the size of networks like figure 8.2 and 8.3, these images are limited to only those preachers who were in the top fourth of featured speakers at these conferences. For example, figure 8.2 shows only 182 of 1,658 total preachers in the network of conferences advertised in *Charisma* between 1990 and 1999. Figure 8.3 shows 182 of the 1,681 total number of preachers advertised between 2000 and 2010.

This is the slow work of exploring the faith movement as a network, calling attention to connectivity and association. I borrow lightly from network theory in attempting to adjudicate significance by interconnection. This book examines diverse leaders, associations, institutions, ideas, and practices to demonstrate not only breadth but also the density of interconnection, weighting significance based on who or what is most linked to others. It must not be thought that the faith movement is static—that the network is an iron grid. As Manuel Vásquez has argued, networks must not be mistaken for "closed, linear systems that automatically integrate constituent parts in a harmonious whole." Rather, a network should be imagined as a circuit board, a template that conducts movement and energy.[12]

Take, for example, the International Pentecostal Holiness Church, once a tiny southern sect and now a denomination of almost 5,000,000 adherents that recently

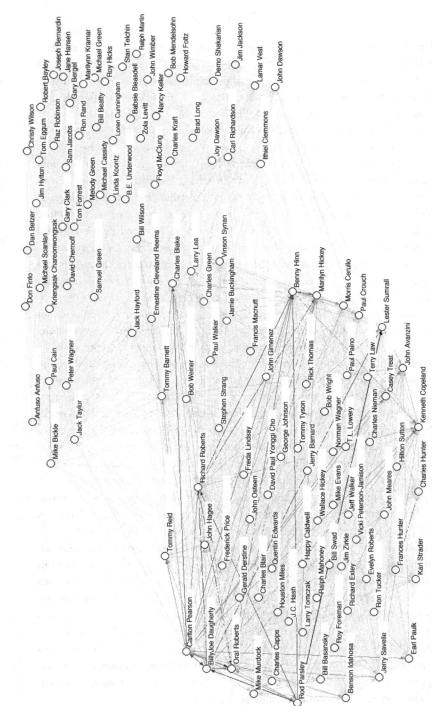

FIGURE 8.2 1990s Conference Participation Advertised in *Charisma* The cluster of conferences on the left suggest that the Word of Faith movement continued to exert a significant influence even after the televangelism scandals toppled many of its stars. But the appearance of new celebrities and diverse conferences showed that the Word of Faith movement no longer occupied the centrality it once enjoyed.

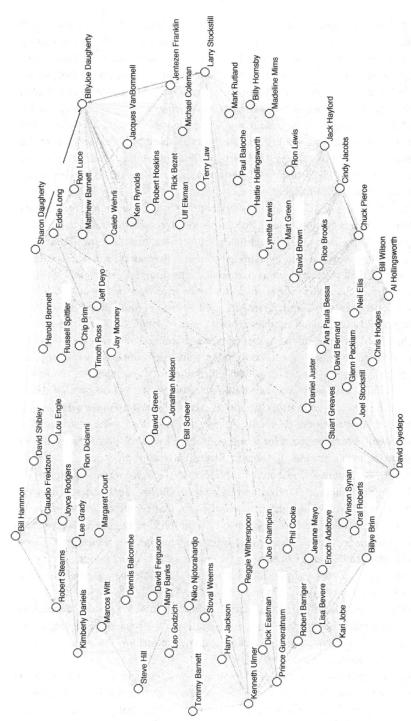

FIGURE 8.3 2000–2010 Conference Participation Advertised in *Charisma* The 2000s saw a great proliferation of international prosperity conferences (see, for example, David Oyedepo, on the bottom left) and a significant number of Latino and African American conference circuits operating independently of any white celebrity.

celebrated their centennial as a miracle of unity. The ceremony in Falcon, North Carolina, marked the renewal of the 1911 covenant that had forged one denomination out of the Fire-Baptized Holiness Church and the Pentecostal Holiness Church. Historically, the socially conservative denomination had little to do with the faith movement, but in 2011 its largest church, under the leadership of Ron Carpenter Jr. (son of IPHC head Ron Carpenter Sr.), serves as a poster child of the prosperity gospel. Junior had grown up in the denomination and gone to its Emmanuel College, but the contrast between his style and his father's could hardly be exaggerated. At the anniversary, Ron Sr. was conservatively dressed in a suit and tie, while the younger Carpenter sported artfully distressed designer jeans, an untucked cowboy shirt, spiked and gelled hair, and a goatee.

In contrast to the tiny clapboard church where the 1911 document had been signed and where celebrants gathered in 2011, Ron Carpenter Jr. presides over a 14,000-member facility complete with a smoke machine, giant screens, and faux-industrial scaffolding. His early efforts at church planting had met with modest success. His church of 500 was marked by an interest in charismatic gifts, liturgical dance, and spiritual warfare. All that changed in 1994 when at a conference, Assemblies of God leader (and prosperity preacher) Tommy Barnett prayed a prayer of multiplication anointing over Carpenter Jr. Carpenter began preaching a form of soft prosperity based on Malachi 3, and his church began to grow. Soon he was holding four services, attended by 4,000, and then he began "sowing into" other ministries connected with the prosperity gospel, attending conferences with more prominent members of the movement. A building campaign produced a new structure with a $5,000,000 sanctuary and a huge for-profit gymnasium. Carpenter's career demonstrates how a denomination that may not preach the prosperity gospel (or may, indeed, even preach against it) can nonetheless make room for flamboyant disciples of the genre. Such figures may be too big to fail, beyond the reach of denominational discipline.

Mainline Protestants—Presbyterians, Methodists, Congregationalists, Episcopalians, Lutherans, American Baptists, and Disciples of Christ—are frequently lumped together as theologically liberal advocates of social justice. Of all denominations, these seem to be the least likely places to find the prosperity gospel. Prosperity's supernaturalism appears too charismatic and unruly for these staid groups; its focus on wealth and health seems unnecessary for such established and wealthy congregations. Yet some of the mainline denominations' largest congregations are now espousing the prosperity gospel in some form.

The prosperity gospel's largest churches exhibited durable regional, denominational, institutional, and associational connections, linking thousands of congregations and millions of believers, not in a uniform, unidirectional whole, but as a highly diverse, multidirectional movement.

From a comprehensive list of all national megachurches, created by Scott Thumma of the Hartford Institute for Religion Research, I identified 115 congregations as "prosperity" churches (see appendix A).[13] It is clear that participation in the faith movement did not preclude involvement in other religious spheres, as each church and pastor simultaneously shared this faith identity with other, overlapping allegiances. I hope that readers will hold the term "prosperity" lightly, seeing it more as an orientation and less as a cattle brand.

Naming Methods and Findings

I adopted a variety of strategies to study this contemporary religious movement. First and foremost, I traveled. I visited 25 percent of all American prosperity megachurches and attended almost all major conferences at least once. These trips included visits to T. D. and Serita Jakes (The Potter's House), Joel and Victoria Osteen (Lakewood Church), Paula White (Without Walls International Place), Joyce and Dave Meyer (traveling ministry), Creflo and Taffi Dollar (World Changers Ministries), Kenneth and Lynnette Hagin (Rhema Bible Church), Casey and Wendy Treat (Christian Faith Center), Kevin and Sheila Gerald (Champions Centre), Sharon Daugherty (Victory Christian Center), Ron and Hope Carpenter (Redemption World Outreach Center), Leroy Bailey Jr. and Vernada Breathett-Bailey (First Cathedral), Willie and Deleva George (Church on the Move), Mac and Lynne Hammond (Living Word Christian Center), Claude Alexander Jr. and Kimberly Nash Alexander (The Park Church), George and Cheryl Cope (Calvary Assembly of God), Brenda Timberlake (Christian Faith Center), Clint Brown (Faith World), Anne Gimenez (Rock Church), Randy Morrison and Roxane Battle Morrison (Speak the Word International), James and Delores Corbett (Greenville Community Christian Church), Mike and Dee Dee Freemen (Spirit of Faith Christian Center), Rob and Laura Koke (Shoreline Christian Center), Joseph Walker III and his wife, Dr. Stephaine Walker (Mount Zion Baptist Church), Remus and Mia Wright (The Fountain of Praise), Steve and Sharon Kelly (Wave Church), Lee and Shonia Stokes (Destiny Christian Center), Benny and Wendy Perez (The Church at South Las Vegas, Henderson, Las Vegas), Shirley Caesar (Mount Calvary), and David and Vicki Shearin (Word of Life Christian Center). The generosity of the Evangelical Fellowship of Canada allowed me to travel to the five-largest prosperity megachurches in Canada. When I could not visit sites, I conducted phone interviews, as was the case with Kenneth Copeland Ministries, Kenneth Hagin Ministries, Cynthia Hale of Ray of Hope, and Frank Reid of Bethel. A Duke University travel grant allowed me to join faith healer Benny Hinn and 900 participants on his 2008 Holy Land Tour. I visited the archives of the Dixon Pentecostal Research Center, the Holy Spirit Research Center at Oral Roberts University, the Assemblies of God Flower Pentecostal Heritage Center, and Regent University's Pentecostal Research Center.

I spent 18 months observing and participating in services at the Victorious Faith Center (VFC), an 80-member African American prosperity church in Durham, North Carolina. In this year and a half of regular Sunday (and frequent Wednesday evening) attendance, I undertook a dozen formal interviews and joined in many more informal conversations over lunch, coffee, and in e-mail exchanges. Initially,

I adopted a collaborative ethnographic model, attempting to involve consultants in a shared interviewing, writing, and editing process.[14] I soon realized that, for many participants, this method was unworkable. Their theology commanded positive speech and some saw providing interviews as tantamount to "negative confession," the naming of disease or misfortune that *causes* unwanted phenomena to be actualized. This led me to switch to a less interactive model, but one that still valued the honesty, vulnerability, and accessibility that marks collaborative ethnography. I solicited feedback from interviewees for whom negative confession was not an issue, either because what they said was positive or because they did not rigorously monitor their speech practices. Though I received signed consent for each of the interviews, I did my best to conceal the identities of the VFC members and the church itself out of respect for the kindness and consideration they extended to me. I did the same for my fellow travelers on the Holy Land tour. Though many generously shared their time and stories, it could hardly be said that they *chose* to be assigned to a bus with an eager researcher.

THE FAITH NETWORK constitutes a complex grid of institutions, ministries, congregations, individuals, and celebrities. Of its millions of participants, a cluster of leaders and megachurches forms the strongest junctions. Most believers and congregations claim some connection to these celebrated pastors, either by watching their television programs, reading their books, attending their conferences, or making financial contributions. Denominations, ministerial associations, and Bible schools structure crucial junctions among scattered participants. Countless churches stand on the periphery of the network. The Victorious Faith Center, for example, evinces weak but discernible connections through use of Rhema Bible publications and attendance at Pastor Creflo Dollar's local appearances. The pathways forged among participants vary in strength and longevity as associations constantly shift. Region matters, with believers concentrated in the Midwest, West, and especially the South. Though marked by differences in theological focus, region, gender, and race, American prosperity churches preach a message of Christian abundance and, big or small, they look to one another for financial support, theological inspiration, and institutional resources.

A marketplace ethos prevails. Connections among churches and pastors remain largely voluntary, as most operate outside an umbrella of supervision. Smaller churches choose their affiliations selectively, often mixing and matching pastors and institutions. Famous pastors lightly hold onto their associations with one another, happy to briefly share a stage but never an organizational platform. As these teachers promote their own ministries, they operate within a network that allows for opportunity but does not enforce conformity. Celebrities who have lost their appeal fall from their perches, while newcomers take their places. Change is constant. Yet their loose associations with one another, bound up in shared ideas, produce a phenomenon called the prosperity movement.

Notes

1. "First lady" refers to the traditional title given to the male pastor's wife among many African American congregations across denominations.
2. "The black church" typically refers to seven major historical black denominations: The National Baptist Convention (NBC), the National Baptist Convention of America (NBCA), the Progressive National Baptist Convention (PNBC), the African Methodist Episcopal Zion (A.M.E.Z.), the African Methodist Episcopal Church (A.M.E.), the Christian Methodist Episcopal Church (C.M.E.), and the Church of God in Christ (COGIC). Many scholars have pointed to the problematic reduction of African American religious experiences into a single entity called the "black church," though it continues to be a powerful and much-used tool in studying black religious thought and practice. For an example of its use see Lincoln and Mamiya, *The Black Church in the African-American Experience*. For its deconstruction see Anderson, *Beyond Ontological Blackness*.
3. Throughout this book I will treat these self-reported numbers at face value because I have no objective means of verifying or contradicting them. However, because large numbers are in themselves signs of prosperity and victory for the churches in question, the figures may have aspirational rather than quantitative value. Readers, therefore, may wish to take this data with a grain of salt.
4. See figures at Joel Osteen Ministries, www.joelosteen.com/pages/aboutjoel.aspx or www.lakewood.cc (accessed October 2012).
5. Van Biema, "Spirit Raiser."
6. Ever Increasing Faith Ministries, "Leaders—Dr. Price Biography," Crenshaw Christian Center, http://www.crenshawchristiancenter.net/drprice.aspx?id=876 (accessed June 21, 2011).

7. In 2007, Sen. Chuck Grassley of the Senate Finance Committee launched an investigation of six famous prosperity teachers: Joyce Meyer, Benny Hinn, Creflo Dollar, Paula White, Eddie Long, and Kenneth and Gloria Copeland. In 2009, according to Grassley, Joyce Meyer and Benny Hinn had been cleared of charges. Eddie Long and the Copelands submitted "incomplete responses." Creflo Dollar declined to comply with the investigation. See U.S. Senate Committee on Finance, *Memorandum.*

8. Van Biema and Chu, "Does God Want You To Be Rich?" In 2006, the *Yearbook of American and Canadian Churches* estimated that Word of Faith members numbered from 4,600,000 to 4,800,000. At less than 2 percent of the population, this total likely only included those churches affiliated with a Word of Faith denomination. See Lindner, *Yearbook of American and Canadian Churches*, 365–77.

9. Pew Hispanic Center, "Changing Faiths."

10. See also Bowler, "Blessed Bodies."

11. Douthat, *Bad Religion.*

CHAPTER 1

Epigraph is from Warren Meyer and Phoebe P. Knapp, "Confident Living," in Unity School of Christianity, *Wings of Song* quoted in Albanese, *Republic of Mind*, 423.

1. *Material magic* employed spells, symbols, artifacts, and actions to effect change, whereas *mental magic* made use of vision, reverie, meditation, and affirmative prayer. Albanese, *Republic of Mind*, 7–16.

2. Following the historian Catherine Albanese, metaphysical religion replaces "occultism," "gnosticism," or "harmonialism" as the umbrella term for the European magical-religious traditions that, since colonial times, have been practiced on American shores. Encompassing elite and lay expressions, blended with American Indian, African American, and, later, Asian customs, metaphysical religion found expression in individual and communal pursuits of spiritual power. Drawing from Albanese, I describe metaphysical religion as the use of spiritual power to manipulate material and spiritual realms, and draw believers to a personal restoration and connection to a greater spiritual plane.

3. Ahlstrom, *A Religious History of the American People*, 1019.

4. Satter, *Each Mind a Kingdom*, 2.

5. Early health reformers adopted a variety of treatments and regimens. Some revolutionized diets, like Grahamism and Adventism (vegetarianism) and hydropathy (water). Homeopathy developed a philosophy of *similia similibus curantur*, or like cures like.

6. James, *The Varieties of Religious Experience*, 78–126. See Albanese, *Republic of Mind*, 413–23.

7. Kenyon's relationship to metaphysical religion, and particularly to New Thought, has been the topic of heated debate. Scholars like Dan McConnell argue for the

"Kenyon Connection" to New Thought, a direct appropriation of metaphysical religion learned at Emerson College. In this analysis, the resulting prosperity gospel became a "facade of orthodoxy" applied to a cultic religion, making "Kenyonism" a "different Gospel." See McConnell, *A Different Gospel*, 15–56. Others situated it firmly within the confines of radical evangelicalism, free from nonorthodox influences. Following Kenyon biographers Dale Simmons and Geir Lie, I find compelling evidence that Kenyon appropriated metaphysical religion more selectively and "evangelically" than McConnell and others have detailed. Simmons, *E. W. Kenyon and the Postbellum Pursuit of Peace, Power, and Plenty*, and Lie, *E. W. Kenyon, Cult Founder or Evangelical Minister?*

8. Simmons, *E. W. Kenyon*, xii.

9. Kenyon, *The Two Kinds of Faith*, 21.

10. Kenyon's gospel was certainly not the first evangelical brush with metaphysical religion. In the 1850s, Holiness revivalism caught wind of Swedenborg's writings, whose theology of correspondence swept over Oberlin (see Simmons, *E. W. Kenyon*, 90.) As Candy Gunther Brown pointed out, Methodist leader Phoebe Palmer's husband, Walter, and the divine health advocate Charles Cullis were homeopathic physicians, suggesting an unexplored connection between the Holiness movement and homeopathy (Candy Gunther Brown, personal communication, June 15, 2009). For more on early evangelicals' ties to vitalist movements, see Ward, *Early Evangelicalism*. Catherine Albanese argued that a Holiness suspicion of "matter" led some to embrace "spirit" in metaphysical ways. Nazarene founder Phineas F. Bresee, for example, eventually drifted into theosophy. See Frankiel, "Ritual Sites in the Narrative of American Religion," 42.

11. Lie, *E. W. Kenyon*, 29.

12. The historian Grant Wacker offers the label "radical evangelicals" for the sundry believers (Baptists, Methodists, Presbyterians, Quakers, and Mennonites among them) who, at the turn of the twentieth century, formed the lively denominational precursors to the pentecostal movement. See Wacker, *Heaven Below*, 1.

13. As Dale Simmons argues, Kenyon met Durham in 1907 (three years prior to Durham's published treatise on the subject) and considered Durham's Finished Work theology indebted to his own. Simmons, *E. W. Kenyon*, 293–94.

14. Holiness, Higher Life, and (later) pentecostal and charismatic adherents commonly held to the idea that God empowered Holy Spirit–led believers to lives of extraordinary witness and service, filled with power above and beyond the ordinary abilities granted to Christians.

15. "Man is a spirit and possesses a soul and has a body. His soul and spirit constitute his personality. Above this soul, is he, himself, spirit. This is the real Man." Kenyon, *The Father and His Family*, 53. For a historical treatment of this theme in Kenyon's work, see Simmons, *E. W. Kenyon*, 97; Lie, *E. W. Kenyon*, 37–38.

16. Lie, *E. W. Kenyon*, 37.
17. Kenyon, *The Two Kinds of Life*, 101.
18. Lie, *E. W. Kenyon*, 43.
19. Simmons, *E. W. Kenyon*, 99.
20. Kenyon, *Advanced Bible Course*, 133. I was not able to locate an original edition of this work, but evidence suggests that later editions varied little.
21. Kenyon, *New Creation Realities*, 51.
22. For more on the roots of the healing movement see Dayton, *Theological Roots of Pentecostalism*; Williams, "The Transformation of Pentecostal Healing: 1906–2006."
23. Curtis, *Faith in the Great Physician*, 8–9.
24. The Keswick tradition, alternatively "Higher Christian Life" and "Victorious Christian Life," named for its 1875 holiness conference in Keswick, England, argued that sanctification (begun in conversion) allowed believers to live out a victorious (higher) life of Christian service. Some saw the experience as progressive and others as episodic. Yet the Holiness, Higher Life, pentecostal, and charismatic traditions that poured in to the modern prosperity gospel agreed the Holy Spirit gave believers extraordinary power for witness and service. See Wacker, "Pentecostalism."
25. Simmons, *E. W. Kenyon*, 236.
26. For Kenyon's reservations see Lie, *E. W. Kenyon*, 22–23; for an account of Evva's first healing, see McIntyre, *E. W. Kenyon and His Message of Faith*, 62.
27. Curtis, *Faith in the Great Physician*, 10. For more on faith homes, see Hardesty, *Faith Cure*; Blumhofer, "Life on Faith Lines," 10–12, 22.
28. Curtis, *Faith in the Great Physician*, 12.
29. See Kenyon, *The Two Kinds of Faith*, 10–31.
30. Simmons, *E. W. Kenyon*, 150.
31. See, for example, Fillmore, *Christian Healing*, 55–65.
32. Kenyon, *The Two Kinds of Faith*, 20.
33. Ibid., 65.
34. Simmons, *E. W. Kenyon*, 101.
35. Ibid., 237.
36. Ibid., 167.
37. Oneness pentecostalism emerged in the late 1910s as a minority tradition within pentecostalism; it always placed more emphasis on the word *Jesus* than their Trinitarian counterparts. See Wacker, *Heaven Below*, 88.
38. Lie, *E. W. Kenyon*, 30. By the 1970s, Kenyon's Gospel Publishing Society sold 100,000 of his books per year. Simmons, *E. W. Kenyon*, x.
39. Lake, *Spiritual Hunger and Other Sermons*, 19.
40. Lie, *E. W. Kenyon*, 50; Simmons, *E. W. Kenyon*, 41.
41. Kenyon's daughter claims that though he maintained strong ties to pentecostalism, he never spoke in tongues and did not consider himself a pentecostal.

42. Lie, *E. W. Kenyon*, 49. Kenyon's biographer Dale Simmons writes, "Precisely when Bosworth came into contact with the teachings of E. W. Kenyon is uncertain; however, Kenyon's daughter relates that the two met during one of Kenyon's visits to Chicago. Most likely, then, the two met before 1910" (Simmons, *E. W. Kenyon*, 295). Further, Bosworth contributed articles to *Kenyon's Herald of Life*. Bosworth, like Kenyon, hovered on the margins of pentecostalism. He withdrew from the Assemblies of God in 1918 because he could not endorse the hallmark doctrine that speaking in tongues was the initial physical evidence of the baptism of the Holy Spirit.

43. Bosworth, *Christ the Healer: Sermons on Divine Healing*, 1924 edition, 188. He devotes two chapters to the act of believing, declaring, and acting faith before it is perceived by the senses. See 84–114, 181–89.

44. Bosworth, *Christ the Healer: Messages on Divine Healing*, 1948 edition, 151. The first edition of *Christ the Healer* advocates the same process for the outworking of faith. In the 1924 edition, he calls these declarations "praise." By 1948, infused with Kenyon's confidence in words, he calls them "confessions." For reference to the "prayer of faith," see page 15; see 22–47 for references to higher life/faith cure leaders.

45. Bosworth, *Christ the Healer*, 2nd ed., 155, 144, 135 (italics in the original).

46. Bosworth, *Christ the Healer*, 1st ed., 98–99.

47. Unlike many others, Bosworth credited Kenyon for his words. The conclusion of "Our Confession" of *Christ the Healer* states: "Most of the thoughts expressed in this sermon I have brought together, by permission, from the writings of Rev. E. W. Kenyon" (*Christ the Healer*, 2nd ed., 156). See also Kenyon, *The Two Kinds of Faith*, 67.

48. Weaver, *The Healer–Prophet, William Marrion Branham*, 68. For his role as advisor, see Harrell, *All Things Are Possible*, 14–15. For early accounts of his tours with Branham and Lindsay, see "Rev. and Mrs. F. F. Bosworth Work With Branham Party," *The Voice of Healing*, 1, 5.

49. Simmons, *E. W. Kenyon*, 174.

50. Wacker, *Heaven Below*, 96.

51. Lake, *Spiritual Hunger*, 20. See also pages 86, 90.

52. Burpeau, *God's Showman*, 152–53.

53. For more on Lake's healing theology, see Susanto, "A Practical Theological Evaluation."

54. Darrin Rodgers, personal correspondence, December 7, 2009.

55. The historian Jonathan R. Baer offered the strongest reading of the materiality of pentecostal salvation. As he wrote, "Pentecostalism originated in the body as much as the spirit. . . . Glossolalia and other ecstatic manifestations authenticated God's presence and power, reflecting the reality of the Holy Spirit within believers. But the materiality of the culture that gave rise to Pentecostalism received its fullest expression in 'divine healing.'" See Baer's "Redeemed Bodies," 735.

56. See Ma and Menzies, *The Spirit and Spirituality*, 224.

57. Jacobsen, *Thinking in the Spirit*, 94–98.

58. Wacker, *Heaven Below*, 25–28. Early pentecostals transformed prayer into a divine contract. Yet subsequent generations exhibited a diversity of opinions on the uses of prayer. Prayer became, among other things, supplication, assurance, strength, and discipline.

59. Bosworth, *Christ the Healer*, 1st ed., pages 10–12, 24–27, 63, 64, 72, 89, 94, 95.

60. James, *The Varieties of Religious Experience*, 95.

61. Watts, *God, Harlem, U.S.A*, 22. Albanese, *Republic of Mind*, 472–78.

62. The origins of New Thought in the African American community are difficult to pinpoint. While New Thought historian Beryl Satter argued for its significance within African American spirituality, she lamented that she was unable to recover its history because it operated in separate networks (*Each Mind a Kingdom*, 16).

63. For more on the connection between New Thought and African American self help, see Beryl Satter's examination of W. E. B. Du Bois and race uplift manuals (*Each Mind a Kingdom*, 16), and Jill Watts's examination of New Thought's influence on the black self-help philosophies of Reconstruction (*Father Divine*, 22).

64. For accounts of alternative black prosperity theologies, see Watts, *Father Divine*; Walton, *Watch This!* 47–74; Dallam, *Daddy Grace*; Moses, "Chosen Peoples of the Metropolis"; and Hardy, "'No Mystery God.'"

65. For a history of black spiritualism see Baer and Singer, *African-American Religion in the Twentieth Century*, 183–215, and for a discussion of the interaction of New Thought with black spiritualism see Martin, *Beyond Christianity*, 37–59.

66. Best, *Passionately Human*, 41.

67. See Walton, *Watch This!* 69; Best, *Passionately Human*, 40–3; Baer, *The Black Spiritual Movement*, 26.

68. Albanese, *Republic of the Mind*, 474.

69. Baer, "Universal Hagar's Spiritual Church."

70. Griffith, *Born Again Bodies*, 141; Watts, *Father Divine*, 106.

71. Michaux was a popular revivalist and broadcaster, who had the longest continuous broadcast in radio history from 1929 to 1968. He regularly preached against materialism, with witty slogans like "When you begin to think of gold, you get cold" (Michaux and Lark, *Sparks from the Anvil of Elder Michaux*, 85).

72. Walton, *Watch This!* 71.

73. "Couple Admits Extortion Against 'Prophet,'" *Jet*, 29.

74. See Best, *Passionately Human*, 41; Walton, *Watch This!* 69.

75. See Baer, *The Black Spiritual Movement*, 26, and Harold A. Carter, *The Prayer Tradition of Black People*, 87. With regard to mainstream acceptability, see "5-Year-Old Boy Directs Choir," *Jet*, 17.

76. Walton, *Watch This!* 69.

77. Anderson, *Vision of the Disinherited*, esp. 114–36. Refuted by Wacker, *Heaven Below*, esp. chap. 12.

78. Kenyon used finances as a testing ground for faith but seldom as a measure. For example, Kenyon gave up his pastoral salary early in his ministry, depending on God for provision. This decision led to a break with his first congregation (Lie, *E. W. Kenyon*, 18, 22).

79. "Adversity," *The Latter Rain Evangel*, 11.

80. Meyer, *Positive Thinkers*, 259–89.

81. Conwell, *Acres of Diamonds*, 22. Conwell tempered his stress on accumulated wealth by instructing those of good fortune to be generous stewards. See Hutchison, *Religious Pluralism in America*, 93–100.

82. For more on religious interpretations of wealth, see Cherry, *God's New Israel*, prologue to part 5 and 249–59.

83. See, for example, Brands, *The Age of Gold*, 441–91.

84. Barton, *The Man Nobody Knows*, 170.

85. Satter dissected the notion that New Thought was solely an economic message, but my study focuses on this single (though not totalizing) characteristic.

86. Albanese, *America: Religion and Religions*, 271.

87. Harley, *Emma Curtis Hopkins*, 71–74; Albanese, *Republic of Mind*, 320.

88. Fillmore, *Prosperity*, 69.

89. Albanese, *Republic of Mind*, 394–99.

90. Simmons, *E. W. Kenyon*, 216.

91. Critics often depicted New Thought as a garish "cult of success" (Griswold, "New Thought: A Cult of Success,"). See also Weiss, *The American Myth of Success*; Meyer, *The Positive Thinkers*.

92. Satter, *Each Mind a Kingdom*, 226.

93. Simmons, *E. W. Kenyon*, 216. The organization The Full Gospel Business Men did much the same for charismatic Christianity a half century later.

94. Satter, *Each Mind a Kingdom*, 240. For the intersection of popular psychology and New Thought at the turn of the twentieth century, see Satter, *Each Mind a Kingdom*, 239–47, and Meyer, *Positive Thinkers*, 164–67.

95. New Thought by no means dissolved, however. A series of small but sturdy sects—Divine Science Federation International, Religious Science, and the Unity School of Christianity—continued into the twenty-first century.

96. Albanese, *Republic of Mind*, 436.

97. Ibid.

98. Holifield, *God's Ambassadors*, 160.

99. Elson, *Myths and Mores in American Best Sellers*, 186. That is not to say, however, that Bruce Barton and Charles Sheldon (author of the bestselling *In His Steps*) dismissed social problems with trite individualism. Like the advocates of the social gospel, these authors urged Christians to remake sinful institutions by taking the hard road through personal sacrifice. See Hutchison, *Religious Pluralism*, 100.

100. Meyer, *Positive Thinkers*, 170.
101. Albanese, *Republic of Mind*, 441.
102. Satter, *Each Mind a Kingdom*, 251.
103. "Happy Am I," *Time*.
104. Holifield, *God's Ambassadors*, 219.
105. Meyer, *Positive Thinkers*, 129.

CHAPTER 2

Epigraph is from Agnes Sanford, *The Healing Light*, 14th ed. (St. Paul, MN: Macalester Park, 1952), 21–22.

1. Margaret Poloma and others argue that pentecostalism's increased institutionalization may have set off this burst of independent revival. See Poloma, *The Charismatic Movement*, 193–97.
2. David Harrell introduced this chronology to describe the two waves of revival, first healing, then the charismatic. See Harrell, *All Things Are Possible*. This pioneering and elegant work remains one of the most important contributions to the study of this period.
3. Ibid., ch. 5.
4. Ibid., 6.
5. Jaggers, *Everlasting Physical and Spiritual Health*, 100–110. Also "The Irresistible Faith of God," 17.
6. By the mid-1950s, these assertions divided the healing revival. See Harrell, *All Things Are Possible*, 89; Shemeth, "Asa Alonso Allen," 311–12.
7. Allen, "The Miracle of Outpoured Oil," 2–3.
8. See "Amazing Testimonies of Cancers Passing," *The Voice of Healing*, 17. Allen example, see *Miracle Magazine*, 1, 7.
9. J. M. from Florida, "Special Miracles," 11.
10. "Coat Never Needed Cleaning," *Miracle Word*, 22.
11. Hayden, "The Lord's Work . . . Henry Ford and I," 4.
12. Their magazines republished Kenyon and Bosworth with regularity as the gold standard for positive confession.
13. Jones, "We Are What We Say!" 9; Bosworth, "The Faith That Takes," 11.
14. Walters, *Power: A Matter of Choice*, 1–8. (The book was in Oral Roberts's possession by 1962, and the typeset and photograph suggest a late 1950s print date.)
15. Kenyon, *Two Kinds of Faith*, 7.
16. Osborn, "Divine Healing Through Confession," 12. For "expect a blessing," see Osborn, "Faith," 14. He repeated variations of this sermon often throughout *Faith Digest*.
17. Miller, *Grappling with Destiny*, 31–32.
18. Ibid., 33.
19. Simmons, *E. W. Kenyon*, 158.

20. Jaggers, "Irresistible Faith of God," 17.

21. Quoted in Wacker, "The Pentecostal Tradition," 526.

22. An excerpt from Gardner, *Healing For You!* 23.

23. He drew from a bevy of radical evangelicals and pentecostals—Charles Price, John MacMillan, F. F. Bosworth, and John G. Lake—but sounded most like Kenyon as he promulgated a heavily mechanical vision of flipping the switch of faith. See also King, *Only Believe*, chapters 2 and 3 for his treatment of Hagin's influences. For the most helpful account of the impact of Hagin's ministry, see Billingsley, "The Midas Touch."

24. R. C. Dearman, letter to J. Roswell Flower, 10 January, 1956, Assemblies of God Archives, Springfield, MO. For an example of how comparatively small Hagin's ministry was, see Braune, "God's Power Mightily Manifested Through Kenneth Hagin Ministry," 16.

25. Kenyon, *The Father and His Family*, 244.

26. Kenyon, *The Wonderful Name of Jesus*, 4. See also Gardner, *The God of Miracles Lives Today!* 40–48.

27. Kenyon, *The Two Kinds of Faith*, 7.

28. For an example of the contemporary use of legal language in faith theology, see Harrison, *Righteous Riches*, 8–10. For an example of condemnation for those living "beneath our privileges," see Hagin, "Is Your Profit Showing?" 4–5.

29. See also Lake, *The John G. Lake Sermons on Dominion over Demons, Disease, and Death*, 56. The growing authority of science likely prompted Christians to take up scientific language to describe the operation of spiritual power. Porterfield, *Healing in the History of Christianity*, 159. As the sociologist Mark Chaves argued, the rise of scientific authority circumscribed religious authority, but did not snuff it out. See Chaves, "Secularization as Declining Religious Authority."

30. King, *Only Believe*, chapters 8 and 9. For another example of earlier radical evangelical uses of the spiritual laws, see Dixon, *The Person and Ministry of the Holy Spirit*, 2.

31. Jones, *The Golden Key*, 1. Many more revivalists preached in a similar legal vein. See Jackson, "What is Faith?" 17; Jaggers, "The Irresistible Faith of God" 17; Osborn, "The Miracle at Bethesda," 15–23.

32. Grant, "The Word of Wisdom," 8.

33. Allen, *The Secret to Scriptural Financial Success*, 10. Olmstead, "God Told Me to Mortgage My Home," 4.

34. A year after Allen's book, the Portland-based *March of Faith* published some of the first testimonials about supernatural money-back guarantees. See Mrs. Thomas (Evelyn) Wyatt, "As I See It," 3.

35. See, for example, *Abundant Life*, June 1958.

36. Harrell, *Oral Roberts*, 152.

37. Roberts, *Oral Roberts' Life Story*, 70–75.

38. The two first crossed paths in 1948 when Hagin attended Roberts's Dallas crusade (Harrell, *Oral Roberts*, 152).

39. Dowell, *Material and Financial Blessings For You.*

40. W. T. Gaston, letter to Ralph Riggs (Executive Files Correspondence), 23 March 1956; R. C. Dearman, letter to J. Roswell Flower, 10 January 1959; Curtis W. Ringness, letter to R. C. Dearman, 26 January 1959; E. B. Crump, letter to Curtis W. Ringness, 29 January 1959. Assemblies of God Archives.

41. Hampel, *Your Faith Is Power*, 18–19.

42. Sylva Iverson's *Releasing the Power Within* and Thomas and Evelyn Wyatt's growing library of the subject of financial miracles stood as only a few examples of the Latter Rain contribution to the prosperity gospel. Oral Roberts's admiring scrawl on his own copy of Thomas Wyatt's *Wings of Healing*, dated 1947, suggests a shared theological conversation. For more on the Latter Rain's relationship to the prosperity gospel, see McClymond, "Prosperity Already and Not Yet."

43. Miller, *Grappling With Destiny*, 100 for "the faith principle," and 134–135 for "spiritual laws."

44. Ibid., 62.

45. Roberts was the only one with widespread national coverage, as Humbard and Allen's presence was a bit spotty. Synan argues that, in a sense, Roberts sanctified television for pentecostals. Synan, *An Eyewitness Remembers the Century of the Holy Spirit*, 197. In the late 1950s, Roberts could be heard on hundreds of radio stations and seen on dozens of television stations. See any issue of *Abundant Life* in 1958 for his radio and television guide.

46. See Hayford and Moore's *The Charismatic Century*, 163, 171, 198–202.

47. Jones, "Down the Years!" 12–13.

48. Rammell, "This is Revival," 7.

49. Their invitation to join the National Association of Evangelicals allowed them to join a broader religious conversation, progress furthered in the 1950s by pentecostal ecumenists like David du Plessis.

50. Montgomery, "God's Contract with Us," 6–7; Nickel, "Religion in Business Brings Sure Success," 10–11.

51. Demos Shakarian, "A Call to the Business Men of Our Nation," 13.

52. This early logo for the FGBMFI comes from the advertisements for the 1957 Fifth Annual Convention in Chicago, Illinois.

53. Menchaca, "Deliverance in Spanish Churches with Evangelist Harry Hampel," 16.

54. Ramirez, "Borderlands Praxis"; Espinoa, "Francisco Olazábal and Latino Pentecostal Revivalism in the North American Borderlands," 125–46, 305–9.

55. For statistics on this economic disparity, see Thernstrom and Thernstrom, *America in Black and White*, 183–202.

56. W. T. Gaston, letter to Ralph Riggs, 23 March 1956, Assemblies of God Archives.

57. Robins, *Pentecostalism in America*, 73–103.

58. Provocateurs like A. A. Allen depicted the denominational preacher as the Catholic taskmaster, a chain around every parishioner's neck (Allen, *God Said Let My People Go!*).

59. Assemblies of God, letter to A. A. Allen, 4–5.

60. Harrell, *All Things Are Possible*, 99–116. Gaston, letter to Ralph Riggs, 23 March 1956, Assemblies of God Archives.

61. Synan, *Eyewitness Remembers*, 36–41.

62. Gee, "Living By Faith," 10.

63. Harrell, *All Things Are Possible*, 139.

64. W. T. Gaston, letter to Ralph Riggs, 23 March 1956, Assemblies of God Archives.

65. Finstuen, 21.

66. Anker, *Self-Help and Popular Religion in Modern American Culture*, 110–11.

67. Holifield, *God's Ambassadors*, 224.

68. Coontz, *Marriage, a History*, 213, 214, 233–35.

69. The show ran from 1951 to 1957, earning an Emmy and an estimated 30 million weekly viewers. Koester, *Fortress Introduction to the History of Christianity in the United States*, 177–78.

70. Peale, *The Power of Positive Thinking*, vii, 2, 6.

71. Ibid., 39, 41.

72. See, for example, ibid., 15, 107, 112, 201, 204.

73. Ibid., 55.

74. Among faith teachers, see Osborn's *Soulwinning Out Where the Sinners Are*.

75. George, *God's Salesman*, 104, 138.

76. For an excellent treatment of Protestant engagement with the 1950s, see Andrew Finstuen's *Original Sin and Everyday Protestants*, especially 13–46.

77. Here I am indebted to Philip Sintiere, who made the connection between the prosperity gospel and Cold War politics.

78. Harrell, *Oral Roberts*, 115.

79. Ibid., 42. Robertson did not persuade Peale.

80. Grant, *Must I Pray for a Miracle?* 3.

81. Harrell, *All Things Are Possible*, 92. The term "point of contact" surfaces in Andrew Murray's book *Divine Healing* (1884) in reference to anointing oil and the laying on of hands. See King, *Only Believe*, 272.

82. See Osborn, "Don't Eat It All," 16–19; Gardner, "Faith for Finances," 4–9; Grant's *How to Receive Without Asking*; Ford, "God's Divine Law of Compensation," 5; Culpepper, "R. W. Culpepper Says." 6–7; Hardy, "Testimonies of Prosperity," 5, 12–13 (references Brother Hardy's initiation of the blessing covenant in 1964); Cerullo, cover; Nunn, "Faith for Finances," 4–5; Kenyon, "Giving Is the Way to Receive," 2; Kenyon, "If We Receive from God!" 1.

83. Harrell, *All Things Are Possible*, 105.

84. Advertisement in David Nunn's *The Healing Messenger*, February 1964.

85. For the most part, preachers republished Kenyon's teachings as the authority on positive confession. See, for example, Kenyon, "Count It Done," 6, and Mattsson-Boze, "The Giver and The Givers," 3–4.

86. See, for example, Thomas Wyatt's expanding strategies from his own miracle crusades in Africa, to sending "crash" teams, to paying for the education of local pastors. Miller, *Grappling With Destiny*, 164–80.

87. Nunn, *The Healing Messenger*, March 1977, 10–11.

88. Ford, "God's Divine Law," 5. For his shared language of faith as activator, see Pope, "Your Faith Can Make It Happen," 4–5.

89. Wyatt, "Prosperity's Hidden Secrets . . . Revealed," 10–11.

90. Gardner, "Faith for Finances," 4–9.

91. Jenkins published *Three Easy Steps to Prosperity* (1965) depicting him in his suburban home explaining how "God has a law established in the Universe which tells us that we must give before we can receive," 3.

92. See Osborn, "Put God to the Test," 8–13.

93. Ewing, *A Miracle For You*, 16.

94. Osborn, "Plant your FIRSTfruits," 8–9.

95. See *The Voice of Healing*, November 1965, 1.

96. Oral Roberts, *Daily BLESSING*, 2–3.

97. See also Osborn, *One Hundred Divine Healing Facts*, 19; Osteen, *What To Do When Nothing Seems to Work*, 20.

98. Copeland, *The Laws of Prosperity*, 27.

99. Hagin, *In Him*, 1. Like many others, this quotation came from Kenyon's *Two Kinds of Faith*.

100. Hagin, *In Him*, 12.

101. Faith teachers parted company with evangelicals and other "born-agains" over their approach to the Word. Traditionally, the Word—the Logos—had been equated with the divinity of Jesus but faith believers conflated "the Word" with positive confession.

102. Copeland, *Laws of Prosperity*, 26–27.

103. For an example of Jesus using positive confession, see Hagin, *In Him*, 6.

104. Hagin, *In Him*, 9.

105. Billingsley, *It's a New Day*, 67.

106. Harrell, *All Things Are Possible*, 235.

107. Walton, *Watch This!* 50.

108. Don Stewart latter recalled that Reverend Ike studied the ministries of Oral Roberts, Kathryn Kuhlman, and A. A. Allen. Don Stewart, see *Only Believe*, 111.

109. Harrell, *All Things Are Possible*, 200.

110. Two issues of the newsmagazine *Time*—October 22, 1965, and April 8, 1966—did much to stoke this debate.

111. Transcendental Meditation, for example, conducted some of its activities under the banner of the Natural Law Party.

112. For helpful surveys of this literature, see Cerillo, "The Beginnings of American Pentecostalism." Hocken, "Charismatic Movement."

113. Synan, *The Century of the Holy Spirit*, 362.

114. Harrell, *All Things Are Possible*, 146.

115. William De Arteaga also argues for an earlier intersection between mainline and metaphysical healing traditions. He suggests that one reason why charismatics gravitated toward the movement was they had already been steeped in the metaphysically inflected Christian healing of Glenn Clark and *The Thought Farthest Out*. De Arteaga, "Glenn Clark's Camps Furthest Out."

116. Sanford, *The Healing Light*.

117. Balmer, *The Encyclopedia of Evangelicalism*, 744; Synan, *An Eyewitness Remembers*, 57–58; J. R. Williams, "Wilkerson, Ralph A.," 1196–97; Roberts, *Holy Spirit in the Now*, 60.

118. Hocken, "Charismatic Movement."

119. McDonnell, "Lutheran Church—Missouri Synod, USA, 1977," 2:307–24.

120. McDonnell, "Lutheran Church in America, USA, 1962: Anointing and Healing," 2:21–55.

121. Synan, *Century of the Holy Spirit*, 363.

122. This estimate comes from the historian David Harrell, *All Things Are Possible*, 3.

123. Charles Green, with an honorary doctorate from ORU, was also on their board of regents. Caldwell, "Charles Green," 54–63.

124. Haggerty, "A Pastor's Heart Opens and his Church Overflows," 57–60. See Poloma's *The Assemblies of God at the Crossroads*, 73–75.

125. To be sure, the charismatic revival did not snuff out the pentecostal healing revivals. They persisted in independent venues and in traditional pentecostal churches.

126. Harrell, *Oral Roberts*, 175–230.

127. Harrell, *All Things Are Possible*, 173.

128. "Full Gospel Business Men's Fellowship International chapter directory: USA, California, Hawaii, and Nevada district," 1967, Regent University Library, Virginia Beach, VA.

129. Mansfield, *Derek Prince*, 214.

130. Harrell, *All Things Are Possible*, 147. Griffith, *God's Daughters*.

131. Hadden, "Religious Broadcasting," 42.

132. Jimmy Swaggart's *Jimmy Swaggart*, Richard De Haan's *Day of Discovery*, Jerry Falwell's *Old Time Gospel Hour*, the Paulist Fathers' *Insight*, the Bakkers' *PTL Club*, and Pat Robertson's *The 700 Club* rounded out the top ten. See Horsfield, *Religious Television*, 103–4.

133. Horsfield, *Religious Television*, 88–100.

134. Blumhofer, *Restoring the Faith*, 217.

135. Harrell, *All Things Are Possible*, 45.

136. Melton, "Rex Humbard," 263.

137. Hadden, "Religious Broadcasting," 41.

138. Ibid., 41.

139. Harrell, *Pat Robertson*, 59.

140. See Lilly, "Lester Sumrall," 48–52.

141. The 1977 Kansas City Conference was arguably the last surge in bringing together Catholics, Pentecostals, and mainline Protestants in shared purpose. It attracted 45,000 attendees and featured a veritable who's who of ecumenical and charismatic leaders. To be sure, ecumenism faded but did not die. Popular ecumenical conferences like the North American Congress on the Holy Spirit and World Evangelization continue (1986–).

142. See Synan, *An Eyewitness Remembers*, 77–94.

143. The 1970s wrangling with questions of spiritual authority tested the pentecostal and charismatic communities' willingness to share, defer, and finance one another's projects. Christian Growth Ministries, based in Fort Lauderdale, Florida, generated a national ministerial network led by five prominent ministers: Derek Prince, Charles Simpson, Ern Baxter, Don Basham, and (most memorably) Bob Mumford. Its flagship publication, *New Wine*, and its leaders' near-constant presence on national platforms and Christian television carried their voices clear across the country. Rumors spread that its disciples were organized into a pyramid of "sheep," each submitting to a "shepherd" with the Ford Lauderdale Five at the top issuing orders and gathering tithes. For this, it was called the Shepherding Controversy. Pat Robertson banned them from his airwaves; Demos Shakarian blacklisted them from FGBMFI conventions; and ecumenical meeting after meeting met to assess its threat to individual conscience and ecclesial autonomy.

CHAPTER 3

1. Copeland, *Poverty*, 10.

2. Copeland, "God Wants You to Prosper," 38–41.

3. Quoting Derek Prince in Harrell, *All Things Are Possible*, 237.

4. Strang, "Kenneth Copeland," 16.

5. Even raucous New Orleans celebrated their own prosperity success story in Charles Green by pronouncing June 14, 1983, Charles Green Day. Terry Meeuwsen (Miss America 1973) and later Cheryl Prewitt (Miss America 1980) became CBN favorites.

6. Andrew, "The Controversy over Faith," 44–49.

7. Strang, "Bridge Builders or Stone Throwers?"

8. Strang, "10 Growth Stages for Charisma," 172; Harrell, *Pat Robertson*, 67.

9. "Demos Shakarian Memorial Issue," *Voice*, 11.

10. For the former, consider A. A. Allen's miraculous money in the healing revival, and for the latter, Morris Cerullo's financial focus on the deliverance circuit.

11. A 1985 *Charisma* poll named Pat Robertson, Kenneth Copeland, and Kenneth Hagin as the three most influential leaders in the charismatic community.

12. Association of Faith Churches and Ministers website, "Dr. Jim Kaseman."

13. These proponents include Tommy Barnett, Happy Caldwell, Kenneth Copeland, Billy Joe Daugherty, John Gimenez, Kenneth Hagin Sr., Buddy Harrison, Marilyn Hickey, Freda Lindsay, John Meares, Mike Murdock, John Osteen, Earl Paulk, Tommy Reid, Evelyn Roberts, Oral Roberts, Richard Roberts, Jerry Savelle, Karl Strader, Stephen Strang, Lester Sumrall, Hilton Sutton, and Robert Tilton. The eminent historian Vinson Synan was one of the founding members and appears on these network pictures only because of the ICBM's habit of annually advertising the appearance of its trustees and founding members.

14. Strang, "The Christian Book Boom," 14.

15. Towns, *Say-It-Faith*; Houghton, *Power of Agreement*; Swann and Swann, *Guarantee Your Child's Success*; Thomas, *Change Your Life with Confession*, 1.

16. Overcoming Faith Christian Center, "Church History."

17. See Hash, *Building God's House*.

18. "TV's Rev. Fred Price Opens $9 Million FaithDome in L.A.," *Jet*, 32–33.

19. Billingsley, *It's a New Day*, 13.

20. Pearson, *Breaking the Curse*, 34.

21. Montgomery, *Breaking the Spirit of Poverty*, 151.

22. Thigpen, "The New Black Charismatics," 58–67.

23. Walsh, "Santidad, Salvación, Sanidad, Liberacion," 154.

24. Bowler, "From Far and Wide."

25. See Fast, "Is Faith a Farce or Force?" 2; Warner, "Roy Hicks," 390. Hicks was also a guest writer for *Charisma* and instructor at Rhema Bible Training Center and Christ for the Nations.

26. "New Role for Swaggart?" *Charisma*, 60.

27. Hayford, *Prayer Is Invading the Impossible*, 138. See page 146 for "authority"; 138 for God's words. Hayford's conflicted relationship to the prosperity gospel can be seen in the discrepancy between his publications (absent of positive confession and money) and his personal relationships. He is the personal pastor of Paul Crouch.

28. Hagin, "Trend Toward Faith Movement," 67–70.

29. Lea, *Spiritual Authority*.

30. Osborn, *Go For It!*

31. Winch, "Jehovah Jireh."

32. Parsley, *Daily Breakthrough*, 295.

33. John 10:10.

34. Thompson, *Money Cometh!* 250 (emphasis in the original).

35. Ibid.

36. Dollar, *Total Life Prosperity*, 15. Some faith teachers rebutted this line of reasoning. See Robison, *True Prosperity*, 44.

37. For the most detailed treatment of Jesus' wealth, see Hagin, *Midas Touch*, 42–65.

38. For one of many lists of Jesus' wealth, see Avanzini, *The Wealth of the World*, 81–86.

39. Hagin, *The Biblical Keys to Financial Prosperity*, 19. See also Roberts, *How I Learned Jesus Was Not Poor*.

40. God promised the land as an everlasting possession, numerous progeny, and a special relationship between God and the descendants of Abraham and Sarah (Genesis 17:7–8).

41. Hagin, *Biblical Keys*, 17.

42. Gilfillan, *Unlocking the Abraham Promise*, 5.

43. Copeland and Copeland, *Prosperity Promises*, vi. See also Hagin, *Biblical Keys*, 45–68.

44. Capps and Capps, *God's Creative Power for Finances*, 27–28. See also Capps, *The Tongue: A Creative Force*.

45. Capps Ministries, "Charles and Peggy Capps," website, http://charlescapps.com (accessed November 22, 2012).

46. Harrison, *Righteous Riches*, 4; Hagin, *Midas Touch*, 173; Basham, *Lead Us Not Into Temptation*, 108.

47. Avanzini, *It's Not Working, Brother John*, 145.

48. Victorious Faith Center. April 4th, 2008.

49. For an early example, see Lindsay, *God's Master Key to Prosperity*, 46. Frederick Price, Joel Osteen, Kenneth Copeland, Frances Hunter, Marilyn Hickey, and many others promoted the hundredfold blessing in print.

50. "But he shall receive an hundredfold now in this time, houses, and brethren, and sisters, and mothers, and children, and lands, with persecutions; and in the world to come eternal life" (Mark 10:30). Copeland, *God's Will Is Prosperity*, 54.

51. See, for example, Avanzini, *30, 60, Hundredfold*, 13–14.

52. Swaggart, "Clean Up Our Act," 25–29.

53. Hagin, *Midas Touch*, 153.

54. Schulman, *The Seventies*, 35.

55. Sagert, *The 1970s*, 4–5.

56. Albert, *Jim Bakker*, 108.

57. Jimmy Carter's "Crisis of Confidence" speech of 1979.

58. Thumma and Travis, *Beyond Megachurch Myths*, 7.

59. Strang, "Oral Roberts Shares His Heart," 56.

60. Shemeth, "Asa Alonso Allen," 311–12. The growth is even more remarkable considering Allen's early death from alcoholism.

61. Loveland and Wheeler, *From Meetinghouse to Megachurch*, 127.

62. Lindsay, *Freda*.

63. Chaves, "All Creatures Great and Small."

64. Loveland and Wheeler, *From Meetinghouse to Megachurch*, 114–20.

65. Bill Hybels and Willow Creek Community Church in South Barrington, Illinois, with its pared-down Christian vocabulary, business casual dress, and corporate architecture, served as the prototype of seeker-sensitive churches. Loveland and Wheeler, *From Meetinghouse to Megachurch*, 127.

66. Historically, African American churchgoers have dressed up more than their white counterparts. See White and White, *Stylin'*. Prosperity churches' theology of demonstrative wealth amplified the importance of such practices.

67. See Munroe, *Kingdom Principles*.

68. Schuller, *Your Church Has Real Possibilities!*

69. Robert Schuller, interviewed by Paul Crouch. See Anker, *Self-Help*, 154.

70. The 1980s televangelists borrowed time-tested techniques. From 1957, Billy Graham broadcast his crusades to vast audiences.

71. Hadden, "Religious Broadcasting," 41–42. Once established, many decided to forego satellite for the larger market of television syndication.

72. Harrell, *Pat Robertson*, 57.

73. Crouch, *Hello World!* 70.

74. Viewers knew better. A 1980 ethnography of PTL viewers found that even among ardent supporters, observers remained critical of their constant financial requests. See Bourgault, "An Ethnographic Study of the 'Praise the Lord Club,'" 179.

75. Roberts, "Trinity Broadcasting Network," 21.

76. Avanzini, *It's Not Working*, 155–56.

77. Meyer, "Enjoying Everyday Life."

78. Bourgault, *Ethnographic Study*, 165–66, 184.

79. Bakker, *We're Blest*.

80. Frame, "Fund Raising: Did Oral Roberts Go Too Far?"

81. Stephens, "Oral Tells His Side," 70–75.

82. Kaufman, "The Fall of Jimmy Swaggart," 37.

83. Lawson, "PTL Plans World's Largest Church," 86.

84. Buckingham, "PTL Meets the Press," 25.

85. Gorman, *Called to Victory*.

86. *ALF*, 1990, season 4, ep. 17.

87. Hadden, "The Rise and Fall of American Televangelism," 113–130.

88. Lea, "Why Have Christians Been Holding Back?" 39–42.

89. Hadden, "The Rise and Fall of American Televangelism," 113–30.

90. Buckingham, "God Is Shaking His Church," 20–23.

91. Montgomery, *Breaking the Spirit of Poverty*, 31.

92. See Tucker-Worgs, *The Black Megachurch*, 85, for educational levels.

93. Walton, *Watch This!* 75–102.

94. Tucker-Worgs, *Black Megachurch*, 61–66.

95. Here I follow Jonathan Walton's helpful parsing of the cultural and aesthetic distinctions between classic pentecostal, neopentecostal, historic black denominations, and Word of Faith traditions drawn directly from Haginite influences.

96. See Lincoln and Mamiya, *The Black Church in the African-American Experience*, 384.

97. See Billingsley, *It's a New Day*, 104–29; Tucker-Worgs, *Black Megachurch*, 4, 48.

98. For an excellent summary of this complicated phenomenon related to mega-church growth, see Walton, "Megachurch Phenomenon," 2:463–76.

99. Tucker-Worgs, *Black Megachurch*, 29, 46–52. These findings match data by the author based on a survey of the 50 black megachurches deemed to be prosperity churches.

100. Tucker-Worgs, *Black Megachurch*, 42–50.

101. See Du Bois, *On Sociology and the Black Community*, 228.

102. Lincoln and Mamiya, "The Black Church and Economics," in *Black Church in the African-American Experience*, 241.

103. The pioneering work of E. Franklin Frazier on the social and economic functions of black churches have been the kindling for over a half-century of debate. See, for example, *The Negro Church in America*.

104. C. Eric Lincoln and Lawrence Mamiya famously parsed the social roles of black churches as the dialectic between the 1. other-worldly and this-worldly, 2. the communal and the privatistic, 3. resistance versus accommodation, 4. charismatic versus bureaucratic, 5. universalism and black theology, and 6. the priestly and prophetic (preservation vs. critique). See Lincoln and Mamiya, *Black Church in the African-American Experience*.

105. Baer, *African American Religion*, 183–215; Floyd-Thomas, *Black Church Studies*, 138–40.

106. C. Eric Lincoln and Lawrence Mamiya's landmark study, published in 1990, observed the growing division within black churches between poor and middle-class churchgoers. See Lincoln and Mamiya, *Black Church in the African-American Experience*, 382–85.

107. Interview with Cynthia Hale, October 12, 2010.

108. Theologically, she describes herself as similar to neopentecostal Baptists like Paul Morton and Kenneth Ulmer.

109. Ray of Hope Christian Church website, http://www.rayofhope.org (accessed July 21, 2011).

110. Eventually, the strained ties between the denomination and McClendon broke. He cited racism and real estate disagreements while the denomination countered that it was the six-month required leave he would have to take owing to his divorce. For prosperity preaching, see McClendon, *Beyond Personal Power*; and "Clarence Mcclendon Cuts Ties with Foursquare After Divorce News," *Charisma*, July 31, 2000. http://www.charismamag.com/index.php/component/content/article/248-people-events/469-clarence-mcclendon-cuts-ties-with-foursquare-after-divorce-news.

111. Best, "Church of God in Christ," in *African American Religious Cultures*, 1:165.

112. The denomination's changing relationship to the wider pentecostal world (and its growing contributions to televangelism) deserves much greater attention. In

particular, G. E. Patterson's televangelist career and presence in popular pentecostal conferences should be explored.

113. West Angeles Community Development Corporation, www.westangelescdc.org (accessed July 20, 2011). See also Raboteau, *Canaan Land*, 132–35.

114. The 1994 Young Evangelists Conference "Pure Power," *Charisma*, n.p.

115. Blake, *Dreamers Are Coming!* 37. He warned readers against the "twisted doctrine" of instantaneous victory in *Free to Dream*, 125.

116. Tamelyn Tucker-Worgs's *The Black Megachurch* discusses a spectrum of ideologies in these churches, contrasting a color-blind vs. black theology, denomination vs. nondenominational, communal vs. privatistic, and social gospel vs. prosperity gospel.

117. Evangel Fellowship COGIC website, "Apostle Otis Lockett biography."

118. Bonner, *Positive Thinking Changed My Life.*

119. Take, for example, Bishop Norman Wagner's fellow speakers at Azusa '88: Carlton Pearson, Oral Roberts, R. W. Schambach, Bishop Charles Blake, Iverna Tompkins, Richard Roberts, Shirley Caesar, Becky Fender, and Jerone Lee. See also Horrace Smith's 2001 FaithWorks Conference hosting Bishop Tudor Bismark, Bishop George Bloomer, Elder Robert Evans, Bishop Noel Jones, and Dr. Carolyn Showell.

120. Ellis, "I Shall Prosper, Part II."

121. In 2010, Charles Ellis appeared daily on the Word Network alongside the biggest names in the prosperity movement. He was not a frequent face on the conference circuit, though he did host his own pastor's conference. He often featured the ministries of Noel Jones and Jamal Bryant, whose messages closely mirrored his own.

122. Here I agree with Shayne Lee's assessment of T. D. Jakes' identity as a "prosperity preacher." See Lee's helpful biography, *T. D. Jakes: America's New Preacher*, 98–122. Jonathan Walton disagrees, arguing further that there must be a clear distinction between the prosperity gospel and an aesthetic demonstration of material wealth. See Walton, *Watch This!* 103–24. Participation in the wider prosperity movement should not be read as a totalizing commitment as many neopentecostal leaders have crossed over into (and out of) theological arguments for divine wealth. See appendix B.

123. T. D. Jakes, *The Great Investment.* See pages 159–61 for "the formula," and page 22 for the quotation.

124. Congregational visit. Redemption World Outreach Center, 17 April, 2011.

125. Walton, *Watch This!* 79.

126. Rush, "May I Have Your Order Please."

127. Walton, *Watch This!* 86; Harrison, *Righteous Riches*, 89–90.

128. See *The Black Church in the African-American Experience*, 385–88.

129. Available from http://www.empowermenttemple.org/ (accessed November 11, 2010).

130. Methodism's early history of making the English middle class out of newly dis-cipled poor or granting economic opportunities to African slaves formed the backbone of this Methodist version of "redemption and lift." "Methodists, some would say, laid the foundations for what some incorrectly call the prosperity gospel" (Frank Reid, interview with the author, September 30, 2011).

131. Reid, "I Am a Winner."

132. For example, he was a mainstay of Tommy and Rachel Burchfield's annual meeting featuring Word of Faith teachers like T. L. Osborn, Charles Nieman, and R. W. Schambach.

133. Maxwell, "The Calm after the Storm."

134. Morris and Lee, "The National Baptist Convention."

135. Osteen, *Become a Better You*, 109; 109; 115; 208–9, 113.

136. Jones and Chaplain, *Vow of Prosperity*, 30.

137. See Lee and Sinitiere, *Holy Mavericks*, 107–28.

138. White, *Birthing Your Dreams*, 104.

139. Ibid. Some approximation of this quotation can be traced to Aristotle's *Ethics*.

140. Congregational visit, VFC, Durham, NC, July 29, 2007.

141. "Will a man rob God? Yet ye have robbed me. But ye say, Wherein have we robbed thee? In tithes and offerings. Ye are cursed with a curse: for ye have robbed me, even this whole nation" (Malachi 3:8–9).

142. Vergara, *How the Other Half Worships*, 153.

143. Given that many of these faith churches came from the sanctified fold, this was simply a matter of continuity. Filing past the offertory plate had long been the normative practice in many working-class African American churches.

144. Hagin, "Offering Prayer." This practice served as a continuation of the historic pentecostal emphasis on palpability, contrary to the common assumption that this was a movement characterized only by spirit.

145. "Alternative Giving from the Heart." Handout, Speak the Word Church Interna-tional, Minneapolis, Minnesota. Congregational visit, May 8, 2011.

146. Congregational visit, November 14, 2010.

147. Church Financial Seminar, *Charisma*, May 2000, n.p. (emphasis in the original).

148. Congregational visit, Winston Salem, NC, August 1, 2010.

149. Vergara, *How the Other Half Worships*, 220.

150. Ibid., 153.

151. Congregational visit, VFC, Durham, NC, March 29, 2007.

152. Hagin, *Obedience in Finances*, 9–15.

153. White, *Birthing Your Dreams*, 68.

154. Meyers, "Thanksgiving."

155. Congregational visit, VFC, Durham, NC, July 29, 2007.

156. Ask Marilyn, "Profitable Words," 10.

157. Copeland, *No Deposit, No Return*, 4–5 (emphasis in the original).

158. Wangenye, *God's Will Still Is Prosperity!* 123.

159. Copeland, *Dear Partner*, 61.

160. White, *Birthing Your Dreams*, 70.

161. Bynum, "I Don't Mind Waiting."

162. Sanneh, "Pray and Grow Rich," 48–58.

163. Potter, "The Prosperity Gospel," *Religion & Ethics Newsweekly.*

164. Dollar, "How It All Began," 6–9.

165. Billingsley, *It's a New Day*, 125.

166. Creflo Dollar Ministries, http://www.creflodollarministries.com (accessed August 15, 2008).

167. Dollar, *Changing Your World.*

168. Keteyian, "Televangelists Living Like Kings?"

169. Ghiringhelli, "ORU Leader Resigns, $70 Million Pledged," 29.

170. Solum, *The Balanced Faith Life.* See "New Role for Swaggart?" *Charisma*, 60.

171. Jakes, *Reposition Yourself*, 221.

172. Hagin, *Midas Touch*, 94–95.

CHAPTER 4

1. In some African American churches, older women who exercised authority and influence in church matters are granted the honorific title "mother of the church."

2. Hanby, "Look What the Lord has Done."

3. See Brown, introduction to *Global Pentecostal and Charismatic Healing.*

4. Pastor John Walton, interview by author, Durham, NC, 3 February, 2007.

5. Hagin, *In Him*, 11.

6. Isaiah 53:5. Pentecostal, charismatic, and faith believers embraced other biblical rationales for healing, but the Isaiah passage remained paramount.

7. Both Oral Roberts and David Yonggi Cho claimed healing from tuberculosis, Nasir Saddiki from shingles, and Benny Hinn from stuttering.

8. Robert Bowman quoting Kenneth Hagin, *The Name of Jesus*, 133.

9. The divine healing movement of the late nineteenth century paved the way for the rejection of pious suffering. See Curtis, "Global Character," 34.

10. Faith teachers frequently advocated this unflinching denial in the face of illness. As Kenneth Copeland argued, "No matter what it looks like, even if I die, I'll go to heaven shouting, 'By His stripes I'm healed'" (*Dear Partner*, 48).

11. Hagin, "Good Confessions," 10.

12. Dollar, *How to Obtain Healing*, 7.

13. Osteen, *This Awakening Generation*, 15.

14. Lawson, "Copeland Reaches Out to AIDS Victims," 61. See also Copeland, *Dear Partner*, 55–56.

15. It was officially endorsed by John Bevere, Joseph Garlington, and Jack Hayford. See Davis, *Cleansing Stream Ministries.*

16. Strang, "Larry Lea," 16–20.
17. For example, Dodie Osteen, John Osteen's wife, taught vast audiences to "take their medicine" in her famous testimony of being healed in the terminal stage of pancreatic cancer. Osteen, "Dodie Osteen's Faith and Healing."
18. Mitchem, *Name It and Claim It?* 76–77. In African American vernacular belief (as linked in the loose system of rootwork), placing a coin in your shoe—often a silver dime—has long been said to bring good luck.
19. Strang, "Expecting a Miracle," 30.
20. "Letters to R. G. Hardy," *Faith in Action*, 10.
21. Avanzini, *It's Not Working*, 144.
22. "My people are destroyed for lack of knowledge: because thou hast rejected knowledge, I will also reject thee, that thou shalt be no priest to me: seeing thou hast forgotten the law of thy God, I will also forget thy children" (Hosea 4:6).
23. Price, *Is Healing for All?* 122.
24. Based on Isaiah 53:5 (NIV).
25. Congregational visit, World Harvest Church, Greensboro, NC, October 9, 2007.
26. The term *praise cure* may have been borrowed from Dr. Lilian Yeomans, *His Healing Power*, 45–52.
27. Hillsong United, "Shout Unto God," Hillsong Music Australia, 2008.
28. Hagin, "Good Confessions," 10.
29. Brazee, *365 Days of Healing*, 244.
30. Benny Hinn, Travel to Israel, September 15, 2008.
31. Ask Marilyn, May 1987, 13.
32. Congregational visit. Destiny Christian Center, Greensboro, NC. July 4, 2010. His ministry is under the "covering" of I. V. and Bridget Hilliard's Associated Independent Ministries. See Destiny Christian Center, http://www.leestokes. org/ (accessed July 5, 2010).
33. This interpretation is drawn from 1 Corinthians 11:30: "For this cause many are weak and sickly among you, and many sleep."
34. Murphy, "Overflow."
35. Andrews, "Anointed to Heal," 14–17.
36. Price, *Azusa Street Centennial General Sessions* (CD). Price likely received this teaching from Kenneth E. Hagin (Hagin, *What to Do When Faith Seems Weak*, 113). For a theological comparison with late nineteenth-century evangelicalism, see King, *Only Believe*, 268–76.
37. The decision to approach the stage of a Benny Hinn crusade involves commitment and physical exertion. Believers who are not chosen to get on stage frequently jockey with others to make their way to the front.
38. Basham, *Can A Christian Have A Demon?*; Basham, *A Manual for Spiritual Warfare*.
39. The church used this Baptist handbook as a deliverance manual: Hammond and Hammond, *Pigs in the Parlor*.

40. For more on this view of purging, see Basham *Deliver Us from Evil*, 206–207; Prince, *They Shall Expel Demons*, 212–14.

41. For an overview of deliverance rituals, see Csordas, *The Sacred Self*, 165–99.

42. With the international success of the prosperity gospel, deliverance ministries adopted and adapted local views of the demonic. For example, Rosalind Hackett has argued that particularly in the area of healing and deliverance, West Africans offered creative variations and themes on American prosperity theology (Hackett, "The Gospel of Prosperity in West Africa").

43. Ernest Leonard Advertisement, *Charisma*, April 2004.

44. The term "apostolic" had been used to describe African American "Oneness" denominations but these new apostolic networks were distinguished by a Trinitarian view and the use of fivefold titles in a flexible non-denominational hierarchy.

45. Wagner, "God's Kingdom Wealth Shall Be Released!"

46. Basham, *Deliver Us from Evil*, 206–207; Prince, *They Shall Expel Demons*, 212–14. For an excellent example of the argument from within the charismatic tradition against Christians requiring exorcism, see du Plessis, *Simple and Profound*, 61–63.

47. Following Melville Herskovits's *The Myth of the Negro Path* and Albert Raboteau's *Slave Religion*, most scholars agree that African religions as systems collapsed but that fragments ("survivals") of an African spiritual heritage remained. For an excellent historiographical summary see Harvey, "Black Protestantism." I am persuaded by Yvonne P. Chireau's argument in *Black Magic: Religion and the African American Conjuring Tradition*, 151, that the African American conjure tradition "coexist[ed] with Christianity as an alternative strategy for interacting with the spiritual realm."

48. Long, *Spiritual Merchants*, 74.

49. Ibid., xvi.

50. Ibid., 75.

51. "Witchcraft" was an inclusive category. Beside hoodoo and voodoo, it included a variety of "alternative" therapies such as yoga, acupuncture, and meditation. Pastor Walton preached vigorously against such practices, though it did not surface in any interviews with congregants as a concern. Regardless of whether VFC congregants ever encountered hoodoo directly, I draw on their familiarity with it as a spiritual alternative.

52. In these Low Country black communities, African religion survived, in part, because of the greater autonomy afforded to slaves. See Long, *Spiritual Merchants*, 71–96.

53. Rev. Ike, "THE ENEMY-FIXER!"

54. Vergara, *How the Other Half Worships*, 184.

55. The overlapping influences of pentecostalism, conjure (including hoodoo and voodoo), and black spiritualism have infused a minority of black Protestant

traditions with strong doses of pentecostal, African, and metaphysical magic. For instance, Bishop Charles Mason, the founder of the Church of God in Christ, the largest black pentecostal denomination, moved between conjure and pentecostalism to gain spiritual guidance. Mason divined spiritual direction from his collection of sacred objects, including "roots, branches, and vegetables that he consulted as 'sources for spiritual revelations,' revisiting the tradition of conjuring charms" (Chireau, *Black Magic*, 109–111). As mentioned earlier, black spiritualism added metaphysical categories to black supernaturalism; see Martin, *Beyond Christianity*, 37–59.

56. Lawson, "Faith Preacher Hobart Freeman Dies," 110; Andrews, "The Controversy over Faith," 44.

57. See Williams, "The Transformation of Pentecostal Healing 1906–2006."

58. A few examples serve to illustrate faith teachers' acceptance of "naturalistic" remedies: Benny Hinn's ongoing partnership with Dr. Eric Braverman; Joel Osteen's *Healthy Living* DVD series; Paula White's co-authored book with her fitness trainer, *The Ten Commandments of Health and Wellness*.

59. Williams, "Is There a Doctor in the House?" 97.

60. Byrd and Clayton, *An American Health Dilemma*.

61. Brittany S. Carlton, "Mental Illness in the African American Community," unpublished paper, 2009. In author's possession.

62. At times, spiritual causation trumped medical diagnosis. For example, Pastor Walton argued that a condom could not prevent the spread of AIDS because it could not block the demonic forces that caused AIDS.

63. See Harrison, *Righteous Riches*, 54–55.

64. Hagin, "Is Your Profit Showing?" 4–5.

65. Harrison, *Righteous Riches*, 64.

66. Williams, "Pentecostal Healing."

67. Ibid., 61.

68. Ibid., 66.

69. Roberts, "Staying Well Is Easier than Getting Well," 8–9.

70. Williams, "Pentecostal Healing," 69

71. Ibid., 71.

72. Whorton, *Nature Cures*, 245–49. See also Sagert, *The 1970s*, 8–9.

73. Williams, "Pentecostal Healing," 73–74.

74. Ibid., 100, 139.

75. See, for example, Williams, *The Miracle Results of Fasting*, 5.

76. Jentezen Franklin, *Fasting*, 12.

77. Jentezen Franklin Ministries website. "First Fruits Fast at Jentezen Franklin's Free Chapel, Atlanta." http://www.jentezenfranklin.org/fasting

78. Pat's Diet Shake, www.patsshake.com (accessed November 17, 2009).

79. Michael Sasso, "Preachers of Profit," *The Tampa Tribune*, May 14, 2006.

80. James Robison, www.jamesrobison.com/trivita/ (accessed November 17, 2009).

81. Prosperity Nutrition, www.prosperitynutrition.com/ (accessed January 3, 2008).

82. Reginald Cherry, www.drcherry.com/ (accessed November 17, 2009).

83. Hunter, *God's Answer to Fat*, 24–25.

84. Williams, "I Lost over 200 Pounds When I Used God's Reducing Plan," 3.

85. Hunter, *God's Answer to Fat*, 24–25.

86. Jakes, *Lay Aside the Weight*, 18–19.

87. Williams, "Pentecostal Healing," 160.

88. Meyer, *Eat & Stay Thin*, 77.

89. White, *Ten Commandments for Health and Wellness*, 39–53.

90. Bill Winston Ministries website, http://www.livingwd.org/ministries/prayer-ministry/confessions (accessed November 18, 2009).

91. Osteen, *Healthy Living*.

92. Williams, "Pentecostal Healing," 117.

93. Sampson's Health and Fitness, www.newbirth.org/samsons/ (accessed November 17, 2009).

94. World Changers Ministries Body Sculpting Center, www.worldchangers.org/Body-Sculpting.aspx (accessed November 17, 2009).

95. Roberts, "Trinity Broadcasting Network," 23.

96. See, for example, the World Redemption Center in Greenville, SC.

97. Billingsley, *It's a New Day*, 84.

98. "Nature of the Gifts of Healing," *The Voice of Healing*, 11.

99. Copeland, *Live Long, Finish Strong*.

100. Copeland, "This is the first day of your unlimited life!"

101. Copeland, *Walking in the Realm of the Miraculous*, 72–73.

102. Wendell Smith Memorial, Handout at the Church at South Las Vegas, 2010.

103. "As for the days of our life, they contain seventy years, or if due to strength, eighty years" (Psalm 90:10). For a theological examination of long life in Word of Faith theology, see King, *Only Believe*, 300–308.

104. Harrell, *All Things Are Possible*, 85, 199.

105. Healing practices varied widely among African Americans who participated in the faith movement. For a comparison of traditional and Word of Faith black healing practices, see Williams, "Is There a Doctor in the House?"

106. Congregational visit, February 4, 2007; congregational visit, February 3, 2008.

107. Other theological explorations of the faith movement have made similar critiques. As D. R. McConnell argued in *A Different Gospel*, 166, "The time when a dying believer needs his faith the most is when he is told that he has it the least . . . Perhaps the most inhuman fact revealed about the Faith movement is this: when its members die, they die alone." See also King, *Only Believe*, 301; Hanegraaff, *Christianity in Crisis*, 259–60.

108. Wigglesworth, *Smith Wigglesworth on Healing*.

CHAPTER 5

1. Conference Visit, Joel Osteen's "A Night of Hope," Greensboro Convention Center, NC, April 18, 2008.
2. Winners Church, http://www.winnerstoday.net (accessed January 11, 2010).
3. Simmons, *E. W. Kenyon*, 88.
4. Hagin, *In Him*, 18.
5. For many teachers, this act lowered Jesus to a humanly achievable level of glory. Believers may *become* Jesus, rather than follow him. Kenneth Copeland once claimed that Jesus never said he was God, only that Jesus "walked with Him and that He was in [Jesus.] That's what you are doing" ("Believers' Voice of Victory," 3).
6. Simmons, *E W. Kenyon*, 54.
7. Sanneh, "Pray and Grow Rich," 57.
8. Impacting Your World Christian Center, http://www.iywcc.org (accessed January 11, 2010).
9. These numbers are a composite of the self-reported attendance of prosperity megachurches (see appendix A) and the master list of American megachurches of the Hartford Institute Religion Research (http://hirr.hartsem.edu/).
10. Chaves, *Congregations in America*, 17–21.
11. Thumma and Travis, *Beyond Megachurch Myths*, 5–6.
12. The total number of prosperity megachurches was meager in comparison with the total of megachurches (and the 335,000 of all American congregations) (Thumma and Travis, *Beyond Megachurch Myths*, 2).
13. Ibid.
14. Ibid., 26.
15. In 2009, New England supported nine megachurches, the smallest percentage of megachurches in the country. Of those, three professed faith theology. Given the average New England Catholic parish holds 3,000 members, these numbers are humbling. Yet the region may show some promise. See Thumma and Travis, *Beyond Megachurch Myths*, 26.
16. See Wellman, "The Church of the Pacific Northwest," 87.
17. Bishop, *Our Covenant of Prosperity*, 69.
18. Bynum, *Matters of the Heart*, 202.
19. Earl, "Tuning in on New Technologies," 34–38; Lawson, "Uplinking the Gospel," 62–65.
20. "Couple Claims Opposing Promises," *Lark News*.
21. Congregational visit, Victorious Faith Center, Durham, NC, March 16, 2008.
22. Munizzi, "Say the Name."
23. See Hagin, *The Precious Blood of Jesus*, 27.
24. Hilliard, *My Strong Tower*.
25. Capps and Capps, *Angels*, 94.

26. Osteen, *Unraveling the Mystery of the Blood Covenant*, 45. Benny Hinn, Kenneth Copeland, Gloria Copeland, Norvel Hayes, Marilyn Hickey, John Osteen, and Kenneth Hagin, among others, promoted angels as a significant aspect of living prosperously and victoriously. See, for example Hickey, *Your Miracle Source*, 75.

27. Interview, VFC, Durham, NC, February 3, 2007.

28. Dollar, "Angel Power Confession."

29. See Holvast, *Spiritual Mapping* for the background to this phenomenon.

30. White, *Birthing Your Dreams*, 24.

31. Congregational Visit, VFC, Durham, NC, February 17, 2008.

32. Clark-Sheard, "Blessed and Highly Favored."

33. Jakes and Jakes, *God's Trophy Women*.

34. Osteen, *Become a Better You*, 109.

35. Osteen, *Your Best Life Now*, 3.

36. Jakes, *Reposition Yourself*, 21, 95–96.

37. Mitchem, *Name It and Claim It?* 76–77.

38. Harrison, *Righteous Riches*, 129.

39. Loveland and Wheeler, *From Meetinghouse to Megachurch*, 180.

40. Congregational visit, VFC, Durham, NC, March 24, 2008.

41. Congregational visit, VFC, Durham, NC, April 1, 2007.

42. Congregational Visit, Destiny Christian Center, Greensboro, NC, July 4, 2010.

43. Wellman, *High on God*.

44. More lyrics can be found at http://www.lyricsmania.com/this_is_our_god_lyrics_hillsong.html All about Hillsong: http://www.musictory.com/music/Hillsong.

45. Harrison, *Righteous Riches*, 107–29.

46. Meyer, "At a Glance."

47. Billingsley, *It's a New Day*, 80.

48. Frederick, *Between Sundays*.

49. Loveland and Wheeler, *Meetinghouse to Megachurch*, 128.

50. Ibid.

51. Mitchem, *Name It and Claim It?* 72–74.

52. See, for example, Destiny Christian Center (Greensboro, NC).

53. Mitchem, *Name It and Claim It?* 78.

54. Goh, "Hillsong and 'Megachurch' Practice."

55. Thumma and Travis, *Beyond Megachurch Myths*, 56–57.

56. Ibid., 56.

57. Goh, "Hillsong and 'Megachurch' Practice," 295.

58. Congregational visit, Charlotte, NC, November 3, 2007.

59. T. D. Jakes, B.E.S.T. conference series.

60. Deuteronomy 8:18: "But thou shalt remember the LORD thy God: for it is he that giveth thee power to get wealth, that he may establish his covenant which he sware unto thy fathers, as it is this day."

61. Dollar, *The Color of Love*, 5.
62. Ibid., 22.
63. Ibid., 157.
64. Bronner, "The Father of the 'Prosperity Gospel' Talks About Fatherhood."
65. Emerson and Smith, *Divided by Faith*.
66. For more on the political and social thought of T. D. Jakes, see Walton, *Watch This!* 114–23.
67. Billingsley, *It's a New Day*, 107–8.
68. Jakes, *Reposition Yourself*, 190.
69. Billingsley, *It's a New Day*, 111.
70. Ibid., 112.
71. Ibid.
72. Harrison, *Righteous Riches*, 17.
73. As Grant Wacker demonstrated, racial harmony never prevailed in pentecostalism's origins. For a brief summary of pentecostal racial relations, see Priest and Nieves, *This Side of Heaven*, 26–28; Wacker, *Heaven Below*, 226–39.
74. Synan, *The Century of the Holy Spirit*, 186. Several prosperity teachers, including Paula White, Billy Joe Daugherty, and Ron Carpenter, participated in wider pentecostal attempts to bring unity to their segregated denominations.
75. Billingsley, *It's a New Day*, 113.
76. Ibid., 42.
77. John Dart, "Issue of Racism Breaks Ties That Bound Two Churches," *Los Angeles Times*, March 28, 1998.
78. Though Price kept his honorary doctorate from Rhema Bible Training Center (1976), he removed Kenneth Hagin Sr.'s name from a building named after him on the Crenshaw Christian Center campus.
79. Price, *Race, Religion & Racism*, 29.
80. Ibid., 131.
81. Billingsley, *It's a New Day*, 116.
82. Joshua Levs, "African American Churches Weigh Gospel Debate," July 31, 2005, npr.org (accessed October 26, 2012).
83. Hannah Elliott, "National Baptist Speakers Criticize Prosperity Gospel, 'Seeker' Churches," *Associated Baptist Press*, September 8, 2006.
84. Reaves, "Black Baptists Eschew 'Prosperity Preaching.'"
85. Flake, *The Way of the Bootstrapper*. Though Flake himself focused on neither entrepreneurism nor prosperity, he regularly associated on the speaking circuit with some of its most prominent prosperity leaders in recent years.
86. Associated Press, "Megachurches Have Wrong Focus, Black Leaders Say," July 2, 2006, chron.com (accessed January 20, 2012).
87. Walsh, "Santidad, Sanación, Salvacion, Liberación."
88. Ibid., 154.
89. Author's data.

90. Winslow, "Go with the Flow."
91. See Dollar, *The Color of Love*, 80–95.
92. Kirk MacGregor argues that faith theology's high anthropology is better attributed to Nation of Islam and Mormon sources. MacGregor's provocative thesis attributes a late start date for faith theology's crystallization (1995) and minimizes the movement's rich prewar pentecostal cosmology. MacGregor, "The Word-Faith Movement," 91.
93. Rosin, "Did Christianity Cause the Crash?"
94. Pew Hispanic Center, "Changing Faiths."
95. I have identified 17 prosperity megachurches as multiracial. Most churches dated their founding or rapid growth to the mid-1980s and 1990s when they intentionally cultivated an ethnically diverse ministry.
96. Eric Gorski. "Sold on the Spirit." *Denver Post*. Last updated Oct. 25, 2006. http://www.denverpost.com/specialreports/ci_4462706 (accessed January 20, 2010).
97. Martin, "Lakewood Church, Servicio en Español."
98. The 7 percent figure can be found in DeYoung et al., *United by Faith*. I found 44 of the 115 prosperity megachuches claimed to have multiethnic congregations. See Thumma and Travis, *Beyond Megachurch Myths*, 30–43, 140–41.
99. DeYoung et al., *United by Faith*, 76.
100. Fischer and Hout, *Century of Difference*, 26–27. For an excellent treatment of the functions and construction of multiethnic congregations, see Marti, *A Mosaic of Believers*.
101. In the past, messengers of a prosperity gospel had occasionally deemed themselves "above" any race or dismissed its obstacles as incidental to spiritual (rather than "sensory") ways of seeing the universe. Elder Lightfoot Solomon Michaux and Sweet Daddy Grace, for example, both considered themselves as beyond racial categorization, or, if pressed, a variety of white.
102. Copeland, "Branson Victory Campaign."
103. Acts 10:34: "Then Peter opened his mouth, and said, 'Of a truth I perceive that God is no respecter of persons.'"
104. Kathryn Kuhlman, the nation's most famous healing evangelist, assumed a prominent place in the charismatic movement but not the faith movement. Though Benny Hinn famously claimed Kuhlman as his spiritual parent, she neither met him nor espoused prosperity theology.
105. Billingsley, *It's a New Day*, 51.
106. Ibid., 50.
107. "How to Stay Young and Grow More Beautiful," *Faith Digest*, 20.
108. Unknown author, *Believer's Voice of Victory* (Canadian edition), October 2007, 25.
109. Billingsley, *It's a New Day*, 67.
110. Ibid., 56–64.
111. Quoted in Osborn, *The Woman Believer*, 17.

112. Lindsay, *Freda: The Widow Who Took up the Mantle.*
113. For example, Anne Gimenez founded the International Women in Leadership conference with famous evangelical, charismatic, and pentecostal speakers crowding the advisory board.
114. Hubbard and Ryan, "Turning Trash into Treasure."
115. Ask Marilyn, "What Comes First?" 1.
116. Paula White, interviewed by Larry King.
117. Millner, "Juanita Bynum." See also Lee and Sinitiere, *Holy Mavericks,* 109–110.
118. Lowe, "Florida Megachurch Pastors End Marriage."
119. Hubbard and Ryan, "Turning Trash into Treasure."
120. A Renewed Covenant, http://www.youtube.com/watch?v=BCH_6zin2WU&feature=relmfu (accessed October 26, 2012).
121. Hagin, *The Woman Question,* 65–66.
122. Gimenez, "Taking the Lead from Esther," 30–34.
123. Conference visit, Joyce Meyer Conference, Lawrence Coliseum, Winston Salem, NC, March 13, 2008.
124. Maxwell, "The Calm after the Storm," 46–51.
125. See, for example, Hagin, "The Ultimate Bailout Plan," 9–11.
126. People & Events, *Charisma,* November 1998, n.p.
127. Lowery, *Living in God's Economy in a Time of Financial Meltdown,* back cover.
128. Gilfillan, *Unlocking the Abraham Promise,* front cover.
129. Shirley Caesar Ministerial Anniversary, Lawrence Joel Veterans Memorial Coliseum, Winston-Salem, NC, July 18, 2008.
130. Benny Hinn's Holy Land Tour, Israel, September 11, 2008.
131. Conference visit, Joel Osteen's "A Night of Hope," Greensboro Convention Center, April 18, 2008. Word of Faith Christian Center, Nashville, http://www.wofcc-nash.org/ (accessed January 17, 2011).
132. Osteen, *Become a Better You,* 34.
133. Prince, *Blessings and Curses,* 8.
134. Congregational visit, VFC, Durham, NC, March 9, 2008.
135. Hagin, *Godliness is Profitable,* 5. Copeland, *Dear Partner,* 9.
136. See also Archer, *A Pentecostal Hermeneutic,* 49–57; Miller, *Piety and Profession,* 179–200.
137. Avanzini, *The Wealth of the World,* 123. Ibid., 148.
138. Late in life, the elderly Hagin fretted over the frenzy surrounding end-time wealth transfers. "I think we need to be careful about coveting the world's money," he warned (*Midas Touch,* 171).
139. Benny Hinn Ministries, "Prosperity . . . Is It Biblical?" Stone, *Entering the Time of Double Portion Blessing.*
140. Copeland, *Azusa Street Centennial General Sessions.*
141. Ephesians 5:27.

142. Taping of *This Is Your Day!* Benny Hinn's Holy Land Tour, Israel, September 12, 2008.
143. Genesis 12:3 (NIV). See Frykolm, "Calculated Blessing."
144. Interview. Benny Hinn's Holy Land Tour, Israel, September 12, 2008.
145. Hagee, *Financial Armageddon.*
146. Frykholm, "Calculated Blessing."
147. Its board and directors included CBN network executives, Rhema and ORU administrators, and prosperity megachurch leaders. Christians United for Israel, http://www.cufi.org (accessed January 20, 2010). For more on their opposition to the two-state solution see Mearsheimer, *The Israel Lobby and U.S. Foreign Policy*, 132–39.
148. Robertson,"The Land of Israel."
149. Harrison, *Righteous Riches*, 101.
150. "The New Mega Churches: Huge Congregations with Spectacular Structures Spread Across the U.S.," *Ebony.*
151. Anastas, "Mammon from Heaven," 61.
152. Tucker-Worgs, *The Black Mega-Church*, 82–102.
153. The Clark Sisters, "Name It, Claim It."

CONCLUSION

1. Hutchinson, *Religious Pluralism in America*, 59–83.
2. Anker, *Self-Help and Popular Religion*, 14.
3. Horatio Alger Association of Distinguished Americans, Inc., Horatio Alger Award, http://www.horatioalger.com/aboutus.cfm (accessed December 1, 2012).
4. Marti, *Hollywood Faith.*
5. Swaggart, *The Confession Principle and the Course of Nature*, 23.
6. Bercht, *My Husband's Affair.*
7. Ehrenreich, *Bright-Sided*, 1–13.
8. Ibid., 45–73.
9. Budde and Brimlow, *Christianity Incorporated*, 27–54.
10. Cerulo, *Never Saw It Coming.*
11. Jones, *Jesus Inc.*
12. Iverson, *Releasing the Power Within.*
13. See, for example, Frederick Price's argument that non-Christians cannot understand the Bible. "It's a coded book, with a coded message . . . the Bible is not for everyone. It's only for God's people. And you have to be connected to God to have the spiritual insight to be able to understand what you are reading" (*Race, Religion & Racism*, volume 3, 40).
14. Macro R. Della Cava, "Secret History of 'The Secret,'" *USA Today*, March 29, 2007.

15. Coleman, *The Globalisation of Charismatic Christianity*.

16. The term "Global South" replaces "third world" and "developing countries" as the preferred descriptor for Africa, Central and South America, and most of Asia.

17. Wiegele, *Investing in Miracles*, 4.

18. New Creation Church website, "History."

19. "Riverview Church," Wikipedia.

20. Hagin, *Midas Touch*, 200.

21. Brouwer, Gifford, and Rose, *Exporting the American Gospel*, 1–46.

22. Warner, "Immigrants and the Faith They Bring," 20–23.

23. Yoido Full Gospel Church website, "Yoido Full Gospel Church Story."

24. Universal Church of the Kingdom of God website, universal.org "Our Locations."

25. Brown, "Global Awakenings."

26. Myles Munroe Ministries, www.bfmmm.com (accessed February 8, 2010).

27. Redeemed Christian Church of God, www.rccg.org (accessed February 8, 2010).

28. Wave Church, www.wavechurch.com (accessed February 8, 2010).

29. See, for example, the transnational web of influence exerted by one Guatemala megachurch. O'Neill, *City of God*.

30. Interviews with VFC members. See also Harrison, *Righteous Riches*, 51–54.

31. Harrison, *Righteous Riches*, 148–52; Alexander, *Signs and Wonders*, 25–32; Berger, "You Can Do It."

32. Millionaire University website, "Homepage."

33. Leonhardt, "Is Your Religion Your Financial Destiny?" http://www.nytimes.com/2011/05/15/magazine/is-your-religion-your-financial-destiny.html (accessed December 3, 2012).

34. Thomas, "The Route to Redemption."

35. Hoover, *The 700 Club*, 36.

36. Thumma and Travis, *Beyond Megachurch Myths*, 139. See also Harrison, *Righteous Riches*, 148–49, for the movement's middle-class appeal.

37. As the sociologists Donald E. Miller and Tetsuano Yamamori in *Global Pentecostalism: The New Face of Christian Social Engagement* demonstrated of pentecostal prosperity churches worldwide, the greatest beneficiaries of these churches' outreach may be the churchgoers themselves. Miller and Tamamori's helpful discussion of pentecostalism and social transformation addresses the social benefits of the pentecostal experience (31–34).

38. McGavran, *Understanding Church Growth*, 209–37. See too Vinson Synan's similar argument about its effectiveness, *An Eyewitness Remembers the Century of the Holy Spirit*, 123.

39. Synan, "Word of Faith Movement has Deep Roots in American History." http://www.believersstandunited.com/word-of-faith-movement-has-deep-roots-in-american-history (accessed October 26, 2012).

40. "Dear R. G. Hardy," *Faith in Action*.

41. Hayford and Moore, *The Charismatic Century*, 161.

42. Bishop, "You Are Rich," October 27, 2010. http://livinghopechurch.com (accessed October 28, 2012)

43. See, for example, Oasis Church, "90 Day Tithing Challenge," http://www.myoasis.tv/giving/index.html (accessed October 28, 2012).

44. Copeland, *Azusa Street Centennial General Sessions.*

APPENDIX B

1. Stephens. "Prosperity in a Bad Economy."

2. I use the terms faith movement, prosperity movement, prosperity theology, and prosperity gospel interchangeably.

3. Impacting Your World Christian Center, http://www.iywcc.org (accessed January 11, 2010). Though church naming is often helpful, at times no clues can be found on the church sign. There are prosperity churches called The Park Church and the City Church.

4. The exception lies with African American denominational churches, which frequently adopted prosperity theology long after the church's founding.

5. The road connecting the megachurch to the highway was named after Cam Fontaine, Leon's father. Leon Fontaine actually stepped into the church passed down from several pastors and aided its growth to its present 3,000-person stature.

6. Data from the author.

7. Walton, *Watch This!* 5.

8. See, for example, I.V. Hilliard, Noel Jones, and Jentezen Franklin as examples of the pastor's face as the primary advertisement.

9. Rhema Bible Training Center, www.rhema.org (accessed August 1, 2008).

10. Kennedy, "Healing ORU."

11. According to scholars Thumma and Travis, 83 percent of all megachurches grew dramatically during the tenure of their current pastor (*Beyond Megachurch Myths*, 59).

12. The concept of network emphasizes nodes, power, and authority concentrated in particular ideas, practices, institutions, and personalities. Theorists of religion would happily supply other analogies, each with distinct advantages. Spatial metaphors, charting maps, geographies, or landscapes, emphasize the location of religion, adding texture to arguments about context and embodiment. Fluid metaphors, following flows, currents, or streams call attention to the dynamism and mobility of religion. Vasquez, "Studying Religion in Motion."

13. This list of megachurches was assembled by Scott Thumma, Hartford Institute for Religion Research, http://hirr.hartsem.edu/index.html (accessed January 1, 2010).

14. Lassiter, *The Chicago Guide to Collaborative Ethnography*, especially chapters 5 and 6: "Ethics and Moral Responsibility," and "Ethnographic Honesty." See also American Anthropological Association website, Code of Ethics of the American Anthropological Association (1998); Hinson, "Stepping Around Experience and the Supernatural."

Bibliography

"Adversity." *The Latter Rain Evangel*, February 1909, 11.

Ahlstrom, Sydney. *A Religious History of the American People*. London: Yale University Press, 2004.

Albanese, Catherine. *America: Religion and Religions*. Belmont, CA: Wadsworth, 1992.

———. *A Republic of Mind and Spirit: A Cultural History of American Metaphysical Religion*. New Haven, CT: Yale University Press, 2007.

Albert, James A. *Jim Bakker: Miscarriage of Justice?* Chicago: Carus, 1998.

Alexander, Paul. *Signs and Wonders: Why Pentecostalism is the World's Fastest-Growing Faith*. San Francisco: Jossey-Bass, 2009.

Allen, A. A. *God Said Let My People Go!: Exodus 8:1*. Miracle Valley, AZ: A. A. Allen Revivals. N.d.

———. *How to Renew Your Youth*. Miracle Valley, AZ: A. A. Allen Pub., 1953.

———. "I Took My Cancer to Church in a Jar," *Miracle Magazine*. January 1960, 1, 7.

———. "The Miracle of Outpoured Oil." *Miracle Magazine,* January 1956.

———. *The Secret to Scriptural Financial Success*. Denver, CO: A. A. Allen Pub., 1953.

"Alternative Giving from the Heart." Handout. Speak the Word Church International, Minneapolis, MN. May 8, 2011.

"Amazing Testimonies of Cancers Passing." *The Voice of Healing*, March 1954.

American Anthropological Association. Code of Ethics of the American Anthropological Association (1998). http://www.aaanet.org/committees/ethics/ethcode. htm (accessed February 2, 2010).

Anastas, Benjamin. "Mammon from Heaven." *Harper's*, March 2010.

Anderson, Robert Mapes. *Vision of the Disinherited: The Making of American Pentecostalism*. Oxford: Oxford University Press, 1979.

Anderson, Victor. *Beyond Ontological Blackness: An Essay on African-American Religious and Cultural Criticism*. New York: Continuum, 1995.

Andrews, Sherry. "Anointed to Heal." *Charisma*, April 1979.

——. "The Controversy over Faith." *Charisma*, January 1982.

Anker, Roy. *Self-Help and Popular Religion in Early American Culture: An Interpretive Guide*. Westport, CT: Greenwood Press, 1999.

Archer, Kenneth. *A Pentecostal Hermeneutic for the Twenty-first Century: Spirit, Scripture and Community*. New York: T&T Clark, 2004.

Ashcraft-Eason, Lillian. "Lightfoot Solomon Michaux." In *African American Lives*. Edited by Henry Louis Gates Jr. and Evelyn Brooks Higginbotham. New York: Oxford University Press, 2004.

Ask Marilyn. *Charisma*, May 1987.

——. "Profitable Words." *Charisma*, November 1987.

——. "What Comes First?" *Charisma*, January 1985.

Assemblies of God. Letter to A. A. Allen. *Miracle Magazine*, December 1955.

Assemblies of God Archives, Springfield, MO.

Association of Faith Churches and Ministers. "Jim Kaseman." http://www. afcminternational.org/aboutus.php?page=jk (accessed November 10, 2009).

Atkinson, William. *Mind-Power: The Secret of Mental Magic*. Chicago: Advanced Thought, 1912.

Avanzini, John. *30, 60, Hundredfold: Your Financial Harvest Released*. Tulsa, OK: Harrison House, 1989.

——. *It's Not Working, Brother John: 25 Things That Close the Windows of Heaven*. Tulsa, OK: Harrison House, 1992.

——. *The Wealth of the World: The Proven Wealth Transfer System*. Tulsa, OK: Harrison House, 1989.

Baer, Hans A. *The Black Spiritual Movement: A Religious Response to Racism*. Knoxville: University of Tennessee Press, 1984.

——. "Elder Solomon Michaux's Church of God." In *Encyclopedia of African and African-American Religions*. Edited by Stephen D. Glazier. New York: Routledge, 2001.

——. "Universal Hagar's Spiritual Church." In *Encyclopedia of African and African-American Religions*. Edited by Stephen D. Glazier. New York: Routledge, 2001.

Baer, Hans A., and Merrill Singer. *African-American Religion in the Twentieth Century: Varieties of Protest and Accommodation*. 2nd ed. Knoxville: University of Tennessee Press, 2002.

Baer, Jonathan R. "Redeemed Bodies: The Functions of Divine Healing in Incipient Pentecostalism." *Church History* 70, no. 4 (Dec. 2001): 735–71.

Balmer, Randall H. "Benny Hinn." In *The Encyclopedia of Evangelicalism*. Rev. ed. Edited by Randall Balmer, 336–37. Waco, TX: Baylor University Press, 2004.

——. *Encyclopedia of Evangelicalism*. Rev. ed. Waco, TX: Baylor University Press, 2004.

Barton, Bruce. *The Man Nobody Knows*. N.p.: Lewis Press, 2011.

Basham, Don. *Can A Christian Have A Demon?* Monroeville, PA: Whitaker Books, 1971.

———. *Deliver Us from Evil.* Washington Depot, CT: Chosen Books, 1972.

———. *Lead Us Not Into Temptation.* Old Tappan, NJ: Chosen Books, 1986.

———. *A Manual for Spiritual Warfare.* Greensburg, PA: Manna Books, 1974.

Bender, Courtney. *The New Metaphysicals: Spirituality and the American Religious Imagination.* Chicago: University of Chicago Press, 2010.

Benny Hinn Ministries. "Prosperity . . . Is It Biblical?" http://www.bennyhinn.org/articles/articledesc.cfm?id=986 (accessed December 19, 2010).

Bercht, Anne. *My Husband's Affair Became the Best Thing That Ever Happened to Me.* Victoria, BC: Trafford, 2004.

Berger, Peter. "You Can Do It." Books & Culture: A Christian Review. September/October 2008. http://www.booksandculture.com/articles/2008/sepoct/10.14.html (accessed December 1, 2012).

Best, Wallace. "Church of God in Christ." *African American Religious Cultures.* Edited by Anthony B. Pinn. 2 vols. 1:165. Santa Barbara, CA: ABC-CLIO, LLC, 2009.

———. *Passionately Human, No Less Divine: Religion and Culture in Black Chicago, 1915–1952.* Princeton: Princeton University Press, 2005.

Bettger, Frank. *How I Raised Myself from Failure to Success in Selling.* London: Cedar, 1949.

Bill Winston Ministries website. "Prayers and Confessions for a Healthier Lifestyle," http://www.livingwd.org/ministries/prayerministry/confessions (accessed December 1, 2012).

Billingsley, Scott. *It's a New Day: Race and Gender in the Modern Charismatic Movement.* Tuscaloosa: University of Alabama Press, 2008.

———. "The Midas Touch: Kenneth E. Hagin and the Prosperity Gospel." In *Recovering the Margins of American Religious History.* Edited by B. Dwain Waldrep and Scott C. Billingsley. Tuscaloosa: University of Alabama Press, 2012.

Bishop, John. "You Are Rich." October 27, 2010, http://livinghopechurch.com (accessed October 28, 2012)

Bishop, Markus. *Our Covenant of Prosperity: Crossing the Threshold of Supernatural Abundance.* Tulsa, OK: Harrison House, 1997.

Blake, Charles E. *Dreamers Are Coming!* Tulsa, OK: Albury, 1999.

Blumhofer, Edith. "Life on Faith Lines: Faith Homes and Early Pentecostal Values." *Assemblies of God Heritage* 10 (Summer 1990): 10–12.

———. *Restoring the Faith: The Assemblies of God, Pentecostalism, and American Culture.* Urbana, IL: University of Illinois Press, 1993.

Bonner, William Lee. *Positive Thinking Changed My Life.* Nashville, TN: True Vine, 2007.

Bosworth, F. F. *Christ the Healer.* Old Tappan, NJ: Fleming H. Revell, 1973.

———. *Christ the Healer: Sermons on Divine Healing.* S.I.: F. F. Bosworth, 1924.

———. *Christ the Healer: Sermons on Divine Healing.* Miami Beach: F. F. Bosworth, 1948.

———. "The Faith That Takes." *The Voice of Healing,* June 1948.

Bourgault, Louise Manon. *An Ethnographic Study of the "Praise the Lord Club."* PhD diss., Ohio State University, 1980.

Bowler, Catherine. "Blessed Bodies: Healing within the African American Faith Movement." In *Global Pentecostal and Charismatic Healing.* Edited by Candy Gunther Brown, 81–105. New York: Oxford University Press, 2011.

———. "From Far and Wide: The Canadian Faith Movement." *Church & Faith Trends,* February 2010.

———. "Positive Thinking." In *The Encyclopedia of Religion in America.* Edited by Charles H. Lippy and Peter W. Williams. Washington, D.C: CQ Press, 2010.

Braden, Charles Samuel. *Spirits in Rebellion: The Rise and Development of New Thought.* Dallas: Southern Methodist University Press, 1963.

Brands, W. H. *The Age of Gold: The California Gold Rush and the New American Dream.* New York: Anchor, 2003.

Braune, O. B. "God's Power Mightily Manifested Through Kenneth Hagin Ministry." *The Voice of Healing,* May 1954.

Braxton, Lee. "A Pattern for Prosperity." *Full Gospel Men's Voice,* May–June 1953.

Brazee, Mark. *365 Days of Healing.* Tulsa, OK: Harrison House, 2006.

Bronner, Angela. "The Father of the 'Prosperity Gospel' Talks About Fatherhood." http://www.blackvoices.com/black_lifestyle/soul_spirit_headlines_features/canvas/feature_article/_a/which-master-do-you-follow/20060614165609990001 (accessed January 18, 2010).

Brouwer, Steve, Paul Gifford, and Susan Rose. *Exporting the American Gospel: Global Christian Fundamentalism.* New York: Routledge, 1996.

Brown, Candy Gunther. "Global Awakenings: Divine Healing Networks and Global Community in North America, Brazil, Mozambique, and Beyond." In *Global Pentecostal and Charismatic Healing.* Edited by Candy Gunther Brown, 351–70. Oxford: Oxford University Press, 2011.

———. *Global Pentecostal and Charismatic Healing.* Oxford: Oxford University Press, 2011.

Brown, Michael F. *The Channeling Zone: American Spirituality in an Anxious Age.* Cambridge, MA: Harvard University Press, 1997.

Buckingham, Jamie. "God Is Shaking His Church." *Charisma,* June 1987.

———. "PTL Meets the Press." *Charisma,* May 1986.

Budde, Michael L., and Robert Brimlow. *Christianity Incorporated: How Big Business Is Buying the Church.* Grand Rapids, MI: Brazos Press, 2002.

Burpeau, Kemp Pendleton. *God's Showman: A Historical Study of John G. Lake and South African/American Pentecostalism.* Oslo: Refleks, 2004.

Butler, Jon. *Awash in a Sea of Faith.* Cambridge, MA: Harvard University Press, 1990.

Bynum, Juanita. *Matters of the Heart.* Lake Mary, FL: Charisma House, 2002.

Byrd, W. Michael, and Linda A. Clayton. *An American Health Dilemma.* 2 vols. New York: Routledge, 2000–2002.

Byrne, Rhonda. *The Secret.* New York: Atria Books, 2006.

Caldwell, E. S. "Charles Green: Called to Win a Sinful City." *Charisma,* February, 1985.

Capps Ministries Website. http://charlescapps.com.

Capps, Charles. *The Tongue: A Creative Force.* England, AR: Capps Pub., 1976.

———. "Without Hope There Is No Faith." *Charisma,* August 1984.

Capps, Charles, and Annette Capps. *Angels.* Tulsa, OK: Harrison House, 1984.

———. *God's Creative Power for Finances.* Tulsa, OK: Harrison House, 2004.

Carter, Harold A. *The Prayer Tradition of Black People.* Valley Forge, PA: Judson Press, 1976.

Carter, Jimmy. "Crisis of Confidence." Televised speech, July 15, 1979. http://www.pbs.org/wgbh/americanexperience/features/primary-resources/carter-crisis/.

Carter, Paul A. *The Spiritual Crisis of the Gilded Age.* DeKalb: Northern Illinois University Press, 1971.

Cerillo, Augustus. "The Beginnings of American Pentecostalism: A Historiograpical Overview." In *Pentecostal Currents in American Protestantism.* Edited by Edith Blumhofer, Russell Spittler, and Grant Wacker, 229–60. Chicago: University of Illinois Press, 1999.

Cerullo, Morris. Cover. *Deeper Life,* May 1967.

Cerulo, Karen. *Never Saw It Coming: Cultural Challenges to Envisioning the Worst.* Chicago: Chicago University Press, 2006.

Chaves, Mark. "All Creatures Great and Small: Megachurches in Context." *Review of Religious Research* 47, no. 4 (June 2006): 329–46.

———. *Congregations in America.* Cambridge, MA: Harvard University Press, 2004.

———. "Secularization as Declining Religious Authority." *Social Forces* 72, no. 3 (March 1994): 749–74.

Cherry, Conrad. *God's New Israel: Religious Interpretations of American Destiny.* Rev. ed. Chapel Hill: University of North Carolina Press, 1998.

Chireau, Yvonne P. *Black Magic: Religion and the African American Conjuring Tradition.* Berkeley: University of California Press, 2003.

Chrystyn, Julie. *The Secret to Life Transformation: How to Claim Your Destiny Now!* Beverly Hills, CA: Dove Books, 2009.

"Coat Never Needed Cleaning." *Miracle Word,* Fall 1975.

Coleman, Simon. *The Globalisation of Charismatic Christianity: Spreading the Gospel of Prosperity.* Cambridge: Cambridge University Press, 2000.

Conwell, Russell H. *Acres of Diamonds.* Philadelphia: Temple University Press, 2002.

Coontz, Stephanie. *Marriage, a History: How Love Conquered Marriage.* New York: Penguin Books, 2005.

Copeland, Gloria. "Branson Victory Campaign." March 6–8, 2008. http://www.bvov.tv/kcm/ondemand/index.php (accessed December 3, 2012).

———. "God Wants You to Prosper, as Your Soul Prospers." *Charisma*, September 1980.

———. *God's Will Is Prosperity*. Tulsa, OK: Harrison House, 1978.

———. *Live Long, Finish Strong: The Divine Secret to Living Healthy, Happy, and Healed*. New York: FaithWords, 2010.

———. *No Deposit, No Return*. Fort Worth, TX: Kenneth Copeland Publications, 1995.

———. "This Is the First Day of Your Unlimited Life!" Web mailing, from kennethcopelandministries@e.kcm.org. August 9, 2011.

Copeland, Kenneth. "Believers' Voice of Victory." September 1991. Impacting Your World Christian Center. http://www.iywcc.org.

———. *Dear Partner*. Fort Worth, TX: Kenneth Copeland Pub., 1997.

———. *The Laws of Prosperity*. Greensburg, PA: Mann Christian Outreach, 1974.

———. *Poverty: The Choice Is Yours*. Fort Worth, TX: Kenneth Copeland Pub., 1985.

———. *Walking in the Realm of the Miraculous*. Fort Worth, TX: Kenneth Copeland Pub., 1979.

Copeland, Kenneth, and Gloria Copeland. *Prosperity Promises*. Tulsa, OK: Kenneth Copeland Pub., 1997.

"Couple Admits Extortion Against 'Prophet.'" *Jet*, March 6, 1952.

"Couple Claims Opposing Promises." *Lark News*, August 2007. http://www.larknews.com/archives/695

Creflo Dollar Ministries website. "About Creflo Dollar." http://www.creflodollarministries.com.

Crenshaw Christian Center website. "About Frederick Price." http://www.crenshawchristiancenter.net/drprice.aspx?id=876.

Crouch, Paul F. *Hello World!: A Personal Message to the Body of Christ*. Nashville, TN: Thomas Nelson, 2003.

Csordas, Thomas J. *The Sacred Self: A Cultural Phenomenology of Charismatic Healing*. Berkeley: University of California Press, 1994.

Culpepper, R. W. "R. W. Culpepper Says . . . God Wants You to Be Happy, Healthy, and Prosperous." *World-Wide Revival Reports*, January 1963.

Curtis, Heather. *Faith in the Great Physician: Suffering and Divine Health in American Culture, 1860–1900*. Baltimore: Johns Hopkins University Press, 2007.

———. "The Global Character of Nineteenth-Century Divine Healing." In *Global Pentecostal and Charismatic Healing*. Edited by Candy Gunther Brown, 29–45. Oxford: Oxford University Press, 2011.

Dallam, Marie. *Daddy Grace: A Celebrity Preacher and His House of Prayer*. New York: New York University Press, 2007.

Davis, T. *Cleansing Stream Ministries: Cleansing Seminar Workbook*. Northridge, CA: Glory Communications International, 1995.

Dayton, Donald W. *Theological Roots of Pentecostalism*. Metuchen, NJ: Scarecrow Press, 1987.

De Arteaga, William L. "Glenn Clark's Camps Furthest Out: The Schoolhouse of the Charismatic Renewal." *PNEUMA: The Journal of the Society for Pentecostal Studies* 25, no. 2 (2003): 265–88.

"Dear R.G. Hardy." *Faith in Action*, June 1973.

"Demos Shakarian Memorial Issue." *Voice*, October 1993.

DeYoung, Curtiss Paul, Michael O. Emerson, George Yancey, and Karen Chai Kim. *United by Faith: The Multiracial Congregation As the Answer to the Problem of Race.* New York: Oxford University Press, 2003.

Dixon, A. C. *The Person and Ministry of the Holy Spirit.* New York: Garland, 1988 (1890).

Dollar, Creflo. "Angel Power Confession." http://www.creflodollarministries.org/BibleStudy/DailyConfessions.aspx?id=2 (accessed January 10, 2010).

———. *Changing Your World.* http://www.streamingfaith.com (accessed November 24, 2004).

———. *The Color of Love: Understanding God's Answer to Racism, Separation, and Division.* Tulsa, OK: Harrison House, 1997.

———. "How It All Began." *Changing Your World*, August 2001.

———. *How to Obtain Healing . . . the Final Authority.* College Park, GA: Creflo Dollar Ministries, 1999.

———. *Jehovah M'Kaddesh.* Atlanta: Creflo Dollar Ministries, 2001.

———. *Jehovah Nissi.* Atlanta: Creflo Dollar Ministries, 2000.

———. *Jehovah Rophe.* Atlanta: Creflo Dollar Ministries, 2000.

———. *Jehovah Shammah.* Atlanta: Creflo Dollar Ministries, 2000.

———. *Jehovah Tsidkenu.* Atlanta: Creflo Dollar Ministries, 2000.

———. "Making a Change." World Changers Broadcast. http://www.streaming-faith.com.

———. *Total Life Prosperity: 14 Practical Steps to Receiving God's Full Blessing.* Nashville: Thomas Nelson, 1999.

Donnally, Ed. "Clarence McClendon Cuts Ties with Foursquare after Divorce News." *Charisma*, July 31, 2000. http://www.charismamag.com/index.php/component/content/article/248-people-events/469-clarence-mcclendon-cuts-ties-with-foursquare-after-divorce-news.

Dowell, Oscar Buford. *Material and Financial Blessings for You.* San Diego, CA: Revival Time Evangelistic Campaigns, 195[?].

Douthat, Ross. *Bad Religion: How We Became a Nation of Heretics.* New York: Free Press, 2012.

Du Bois, W. E. B. *On Sociology and the Black Community.* Edited by Dan Green and Edwin Driver. Chicago: University of Chicago Press, 1978.

du Plessis, David. *Simple and Profound.* New Orleans: Paraclete Press, 1986.

Earl, Howard. "Tuning in on New Technologies That Communicate the Gospel." *Charisma*, June 1982.

Ehrenreich, Barbara. *Bright-Sided: How the Relentless Promotion of Positive Thinking Has Undermined America.* New York: Metropolitan Books, 2009.

Ellis, Charles H. "I Shall Prosper, Part II." Video posted by Greater Grace TV, September 2, 2009. http://www.youtube.com/user/greatergracetv#p/u/16/pLT_OOiGsok.

Elson, Ruth Miller. *Myths and Mores in American Best Sellers, 1865–1965*. New York: Garland, 1985.

Emerson, Michael O., and Christian Smith. *Divided by Faith: Evangelical Religion and the Problem of Race in America*. New York: Oxford University Press, 2000.

Empowerment Temple. "40 Days of Triumph." http://www.empowermenttemple.org/.

Espinosa, Gastón. "Francisco Olazábal and Latino Pentecostal Revivalism in the North American Borderlands." In *Embodying the Spirit: New Perspectives on North American Revivalism*. Edited by Michael J. McClymond, 125–46. Baltimore: Johns Hopkins University Press, 2004.

Evangel Fellowship Church of God in Christ. "Apostle Otis Lockett Biography." http://www.evangelword.org/.

Ewing, Gene. *A Miracle for You*. Fort Worth, TX: Campmeeting Revivals Inc., 1964.

Fast, Clarence E. "Is Faith a Farce or Force?" *Foursquare World Advance*, May 1977.

Faupel, D. William. "The New Order of the Latter Rain: Restoration or Renewal?" In *Winds from the North: Canadian Contributions to the Pentecostal Movement*. Edited by Michael Wilkinson and Peter Althouse, 239–64. Leiden: Brill, 2010.

Fillmore, Charles. *Christian Healing: The Science of Being*. Unity Village, MO: Unity School of Christianity, 1919.

———. *Prosperity*. Kansas City, MO: Unity School of Christianity, 1936.

Finstuen, Andrew S. *Original Sin and Everyday Protestants: The Theology of Reinhold Niebuhr, Billy Graham, and Paul Tillich in an Age of Anxiety*. Chapel Hill, NC: University of North Carolina Press, 2009.

Fischer, Claude S., and Michael Hout. *Century of Difference: How America Changed in the Last One Hundred Years*. New York: Russell Sage, 2008.

"5-Year-Old Boy Directs Choir." *Jet*, November 1, 1951.

Flake, Floyd. *The Way of the Bootstrapper: Nine Action Steps for Achieving Your Dreams*. New York: HarperCollins, 1999.

Floyd-Thomas, Stacy M. *Black Church Studies: An Introduction*. Nashville, TN: Abingdon Press, 2007.

Ford, C. C. "God's Divine Law of Compensation." *World Harvest*, January 1963.

Frame, Randy. "Fund Raising: Did Oral Roberts Go Too Far?" *Christianity Today*, February 20, 1987.

Frankiel, Tamar. "Ritual Sites in the Narrative of American Religion." In *American Spiritualities: A Reader*. Edited by Catherine Albanese, 23–55. Bloomington: University of Indiana Press, 2001.

Frazier, E. Franklin. *The Negro Church in America*. New York: Schocken Books, 1963.

Frederick, Marla F. *Between Sundays: Black Women and Everyday Struggles of Faith*. Berkeley: University of California Press, 2003.

Frykolm, Amy. "Calculated Blessing: A Visit to John Hagee's Church." *Christian Century* 125, no. 20 (Oct. 7, 2008): 35–37.

"Full Gospel Business Men's Fellowship International Chapter Directory: USA, California, Hawaii, and Nevada District." Regent University Library, Virginia Beach, VA. 1967.

Gardner, Velmer. "Faith for Finances." *Voice,* September 1963.

———. *The God of Miracles Lives Today!* Wenatchee, WA: V. J. Gardner, 1950. http://www.johncarverministries.org/pof/gardner/index.cfm

———. *Healing For You!* Springfield, MO: V. J. Gardner, 1952.

Gee, Donald. "Living By Faith." *The Voice of Healing,* February 1952.

George, Carol V. R. *God's Salesman: Norman Vincent Peale & the Power of Positive Thinking.* New York: Oxford University Press, 1993.

Ghiringhelli, Paul Steven. "ORU Leader Resigns, $70 Million Pledged." *Charisma,* January 2008.

Gifford, Paul. "The Complex Provenance of Some Elements of African Pentecostal Theology." In *Between Babel and Pentecost: Transnational Pentecostalism in Africa and Latin America.* Edited by André Corten and Ruth R. Marshall-Fratani, 62–79. Bloomington: Indiana University Press, 2001.

———. *Ghana's New Christianity: Pentecostalism in a Globalizing African Economy.* Bloomington: Indiana University Press, 2004.

Gilfillan, Berin. *Unlocking the Abraham Promise.* Fawnskin, CA: Powerhouse, 2004.

Gimenez, Anne. "Taking the Lead from Esther." *Charisma,* June 1986.

Giuliano, Michael James. *Thrice-Born: The Rhetorical Comeback of Jimmy Swaggart.* Macon, GA: Mercer University Press, 1999.

Gladwell, Malcolm. *Outliers: The Story of Success.* New York: Little, Brown, 2008.

Goh, Robbie B. H. "Hillsong and 'Megachurch' Practice: Semiotics, Spatial Logic and the Embodiment of Contemporary Evangelical Protestantism." *Material Religion* 4, no. 3 (Nov. 2008): 284–304.

Göransson, Kristina. *The Binding Tie: Chinese Intergenerational Relations in Modern Singapore.* Honolulu: University of Hawaii Press, 2009.

Gorman, Marvin. *Called to Victory.* New Orleans, LA: Marvin Gorman Ministries, 1982.

Grant, W. V. *How to Receive Without Asking.* Dallas: Grant's Faith Clinic, 1963.

———. *Must I Pray for a Miracle?* Dallas: Grant's Faith Clinic, 195[?].

———. "The Word of Wisdom." *The Voice of Healing,* January 1954.

Griffith, R. Marie. *Born Again Bodies: Flesh and Spirit in American Christianity.* Berkeley: University of California Press, 2004.

———. *God's Daughters: Evangelical Women and the Power of Submission.* Berkeley, CA: University of California Press, 1997.

———. "Material Devotion: Pentecostal Prayer Cloths." Interview in the Material History of American Religion Project *Newsletter* (Spring 1997): 1–3, http://www.materialreligion.org/journal/handkerchief.html.

Griswold, Whitney. "New Thought: A Cult of Success." *American Journal of Sociology* 40 (November 1934): 309–18.

Hackett, Rosalind I. J. "The Gospel of Prosperity in West Africa." In *Religion and the Transformations of Capitalism: Comparative Approaches.* Edited by Richard H. Roberts, 199–214. London: Routledge, 1995.

Hadden, Jeffrey K. "Religious Broadcasting." In *The New Encyclopedia of Southern Culture.* Vol. 1: *Religion.* Edited by Samuel S. Hill and Charles Reagan Wilson, 39–43. Chapel Hill, NC: University of North Carolina Press, 2006.

———. "The Rise and Fall of American Televangelism." *The ANNALS of the American Academy of Political and Social Science* 527, no. 1 (May 1993): 113–30.

Hagee, John. *Attack on America.* Nashville: Thomas Nelson, 2001.

———. *The Battle for Jerusalem.* Nashville: Thomas Nelson, 2003.

———. *Financial Armageddon: We are in a Battle for our Very Survival.* Lake Mary, FL: FrontLine, 2008.

———. *From Daniel to Doomsday.* Nashville: Thomas Nelson, 2000.

———. *In Defense of Israel.* Lake Mary, FL: FrontLine, 2007.

———. *Jerusalem Countdown.* Lake Mary, FL: FrontLine, 2006.

Haggerty, Steve. "A Pastor's Heart Opens and His Church Overflows." *Charisma,* March 1985.

Hagin, Craig W. "The Ultimate Bailout Plan." *Word of Faith,* July 2009.

Hagin, Kenneth E. *The Biblical Keys to Financial Prosperity.* Tulsa: Kenneth Hagin Ministries, 2005.

———. *El Shaddai: The God Who Is More Than Enough.* Tulsa, OK: Kenneth Hagin Ministries, 1987.

———. *Godliness is Profitable.* Tulsa, OK: Kenneth Hagin Ministries, 1982.

———. "Good Confessions." *The Word of Faith,* December 1978.

———. *In Him.* Tulsa, OK: Kenneth Hagin Ministries, 2006.

———. "Is Your Profit Showing?" *Word of Faith,* January 1976.

———. *Obedience in Finances.* Tulsa: Kenneth Hagin Ministries, 1983.

———. *The Midas Touch: A Balanced Approach to Biblical Prosperity.* Tulsa, OK: Kenneth Hagin Ministries, 2000.

———. *The Name of Jesus.* Tulsa, OK: Kenneth Hagin Ministries, 1979.

———. *The Precious Blood of Jesus.* Tulsa, OK: Kenneth Hagin Ministries, 1984.

———. "Trend Toward Faith Movement." *Charisma,* August 1985.

———. *What To Do When Faith Seems Weak & Victory Lost.* Tulsa, OK: Kenneth Hagin Ministries, 1979.

———. *The Woman Question.* Tulsa, OK: Faith Library, 1983.

Hagin, Lynette. "Offering Prayer." http://www.rhemabiblechurch.com/PDFs/Bulletins/Bulletin112209.pdf.

Hall, David. *Worlds of Wonders, Days of Judgment.* New York: Knopf, 1989.

Hammond, Frank, and Ida Mae Hammond. *Pigs in the Parlor: The Practical Guide to Deliverance.* Kirkwood, MO: Impact Books, 1973.

Hampel, Harry. *Your Faith Is Power.* Dallas, TX: Harry Hampel Deliverance Revivals, n.d.

Hanegraaff, Hank. *Christianity in Crisis.* Eugene, OR: Harvest House, 1993.

"Happy Am I." *Time*, June 11, 1934. http://www.time.com/time/magazine/article/0,9171,762188,00.html#ixzz1EK5wcVNn.

Hardesty, Nancy. *Faith Cure: Divine Healing in the Holiness and Pentecostal Movements*. Peabody, MA: Hendrickson, 2003.

Hardy, Clarence E., III. "'No Mystery God': Black Religions of the Flesh in Pre-War Urban America." *Church History* 77, no. 1 (2008): 128–50.

Hardy, R. G. "Testimonies of Prosperity." *Faith in Action*, March 1967.

Harley, Gail M. *Emma Curtis Hopkins: Forgotten Founder of New Thought*. Syracuse, NY: Syracuse University Press, 2002.

Harrell, David Edwin, Jr. *All Things Are Possible: The Healing and Charismatic Revivals in Modern America*. Bloomington: Indiana University Press, 1975.

———. *Oral Roberts: An American Life*. Bloomington: Indiana University Press, 1985.

———. *Pat Robertson: A Life and Legacy*. Grand Rapids, MI: Eerdmans, 2010.

———. *Pat Robertson: A Personal, Religious, and Political Portrait*. San Francisco: Harper & Row, 1987.

Harrison, Milmon F. *Righteous Riches: The Word of Faith Movement in Contemporary African-American Religion*. New York: Oxford University Press, 2005.

Hartford Institute Religion Research. Database of megachurches in the United States. http://hirr.hartsem.edu/.

Harvey, Paul. "Black Protestantism: A Historiographical Appraisal." In *American Denominational History: Perspectives on the Past, Prospects for the Future*. Edited by Keith Harper et al., 120–45. Tuscaloosa: University of Alabama Press, 2008.

Hash, Francene. *Building God's House: Seven Strategies for Raising a Healthy Church*. Longwood, FL: Xulon Press, 2005.

Hayden, Perry. "The Lord's Work . . . Henry Ford and I." *The Voice of Healing*, June 1954.

Hayes, Norvel. *Putting Your Angels to Work*. Tulsa, OK: Harrison House, 1989.

Hayford, Jack W., and David Moore. *The Charismatic Century: The Enduring Impact of the Azusa Street Revival*. New York: Warner Faith, 2006.

Hayford, Jack. *Prayer Is Invading the Impossible*. Plainfield, NJ: Logos International, 1977.

"Healing in Sub-Saharan Africa." In *Encyclopedia of African and African-American Religions*. Edited by Stephen D. Glazier. New York: Routledge, 2001.

Herskovits, Melville. *The Myth of the Negro Path*. New York: Harper & Bros., 1941.

Hickey, Marilyn. *Your Miracle Source*. Tulsa, OK: Harrison House, 1982.

Hilliard, Bridget. *My Strong Tower: Power in Knowing the Names of God*. Houston: Hilliard Ministries, 2009.

Hinson, Glenn. "Stepping Around Experience and the Supernatural." In *Fire in My Bones: Transcendence and the Holy Spirit in African American Gospel*, 327–334. Philadelphia: University of Pennsylvania Press, 2000.

Hocken, P. D. "Charismatic Movement." In *Dictionary of Pentecostal and Charismatic Movements*. Edited by Stanley M. Burgess and Gary B. McGee, 130–60. Grand Rapids, MI: Zondervan, 1993.

Hoffman, Brett. "Schuller and Robertson Together at Word of Faith." *Charisma,* March 1985.

Holifield, Brooks. *God's Ambassadors: A History of the Christian Clergy in America.* Grand Rapids, MI: Eerdmans, 2007.

Holvast, René. *Spiritual Mapping in the United States and Argentina, 1989–2005: A Geography of Fear.* Leiden: Brill, 2008.

Hood, Kregg. *Take God at His Word: Expect a Harvest.* Hurst, TX: Sweet, 2001.

Hoover, Stewart Mark. *The 700 Club as Religion and as Television: A Study of Reasons and Effects.* PhD diss., University of Pennsylvania, 1985.

Horatio Alger Association of Distinguished Americans, Inc., Horatio Alger Award, http://www.horatioalger.com/aboutus.cfm (accessed December 1, 2012).

Horsfield, Peter G. *Religious Television: The American Experience.* New York: Longman Inc., 1984.

Horton, Harold. "The Gift of Faith." *The Voice of Healing,* February 1950.

Houghton, Al. *Power of Agreement.* Plainfield, NJ: Logos International, 1981.

"How to Stay Young and Grow More Beautiful." *Faith Digest,* August 1964.

Hubbard, Stephen, and Lisa Ryan. "Turning Trash into Treasure: The Testimony of Paula White." *The 700 Club.* CBN. http://www.cbn.com/700club/Guests/Interviews/Paula_White063005.aspx (accessed January 23, 2010).

Hudnut-Beumler, James David. *In Pursuit of the Almighty's Dollar: A History of Money and American Protestantism.* Chapel Hill, NC: University of North Carolina Press, 2007.

Hunter, Frances. *God's Answer to Fat: Loose It.* Houston: Hunter Ministries, 1976.

Hutchinson, Mark. "The Latter Rain Movement and the Phenomenon of Global Return." In *Winds from the North: Canadian Contributions to the Pentecostal Movement.* Edited by Michael Wilkinson and Peter Althouse, 265–84. Leiden: Brill, 2010.

Hutchinson, William R. *Religious Pluralism in America: The Contentious History of a Founding Ideal.* New Haven, CT: Yale University Press, 2003.

Iverson, Dick. *Team Ministry: Putting Together a Team That Makes Churches Grow.* Portland, OR: City Bible, 1984.

Iverson, Sylva F. *Releasing the Power Within.* Portland: Bible Press, 1957.

J. M. from Florida. "Special Miracles." *Miracle Magazine,* October 1955.

Jackson, Gayle. "What is Faith?" *The Voice of Healing,* September 1952.

Jacobsen, Douglas Gordon. *Thinking in the Spirit: Theologies of the Early Pentecostal Movement.* Bloomington: Indiana University Press, 2003.

Jaggers, O. L. *Everlasting Physical and Spiritual Health.* Dexter, MO: Kessinger, 1949.

———. "The Irresistible Faith of God." *The Voice of Healing,* February 1952.

Jakes, Jacqueline, and T. D. Jakes. *God's Trophy Women: You are Blessed and Highly Favored.* New York: FaithWords, 2006.

Jakes, T. D. B.E.S.T. Conference Series. http://www.nationwideministry.com/eblasts.php?name=best (accessed December 3, 2012).

————. *The Great Investment: Faith, Family, and Finance.* New York: Putnam's Sons, 2000.

————. *Lay Aside the Weight: Take Control of It before It Controls You.* Tulsa, OK: Albury, 1997.

————. *Reposition Yourself: Living Life Without Limits.* New York: Atria Books, 2008.

James, William. *The Varieties of Religious Experience: A Study in Human Nature.* London: Longmans, Green, 1911.

Jenkins, Leroy. *Three Easy Steps to Prosperity.* Tampa, FL: Leroy Jenkins Evangelistic Association, 1965.

Jenkins, Phillip. *Mystics and Messiahs: Cults and New Religions in American History.* New York: Oxford University Press, 2000.

————. *The Next Christendom: The Coming of Global Christianity.* New York: Oxford University Press, 2007.

Jentezen Franklin Ministries website. "The Fasting Movement," http://www. jentezenfranklin.org/fasting/index.php (accessed December 3, 2012).

Joel Osteen Ministries. www.joelosteen.com or www.lakewood.cc.

Jones, Laurie Beth. *Jesus Inc.: The Visionary Path.* Promotional book insert. Crown Public Group, 2001.

Jones, Len J. "Down the Years!" *The Voice of Healing,* October 1953.

————. "We Are What We Say!" *The Voice of Healing,* January 1954.

Jones, Noel, and Scott Chaplan. *Vow of Prosperity: Spiritual Solutions for Financial Freedom.* Shippensburg, PA: Destiny Image, 2007.

Jones, Thea F. *The Golden Key.* Philadelphia, PA: Philadelphia Evangelic Centre, 195[?]

Kaufman, Joanne. "The Fall of Jimmy Swaggart." *People,* March 1988. http://www. people.com/people/archive/article/0,,20098413,00.html.

Kennedy, John W. "Healing ORU." *Christianity Today,* September 2008.

Kenyon, E. W. *Advanced Bible Course: Studies in the Deeper Life.* 5th ed. Lynnwood, WA: Kenyon's Gospel Publishing Society, 1970.

————. "Count It Done." *Herald of Faith/Harvest Time,* Christmas 1970.

————. *The Father and His Family.* Spencer, MA: Reality Press, 1916.

————. *The Father and His Family: A Restatement of the Plan of Redemption.* Lynnwood, WA: Kenyon's Gospel Publishing Society, 1998.

————. "Giving Is the Way to Receive." *Shield of Faith,* Nov.–Dec. 1969.

————. "If We Receive From God . . . We Must Give!" *Shield of Faith,* May–June 1969.

————. *New Creation Realities.* Lynnwood, WA: Kenyon's Gospel Publishing Society, 1970.

————. *The Two Kinds of Faith: Faith's Secret Revealed.* Lynnwood, WA: Kenyon's Gospel Publishing Society, 1998 (1942).

————. *The Two Kinds of Life.* Lynnwood, WA: Kenyon's Gospel Publishing Society, 1983.

―――. *The Wonderful Name of Jesus*. Lynnwood, WA: Kenyon's Gospel Publishing Society, 1998.

Keteyian, Armen. "Televangelists Living Like Kings?" CBS News, November 6, 2007. http://www.cbsnews.com/stories/2007/11/06/cbsnews_investigates/main3462147. shtml?tag=mncol;lst;2 (accessed May 3, 2010).

King, Paul L. *Only Believe, Examining the Origin and Development of Classic and Contemporary "Word of Faith" Theologies*. Menlo Park, CA: Word and Spirit Press, 2009.

Koester, Nancy. *Fortress Introduction to the History of Christianity in the United States*. Minneapolis: Fortress Press, 2007.

Lake, John G. *The John G. Lake Sermons on Dominion over Demons, Disease, and Death*. Dallas: Christ for the Nations, 1982 (1950).

―――. *Spiritual Hunger and Other Sermons*. Edited by Gordon Lindsay. Dallas: Christ for the Nations, 1994.

Lassiter, Luke. *The Chicago Guide to Collaborative Ethnography* (Chicago: University of Chicago Press, 2005).

Lawson, Steven. "Copeland Reaches Out to AIDS Victims." *Charisma & Christian Life*, January 1988.

―――. "Faith Preacher Hobart Freeman Dies." *Charisma*, February 1985.

―――. "PTL Plans World's Largest Church." *Charisma*, March 1987.

―――. "Uplinking the Gospel: What's Happening with Satellite Ministries." *Charisma*, December 1985.

Lea, Larry. *Spiritual Authority*. Rockwall, TX: Church on the Rock, 1986.

―――. "Why Have Christians Been Holding Back?" *Charisma & Christian Life*, April 1988.

Lee, Shayne. *T. D. Jakes: America's New Preacher*. New York: New York University Press, 2005.

Lee, Shayne, and Phillip Luke Sinitiere. *Holy Mavericks: Evangelical Innovators and the Spiritual Marketplace*. New York: New York University Press, 2009.

Leonhardt, David. "Is Your Religion Your Financial Destiny?" *The New York Times*, May 2011 http://www.nytimes.com/2011/05/15/magazine/is-your-religion-your-financial-destiny.html (accessed December 1, 2012).

"Letters to R. G. Hardy." *Faith in Action*, April 1973.

Levs, Joshua. "African-American Churches Weigh Gospel Debate," July 31, 2005. http://www.npr.org/templates/story/story.php?storyid=4779412. (accessed December 2012).

Lie, Geir. *E. W. Kenyon, Cult Founder or Evangelical Minister? An Historical Analysis of Kenyon's Theology with Particular Emphasis on Roots and Influences*. Oslo: Refleks, 2003.

Lilly, Fred. "Lester Sumrall: Cathedral of Praise." *Charisma*, November 1985.

Lincoln, C. Eric, and Lawrence H. Mamiya. *The Black Church in the African-American Experience*. Durham, NC: Duke University Press, 1990.

Lindner, Eileen. *Yearbook of American and Canadian Churches.* New York: NCC Communication Department, 2006.

Lindsay, Gordon. *Freda.* Dallas, TX: Christ for the Nations, 1984.

———. *God's Master Key to Success and Prosperity.* Dallas: The Voice of Healing, 1959.

Lindsay, Mrs. Gordon (Freda). *Freda: The Widow Who Took up the Mantle.* Dallas: Christ for the Nations, 1984.

Lipset, Seymour Martin. *Continental Divide: The Values and Institutions of the United States and Canada.* New York: Routledge, 1990.

Long, Carolyn. *Spiritual Merchants: Religion, Magic, and Commerce.* Knoxville: University of Tennessee Press, 2001.

Loveland, Anne C., and Otis B. Wheeler. *From Meetinghouse to Megachurch: A Material and Cultural History.* Columbia: University of Missouri Press, 2003.

Lowe, Valerie G. "Florida Megachurch Pastors End Marriage." *Charisma,* August 14, 2009. http://www.charismamag.com/index.php/news-old/22954-florida-megachurch-pastors-end-marriage.

Lowery, T. L. *Living in God's Economy in a Time of Financial Meltdown.* N.p.: T. L. Lowery, 2009.

Lutheran Church in America, USA, 1962. "Anointing and Healing." In *Presence, Power, Praise: Documents on the Charismatic Renewal.* Edited by Kilian McDonnell, 2:21–55, Collegeville, MN: Liturgical Press, 1980.

Lutheran Church-Missouri Synod, USA, 1977. "The Lutheran Church and the Charismatic Movement: Guidelines for Congregations and Pastors." In *Presence, Power, Praise: Documents on the Charismatic Renewal.* Edited by Kilian McDonnell, 2:307–24, Collegeville, MN: Liturgical Press, 1980.

Ma, Wonsuk, and Robert P. Menzies, eds. *The Spirit and Spirituality: Essays in Honour of Russell P. Spittler.* New York: T&T Clark International, 2004.

MacGregor, Kirk. "The Word-Faith Movement: A Theological Conflation of the Nation of Islam and Mormonism?" *Journal of the American Academy of Religion* 75 (2007): 87–120.

Mansfield, Stephen. *Derek Prince: A Biography.* Lake Mary, FL: Charisma House, 2005.

Marshall, Ruth. *Political Spiritualities: The Pentecostal Revolution in Nigeria.* Chicago: University of Chicago Press, 2009.

Marti, Gerardo. *Hollywood Faith: Holiness, Prosperity, and Ambition in a Los Angeles Church.* New Brunswick, NJ: Rutgers University Press, 2008.

———. *A Mosaic of Believers: Diversity and Innovation in a Multiethnic Church.* Bloomington: University of Indiana Press, 2005.

Martin, Darnise C. *Beyond Christianity: African Americans in a New Thought Church.* New York: New York University Press, 2005.

Martin, William. "Lakewood Church, Servicio en Español." *Texas Monthly.* December 9, 2007.

Mason, John. *An Enemy Called Average.* Tulsa, OK: Insight International, 1990.

Mattsson-Boze, Joseph. "The Giver and the Givers." *Herald of Faith/Harvest Time,* Christmas 1970.

Maxwell, Joe. "The Calm after the Storm." *Charisma,* August 2008. http://www. charismamag.com/index.php/features2/477-heroes-of-faith/17479-the-calm-after-the-storm.

McClendon, Clarence E. *Beyond Personal Power: Experiencing the "God Kind of Faith."* Denver, CO: Legacy, 2003.

McClymond, Michael J. "Prosperity Already and Not Yet: An Eschatological Interpretation of the Health and Wealth Teaching in North American Pentecostalism." Paper presented at the annual meeting for the American Academy of Religion, Chicago. November 1–3, 2008.

McConnell, D. R. *A Different Gospel.* Peabody, MA: Hendrickson, 1988.

McGavran, Donald. *Understanding Church Growth.* 3rd ed. Grand Rapids, MI: Eerdmans, 1990.

McGee, Micki. *Self-Help, Inc.: Makeover Culture in American Life.* New York: Oxford University Press, 2005.

McIntyre, Joe. *E. W. Kenyon and His Message of Faith: The True Story.* Lake Mary, FL: Creation House, 1997.

Mearsheimer, John J. *The Israel Lobby and U.S. Foreign Policy.* New York: Farrar, Straus and Giroux, 2007.

Menchaca, H. M. "Deliverance in Spanish Churches with Evangelist Harry Hampel." *The Voice of Healing,* April 1955.

Meyer, Donald. *The Positive Thinkers: Popular Religious Psychology from Mary Baker Eddy to Norman Vincent Peale and Ronald Reagan.* Middletown, CT: Wesleyan University Press, 1988.

———. *The Positive Thinkers: Religion as Psychology from Mary Baker Eddy to Oral Roberts.* New York: Pantheon Books, 1980 (1965).

Meyer, Joyce. "At a Glance." http://www.JoyceMeyer.org (accessed February 21, 2011).

———. *Eat & Stay Thin: Simple, Spiritual, Satisfying Weight Control.* Tulsa, OK: Harrison House, 1999.

———. "Enjoying Everyday Life." Channel 49, New Haven, CT, November 26, 2004, 9:30–10:00.

———. "Thanksgiving." http://www.streamingfaith.com (accessed November 26, 2004).

Michaux, Lightfoot, and Pauline Lark. *Sparks from the Anvil of Elder Michaux.* New York: Vantage Press, 1950.

Miller, Basil. *Grappling With Destiny.* Los Angeles: Wings of Healing, 1962.

Miller, Donald E., and Tetsuano Yamamori. *Global Pentecostalism: The New Face of Christian Social Engagement.* Berkeley: University of California Press, 2007.

Miller, Glenn. *Piety and Profession: American Protestant Theological Education, 1870–1970.* Grand Rapids, MI: Eerdmans, 2007.

Millionaire University. "Homepage." http://web.mac.com/davanzini/Millionaire_University/Curriculum.html (accessed December 21, 2011).

Millner, Denene. "Juanita Bynum: I've Come This Far by Faith." *Essence,* December 2008.

Mitchem, Stephanie Y. *Name It and Claim It? Prosperity Preaching in the Black Church.* Cleveland, OH: Pilgrim Press, 2007.

Montgomery, Ed. *Breaking the Spirit of Poverty.* Shippensburg, PA: Destiny Image, 1988.

Montgomery, G. H. "God's Contract with Us." *Full Gospel Men's Voice,* February 1953.

Moore, R. Laurence. *Religious Outsiders and the Making of Americans.* New York: Oxford University Press, 1986.

Morris, Aldon D., and Shayne Lee. "The National Baptist Convention: Traditions and Contemporary Challenges." In *Church, Identity, and Change: Theology and Denominational Structures in Unsettled Times.* Edited by David A. Roozen and James R. Nieman, 336–79. Grand Rapids, MI: Eerdmans, 2005.

Moses, Wilson Jeremiah. "Chosen Peoples of the Metropolis: Black Muslims, Black Jews, and Others." In *African American Religious Thought: An Anthology.* Edited by Cornel West and Eddie S. Glaude Jr., 535–49. Louisville, KY: Westminster John Knox Press, 2003.

Munroe, Myles. *Kingdom Principles: Preparing the Kingdom Experience and Expansion.* Shippensburg, PA: Destiny Image, 2006.

"Nature of the Gifts of Healing." *The Voice of Healing,* July 1948.

New Creation Church. "History." http://www.newcreation.org.sg/about-us/history (accessed July 4, 2010).

"New Mega Churches: Huge Congregations with Spectacular Structures Spread across the U.S." *Ebony,* December 2001.

"New Role for Swaggart?" *Charisma,* June 1987.

Nickel, Thomas. "Religion in Business Brings Sure Success." *Full Gospel Men's Voice,* February 1953.

Nunn, David. "Faith for Finances." *The Healing Messenger,* February 1965.

Olmstead, Ralph. "God Told Me to Mortgage My Home." *Miracle Magazine,* November 1955.

O'Neill, Kevin. *City of God: Christian Citizenship in Postwar Guatemala.* Berkeley: University of California Press, 2009.

Osborn, Daisy Washburn. *The Woman Believer.* Tulsa, OK: OSFO, 1990.

Osteen, Dodie. "Dodie Osteen's Faith and Healing." iamawtness.com. http://community.imawitness.com/_Dodie-Osteens-Faith-Healing/video/350741/54126.html (accessed November 12, 2009).

Osborn, T. L. "Divine Healing Through Confession." *The Voice of Healing,* July 1950.

———. "Don't Eat It All." *Faith Digest,* October 1960.

———. "Faith." *Faith Digest,* May 1956.

———. *Go For It!: Get the Best Out of Life*. Tulsa, OK: Osborn Foundation International, 1983.

———. "The Miracle at Bethesda." *Faith Digest*, August 1957.

———. *One Hundred Divine Healing Facts*. Tulsa, OK: Harrison House, 1983.

———. "Plant your FIRSTfruits." *Faith Digest*, August 1976.

———. "Put God to the Test." *Faith Digest*, March 1970.

———. *Soulwinning Out Where the Sinners Are*. Tulsa, OK: T. L. Osborn Ministries, 1967.

Osteen, Joel. *Become a Better You: 7 Keys to Improving Your Life Every Day*. New York: Free Press, 2007.

———. *Healthy Living: Discover God's Plan for a Stronger, Happier, Younger Looking You!* Houston: Joel Osteen Ministries, 2006.

———. *Your Best Life Now: 7 Steps to Living at Your Full Potential*. New York: Faith-Words, 2004.

Osteen, John. *This Awakening Generation*. Houston: John Osteen Ministries, 1964.

———. *Unraveling the Mystery of the Blood Covenant*. Houston: John Osteen Pub., 1987.

———. *What to Do When Nothing Seems to Work*. Houston: Lakewood Church, 1981.

Overcoming Faith Christian Center. "Church History." http://www.overcomingfaith. com/church/history.html (accessed July 28, 2011).

Parsley, Rod. *Daily Breakthrough: Daily Devotions to Take You into God's Promise*. Orlando, FL: Charisma House, 1998.

Patterson, Eric, and Edmund John Rybarczyk. *The Future of Pentecostalism in the United States*. Lanham, MD: Lexington Books, 2007.

Peale, Norman Vincent. *The Power of Positive Thinking*. New York: Fireside/Simon & Schuster, 2003.

Pearson, Carlton. *Breaking the Curse: The Ultimate Act of Devotion*. Tulsa, OK: Harrison House, 1991.

Pew Hispanic Center and Pew Forum on Religion & Public Life. "Changing Faiths: Latinos and the Transformation of American Religion." 2007. http://pewforum. org/newassets/surveys/hispanic/hispanics-religion-07-final-mar08.pdf (accessed January 7, 2010).

Pinn, Anthony B. *The African American Religious Experience in America*. Westport, CT: Greenwood Press, 2007.

Poloma, Margaret M. *The Assemblies of God at the Crossroads: Charisma and Institutional Dreams*. Knoxville, TN: University of Tennessee Press, 1989.

———. *The Charismatic Movement: Is There a New Pentecost?* Boston: Twayne, 1982.

Pope, Gerald. "Your Faith Can Make It Happen." *World Harvest*, April 1964.

Porterfield, Amanda. *Healing in the History of Christianity*. New York: Oxford University Press, 2005.

Potter, Deborah. "The Prosperity Gospel." *Religion & Ethics Newsweekly*, August 17, 2007. http://www.pbs.org/wnet/religionandethics/week1051/feature.html.

Price, Frederick. *Is Healing for All?* Tulsa, OK: Harrison House, 1976.

———. *Race, Religion & Racism*. Los Angeles, CA: Faith One, 1999-2002.

Priest, Robert, and Alvaro L. Nieves. *This Side of Heaven: Race, Ethnicity, and Christian Faith*. New York: Oxford University Press, 2007.

Prince, Derek. *Blessings and Curses*. Grand Rapids, MI: Chosen Books, 2003.

———. *They Shall Expel Demons: What You Need to Know about Demons—Your Invisible Enemies*. Washington Depot, CT: Chosen Books, 1998.

Quebedeaux, Richard. *The New Charismatics II*. San Francisco: Harper & Row, 1983.

Raboteau, Albert. *Canaan Land: A Religious History of African Americans*. Oxford: Oxford University Press, 2001.

———. *Slave Religion*. New York: Oxford University Press, 1978.

Ramirez, Daniel. "Borderlands Praxis: The Immigrant Experience in Latino Pentecostal Churches." *Journal of the American Academy of Religion* 67, no. 3 (1999): 573–96.

Rammell, Peter J. "This is Revival." *The Pentecostal Evangel*, January 26, 1969, 7.

Ray of Hope Christian Church website. http://www.rayofhope.org (accessed July 21, 2011).

Reaves, Gary. "Black Baptists Eschew 'Prosperity Preaching.'" ReligionNewsBlog. com, September 8, 2006.

Redeemed Christian Church of God Website. http://www.rccg.org.

Reid, Frank. "I Am a Winner." http://www.youtube.com (accessed November 10, 2011).

"Renewed Covenant." http://www.youtube.com/watch?v=BCH_6zin2WU&feature =relmfu (accessed October 26, 2012).

"Rev. and Mrs. F. F. Bosworth Work with Branham Party." *The Voice of Healing*, May 1948, 1, 5.

Rev. Ike (Frederick J. Eikerenkoetter II). "THE ENEMY-FIXER!" Mass mailing. 15 April, 1982.

"Rex Humbard." In *Religious Leaders of America: A Biographical Guide to Founders and Leaders of Religious Bodies, Churches, and Spiritual Groups in North America*. Edited by J. Gordon Melton, 263. Detroit, MI: Gale Research, 1999.

"Rice: Israel Must Divide Jerusalem." *Israel Today*, October 15, 2007. http://www. israeltoday.co.il/default.aspx?tabid=178&nid=14294.

Richie, Tony. "Dealing with the Dilemma of Christian Zionism." http://www. christianzionism.org/Article/RichieT02.pdf.

"Riverview Church." Wikipedia. http://en.wikipedia.org/wiki/Riverview_Church (accessed December 21, 2011).

Robbins, Thomas. "Last Civil Religion: Reverend Moon and the Unification Church." *Sociological Analysis* 37, no. 2 (Summer 1976): 111–25.

———. "The Transformative Impact of the Study of New Religion on the Sociology of Religion." *Journal for the Scientific Study of Religion* 27, no. 1 (March 1988): 12–31.

Roberts, Dennis. "Trinity Broadcasting Network: The Dream Almost Didn't Happen." *Charisma*, June 1983.

Roberts, Oral. *Daily BLESSING*, March 1959.

———. *Holy Spirit in the Now*. Tulsa, OK: Oral Roberts University, 1974.

———. *How I Learned Jesus Was Not Poor*. Altamonte Springs, FL: Creation House, 1989.

———. *Oral Roberts' Life Story: As Told by Himself*. Tulsa, OK: Oral Roberts Ministry, 1952.

Roberts, Richard. "Staying Well Is Easier than Getting Well." *Abundant Life*, August/September 1986.

Robertson, Pat. "The Land of Israel." http://patrobertson.com/askpat/bringiton021302.asp (accessed February 2, 2010).

Robins, R. G. *Pentecostalism in America*. Santa Barbara, CA: Praeger, 2010.

Robison, James. *True Prosperity: Truth Matters*. Carol Stream, IL: Tyndale House: 2004.

Rose, Fred. "Toward a Class-Culture Theory of Social Movements: Reinterpreting New Social Movements." *Sociological Forum* 12, no. 3 (September 1997): 461–94.

Rosin, Hanna. "Did Christianity Cause the Crash?" *Atlantic Magazine*, December 2009.

Rudolph, Frederick. *The American College and University: A History*. New York: Knopf, 1962.

Rush, Rick. "May I Have Your Order Please." http://www.youtube.com/watch?v=U-ceYywY9Do.

———. *May I Have Your Order, Please? How To Get What You Want from God!* Cedar Hill, TX: Black Pearl, 2005.

Sagert, Kelly Boyer. *The 1970s*. Westport, CT: Greenwood Press, 2007.

Sanford, Agnes. *The Healing Light*. St. Paul, MN: Macalester Park, 1947.

Sanneh, Kelefa. "Pray and Grow Rich." *New Yorker*, October 11, 2004.

Sanneh, Lamin. *Whose Religion is Christianity? The Gospel Beyond the West*. Grand Rapids, MI: Eerdmans, 1993.

Satter, Beryl. *Each Mind a Kingdom: American Women, Sexual Purity and the New Thought Movement, 1875–1920*. Berkeley: University of California Press, 1999.

Schuller, Robert. Interview by Paul Crouch. *Praise the Lord*, TBN. May 3, 2010. www.tbn.org/index.php/2/37/92.html (accessed May 24, 2010).

———. *Your Church Has Real Possibilities!* Glendale, CA: Regal Books, 1974.

Schulman, Bruce J. *The Seventies: The Great Shift in American Culture, Society, and Politics*. New York: The Free Press, 2001.

Shakarian, Demos. "A Call to the Business Men of Our Nation." *The Voice of Healing*, June 1954.

Shaw, Mark. *Global Awakening: How 20th-Century Revivals Triggered Christian Revolution*. Downers Grove, IL: InterVarsity Press, 2010.

Shemeth, S. "Asa Alonso Allen." In *New International Dictionary of Pentecostal and Charismatic Movements*. Edited by Stanley M. Burgess and Eduard M. van der Maas, 311–12. Grand Rapids, MI: Zondervan, 2002.

Simmons, Dale H. *E. W. Kenyon and the Postbellum Pursuit of Peace, Power, and Plenty*. London: Scarecrow Press, 1997.

Stephens, Carl. "Prosperity in a Bad Economy." June 2, 2010, podcast, www.faithassembly. org/sermons/podcast.php (accessed July 6, 2010).

Stephens, Edward C. "Oral Tells His Side." *Charisma & Christian Life*, November 1987.

Stewart, Don. *Only Believe: An Eyewitness Account of the Great Healing Revivals of the 20th Century*. Shippensburg, PA: Revival Press, 1999.

Strang, Stephen. "10 Growth Stages for Charisma." *Charisma*, August 1985.

———. "Bridge Builders or Stone Throwers?" *Charisma*, August 1993.

———. "The Christian Book Boom." *Charisma*, April 1978.

———. "Expecting a Miracle." *Charisma*, March 1981.

———. "Kenneth Copeland." *Charisma*, June 1979.

———. "Larry Lea: Proof that Prayer Works." *Charisma*, October 1986.

———. "Oral Roberts Shares His Heart." *Charisma*, June 1985.

Summers, Harrison B., ed. *A Thirty-Year History of Programs Carried on National Radio Networks in the United States, 1926–1956*. New York: Arno Press, 1971.

Susanto, Johanes Lilik. "A Practical Theological Evaluation of the Divine Healing Ministries of Smith Wigglesworth and John G. Lake: A Continuationist Reformed Perspective." Doctor of theology thesis, University of South Africa, 2007. http:// uir.unisa.ac.za/xmlui/handle/10500/1737

Swaggart, Jimmy. "Clean Up Our Act." *Charisma*, November 1982.

———. *The Confession Principle and the Course of Nature*. Baton Rouge, LA: Jimmy Swaggart Ministries, 1981.

Swaggart, Jimmy, and Marvin E. Solum. *The Balanced Faith Life*. Baton Rouge, LA: Jimmy Swaggart Ministries, 1981.

Swann, David, and Roxanne Swann. *Guarantee Your Child's Success*. Tulsa, OK: Harrison House, 1990.

Synan, Vinson. *The Century of the Holy Spirit: 100 Years of Pentecostal and Charismatic Renewal, 1901–2001*. Nashville, TN: Thomas Nelson, 2001.

———. *An Eyewitness Remembers the Century of the Holy Spirit*. Grand Rapids, MI: Chosen, 2010.

———. "Word of Faith Movement has Deep Roots in American History." http:// www.believersstandunited.com/word-of-faith-movement-has-deep-roots-in-american-history/

Taves, Ann. *Fits, Trances, & Visions: Experiencing Religion and Explaining Experience from Wesley to James*. Princeton, NJ: Princeton University Press, 1999.

Thernstrom, Stephan, and Abigail Thernstrom. *America in Black and White: One Nation, Indivisible.* New York: Simon and Schuster, 1997.

Thigpen, Paul. "The New Black Charismatics." *Charisma and Christian Life*, November 1990.

Thomas, Benny. *Change Your Life with Confession Calisthenics.* Beaumont, TX: Benny Thomas Evangelistic Association, 1984.

Thomas, Sari. "The Route to Redemption: Religion and Social Class." *Journal of Communication* 35 (1985): 111–22.

Thompson, Leroy, Sr. *Money Cometh! To the Body of Christ.* Tulsa: Harrison House, 1999.

Thumma, Scott, and Dave Travis. *Beyond Megachurch Myths: What We Can Learn from America's Largest Churches.* San Francisco: Jossey-Bass, 2007.

Towns, Elmer L. *Say-It-Faith.* Wheaton, IL: Tyndale House, 1983.

Trachtenberg, Alan. *The Incorporation of America: Culture and Society in the Gilded Age.* New York: Hill and Wang, 2007.

Tucker-Worgs, Tamelyn N. *The Black Mega-Church, Theology, Gender, and the Politics of Public Engagement.* Waco, TX: Baylor Press, 2011.

Ulmer, Kenneth. *Making Your Money Count.* Ventura, CA: Regal Books, 2007.

United States Senate. Committee on Finance. *Memorandum*, March 12, 2009. http://www.finance.senate.gov/newsroom/ranking/release/?id=c11c2bec-5974-4197-a22c-5d75a7fcfcd7 (accessed December 2, 2012).

Universal Church of the Kingdom of God website. "Our Locations." http://universal.org/who-where-how/our-locations.html (accessed January 14, 2010).

Van Biema, David. "Spirit Raiser." *Time*, September 17, 2001. http://www.time.com/time/magazine/article/0,9171,1000836,00.html (accessed June 21, 2011.)

Van Biema, David, and Jeff Chu. "Does God Want You to Be Rich?" *Time*, September 6, 2006. http://www.time.com/time/magazine/article/0,9171,1533448,00.html (accessed January 7, 2010).

Vasquez, M. A. "Studying Religion in Motion: A Networks Approach." *Method and Theory in the Study of Religion* 20 (2008): 151–184.

Vaughan, John N. *The World's Twenty Largest Churches.* Grand Rapids, MI: Baker Book House, 1984.

Vergara, Camilo J. *How the Other Half Worships.* New Brunswick, NJ: Rutgers University Press, 2005.

Wacker, Grant. *Heaven Below: Early Pentecostals and American Culture.* Cambridge, MA: Harvard University Press, 2001.

———. "The Pentecostal Tradition." In *Caring and Curing: Health and Medicine in the Western Religious Traditions.* Edited by Ronald L. Numbers and Darrel W. Amundsen., 514–38. New York: Macmillan, 1986.

———. "Pentecostalism." In *Encyclopedia of the American Religious Experience.* Vol. 2. Edited by Charles H. Lippy and Peter W. Williams. New York, 933–45. Charles Scribner's Sons, 1988.

Wagner, Peter C. "God's Kingdom Wealth Shall Be Released!" Apostolic Decree. Encounter's Network. June 2006. http://www.encountersnetwork.com/pdf/6_9_06_CPW_Decree_4_wealth_transfer.pdf.

Walsh, Arlene Sánchez. "Santidad, Sanación, Salvacion, Liberación: The Word of Faith Movement among Twenty-First-Century Latina/o Pentecostals." In *Global Pentecostal and Charismatic Healing*. Edited by Candy Gunther Brown, 151–68. Oxford: Oxford University Press, 2011.

Walters, Herman W. *Power: A Matter of Choice*. Lodi, CA: Balm of Gilead [late 1950s?].

Walton, Jonathan L. "Megachurch Phenomenon." In *African American Religious Cultures*. Edited by Anthony B. Pinn, 2 vols. 2:463–76. Santa Barbara, CA: ABC-CLIO, LLC, 2009.

———. *Watch This! The Ethics and Aesthetics of Black Televangelism*. New York: New York University Press, 2009.

Wangenye, Stan. *God's Will Still Is Prosperity!* Longwood, FL: Xulon Press, 2009.

Ward, W. R. *Early Evangelicalism: A Global Intellectual History, 1670–1789*. Cambridge: Cambridge University Press, 2006.

Warner, Stephen. "Immigrants and the Faith They Bring." *The Christian Century*, February 10, 2004.

Warner, W. E. "Roy Hicks." In *Dictionary of Pentecostal and Charismatic Movements*. Edited by Stanley M. Burgess, Gary B. McGee, and Patrick H. Alexander. Grand Rapids, MI: Regency Reference Library, 1988.

Watts, Jill. *God, Harlem, U.S.A: The Father Divine Story*. Berkeley: University of California Press, 1995.

Wave Church website. http://www.wavechurch.com.

Weaver, C. Douglas. *The Healer–Prophet, William Marrion Branham: A Study of the Prophetic In American Pentecostalism*. Mason, GA: Mercer University Press, 2000.

Weiss, Richard. *The American Myth of Success: From Horatio Alger to Norman Vincent Peale*. Urbana: University of Illinois Press 1988 (1969).

Wellman, James K., Jr. "The Church of the Pacific Northwest: The Rise of Sectarian Entrepreneurs." In *Religion and Public Life in the Pacific Northwest: The None Zone*. 79–105. Edited by Patricia O'Connell Killen et al. Walnut Creek, CA: AltaMira Press, 2004.

———. *High on God: How the Megachurch Conquered America*. New York: Oxford University Press, forthcoming.

West Angeles Community Development Corporation website. http://www.westangelescdc.org (accessed July 20, 2011).

White, Paula. *Birthing Your Dreams: God's Plan for Living Victoriously*. New York: Thomas Nelson, 2003.

———. *Ten Commandments for Health and Wellness*. Tampa, FL: Paula White Enterprises, 2007.

White, Paula. Interview by Larry King. *Larry King Live*. CNN. November 26, 2007. http://transcripts.cnn.com/TRANSCRIPTS/0711/26/lkl.01.html (accessed January 18, 2010).

White, Shane, and Graham White. *Stylin': African American Expressive Culture, from Its Beginnings to the Zoot Suit*. Ithaca, NY: Cornell University Press, 1999.

Whorton, James C. *Nature Cures: The History of Alternative Medicine in America*. New York: Oxford University Press, 2004.

Wiegele, Katharine. *Investing in Miracles: El Shaddai and the Transformation of Popular Catholicism in the Philippines*. Honolulu: University of Hawaii Press, 2005.

Wigglesworth, Smith. *Smith Wigglesworth on Healing*. New Kensington, UK: Whitaker House, 1999.

Wilkinson, Bruce. *The Dream Giver: Following Your God-Given Destiny*. Portland, OR: Multnomah, 2003.

———. *The Prayer of Jabez: Breaking Through to the Blessed Life*. Portland, OR: Multnomah, 2000.

Williams, Alverster. "I Lost over 200 Pounds When I Used God's Reducing Plan." *Miracle Magazine* 1961, 3.

Williams, Dave. *The Miracle Results of Fasting: Discover the Amazing Benefits in Your Spirit, Soul, and Body*. Tulsa, OK: Harrison House, 2004.

Williams, J. R. "Wilkerson, Ralph A." In *The New International Dictionary of Pentecostal and Charismatic Movements*. Rev. ed. Edited by Stanley M. Burgess, 1196–97. Grand Rapids, MI: Zondervan, 2002.

Williams, Joseph. "The Transformation of Pentecostal Healing 1906–2006." PhD diss., Florida State University, 2008.

Williams, Tammy R. "Is There a Doctor in the House? Reflections on the Practice of Healing in African American Churches." In *Practicing Theology: Beliefs and Practices in Christian Life*. Edited by Miroslav Volf and Dorothy C. Bass, 94–120. Grand Rapids, MI: Eerdmans, 2002.

Winners Church website. http://www.winnerstoday.net.

Winslow, George. "Go with the Flow: Hispanic Religious Channels Grow." *Broadcasting and Cable*. February 20, 2005. http://www.broadcastingcable.com/article/156232-Go_With_the_Flow_Hispanic_Religious_Channels_Grow.php (accessed December 16, 2011).

Word of Faith Christian Center, Nashville, TN, website. http://www.wofcc-nash.org/.

Wyatt, Mrs. Thomas (Evelyn). "As I See It." *The March of Faith*, September 1954.

———. "Prosperity's Hidden Secrets . . . Revealed." *Wings of Healing*, March 1977.

———. *Words That Work Wonders*. Portland, OR: Wings of Healing, 1951.

Wyllie, Irvin G. *The Self-Made Man in America: The Myth of Rags to Riches*. New Brunswick, NJ: Rutgers University Press, 1954.

Yeomans, Lilian. *His Healing Power*. Tulsa, OK: Harrison House, 2003.

Yoido Full Gospel Church. "Yoido Full Gospel Church Story." http://english.fgtv.com/yfgc.pdf (accessed February 5, 2010).

DISCOGRAPHY

Bakker, Tammy Faye. *We're Blest*. PTL Records, 1979.

Bynum, Juanita. "I Don't Mind Waiting." *A Piece of My Passion*. Flow Records, 2006.

Clark Sisters, The. "Name It, Claim It." *Sincerely*. New Birth Records, 1982.

Clark-Sheard, Karen. "Blessed and Highly Favored." *One Last Time*. EMI Gospel, 2007.

Copeland, Gloria. *Azusa Street Centennial General Sessions*. Kingdom Recordings, 2006.

Hanby, Mark David. "Look What the Lord has Done." Exaltation Music, 1974.

Hillsong United. "Shout Unto God." Hillsong Music Australia, 2008.

Hillsong. "This Is Our God." *This Is Our God*. Integrity Media, 2008.

Munizzi, Martha. "Say the Name." *Say the Name*. Sony, 2002.

Murphy, William, III. "Overflow." *The Sound*. M3M Music Group, 2007.

Stone, Perry. *Entering the Time of Double Portion Blessing*. Perry Stone Ministries, 2010.

Winch, Terry. "Jehovah Jireh." EMI Christian Music Publishing, 1978.

Index